~ Obsessive-Compulsive Disorders

Obsessive-Compulsive Disorders

~

A COMPLETE GUIDE TO GETTING WELL AND STAYING WELL

Fred Penzel, Ph.D.

~

OXFORD
UNIVERSITY PRESS

2000

OXFORD
UNIVERSITY PRESS

Oxford New York
Athens Auckland Bangkok Bogotá
Buenos Aires Calcutta Cape Town Chennai Dar es Salaam
Delhi Florence Hong Kong Istanbul Karachi
Kuala Lumpur Madrid Melbourne
Mexico City Mumbai Nairobi Paris São Paolo Singapore
Taipei Tokyo Toronto Warsaw

and associated companies in
Berlin Ibadan

Copyright © 2000 by Fred Penzel

Published by Oxford University Press, Inc.
198 Madison Avenue, New York, New York 10016

Oxford is a registered trademark of Oxford University Press, Inc.

Library of Congress Cataloging-in-Publication Data
Penzel, Fred.
Obsessive-compulsive disorders : a complete guide to
getting well and staying well / Fred Penzel.
p. cm.
Includes bibliographical references
ISBN 0-19-514092-3
1. Obsessive-compulsive disorder—Popular works.   I. Title.
RC533.P35   2000
616.85'227—dc21   00–032419

3 5 7 9 8 6 4 2

Printed in the United States of America
on acid-free paper

*This book is dedicated to all those
who have suffered for so long,
and to those who continue to suffer.*

Pain of mind is worse than pain of body.

—*Publius Syrus, 1st Century* B.C.

ACKNOWLEDGMENTS

I would like to thank the following people for having made this book possible. First, I would like to thank my wife and best friend, Wendy, for her invaluable support and many hours of help as reader, critic, typist, printer, and adviser in the proper use of the King's English, and both her and my wonderful son, Joseph, for generously giving up some of their time with me so that I could write; my parents, Irwin and Harriet Penzel, for instilling in me a love of books, knowledge, and helping others; Barbara Bergstrom, my extremely patient, persistent, and enthusiastic editor and agent, for all her expert help in shaping this small mountain of information into a book; Drs. Richard Schloss and Marc Reitman, my respected friends and colleagues, for their review and advice concerning the medical information presented in this book; Dr. Robert Araujo, my good friend, colleague, and neighbor for his expert advice and support; my personal hero H. N., Patricia Perkins-Doyle, president of the OC Foundation, for her friendship, advice, and support from the beginning; Christina Pearson, founder of the Trichotillomania Learning Center for her intelligent insights, encouragement, and deep understanding; my other friends at the OC Foundation, especially Fran Sydney, Susan Duffy, and Joan Kaylor; Roy C., founder of Obsessive-Compulsive Anonymous, who advised me and who helps so many others; the many persons who generously submitted their stories to me in the hope of helping others; and last, but certainly not least, the hundreds of people I have worked with in therapy over the last eighteen years, for the many aspects of OCSDs, in which they have instructed me on a daily basis, and for sharing their personal agonies and triumphs.

Note to the Reader

This book is meant solely for informational purposes. It is not intended that any of the ideas, procedures, or suggestions mentioned here be regarded as substitutes for expert medical or psychological services where they are required. Personal accounts contained within this book have all been voluntarily submitted. Any names used have been changed to protect the identities of the contributors.

CONTENTS

LIST OF ILLUSTRATIONS

Figure

~ *Advice is judged by results, not by intentions.*
—Cicero

As a psychologist, I have been involved in the treatment of Obsessive-Compulsive Disorders (OCDs) for over eighteen years. During that time, I have found a great deal of fulfillment in working to help sufferers and as a group, I find them to be bright, motivated, and interesting people, living secret lives of incredible pain.

OCDs are an emotionally painful and humiliating experience for sufferers. Many more than we know have suffered in silence for fear of being judged as "crazy." Dr. Michael Jenike of Harvard University has referred to classic OCD as the "hidden epidemic." These disorders cause sociable people to isolate themselves, and bright and talented people to achieve far less than they are capable of. OCDs cause vital people to lose the ability to be spontaneous or take the risks necessary in everyday living. Most important of all, they have the potential to, can, and often do seriously handicap or destroy people's lives.

One medical textbook, Breitner's *Diseases of the Nervous System*, published as recently as 1960, stated of classic OCD that "most of us are agreed that the treatment of obsessional states is one of the most difficult tasks confronting the psychiatrist and many of us consider it hopeless." Until not too long ago, Obsessive-Compulsive Disorders were commonly thought to be rare, untreatable, and caused strictly by psychological factors. They were also believed to be separate and unrelated problems. We now know that the first three beliefs have not proved to be true. The fourth belief, the concept that there are a group of disorders known as Obsessive-Compulsive Spectrum Disorders (OCSDs), is still being argued.

This book takes the view that classic OCD itself is really only a part of a whole family of neurobiological disorders, ranging from symptoms of compulsiveness at one end of the scale, to disorders of impulse control at the other. I have selected five disorders from this OC Spectrum to discuss: Obsessive-Compulsive Disorder (OCD); Body Dysmorphic Disorder (BDD); Trichotillomania (TTM); compulsive nail biting (also known as Onychophagia); and compulsive skin picking. In fact, any one of these could make up a separate book on its own.

This book has been written and organized with several purposes in mind. First, it gives the reader a brief general description of each disorder. Second, it outlines behavioral therapy—what it involves and what can be expected from it. This is followed by self-help instructions for each of the disorders. Next comes a discussion of what medications can do, which ones are useful, and some recommendations for managing them. The last part of the book is designed to be used as a reference guide, in which the various forms of OCD are described so that the reader may identify and understand the categories into which the symptoms fall. This guide will help those who suffer from OCD, and those who love them, to see that they are not the only ones with these particular problems and also to see what their symptoms are all about.

Lack of information is still the greatest obstacle sufferers face as they begin the task of recovery. Over the years, I have tried to educate those with OCSDs and their families via public meetings at my clinic and other locations around the country. Although I can reach several dozen people at a time in this way locally, it still isn't efficient enough to educate and help the majority of those who suffer in silence. I have also written a number of articles for the OC Foundation and TLC newsletters and other publications that have reached a somewhat larger group of people. Articles, however, are always limited to a single topic and can reach only a limited number of readers. My hope is that by writing this book, I can continue to aid in the dissemination of sensible, accurate, and useful information to help sufferers and those close to them understand the disorders and assist them in recovering and having lives that are more livable, productive, and meaningful. I also hope that this book will be an important resource for those who are more independent and prefer to help themselves, as well as for those who have no local resources to help with recovery. Not everyone can afford treatment these days, nor is effective help always nearby. Wherever possible, I have tried to include the actual words of sufferers themselves to better communicate the actual experience of these disorders.

To try to sum up OCSDs and their treatment in just a few words is impossible. Even the meaning of the words "obsession" and "compulsion" can be difficult to pin down, because they are used very loosely in our language. The term "impulsion" will also be discussed. This belongs together with these two terms and is probably not even known or understood by most people.

Until recently, practically everyone with an OCSD suffered in ignorance, not knowing that their problems had names, not understanding the cause of their illness, or that anything could be done about it. Since 1987, many resources for distributing information and providing help have been established. These include the Obsessive-Compulsive Foundation and their excellent newsletter; the Trichotillomania Learning Center and their important publication; a large and active self-help movement, which now also includes 12-Step groups collectively known as Obsessive-Compulsives Anonymous; a number of TV specials; numerous articles; and several fine books on the subject of OCD by distinguished authorities in the field.

Unfortunately, despite all of the above, the information has still not spread far enough to reach all sufferers or the professionals who treat them. I still find many people who believe that they are the only ones who have their particular symptoms; that they cannot be helped; and that mental health professionals have little to offer. I also meet far too many health professionals who are unable to diagnose, understand, or treat these disorders.

Finally, the most important things I hope to communicate through this book are that those with OCSDs are not to be blamed for having these problems, and that there is hope for all those who suffer from them. While I will never claim that it is easy, recovery is possible for anyone willing to work hard and persevere. We are still only in the beginning phases. Only a greater awareness of the benefits of behavioral therapy, together with the growing number of effective medications, will bring the relief and recovery still available only to some sufferers. Hopefully, through the information provided in this book, more sufferers of OCSDs and their loved ones will find their way to the goal of recovery.

∼ Obsessive-Compulsive Disorders

~ *Obsessive-Compulsive Disorders— What They Are*

~ *When the disease is known it is half cured.*
—Erasmus' Colloquies

In defining obsessive-compulsive disorders (OCDs), our language creates problems, because it treats the terms "obsession" and "compulsion" very loosely. You only have to walk into a department store and see a perfume labeled Obsession, hear about "obsessed" fans stalking movie stars, or listen to people talk about their "compulsive" eating to be aware of this. Excessive drinking, compulsive gambling and sexual activity, lying, stalking, shopping, stealing (kleptomania), and firesetting (pyromania), to name a few, have all become wrongly associated in the public mind with OCDs. As you will see, these have nothing to do with the disorder.

With all the juggling of these terms over the years, it is easy to become confused when you start looking for information on the subject. Simply put, obsessions are persistent, repetitive thoughts which seem to intrude upon your mind and which may be either meaningless or frightening in some way. Mostly, they create doubts about whether harm has happened or will happen to oneself or to others. The desire to stop or to be rid of them is also important. Even the most meaningless repetitive thoughts can cause anxiety, simply because they make it seem as if one's mind is out of control.

Obsessive thoughts enter a person's thinking in a way that can be sudden, like an electric shock, or very gradual. At first, the thought may seem to be connected with some real event or issue, but later it appears that it is purposeless, extreme, and would sound "crazy" or bizarre to others. In other cases, the thoughts seem outlandish and ridiculous right from the beginning. Obsessive thoughts are repeated often, and it may be difficult or even impossible to stop thinking them or to switch to other thoughts. Some thoughts have a sort of permanent quality, and each time they happen they are exactly the same. Some people's obsessions may take different forms each time they happen, but both types usually revolve around basic themes that are consistent. For some, the obsessions are a constant part of their thinking. For others, they come and go, either rapidly switching from one to another for no reason or changing each time a new, and seemingly more threatening one comes along (actually, the new ones aren't necessarily more threatening, just different). It is all these qualities that make obsessions different from ordinary worries and anxieties.

One very important feature that often goes along with obsessions is the feeling of doubt or uncertainty. If we had to sum up the majority of obsessions, two words would be sufficient—they would be "pathological doubt." In the last century, in fact, classic OCD was commonly known as "the doubting sickness." The person seems to both believe and not believe in the obsessions at the same time. Obsessives will often be heard to say things like, "I know the thoughts I'm having don't seem to be logical or make any sense, but I worry about them anyway because I can't be totally sure that they aren't true." Or they can be heard to begin their remarks with "How can I be sure that . . . ?" These doubts are very common and often are a large part of what makes it so difficult and agonizing for those with obsessions to function normally, since they cannot seem to decide whether to believe them or not. This is doubly true for thoughts that involve serious harm to the obsessive thinker or to others. The doubt that accompanies this disorder can be so insidious that it can even make you doubt that you have OCD, which will even further weaken your insight.

Obsessive doubts are extremely torturous and stubbornly refuse to quit. The result is often a stream of nonstop compulsive questioning, checking, and looking for reassurance about whether the thought is or isn't true. However, no amount of answering and reassuring ever seems to satisfy someone with this problem. An OCD sufferer's questions could be answered dozens of times, with people eventually losing patience with them. The sufferer may then in turn become angry and upset when the person tires of answering the same question for the hundredth time.

Actually, there are no adequate answers to obsessive questions, because they aren't real questions. Those with OCDs can have more information than the average person would need to be able to arrive at a decision or size up a risk—yet they are unable to do so. In their state of doubt, they mistakenly believe that the problem is that they simply do not have enough information. This leads to such information-gathering activities as excessive questioning and double-checking. They could have enough information to fill an encyclopedia (and sometimes do) yet they would still be in doubt, possibly because they just cannot process the information in a way that could eradicate that doubt. The answers just don't seem to "stick." Many of those with obsessions think that when they are actively obsessing about something, that they are actually "thinking" about it. In reality, obsessing is not thinking as most of us understand it, nor does it seem to be a logical or linear process. One of my patients refers to obsessions as "synthetic thoughts." They go nowhere except in a circle, starting with an intrusive thought that cannot be ignored, to a state of doubt, to an answer that doesn't stick, and then back to the thought again.

One might question the above explanation and ask whether the doubt of OCD is due to faulty information processing, or due simply to the repetition of the doubting and questioning which convinces the sufferer that they do not know the answer, when they actually do. It may actually be a chicken-and-egg type question. Perhaps future research will help to clarify this picture.

Dr. Paul Salkovskis of Oxford University, England, suggests that obsessing actually begins as a normal process, and that all people have intrusive thoughts at times. What may make it escalate into a problem is an individual's cata-strophic rating of these thoughts—thinking that having obsessive thoughts is terrible, as well as thinking that a danger may really exist.

One other view of the problem suggests that those with OCD are unable to screen out thoughts that are irrelevant, something the brain may do automatically when it is working normally. This could explain why the thoughts repeat in the circular way described above. It has been described by some as a faulty "gate" that instead of fully closing, allows stray thoughts to be transmitted to the brain areas responsible for conscious reasoning. All these theories may be correct, in part, or they may all be wrong. Only further investigation will give us the answers.

One important way in which classic OCD sufferers seem to differ from each other is in the degree of belief in their obsessive thoughts. At one end of the spec-trum are found those who can honestly say, "I know these thoughts are ridicu-lous and unbelievable, but I just can't turn them off." At the other end, we find what is called "overvalued ideation," where people find their obsessive thoughts very believable and have a difficult time distinguishing them from reality. A com-ment often made by sufferers about their thoughts is "They seem so real." I will sometimes question a person in treatment, asking, "How can you explain the fact that no one else you know believes or sees things as you do?" Those with overval-ued ideas will say, "That's because they're not as well informed as I am. Most peo-ple are ignorant. If they really knew what I know, they'd think the same way." This sort of thinking can be seen among some of those with classic OCD and especially those with Body Dysmorphic Disorder (BDD).

One type of repetitive thinking that should not be mistaken for OCD is the sort of ruminating that often goes along with serious depressions. Generally, in such cases there is no long-term history of obsessing prior to the start of the depression. Another important difference is that in depression, the thoughts con-sist more of general worries about life, such as relationships, finances, career obstacles, etc. These thoughts tend to be less doubtful and more negative overall about the person and their present, past, and future. Everything seems hopeless

Fig. 1.1 ⁓ The Obsessive-Compulsive Spectrum

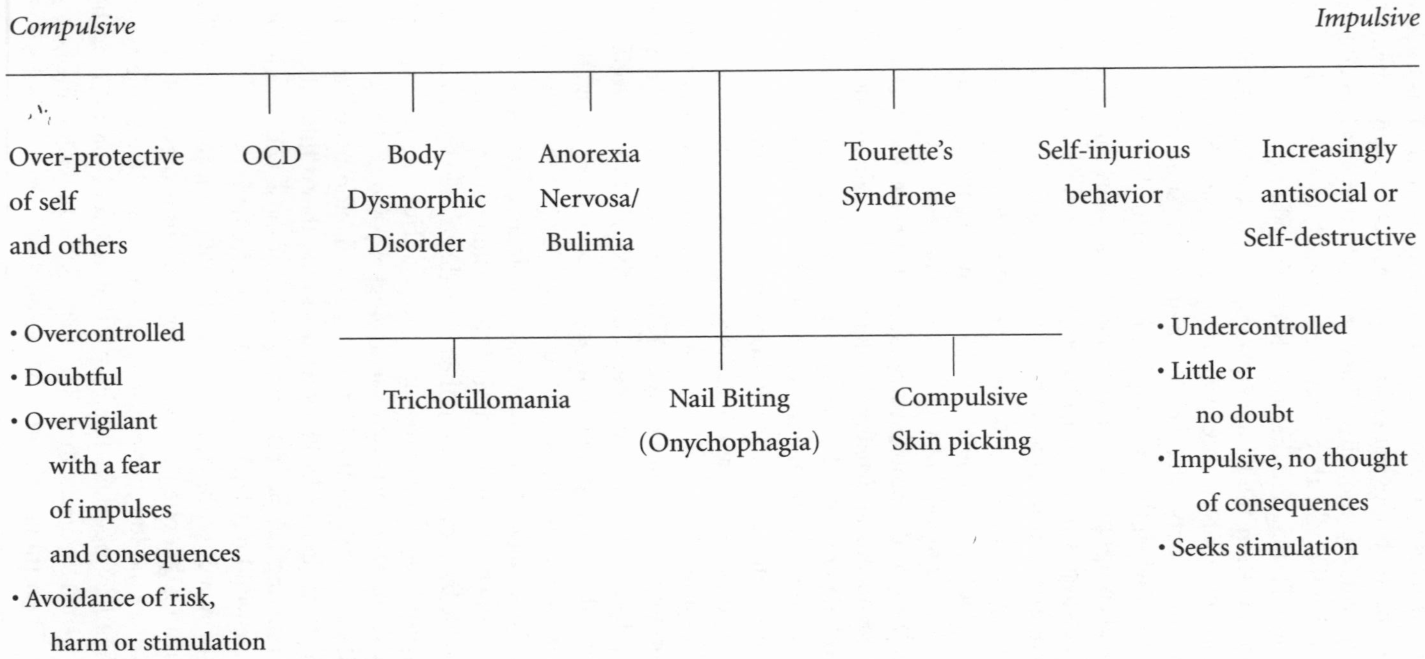

Compulsive					*Impulsive*
OCD	Body Dysmorphic Disorder	Anorexia Nervosa/ Bulimia	Tourette's Syndrome	Self-injurious behavior	Increasingly antisocial or Self-destructive
		Trichotillomania	Nail Biting (Onychophagia)	Compulsive Skin picking	

Over-protective of self and others

- Overcontrolled
- Doubtful
- Overvigilant with a fear of impulses and consequences
- Avoidance of risk, harm or stimulation

- Undercontrolled
- Little or no doubt
- Impulsive, no thought of consequences
- Seeks stimulation

and negative, as if a cloud were hanging over the person's life. Depressive rumi-nations also lack the bizarre or magical quality seen in some obsessions. A dis-cussion of the different forms that obsessions can take will be found in chapter 8.

Compulsions are performed to relieve the anxiety caused by obsessions. They are meant to keep certain bad or unpleasant things from happening, to cancel out things that have already happened, or to relieve doubtfulness about such things. They can be either physical behaviors or thoughts and may or may not have to be carried out according to a set of very exact rules, sometimes over and over again. They may often seem very strange and senseless to others who see them performed or who are told about them (when the activity cannot be seen). People who carry out compulsions are usually able to recognize this too, but they have the urge to per-form them anyway, no matter how difficult it may be for them, simply because they will feel less anxious afterward. It is this rewarding escape from anxiety that gets sufferers to establish these repeating patterns of behavior. They literally train them-selves to do these things without realizing what they are doing (see chapter 12).

Compulsive thinking activities, or mental compulsions, are the urges to carry out some type of special mental activity. This can include counting numbers in special patterns; repeatedly thinking of a word or words; praying in one's mind; making mental arrangements of objects or thoughts; making and reviewing mental lists; repeating in one's head what someone is saying; or drawing pic-tures or creating images in one's mind, etc. Usually, these acts have to be done in a special order, a perfect way, or at a particular time. These are different from obsessions because they are deliberately performed to relieve anxiety. Physical compulsions, on the other hand, involve carrying out some type of observable activity. Compulsions are more fully discussed in chapter 9.

The symptoms of classic OCD make up many categories that have within them a great number of varieties. While obsessions and compulsions are the chief symptoms, there are many other problems and traits that go along with them which have not been written about widely. Often, sufferers themselves may not be aware that what they are going through is connected to their main problem. There are also several other disorders (Body Dysmorphic Disorder, Trichotillomania, compulsive skin picking and nail biting, and Tourette's Syndrome) which together with classic OCD may make up a whole family or spectrum of disorders. Com-pared with classic OCD, the symptoms of these other disorders are even less well known, not only to those who suffer from them, but also to many practitioners. How they may be related to classic OCD will be covered in the next section.

THE OBSESSIVE-COMPULSIVE SPECTRUM

The diagram in Figure 1.1 shows a number of disorders which some now believe make up a group known as the "OC Spectrum." You may wonder why these disorders would belong together, or why they would make up a spectrum. Taken as a group, there appears to be some rather interesting information which suggests that they may have similarities, and that there may be some common cause or mechanism behind all of them. This is not to say that they are all the exact same disorder; however, they may be separate but related disorders. To put it in family terms, BDD might be regarded as a sibling to classic OCD, and TTM, skin picking, and nail biting could be thought of as cousins. It should be noted that with these disorders, sufferers find their symptoms repetitive and intrusive, they attempt to resist their symptoms (at least at times), feel anxious because of them, and have their lives disrupted and damaged by them. Statistics on those who have one disorder in this group show that they are far more likely to have a second one than chance would predict for the average person. Examples of this are:

- that 15 percent of a group of OCD patients was also found to qualify as having BDD according to a 1998 study by Dr. Katharine Phillips, who has conducted extensive research in this area. Another study, published in 1993 by Dr. Eric Hollander and colleagues, found diagnosable BDD in 37 percent of a group of OCD sufferers. Conversely, a study by Dr. Katharine Phillips and others published in 1994 found a lifetime frequency of OCD in 34 percent of a group of BDD patients.

- that 20 percent of those with classic OCD also meet criteria for Tourette's Syndrome (TS) or some other type of tic disorder. The prevalence of TS in the general population is one in one thousand. Conversely, Dr. David Pauls of Yale University has found that as many as 36 percent of those with TS also have OCD. In another study, published in 1994 by Rasmussen and Eisen, OCD was detected in 68 percent of a sample of TS patients.

- that a study by Dr. Gary Christensen of the University of Minnesota Medical School, and others, found a lifetime occurrence for anxiety disorders of 57 percent among those with TTM (OCD is currently classified as an anxiety disorder). A 1995 study by Cohen and colleagues found that 13 percent of a sample of TTM sufferers were also found to have diagnosable OCD. Another study, published in 1994 by Schlosser and associates, found OCD in 27 percent of a sample of those with TTM.

- that a 1996 study by Soriano and colleagues found that 26 percent of a sample of those diagnosed with TTM also met criteria for BDD.

- that in a recent study done at Johns Hopkins University, 23 percent of a sample of OCD sufferers were found to engage in skin picking, compared with 7 percent of controls.

Those whose disorders lie more toward the compulsive end of the spectrum are doubtful, rigid, and overcontrolled, overly vigilant, tend to double-check, constantly seek to avoid harm, and have a fear of their own impulses and the possible consequences. Conversely, those with disorders nearer the impulsive end of the spectrum are untroubled by doubt, are rather undercontrolled in some ways, are likely to act at any particular moment without thinking about consequences, and are more likely to engage in risky behaviors.

The same group of antidepressant drugs known as serotonin specific reuptake inhibitors (SSRIs) is effective in treating the disorders within this spectrum. Serotonin is a brain transmitter chemical that has been implicated in many of these disorders (see chapter 12). This may suggest a biological link between them. A second possible biological connection is suggested by the observation that serotonin levels have been shown to vary from higher at the compulsive end of the spectrum to lower at the impulsive end. This variation in serotonin suggests that these disorders may lie along some type of continuum relating to brain chemistry (see chapter 12). A third possible biological connection is that in the more compulsive disorders, higher-than-normal levels of metabolic activity in the frontal lobes of the brain can be seen, while toward the impulsive end of the spectrum there are lower-than-normal levels.

Due to the compelling nature of these observations, and because it appears to be currently the most logical way of organizing what is a rather broad topic, it was decided to use the theoretical view of an OC Spectrum to approach the disorders dealt with in this book. It should again be stressed that the idea of an OC Spectrum is a theory and is still being debated. There are those who question whether these similarities and connections may perhaps be coincidental and may also be seen in other disorders outside of this spectrum. They also wonder if we may be oversimplifying things by grouping these disorders together, and that by doing so, we may be overlooking other characteristics that are important. We do not yet have answers to these questions. Only further research can answer them.

BODY DYSMORPHIC DISORDER (BDD)

BDD is a little known and poorly understood disorder. It has been officially classified as a Somatoform Disorder in the DSM-IV, but more recently, BDD has come to be considered by some to be a part of the OC Spectrum. (See appendix C. For definition, see appendix E, Glossary.) BDD is the only disorder in this somatoform group that involves appearance, while all the others (hypochondriasis is one) involve either imagined or magnified beliefs that the sufferer is ill or in pain or is suffering actual physical symptoms that are purely psychological.

Another name for BDD is dysmorphophobia, a term originated by the Italian physician Enriqué Morselli in the late nineteenth century.

As in classic OCD, BDD sufferers also have obsessions. In BDD, they obsess about what they believe are defects in the way they look. These defects may seem to be either totally imaginary to others who cannot see what the sufferer is talking about or are so tiny that the sufferer appears to be greatly exaggerating them. The degree of belief in these defects can range from moderate to very strong, is stubbornly held, greater than many other types of obsessions, and almost gives the impression that the sufferer is out of touch with reality. This is one feature that differentiates some cases of BDD from classic OCD.

BDD sufferers can also behave compulsively in that they constantly check their appearance (or conversely, avoid looking at themselves), constantly question others (in some cases), and perfectionistically try to remove or cover up their defect. The feelings of embarrassment and shame that go along with these beliefs actually keep many from seeking help, because they fear having to talk about them. Poor self-image is frequently a problem. Many with BDD avoid socializing with others or even going out in public, for fear of others seeing the imagined defect. Thoughts about their bodies can take up so many hours a day that their lives may be completely taken over by them. Serious difficulties in everyday living are common in BDD and many sufferers stay at home disabled or at least living very limited lives. Many never marry or have relationships and avoid seeking jobs. Hospitalization is not unusual because of the anxiety and depression.

There is no doubt that there are social inputs into BDD, as well as biological ones. We live in an image-conscious society, bombarded by messages from powerful clothing and cosmetic industries dedicated to making people dissatisfied with their appearance so that they will constantly buy more products. Advertisers try to take advantage of the fact that a certain amount of dissatisfaction for particular body parts is normal in many people. Those with BDD may be more heavily influenced by these values.

A sufferer's beliefs can involve any physical defects that can be imagined. Perhaps parts of the body are too large or too small, or the body or parts of it are not symmetrical, or a part of one's body is aging prematurely, or body parts are ugly (scarred or marked with spots, bumps, acne, etc.), misshapen, or disfigured. Areas of the body that are focused on can vary widely. People with BDD may become preoccupied with their hair, eyes, nose, skin, chin, lips, the shape of their head or face, their teeth, breasts, sex organs, legs, buttocks, etc. Also, a BDD sufferer's focus may shift over time, from being obsessed with one part of their body for several months, losing interest in it, and then focusing on another just as strongly. Multiple body areas may be involved. As in OCD, symptoms may ebb and flow, but are always there. (For further discussion, see the sections on "Body-Focused Obsessions" in chapter 8 and "Body-Focused Compulsions" in chapter 9.)

TRICHOTILLOMANIA (TTM)—HAIR PULLING

Trichotillomania (TTM), or Impulsive Hair Pulling, is a disorder which is only just beginning to be appreciated in terms of how complex it is, the number of people who actually have it, and its powerful negative impact on people's lives. (For definitions, see appendices C and E.) TTM was first given its name in 1889 by the French physician, François Henri Hallopeau. The name itself is misleading and creates an unfortunate connection with other disorders to which it is not related. The fact that its name includes the term "mania" wrongly suggests that sufferers are "crazy" or seriously mentally ill. It was, and still is, classified as an "Impulse Control Disorder," lumped together with such problems as kleptomania, pyromania, and pathological gambling in the DSM-IV. Anyone familiar with the disorder can quickly see how little it has in common with the other disorders in its current official category, although it does share problem impulses that can be pleasurable in the short run. It was most likely included in this group because no one really knew where else to put it. Actually, TTM appears to share many different elements with OCD, BDD, and TS. Because of these shared characteristics, there are those who have chosen to include it in this spectrum of OC disorders. More research will help determine into which category it truly belongs. What is most important though is that the individual sufferer knows that they are not alone with this problem, and that help is available.

Recent studies, such as those by Dr. Gary Christensen, have begun to cast doubt on the accuracy of the official diagnostic criteria (see appendix C). In one groundbreaking study by Dr. Christensen and colleagues, it was found that among a large group of college students there were a number who pulled their hair, but without having a particular urge or feeling of tension before doing so. This finding contradicts the official DSM-IV definition. While it is true that the urge to pull out your hair can start with an impulse that cannot be easily controlled, the picture is a lot more complicated. Pulling has many inputs and can be influenced by a wide variety of factors. For some, it can be automatic at least part of the time, and there is often no awareness of the pulling. A study by Drs. Christensen and Mackenzie published in 1994 found that automatic pulling was the major pulling style of about 75 percent of TTM sufferers. Some say that this automatic pulling may at times be closer to a tic of the type seen in Tourette's Syndrome (TS). Another group of TTM sufferers report a pleasurable or soothing feeling when pulling hair, and they may go on to ritualize or play with the hair afterward. There are those who report feeling no particular pleasure. Finally, there are those whose pulling is done deliberately and seems closer to classic OCD. They feel driven to perfectionistically pull hairs that are imperfect or "wrong" in some special way. By pulling out these hairs, they believe that they are *fixing* the way their hair looks and improving its appearance. One thing all these different groups have in common is the upset they feel over what they have done, and the fact that they could not stop themselves.

Exactly what underlies TTM remains unknown. Dr. Judith Rapoport of the National Institute of Mental Health (NIMH) has, in recent years, proposed that TTM may be an ancient leftover grooming program, left behind by evolution and present in everyone, but somehow mistakenly switched on in the brains of those with this disorder. She has also drawn attention to an animal model for the disorder found in certain breeds of dogs and known to veterinarians as Canine Acral Lick. Dogs with this problem are seen to lick their forepaws to excess, removing their fur, and causing great irritation and even skin damage. There is also a similar disorder seen in cats. Antidepressant medications seem to remedy these problems in animals as they do in humans.

Whether this theory is true or not, the fact that certain antidepressant medications alone can sometimes relieve the urge to pull, gives strong evidence that there is some underlying basis in the chemistry of the brain. The story doesn't end here, however. Current theory on TTM suggests that it is a complex disorder that may be both biological and behavioral and can also be strongly influenced by environmental factors. According to Dr. Charles Mansueto, a psychologist and noted TTM theorist, there are both internal and external factors which affect hair pulling. Dr. Mansueto identifies five modalities that act as both cues or signals and sources of feedback that work together to maintain pulling. The first four of these modalities are said to be internal to the sufferer. They are Cognitive (the individual's thoughts and beliefs), Affective (the individual's emotional state), Motoric (physical actions), Sensory (sight, touch, etc.), and External (environmental). To fully understand TTM, Dr. Mansueto believes that all these modalities must be considered in the various ways in which they interact with each other.

TTM is not limited to pulling hair from the scalp. Hair may be pulled from any area of the body: eyelashes, eyebrows, the arms or torso, the legs, under the arms, or even the pubic area. Many of those in this last category may be especially reluctant to go for treatment because of feelings of embarrassment. There are even differences between those who pull only from their scalp. Some may pull exclusively from just one spot to the point of baldness. Others may pull from several sites, and still others may simply allow their hands to generally wander all over their heads in search of special hairs that seem to need removing, resulting in a general thinning. Due to these differences in pulling styles, there are those who show spots which are completely free of hairs, and there are others with wide areas of thinned hair.

Interestingly, some TTM sufferers' urges are not confined to themselves, and they can be seen to habitually pull fibers, hairs, and strands from pets, toys, or objects in their environment. A resemblance to classic OCD can be seen in the way some hair pullers choose which hairs to pull. The decision can sometimes involve perfectionism in terms of finding hairs that are "just right" or "perfect" for pulling, based on certain qualities such as color, texture, location, length, etc. In addition, there may be rituals performed with hairs after they are pulled. This is a less well-known side of TTM that also seems to resemble the ritual behaviors of OCD. Hairs may have to be bitten, rolled up, chewed, knotted, played with, swallowed, etc. The swallowing of hairs may be the most physically hazardous symptom of TTM, as it can result in hairballs known as trichobezoars, which can block the intestinal tract. In the most serious cases, this can require surgery.

Two important differences separate TTM from classic OCD. One is that for many, it has a strong sensory component and can be a pleasurable and relaxing activity, even though the long-term effects are the opposite. In classic OCD, the sensory component plays a lesser role, and compulsions are definitely not pleasurable or relaxing. Those who pull report that while it is happening, it can be very soothing and relaxing, as well as stimulating and satisfying to the person's sense of touch and sight. Hair pullers commonly get feelings of satisfaction from such things as stroking pulled hairs across their cheeks or lips, crunching the root bulb of a hair between their teeth, or in visually inspecting the hairs. The pleasures derived from these sensations are part of what makes TTM a stubborn problem to treat.

Physical problems are sometimes seen among hair pullers. Trichobezoars have already been mentioned above. Others commonly seen are repetitive strain injuries, such as neck, back, and shoulder problems, or tendonitis due to bending and twisting the wrists when pulling. There can also be eye irritations and infections, and dental problems caused by excessive wear of tooth enamel due to chewing hairs or grooves cut in tooth enamel from pulling hairs between the teeth. Women who pull pubic hairs have been known to develop health problems due to avoidance of regular visits to a gynecologist. Those who pull eyebrows or eyelashes often neglect going for eye checkups or corrective lenses.

The emotional impact of TTM cannot be overemphasized. The feelings of shame, helplessness, isolation, and frustration can take a tremendous toll on sufferers. It is not unusual for sufferers to feel that TTM has ruined much of their lives. The experience of TTM is a very lonely and isolating one, with secrecy being almost universal. It is also not unusual to meet many TTM sufferers who actually believe that their symptoms are unique and that they are the only ones who do these things. They may go for years without seeking help, thinking that there is nothing they can do either because of a lack of information, or because they were told that nothing could be done. They also suffer ridicule, anger, and insensitivity from their family members. Sufferers may sometimes turn to alcohol or drug abuse to ease their emotional pain. While we do not currently know the extent of such self-medication, my guess is that it may be widespread. In the more severe cases, those with TTM avoid social contacts, as well as working outside their homes, preferring instead to hide their disorder. Hats, wigs, scarves, glasses, makeup, and other cover-ups must be employed before they can go out into the world—if they go out at all.

Ordinary activities that we take for granted become closed to many with TTM. A simple visit to a hairdresser or barber may be out of the question or conducted with great anxiety and secrecy. Many have not had a haircut in years. Swimming, skiing, bicycling, riding in convertibles or on motorcycles, or taking an amusement park ride are avoided, due to the fear of losing a wig or having their carefully arranged hair blown around to reveal bald spots. Many who depend on hats or scarves miss out on social events or jobs where wearing these would be inappropriate.

In addition to having their activities limited, TTM sufferers face other difficulties. Because of the bad feelings surrounding their appearance, we see poor self-image and a lack of self-confidence in many that can lead to lower levels of achievement in school or at work. Many also fear to have relationships, not wanting others to discover their secret. Some married sufferers live double lives, keeping their hair loss a secret from their spouses. They make sure to never go to bed without a wig or scarf on, their eye makeup complete, or their hair clipped or firmly braided in place to cover any bald spots.

Joanne's account of her TTM communicates the experience of the disorder.

Joanne's Story

∾ *"Please, just one more with a big root." I've said that to myself over and over again, more times than I could ever begin to count. One more what? Well, a dark, kinky hair. Sound crazy? It does to me too. You see, I have a disorder which is referred to as Trichotillomania. It is an uncontrollable urge to pull out my hair, one strand at a time. As if that isn't bad enough, I then proceed to eat it. I don't swallow the hair whole, but rather nibble it down into tiny segments. I concentrate mostly on chewing the root. Something about that feels good. I'm an otherwise normal twenty-six-year-old female. . . . Most people, even close friends, have no idea that I suffer from this disorder. I try very hard to keep it secret. Others would be shocked to learn that I have been pulling out my own hair, including my eyebrows, leg hair, and pubic hair since the age of thirteen. Even though I have three large bald spots, I have become pretty clever at covering them. Anyone who suffers from Trichotillomania knows the pain and suffering it brings. I cannot go swimming without revealing my bald head to the world. Getting my hair cut is an embarrassing nightmare. The wind has become my worst enemy. I constantly fear the thought of being left with so little hair that I have to resort to wearing a wig. Does this make me stop? Of course not! Some days I get by without pulling any hair. Most others, however, are filled with my pulling routine. I sometimes spend four hours or more concentrating only on finding "the right hair." When I have episodes like those, sleep is the only thing that stops my hands from being drawn to my head. I have tried to learn as much as I can about Trichotillomania and OCD. It is reassuring to know that I am not the only person on earth with this odd condition. . . . I've tried wearing gloves, pinning my hair back, and cutting my nails short. I wasn't surprised when all these strategies to alleviate my pulling failed. I am fully aware of my problem. Not one day goes by that I don't think about it. I'm constantly paranoid that people can see my bald spots and think I am strange. I've often wondered "why me?" I feel very unlucky that I have to be affected by this disorder. . . . I recognize my disorder and am trying everything possible to bring it to an end.*

IMPULSIVE SKIN PICKING AND NAIL BITING

While it is true that everyone picks and pulls and scratches and squeezes their skin or bites their nails at times, there are boundaries separating normal from abnormal. In most cases, these things are done out of boredom or as nervous habits and only cause minor problems at most. The point at which these behaviors cross the line into what would be considered a disorder can be determined by how much physical damage has been caused, and whether the behavior is causing noticeable interference with normal, day-to-day activities.

Skin picking and nail biting have only recently come into focus as part of the OC Spectrum. Compulsive nail biting (onychophagia) does not appear in the DSM-IV as an official disorder. Compulsive skin picking is known to dermatologists as "neurotic excoriation"; however, it has no official psychiatric designation in the DSM-IV either, other than put into the category of "Impulse-Control Disorder Not Otherwise Specified." It is clear, however, that either of these problems can become serious enough to disable a sufferer.

Skin picking can involve picking to the point of creating open sores on different body areas and then also picking the resulting scabs. Skin picking can also involve widespread squeezing and digging at pimples and blackheads with fingers or other tools to the point of causing scarring and skin infections. It also can include hours of studying one's face in mirrors. There would appear to be two groups of skin pickers. One group has a strong similarity to BDD, in that sufferers believe that the slightest blemish will totally disfigure their faces. They not only pick at real blemishes, but also at anything even slightly resembling a possible blemish. The goal is to make their faces "perfect." As they examine themselves, they can mentally magnify a small pimple or two into a major case of severe acne.

The other group is more similar to the automatic type of TTM. These sufferers pick to satisfy an urge, much as TTM sufferers get the urge to pull their hair. They will stand before their mirror in an almost trancelike state, picking and squeezing because it "feels good." Picking, for them, relieves tension and stress and relieves their urge.

Serious nail biting, where nails are bitten down to the nail bed, can be severe enough to result in bleeding and disfigured fingertips. Cuticles may also be picked or bitten. Actually, nails can be peeled or picked off, as well as being bitten off. Nails can be destroyed either deliberately or automatically, as in TTM and skin picking. Like TTM, sufferers often report feeling little or no pain and, in fact, can report feelings of satisfaction and calm while they are doing it.

The actual number of people who are afflicted by these behaviors is unknown at the present time. My guess is that there are more sufferers than we may realize. Many probably do not realize that they may have a disorder or that there is anything that can be done about it. Also, many therapists and physicians may not yet be informed enough to identify patients who have these problems.

INCIDENCE OF OBSESSIVE-COMPULSIVE SPECTRUM DISORDERS (OCSDs)

Until recent times, OCSDs were thought to be rather rare. In 1953, it was estimated that just .05 percent of the population had classic OCD. The National Epidemiological Catchment Area Survey (NECA), conducted in 1985, determined that classic OCD had a lifetime occurrence rate among the American population of 2.5 percent, a fiftyfold increase. Other estimates suggest that between four and seven million Americans suffer from classic OCD. This works out to approximately one in forty persons. Other estimates suggest the rate may be higher. It also used to be thought that twice as many persons suffered from schizophrenia as compared to the number of those with OCD. To the surprise of many, the NECA Survey found that the opposite was true. What is striking about current incidence figures is that despite the fact that OC disorders are so common, little is known or understood by the public, professionals, and sufferers.

In the past, reasons for OCSDs' supposed rarity were probably due to:

- misdiagnosis (often as schizophrenia, for instance)

- the finding that over half of those with classic OCD were seen (and still are seen) by practitioners who are not mental health specialists

- many people with OCSDs keeping their "crazy" symptoms a secret, fearing exposure

- many practitioners failing (and they still fail) to routinely screen new patients for OCSDs, even in the presence of obvious warning signs.

The true extent of BDD is unknown at this time. There have, so far, been no surveys, although Dr. Eric Hollander of Mt. Sinai Hospital, an expert in OCSDs, estimates its incidence at 1 percent of the population. Hopefully, someone will make such a scientific survey in the near future. TTM is just beginning to be explored. It was once thought to be rare, but now there are estimates of sufferers in the United States ranging from four to ten million. Other estimates have suggested a prevalence of 1–2 percent of the population. A very interesting survey among college students, carried out by Dr. Gary Christensen and collaborators in Minneapolis, indicated that about .6 percent of both male and female students suffered from TTM (when diagnosed using the now obsolete DSM-IIIR criteria) at some time in their lives. Using a wider definition than the one found in the DSM, they found lifetime occurrences of hair pulling which resulted in visible hair loss in 1.5 percent of the men and 3.4 percent of the women. Another study, carried out by King and colleagues and published in 1995, studied a large group of Israeli seventeen-year-olds and found a lifetime occurrence of hair pulling of 1 percent. It was also found that .5 percent of this group were currently pulling hairs at the time of the study.

Skin picking is not presently classified as a disorder in its own right, and as such, there are no studies on its prevalence in the general population. A study by Griesemor, published in 1978, found that 2 percent of dermatology patients engaged in this behavior. A more recent study presented by Dr. Bernadette Cullen of Johns Hopkins University in Baltimore found that it might be far more common among OCD sufferers than most people realize. In this study of 79 OCD sufferers, 23 percent were found to engage in skin picking as compared with 7 percent of a non-OCD control group.

~ Behavioral Therapy

A Treatment That Works

~ There is nothing which persevering effort and unceasing and diligent care cannot overcome.
—*Seneca*

Habit is habit, and not to be flung out of the window by any man, but coaxed downstairs a step at a time.
—*Mark Twain*

Habit is overcome by habit.
—*Thomas à Kempis, c. 1420*

Recovering from OC disorders is not simply a matter of sheer willpower, resistance, or "just stopping," although these may help. Most sufferers have been told repeatedly to "just snap out of it," or "get a grip on yourself," or even, "why don't you just stop?" However, it is much more difficult and complicated than that. Those with OCSDs need intensive help in retraining themselves, both in terms of behavior and their outlook on life. Many are tagged with the old mental illness stigma of somehow being "morally weak" or defective and are made to feel desperately ashamed of themselves. This is an injustice, pure and simple. No one with an OCSD prefers to do what they are doing, no matter how frantic they may seem as they do it. Obviously, if they could stop, they would. Those who do not have an OCSD cannot fully understand the anxiety and desperation which follows the doubtful thoughts and powerful urges that at times seem so compelling. Some sufferers have described it as feeling like being "possessed."

I believe that one major mistake nonsufferers make is that they somehow look upon OCSDs as merely some annoying thoughts or problem habits, similar to smoking or overeating (actually also very difficult habits to break). People with OCSDs are seen in the public mind as having poor self-control and lacking the will to resist. An OCSD is not just a bad habit or temptation to be "kicked." It is a biological attack on a person's ability to think only their own thoughts and to control their own physical actions. You cannot throw away an OCSD the way you would your pack of cigarettes and go cold turkey. It is inside your thinking and has set itself up there. It has become part of your mental life. When my patients ask me how they can differentiate OCSD symptoms from other habits they may have, I tell them, "If you feel as if you haven't got a choice, it's an OCSD." Interestingly, various researchers have found that when obsessive thinkers try to deliberately stop their thoughts and not think them, they actually end up thinking them more, as a sort of rebound effect.

This is not to say that sufferers are not responsible for themselves. They are at all times. Even though the problem has a biological basis, you can fight back and be responsible to yourself for finding effective therapy and following through with it. A person in the midst of an OCSD simply cannot instantly stop and to expect them to do so is unrealistic. Stopping is the final result of a persistent effort over time, the result of changing both behavior and thinking. It is not a place to start, but a goal—a destination.

PSYCHOTHERAPY AND OCSDs

While psychotherapists of many schools may claim that their particular approaches can help OCSDs, there is still only one group of therapies that has been scientifically demonstrated to be effective—the behavioral therapies. Numerous studies indicate that behavioral therapy is the most effective psychotherapeutic treatment for OCSDs—a claim that no other therapy (with one possible exception) can document. One study published in 1985 by Dr. Edna Foa showed that behavioral therapy was able to produce outcomes in classic OCD, in which greater than 70 percent of patients were recovered or much improved. Another behavioral study, published in 1980 by Dr. Nathan Azrin and colleagues, indicated a success rate of 91 percent in the treatment of TTM. This is not to say that there aren't people out there who can claim to have been helped by other types of therapy. There are. Every treatment has probably worked for at least a few people, but may not work for most. What may have helped a specific person may be due more to factors particular just to that person, factors which may not operate in your own life.

It is always wisest to go with the scientific evidence. The evidence we have tells us that OCSDs are biologically based brain chemical disorders, and because this is so, it will do little good to spend endless sessions reviewing your childhood experiences and the behavior of your parents in raising you. We have no evidence that there is a psychological "root" underlying these problems which must be fixed before progress can be made.

COGNITIVE THERAPY

Cognitive therapy is a type of treatment that has been around for about the last forty years but was not thought to be helpful for treating the symptoms of any of the OCSDs. Recent studies conducted in Great Britain and Holland have shown it to be as effective as behavior therapy for classic OCD. It has not been tested with the other OCSDs thus far, although BDD and the eating disorders would probably be the only other disorders in this spectrum for which it would be appropriate. More studies need to be done to confirm its effectiveness; however, the results so far are very interesting.

This type of therapy, briefly, is based on the theory that emotional disturbance is caused by extreme and illogical beliefs and ways of distorted reasoning, which make up an individual's own outlook and "philosophy" of how life ought to be for themselves and others. It further suggests that we human beings have a tendency to think illogically. These beliefs can often be deeply held for most of a person's life and come to mind almost automatically. They can be acquired during one's early years, from one's family, one's later experiences, or may be shaped and influenced by an illness itself. Cognitive therapy teaches essentially that people and things don't upset us, we upset and disturb ourselves as a result of the erroneous views we take of them. Much disturbance comes from beliefs that we ought to be able to control people and situations in order to control ourselves, when in fact the only thing actually under our control is our own thinking and our own behavior.

Beyond the normal amount of faulty reasoning that we all use, those who have had classic OCD and BDD long term seem to have developed more than their share. The cognitive approach to OCD starts with the notion that everyone, even nonsufferers, gets intrusive and unpleasant thoughts at times. Those with OCD tend to make more of these thoughts and believe that they must be acted upon. Once they act, they set a whole cycle in motion, in which they give the thoughts believability, but never test them out because they are too busy doing compulsive things to avoid confronting them.

There are two main areas that cognitive therapy for classic OCD has focused on and which are thought to be central to the disorder. One is the ability of sufferers to estimate the amount of risks in everyday situations in life. It is suggested that those with OCD are much more prone than average to overestimate possible dangers in many ordinary situations. Many people with classic OCD and BDD have difficulty recognizing and admitting they have problems with this and truly need to change their thinking in this respect. Cognitive therapy for OCD and BDD helps sufferers to improve their risk-estimating skills. It is also used to help them accept that taking risks, both great and small, is part of normal everyday existence. Attempting to eliminate risk may mean eliminating large portions of your life itself. Cognitive therapy works to help you regain the ability to accept that although life is not, and cannot be, risk-free, you must take risks in order to become spontaneous and free. Cognitive therapy can't teach you how to get everything you want from life, but it can help you take the chances necessary to maximize what you are able to get, while helping you to accept what you cannot.

Second, many OC sufferers have a highly exaggerated sense of just how responsible they are for the things that go on around them. Along with this come extreme feelings of guilt in reaction to feeling overly responsible. Cognitive therapy seeks to help you be more logical about deciding exactly how much responsibility you really have in the situations you typically worry about.

Cognitive therapy can also be quite helpful in other ways as well. Along with learning to take responsibility for your own emotions, learning to think and reason logically are the keys to coping with everyday life in a world which often seems anxiety provoking, frustrating, and disappointing. As unwanted as anxiety, frustration, and disappointment may be, they can be tolerated and lived with.

Since it appears that stress tends to worsen the symptoms of OCSDs, it is obvious that those who cope best with life in recovery will be more likely to stay recovered. I like to tell my patients that the behavior therapy is what initially gets them well, and the cognitive therapy is what keeps them well.

As yet, cognitive therapy for OCD has not been widely used in the United States, nor are there currently any treatment guides or manuals. Hopefully, we will see and hear more of this valuable treatment in the near future.

It should be mentioned at this point that other types of therapy could be helpful as additional treatments. It stands to reason that since OCSDs are affected by stress, any type of therapy that helps a person cope with frustration, disappointment, anxiety, and sadness ought to be able to make a contribution to getting well. This could also explain how some other types of talk therapies seem, at times, to help lessen OCSDs a bit (although they rarely do a good job).

Other types of therapy may also be useful for problems that have developed as the result of having an OCSD. Examples could include having been disabled by the illness for many years, feeling poorly about yourself for having an OCSD, or having suffered important losses in life due to the illness. Again, I recommend cognitive therapy for such problems.

I have found that cognitive therapy used in this way is useful when combined with behavioral therapy. Often, there are personal issues which must be treated along with OCD and which may interfere with the therapy if not addressed. These issues may involve poor self-acceptance, relationship or family problems, career questions, anger problems, depression, substance abuse, etc. Today most behavioral therapists also practice cognitive therapy as well, in order to help their patients cope with these issues. They are properly referred to as cognitive/behavioral therapists. This provides a talk therapy component for the types of philosophical and emotional issues which behavioral therapy alone cannot address. Changing your behavior can change the way you think, but conversely, changing your thinking can also modify your behavior. These two therapies complement each other and add to each other's effectiveness.

There is one further thing that cognitive therapy can teach you whatever your disorder—that is, how to accept yourself as simply the ordinary, mistake-making human being you are. It tells us that you are basically unratable. You can, however, rate your own behavior as "good" or "bad." This will not get you into trouble. If you rate yourself badly because of your illness, you will most likely get depressed and feel unable to change. If you stick to rating your behavior instead of yourself, you can stay focused on changing that particular behavior and still feel motivated.

As useful as cognitive therapy may be as an additional therapy, I would still not recommend this approach alone for treating OCSDs at this time. While it might be most helpful for those with milder disorders, the OC thought process itself is not one you can easily reason your way out of. Most people with OCD already know that their obsessions are clearly illogical and sound crazy to others. Changing one's behavior is still a more efficient way to change thinking in the case of OCD or BDD. There is no real substitute for directly facing and overcoming fearful situations when it comes to changing the way you think about your obsessions. You end up with an understanding of the truth that is real and not just theoretical.

BEHAVIORAL THERAPY WORKS

Not all behavioral therapies are the same. The scientific evidence we have indicates that different ones are applicable to different types of disorders. This book focuses on two particular types: Exposure and Response Prevention (E&RP) for classic OCD and BDD, and Habit Reversal Training (HRT) for TTM, skin picking, and nail biting.

The only type of behavioral therapy shown to be effective for classic OCD is E&RP. Its use is also being studied for the treatment of BDD and anorexia (see

Fig. 2.1 ∾ Treatment of Obsessive-Compulsive Spectrum Disorders

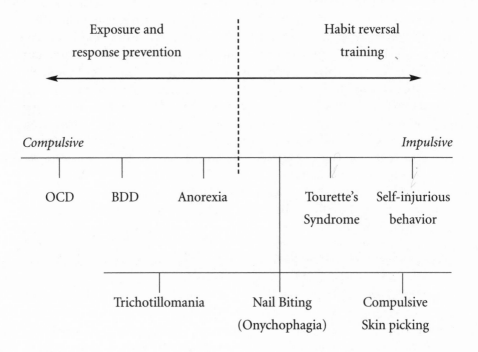

Fig. 2.1). Another and less accurate name for this procedure is "flooding." People with classic OCD typically do not remain in the presence of what they fear long enough to discover that it wasn't really dangerous, that nothing bad would have happened, and that their anxiety would have subsided on its own. Their thinking is concentrated only on short-term avoidance rather than on long-term consequences. They are more concerned with how they will feel in the next five minutes rather than in the next five years.

E&RP encourages participants to expose themselves to their obsessions (or to situations that will bring on the obsessions), while they prevent themselves from using compulsions to get rid of the resulting anxiety. The fearful thoughts or situations are approached in gradually increased amounts over a period of from several weeks to several months (see the next section on the steps in a typical course of behavioral therapy). This results in an effect on the individual that we call "habituation." That is, when you remain in the presence of what you fear over long periods of time, you will soon see that no harm of any kind results. As you do so in slowly increasing amounts, you develop a tolerance to the presence of the fear, and its effect is greatly lessened. By continually avoiding feared situations and never really encountering them, you keep yourself sensitized. By facing them, you learn that the avoidance itself is the "real" threat that keeps you trapped. It puts you in the role of a scientist conducting experiments that test your own fearful predictions, to see what really happens when you don't avoid what you fear. The result is that as you slowly build up your tolerance for whatever is fear-provoking, it begins to take larger and larger doses of frightening thoughts or situations to bring on the same amount of anxiety. When you have finally managed to tolerate the most difficult parts of your OCD, they can no longer cause you to react with fear. By agreeing to face some short-term anxiety, you can thus achieve long-term relief.

Those with classic OCD and BDD are generally overcontrolled individuals. Because of their fears, they have attempted to create lives for themselves that are risk-free, have no spontaneity, and revolve around never having to encounter what they fear. Rather than anything positive, this results in a distorted life with limited functioning in many areas. Engaging in E&RP means gradually giving up that rigid control, but paradoxically, it also means gradually having more control over your OCSD.

Some people question whether it is necessary to do both exposure and response prevention to get the desired result. An interesting study by Dr. Edna Foa and colleagues done in 1980 compared the use of E&RP to the use of either exposure alone or response prevention alone. Exposure alone led to more of a reduction in anxiety, but less improvement of compulsive rituals. The reverse was found to be true for response prevention used alone. When the two treatments were combined as E&RP, the differences between the two groups disappeared. Although this was done with a group of only eight patients, the results do suggest that E&RP should be considered as a complete treatment package that should not be divided up.

Patients often ask whether behavior therapy can eradicate obsessions. In the course of behavior therapy, obsessions may be lessened because the overall anxiety and stress levels are lower, but this is one thing that cannot be guaranteed. After the completion of therapy, obsessions can and do occur. It is realistic to expect them. Sufferers may never enjoy having whatever part of the obsessions remain, but at least they will no longer need to react fearfully and compulsively in ways that destroy or impair their lives. They will have now achieved the ability to tolerate the thoughts. An image I sometimes use with new patients is to compare the therapy to allergy shots, where patients are gradually injected with stronger solutions of the substances to which they are allergic, in order to gradually build up their tolerance and decrease the allergic response.

Some people question E&RP, asking, "How can it help me, since I am already exposed to what I fear many times a day?" The answer to this is that they probably react compulsively at those times, whereas with the E&RP procedure, they resist doing compulsions as they expose themselves to the fears. Also, I believe there is a completely different mind-set when people deliberately expose themselves to what they fear, as opposed to just passively waiting for the fear to come spontaneously. It may actually give the sufferer a new and better sense of control, in a paradoxical sort of way, as they are now giving themselves permission to be anxious. By accepting that they cannot control the things they will see, hear, or encounter in the world, they achieve control of themselves.

In the case of TTM, skin picking, and nail biting, the only treatment for which we have any real scientific data is HRT. Some claims have been made for the use of clinical hypnosis, but there are practically no data to support them. HRT is a multicomponent treatment which includes the use of self-monitoring, self-relaxation, breathing control, and isometric muscle contraction. The combined goal of these techniques is to increase a sufferer's awareness of their own behavior, and to train them in how to center themselves and physically resist urges to perform the destructive habits. The idea is that through repetitive practice, HRT can become almost as automatic as the undesirable behaviors themselves. Participants are also encouraged to discover all the internal and external signals that lead to the behaviors. They can then anticipate the internal ones and change the external ones, thus leading to fewer urges.

THERAPY, THE THERAPIST, AND MY FEELINGS

Contrary to what you may have heard, behavioral therapy is not performed by people in white lab coats who carry clipboards and little hand counters, run rats in mazes, and say they aren't interested in your feelings. Behavioral therapy isn't just for animals. The laws that govern behavior are universal, even if in the case of human beings things seem a little more complicated due to our higher reasoning powers. Behavioral therapy has a very human face and is actually a very personal and humane approach to treating certain problems. As in other forms of therapy, the working relationship between the patient and the behavior therapist is crucial and possibly the single most important factor in accounting for how successful patients respond. It is a partnership, an alliance.

Behavioral therapy is a "doing" therapy, and the therapist must ask the patient to do some extremely difficult and anxiety-provoking things at times. A strong partnership must be established. Unless the patient trusts their therapist to understand what they are experiencing and be sensitive to their limits, the treatment will not succeed. In this type of therapy, people are not forced to do anything they do not wish to do, nor are situations sprung on them by surprise.

All behavioral therapy begins with carefully taking a full history, during which time the therapist gets to know not only about symptoms, but also all the different aspects of the patient's life, including family background, upbringing, career, relationships, current day-to-day existence, etc. The overall impact of the disorder on the patient's life and the lives of others must be understood as well.

Behavioral therapists often use themselves as examples for their patients, share their own feelings, model for them, and actually are generally more involved and self-disclosing than many of the more orthodox analytic therapists. Behavioral therapists do more than just talk to their patients. They share active experiences together, both in and out of the office. Successes and setbacks are shared on a regular basis. Humor and laughter are frequently a part of therapy sessions. Patients of all ages often need to learn to laugh at some of their symptoms as a way of taking control of them. Behavioral therapists can also cry with their patients. You will find the same box of tissues in a behavioral therapist's office, as you will in any other.

Those who tell you about the coldness and impersonality of behavioral therapy, or that it cannot deal with your thoughts or feelings, have probably had no experience or training in this type of treatment.

BEHAVIORAL THERAPY FOR OCSDs

While I realize that this is a self-help book, I believe that you should be aware of what behavioral therapy for this group of disorders is like, in case you do decide to try it, or if you are using this book for information for yourself or another. Here is my own particular approach to treating OCSDs. I do not believe that my methods differ radically from most. The steps are as follows:

1. Intake and history

2. Diagnosis

3. Detailed analysis of the symptoms

4. Creation of a hierarchy (for OCD and BDD only)

5. Creation of a treatment plan

6. Assignment of behavioral homework

7. Regular debriefing of assignments and the assignment of new tasks

8. Teaching and practicing cognitive therapy

9. Maintenance and relapse prevention

Step 1. Intake and History

At your first visit, the therapist will most likely try to get a general idea of what the problem is, establish a rapport with you, and outline what he or she thinks can can be done for you. At the following early visits, the therapist will try to gather and understand as much information about you, your life, and your symptoms, both past and present, as is possible. He or she will need to determine the strengths and weaknesses you bring to therapy, the support you may or may not have from others, the way you live from day to day, and what your goals and motivations are. They will also want to know your treatment history, what has worked for you and what hasn't. It may take the first few sessions to accomplish this.

Step 2. Diagnosis

You can only be properly treated if you have a proper diagnosis. In the past, many of those with OCSDs, particularly OCD and BDD, were misdiagnosed. Even if their disorder was correctly identified, many symptoms were missed or ignored. On the other hand, some of those with OCSDs are not always open in telling professionals about their symptoms. The goal here, obviously, is to see if what is happening to you fits the criteria for one of the OCSDs.

At this point your therapist or physician will question exactly what you mean when you say you are having certain thoughts or performing particular compulsions. As you will see in chapter 9, sufferers can perform similar-looking compulsions for totally different reasons. Even behaviors that look like TTM may actually be another type of compulsion. Questions should also be asked to uncover the presence of mental compulsions. These can sometimes be difficult to diagnose. Quite a few of those with OCSDs do not always realize that some of their behaviors are symptoms. A great deal of questioning may be required. For those with a greater awareness of their symptoms, getting a diagnosis can be an easier process. Your diagnosis may be obvious at the first session or it may only be arrived at after several visits.

Step 3. Detailed Analysis of the Symptoms

Once a history has been obtained and a diagnosis arrived at, your therapist will try to examine the full depth and severity of your disorder in great detail. They may use some type of checklist or special questionnaire, such as those included at the end of this book (see appendices A and B), the Yale Brown Obsessive-Compulsive Scale (YBOCS), or they will question you based on their understanding of your disorder. It can help at this point to see what groups or clusters your symptoms fit into. It may also help if (with your permission) the therapist can question family members or close friends who have been able to observe you in many different situations. Often they can remember or identify symptoms that you cannot.

When a listing of thoughts and behaviors has been put together, it will next be important to identify the conditions under which symptoms can occur. The therapist will ask about the times, places, activities, moods, etc., which can bring on or affect your symptoms. It is important to find out what triggers particular obsessions and, in turn, which obsessions trigger particular compulsions. Information will also be needed to find out if family or others are involved in certain symptoms or are helping you to function. For TTM, skin picking, and nail biting, it is absolutely crucial for the person treating you to understand all factors that can encourage or bring on your symptoms.

Step 4. Creation of a Hierarchy (for OCD and BDD only)

With the creation of a fairly complete list of obsessions, compulsions, and the factors which influence them, finding out exactly which symptoms are worse than others is the next important step. This would be more the case for OCD and BDD. In the case of TTM, nail biting, and skin picking, the task would be to determine which situations, moods, and times are the most difficult or risky when it comes to resisting the urge to perform the behaviors.

In all cases, there are some thoughts or activities which can cause just a little anxiety or discomfort. Others can cause moderate to high levels of anxiety and usually can only be resisted with great effort, if at all. The therapist will ask you to rate each thought or situation in terms of how anxious it might make you. You will also be asked to give ratings for a variety of difficult situations, in which either resisting compulsions or habits will be likely to make you feel anxious or in which you would be likely to have obsessive thoughts. You might typically be asked questions beginning with, "How anxious would you feel if you were to . . . ?" You would then be asked to rate the situation on a 0 to 100 scale, known as a SUDS scale (Subjective Units of Distress). Those who suffer from extreme doubt and have trouble making decisions sometimes find this difficult. With a little guidance, however, everyone eventually completes this. There may only be a couple of dozen items on a list, while others may run several pages. It may take one or two sessions to complete such a hierarchy.

Step 5. Creation of a Treatment Plan

This represents the last step before the actual "doing" part of your therapy begins. It is important to have a treatment plan because you cannot treat every part of the disorder at the same time. Some of your symptoms can't be put off and need to be dealt with first. If you are extremely anxious and agitated a lot of the time or if you are severely depressed, these will have to be dealt with right away if any progress is to be made. If you can't get yourself out of bed each day or if you are jumping out of your seat with anxiety, you probably won't be able to concentrate very much.

There are several things that can be done for anxiety. First, you can be taught techniques to try to control the physical symptoms. The techniques could include deep breathing and muscle relaxation (see the section on "Self-Help for TTM" in chapter 3 for more details about these techniques). Another approach would be for the therapist to refer you to a psychiatrist for some anti-anxiety medication, such as Xanax or Klonopin, with the understanding that you would only take it for a short time until the other parts of your treatment can take hold.

If you are depressed, treatment may depend upon the type of depression (see the section on "Depression" in chapter 11). If your depression is purely a reaction to having OCD itself, your therapist will want to treat your symptoms as soon as possible. If, however, the depression is more of a biological type (also known as endogenous depression) and exists alongside your OCD, it will have to be treated before you can deal with the OCD symptoms. These depressions can be serious. People with this kind of depression usually feel very negative about themselves and everything in life and tend to sleep much of the time. They lack the energy and motivation needed to get started. Endogenous depression is best treated with antidepressant medication, which probably would have been prescribed for the OCSD anyway. Some people seem to only respond to a combination of antidepressants.

Another problem that may have to be dealt with is substance abuse. I make it very clear to new patients that I cannot work with them on their OCSD while they are actively abusing drugs or alcohol to medicate their symptoms. If you have such a problem, becoming drug- or alcohol-free may turn out to be the first step in your treatment. Overcoming this will represent a serious commitment on your part to recovery. You must see your attempts at self-medication as a part of your disorder. It may not be easy to accept and many doubt it at first. If you find that you are unable to stop on your own, there are hospital detoxification programs or 12-Step groups such as Alcoholics Anonymous that can help. Some patients with OCSDs shy away from AA because they sometimes report that it is difficult to find understanding for the disorder there. Perhaps there will be AA groups for those with OCSDs someday, but in the meantime, it is a good place to start.

A common problem, which may get in the way of starting therapy, involves serious family or marital disturbances. Anger, fighting, or emotional abuse either toward you or from you cannot be ignored. These can be so stressful that they can easily undo many of your other positive efforts in treatment. Your therapist may refer you and those others in your life for family or marital therapy. It is usually better to see someone who isn't treating your OCSD so that your spouse or family won't feel that the therapist is mostly on your side and refuse to attend. Therapists do best in these situations when they can be neutral parties. In addition to the counseling, it can be very helpful if a spouse or family can attend an OC family support group (if one is available nearby). People get support and learn from each other in these groups.

Once these other problems have been dealt with or are on their way to being controlled, the next step would be for your therapist to use your hierarchy to make up the order in which your symptoms will be treated. This would apply to OCD and BDD. In the case of TTM, skin picking, and nail biting, this step would be skipped over, and you would move right on to treatment (see the section on behavioral therapy for TTM, skin picking, and nail biting further ahead). Obviously, your therapist will want to start with the easier items from the lower end of your scale, things you feel most able to tackle first. The only exception to this is if you have given most of the items on your list about the same high rating. When this happens, it is best that your therapist simply lets you pick the situations you feel most up to confronting first. You will probably be the best judge of this.

Step 6. Assignment of Behavioral Homework

This is where the actual work on your OCSD begins. The therapist will outline the therapy plan for you and begin assigning the tasks you will do outside therapy sessions. It is important to understand that the responsibility for doing homework is yours alone, and that you must stay with the anxiety-causing situations if you are going to learn to tolerate them. No one is going to do your homework for you and no one can make you do it.

Note: At this point, those with TTM, skin picking, or nail biting should consult the section further ahead on specific behavioral therapy for these problems. The following instructions in this section really apply to classic OCD and BDD. Those with BDD will need to read the next section on behavioral therapy for this specific problem when they finish this section.

The therapist will usually start by having you face situations and thoughts with SUDS levels between 20 and 30. The first goal is to ease into the therapy and help you feel that you are accomplishing something, not to crush you with anxiety. Remember though, if you aren't feeling anxious, the treatment won't be working effectively. Ideally, your therapist will include you in making decisions about which symptoms will be tackled and in what order. You may feel more in control of the process and work harder when you have some say over what is happening to you. Also, letting you pick some of your own assignments will help avoid a common OC trap. This is where you might unintentionally feel relieved of guilt or responsibility over doing the homework because the therapist told you to do it. This supposedly puts the burden on them and lets you off the hook if something bad actually happens.

You may look at your hierarchy and ask, "Why do I have to work to the very top of my list to get well? After all, average people don't have to do these things." You need to understand that in therapy, it is sometimes necessary to do some things that go a bit beyond the ordinary. This is because you may already be doing things that the average person wouldn't do and may now have to go a bit further in the opposite direction. It is also important to understand that in the case of classic OCD and BDD, you tend to have much more doubt and are more at risk than the average person. Therefore, you must do more in order to be stronger and more resistant.

Your homework may be given to you in written form to prevent you from forgetting or misinterpreting it. I believe that this is best. You can post it and look at it daily as a reminder.

The general approach in the case of your obsessions is to learn to confront them on an ongoing basis. This will be done directly, by having you expose yourself to tapes containing the thoughts or writing about them extensively, or indirectly, by putting yourself in situations that will bring them on.

The strategy for dealing with compulsions is to learn to resist them in every way possible. If the compulsion involves contamination, you will be directed to touch things that are increasingly contaminated and to contaminate your environment without washing or cleaning afterward. If checking is your problem, you will be asked to resist doing so in situations that gradually seem more risky. You will be asked to take apart your rituals or to resist doing them under increasingly tougher circumstances. For those of you who hoard, you will need to work your way through what you have been saving and discard more items week by week. In the case of perfectionism or symmetry-making compulsions, your goal will be to methodically mess up your environment and so on.

You will probably find that some symptoms can be tackled in a single step, while others are best confronted in smaller steps. You may only require a single confrontation lasting a few minutes or several contacts lasting an hour or more each. Everyone develops tolerance at his or her own rate. The process for each item on your hierarchy may take a day, several days, or even several weeks. It is important for you to know in advance that this may be the case, to help you to be patient. Time is on your side and sooner or later your fear will give way.

Step 7. Regular Debriefing of Assignments and the Assignment of New Tasks

It is important to the success of your therapy that you keep in mind that each week you will have to report about your progress to someone. It helps keep the idea of your goal before your eyes and keeps you from letting yourself off the hook as you have been in the habit of doing. Don't forget that you are only in therapy for an hour a week and that during the other 167 hours you are on your own. Along with help from your therapist, you need to see that getting well is your responsibility to yourself.

The therapist may start each session by running through the homework list from the previous session. In this way, you can either be praised for what you were able to accomplish or get help in troubleshooting situations where you were not so successful. In the second case, for my own patients, I like to ask the person, "What do you think you should have done?" to first make sure they really did know. If it appears they did not know what to do, we will once again review what should have been done. They may also be asked, "Do you understand what was unhelpful about the way you handled the situation?" If they do not, it is explained to them. Finally, they will be asked, "What do you plan to do the next time you are in a similar situation?" to make sure they are prepared for the next time. If they aren't certain, it is spelled out for them and sometimes written down.

One further aid that can sometimes be of help is what I call a "coaching" tape. This tape is different from an exposure tape in that it contains positive and encouraging messages and you listen to it when you are having trouble remembering what to do or are feeling discouraged. Sometimes, hearing your therapist's voice between sessions can provide a needed boost. Remember that these tapes do not provide reassurance about fears, only encouragement and instructions.

A potential hazard sometimes seen in this phase of therapy is where patients ask the therapist if troubling thoughts could be obsessions. This is really a form of double checking. If the therapist says "yes," your anxiety is then relieved because you now know that the worry wasn't realistic to begin with.

The overall goal in debriefing is to be able to give you constructive criticism without making you feel like a failure for what you have not done. In many of those with OCSDs, feelings of failure and helplessness are usually not far below the surface. The idea must be maintained that failing to do a particular task does not make you an overall failure, and that failure can only happen when you stop trying. Even this may not be final, since you can always start again.

If you tend to be rather perfectionistic, you must also be helped to shift your focus from the things you cannot yet do, to crediting yourself for the things you have been able to accomplish thus far. In many cases I have seen, perfectionistic people are more likely to focus on the one homework assignment they did not do, while ignoring the other six at which they've succeeded.

Step 8. *Teaching and Practicing Cognitive Therapy*

Once behavioral therapy is well under way and you are about 75 percent of the way through the process, it is best for the therapist to introduce cognitive therapy. This is the "talking" part of treatment. You could describe it as "going back to school to learn how to think." Many educational materials are used and include books, prerecorded tapes, and written assignments.

Many of those with OCD need to make some serious changes in the way they think. Their approach to life may have been strongly shaped by OCD, and in many cases, they may have lost their ability to live spontaneously, that is, to be able to act without having to stop and think about each little thing they do. They have tried to create lives without some type of risk for themselves but have ended up with lives that are limited and do not work. In an attempt to eliminate this risk, they have become overcontrolled.

It is best explained that while the behavioral therapy is what initially gets you well, it is the cognitive therapy that gives you the skills to stay well. Living a more functional life where you are able to cope with the inevitable stresses and problems can be your best defense against a relapse.

Patients are instructed in the principles and philosophy of cognitive therapy, and it gradually becomes the major portion of their therapy. (For a more detailed discussion of cognitive therapy, see the earlier section entitled, "Cognitive Therapy.")

Step 9. Maintenance and Relapse Prevention

If your therapist has done the job correctly, you will have become your own therapist at this point. Hopefully, you will be quick to spot oncoming difficulties and assign yourself homework on an ongoing basis. This is not to say that you will not backslide now and then. You probably will since no one can be perfect, and you must be prepared. Preparing for this is known as "relapse prevention."

A program of relapse prevention teaches you how to be ready for your own particular trouble spots and how to face them immediately. You will have to be active in keeping the ground you have gained. You may also find that you may have to "rebalance" your life to keep down the stress that leads to symptoms. For a more detailed explanation of relapse prevention, see chapter 3.

One further help in staying recovered may be the use of periodic booster sessions. Occasional visits to your therapist, if needed, can help you brush up on your skills and be more aware of any possible slippage. Some people return when they are under a lot of stress and their symptoms reappear. This should not be seen as failing, it is just being realistic.

BEHAVIORAL THERAPY FOR BDD

As mentioned earlier, the same Exposure and Response Prevention (E&RP) procedure used to treat OCD is also used to treat BDD (see Fig. 2.1). The focus of the therapy here is usually very specific, as the symptoms in BDD are often very specific as well, limiting themselves to a particular body part or region. Again, the individual is exposed to what they fear, in this case, the thought that a part of their body is ugly or misshapen. This exposure is, of course, done gradually and with a great deal of sensitivity. Those with BDD can be very fixed in their beliefs, and too much exposure too soon can often frighten them away from therapy and make them think the therapist doesn't understand. For the response prevention part of the treatment, patients are discouraged from checking in the mirror or otherwise inspecting themselves. They are also asked to stop questioning others about their appearance or seeking medical opinions or surgery. Covering up the defect and avoiding going out in public are also discouraged.

In my own experience, if you have BDD you may require more time to habituate to the unpleasant thoughts.

BEHAVIORAL THERAPY FOR TTM, SKIN PICKING, OR NAIL BITING

In seeking treatment for your grooming impulsions, you will see many different types of treatments being touted. They range from hypnosis to spiritual healing and to exotic forms of oriental medical practices. You may even know of cases where one of these techniques has worked for someone. Remember, "Everything works for someone, and nothing works for everyone." Just because one of these approaches has worked for an individual, it doesn't mean that it is a surefire help for all sufferers. It is still the best approach to stick with treatments for which there is scientific data. Behavioral treatment is the only treatment we currently have data for. In line with the quote above, it is not being said that because we have data, that the behavioral methods outlined below will work for everyone. They won't. They may, however, have a chance of working for the largest number of people. No technique is perfect, and the future may hold more effective treatment, but for now, it is the most proven approach we have.

While many different behavioral techniques have been used to treat TTM, skin picking, and nail biting, the one which is considered to be superior is known as Habit Reversal Training (HRT) (see Fig. 2.1). Its use has not been strictly limited to these three disorders. HRT has also been used to treat the tics of Tourette's Syndrome, another impulse control problem. This technique was developed and first written about by Dr. Nathan Azrin in 1973. He also published a book about it, entitled *Habit Reversal in a Day*, now out of print. HRT was generally intended to eliminate tics and other "nervous habits," as hair pulling was considered to be. At the time this book was first published, TTM and compulsive skin picking and nail biting were practically unknown as disorders in this country, and like other types of OCSDs, were thought to be both rare and mostly untreatable. As a result, this technique received little notice then and probably only a handful of specialists in this country were aware of its existence. For nearly twenty years it went practically unmentioned in the scientific literature, only cropping up some eight times in different studies, in which a total of only forty-four individuals were treated with it. A study by Azrin, Nunn, and Frantz conducted in 1980 showed a 90 percent improvement in hair pulling behavior. These studies, although imperfect in a number of ways, suggest that HRT may currently be the most effective treatment. Scientists and clinicians agree, though, that much more research still needs to be done on HRT to further establish its effectiveness.

HRT is accomplished in four steps. The first step focuses on developing an awareness of the habit itself. As mentioned earlier, there are those whose pulling, picking, or biting are preceded by a feeling of tension or an urge to do it and this is followed by a feeling of satisfaction. There are also those whose pulling and biting habits are rather automatic and mostly done while their attention is focused on something else they are doing at the time. This automatic behavior takes place during other activities, such as talking on the phone, driving, reading, doing homework, watching TV, etc. Some of those in the latter group describe a feeling similar to going into a trance or being "spaced out." They often do not realize that they have pulled or bitten at all until they are finished and see the discarded hairs or nails nearby. Those in both groups mostly tend to forget incidents after they have happened, because they do not like to think about or remember them. It is because of this that when starting treatment you may only be able to give very little information about your habit. Awareness must be increased before any progress can take place because obviously, it is difficult to learn to control a behavior you are unaware of.

The steps of HRT are:

1. Self-awareness training

2. Teaching self-relaxation

3. Diaphragmatic breathing

4. Muscle tensing action

Step 1. Self-Awareness Training

Self-awareness training is taught via self-monitoring and self-recording of pulling, picking, or biting events, the strength of the urge in each event, the time spent doing it, the approximate number of hairs pulled or nails bitten, and the relevant behaviors and feelings surrounding them. These daily records are often kept using special self-monitoring sheets.

Once enough records have been gathered, it is possible to discover patterns present in the behavior. We can compare situations where habits are practiced to find out which ones tend to be the most repetitive and what is similar about them. We can also discover which ones make it more difficult to resist urges. Interestingly, even many of those with these problems who claim to be aware of their own actions, frequently admit that they are surprised when they discover their own patterns of behavior. It should also be noted that during this aware-ness-training phase, you may already find yourself starting to change certain unhelpful behaviors. These would include things you may have been doing such as shaving your head to remove the temptation to pull newly sprouting hairs or cutting your nails very short. You will quickly realize that if there is nothing to pull or bite, there will be nothing to monitor and become aware of. This behav-ior and others like it would have to be given up eventually, anyway.

Step 2. Teaching Self-Relaxation

The purpose of teaching self-relaxation is to teach you a way of focusing yourself, as well as a way of reducing inner tension. Many episodes happen after tense or stressful events. Additionally, many with these problems report a feeling of ten-sion just before they begin. A longer, progressive muscle relaxation exercise is taught at first. At a later point, when relaxation is mastered, a more abbreviated relaxation exercise is taught, which will be put together with the last two steps.

Step 3. Diaphragmatic Breathing

The techniques of diaphragmatic breathing are now added to your relaxation skills. You are taught to regulate your own breathing in terms of how to breathe evenly and deeply. This further adds to your ability to center and relax yourself and also helps to counter a common tendency to hyperventilate when anxious.

Step 4. Muscle Tensing Action

The teaching of a muscle tensing action is opposite to and incompatible with reaching to pull hair, pick skin, or bite nails. It is referred to as a "competing response." Most commonly, it involves making a fist, tensing your arm muscles, and pressing your bent arm firmly against your side at waist level.

These four steps are practiced over a period of several weeks (for more detailed self-help instructions, see chapter 3), and then assembled into what will become the complete HR response. It is practiced either before, during, or after every episode, and requires much time and patience to learn. It may require weeks or even several months of steady practice. Weekly sessions provide structure, coaching, and morale building. This should not be minimized. Some feel that this is the most important help the therapist can provide. Refer to the TTM self-help section in chapter 3 to see how you may set up your own self-help program should you want to try recovering without professional assistance or if such help is just not available to you.

BEHAVIORAL THERAPY—A TIME FRAME

In determining how long a course of behavioral therapy might take, it must be kept in mind that a lot depends on the individual. Some habituate rather quickly to what they fear, while others change much more slowly. Some can form new habits right away, and some take many repetitions. Different factors may influence the course of your recovery. These include:

- How long you have had symptoms
- How serious your symptoms have become
- How motivated you are to follow treatment instructions
- How avoidant you are in general when facing discomfort
- How patient you are in terms of waiting for results
- How quickly your nervous system is able to habituate to fearful situations or to form new habits
- Whether or not medication is also being used, and how long it takes to find the right one(s)
- How much stress is in your daily environment
- What other problems are present in addition to the disorder.

Sometimes, behavioral therapy can even begin to work the first week, even in small ways, if instructions are followed. I have always believed that a person has already changed by simply making the commitment to face a problem and by getting up the courage to expose their symptoms to another person. People have changed their behaviors the week before therapy actually started, simply because they told themselves that they would have to give them up eventually anyway.

Since everyone is an individual, it is a bit tricky to make predictions about length of treatment. I will go so far as to give you some general observations. Remember that these are not engraved in stone and cannot tell you a lot about yourself in particular. In uncomplicated cases of classic OCD where no other disorders or major problems exist in an individual's life, where they attend therapy steadily and follow all instructions, it is likely that recovery can be achieved in six to nine months, perhaps twelve months at the longest. This would work out to between twenty-four and thirty-six sessions, or perhaps forty to fifty sessions at the most. This is not to say that some cases do not respond more quickly. I have seen recoveries take place within a dozen sessions. Some cases take longer, particularly where other problems exist, or where the sufferer has not been able to function for many years and requires overall rehabilitation. I have found that BDD can sometimes require more time than classic OCD, as the ideas can be so deeply believed.

TTM, skin picking, and nail biting seem to be a little harder to pin down in terms of time. An extremely motivated person who is not too stigmatized by the illness can often recover in six to twelve months. Treatment can take months longer if: you find HRT difficult to stick to; you don't feel you deserve to recover (because of being stigmatized); your urges are so strong that medication is required and you have to go through several different ones before you find one that works; or your habit is of the more automatic variety, and you have very little awareness of when or where it is occurring.

INPATIENT OR OUTPATIENT THERAPY

There are basically two major models for how behavioral therapy for OCD is conducted. The first model is intensive and is taken from the original treatment that was conducted when behavioral therapy for OCD first began. This treatment is done with inpatients in a psychiatric hospital setting. It involves daily treatments of about ninety minutes in length for a period of three to four weeks. The advantages are that:

+ It can lead to rapid change and get you off to a running start.
+ It is useful for the most severe cases to be in an environment that can be totally controlled to prevent relapse or nonadherence to instructions—a kind of brief, total immersion.
+ It can help in cases where you really want to recover, but just feel too demoralized and helpless to bring yourself to follow instructions on your own.
+ It may be a better environment in which to have your physician change or adjust your medications if you are extremely drug sensitive and need careful monitoring.
+ It is often better covered by health insurance, since it is performed in a hospital.

+ It can get you, at least briefly, out of a toxic family environment or one where family members are heavily involved in symptoms, so that stress is reduced more quickly. Being surrounded by encouraging hospital staff on a twenty-four hour basis also helps the morale of the more hopeless and demoralized.

+ It can be practical for you if you do not have any appropriate sources of therapy near where you live and have no option, except to travel to the hospital for briefer, more intensive treatment.

The disadvantages of this model are that:

- It is over after a few weeks, leaving you without support or help with maintenance and open to relapse if you do not live near a source of postdischarge follow-up or booster therapy sessions.

- It is too disruptive if you have a job and family and cannot easily take a month off.

- In many cases the three to four weeks are not sufficient, especially where there are dozens of compulsions and numerous obsessions to be dealt with. Insurance companies are not usually supportive of long stays.

- It rapidly uses up insurance coverage if you have yearly or lifetime limits, leaving you uncovered after discharge or even sometimes without enough time to fully carry out the inpatient treatment.

- It can leave you unprepared to face your own real world environment, since the treatment is conducted in a safe, controlled hospital setting where many feared things from home cannot be brought or reproduced for therapy purposes.

- The ever-present hospital supervision may keep you from developing feelings of self-efficacy that come with doing things on your own.

- If you have no insurance coverage, it is ruinously expensive, requiring large sums to be paid in a short period of time which may be out of the reach of most ordinary people.

- It can be rather stigmatizing to have to undergo a psychiatric hospitalization, perhaps reinforcing for both yourself and those close to you the mistaken notion that you are "crazy" or "insane."

- The three- or four-week time limit of many programs can put unnecessary pressure and stress on you and may make you feel that you will "fail" if you cannot recover sufficiently by the end of your stay.

 − Conversely, the time limit also can create unrealistic expectations on your part or your friends and family members who believe that recovery will be complete by the end of your stay, when often it is not.

The other model, and one that I believe to be a more efficient and realistic one for the majority of people with OCD, is outpatient treatment. This model is based on the familiar one visit per week setup. The advantages of this model are that:

 + It avoids the stigma of going to a psychiatric hospital—something which can be fairly devastating to many people, especially children and adolescents.

 + It allows you to be treated in your own home setting, a place where symptoms have originated, and where the work of therapy really needs to take place.

 + Doing assignments on your own at home is a lot closer to what post-therapy self-maintenance will be like, and teaches you how to be your own therapist and develop your own resources.

 + It boosts personal feelings of effectiveness and self-control by allowing you to take your assignments home and be responsible for doing them without supervision. It is clearly much better for you to be able to say that you did an assignment because you made yourself do it, rather than because a psychologist or other staff person was standing over you.

 + Costs are much lower since you are not paying for hospital room and board. If you are putting it through a health insurance plan, they are more likely to pay for treatment.

 + Costs are spread over a much longer period.

 + It allows sufficient time for those who have numerous compulsions and obsessions to have their symptoms treated in-depth and more completely when visits are spread over a longer time span.

 + It allows more between visit time for assignments to be done a greater number of times, and for greater habituation to occur.

 + The lack of an exact short term time limit discourages you from pressuring yourself about recovering by a particular date, and also helps family and friends to be more patient and realistic about seeing the therapy as a process and not an event.

 + It allows those who work outside the home or those who raise children to keep up their responsibilities while working on a recovery, sparing the family added unnecessary stress and even further expense.

+ It permits the therapist to observe and become acquainted with you over a longer period of time, allowing him or her to spot other problems which also need to be confronted in therapy, and which could have a negative impact on your recovery if not treated.

The disadvantages of the outpatient model are that:

- It may not be suitable for the most seriously ill, who will not be able to follow instructions on their own.
- It is not as economical for those who have inpatient insurance coverage, but little or no outpatient benefits.
- You may not have anyone nearby to see for outpatient therapy, making an inpatient stay away from home more practical (although follow-up will still be a problem).
- It cannot immediately remove you from a stressful home environment the way a hospital stay can.

There are some therapists who offer intensive daily treatment on an outpatient basis, but this seems to be impractical. If an individual is functioning well enough to come to an office and take home assignments in the first place, then they probably don't need to come to the office every day. Conversely, if they are so ill that they need daily supervision in order to succeed, then they probably would be better off in an inpatient setting for a time. One could argue that intensive outpatient treatment is a less costly way for the seriously ill to be treated. I would answer that if costs really were a problem, you could go further and have weekly or, at the most, twice weekly visits, with extended assignments. Daily ninety-minute sessions are still very expensive, although less so than inpatient treatment.

Scientifically speaking, there are studies that have shown self-exposure to be as effective as therapist aided exposure. Two studies by Paul Emmelkamp and colleagues (Emmelkamp & Kraanen, 1977; and Emmelkamp et al., 1989) found that home based treatment resulted in longer lasting and better maintained recoveries.

One further note. Some friends and family see hospitalization as a way to force unmotivated sufferers to enter into therapy and to convince them of the seriousness of their conditions. They think that if they pressure their stubborn loved ones into entering the hospital, that the hospital staff will find a way to either motivate them or "make" them get well. This almost never works. Those who are unmotivated or not yet ready for treatment will probably only be antagonized, feel resentful, and develop a real distaste for any kind of treatment in the future. Getting well is hard work, even when you are motivated. The desire for recovery must come from the individual or it will not happen at all.

NO ADVERSE EFFECTS

Behavioral therapy cannot make you worse if you are already nervous. Properly done, it is a gradual process, exposing a person to no more than they can reasonably handle at a given point in time. It actually increases tolerance for the anxiety. If behavior therapy is carried out poorly by someone who is not well trained, it can sometimes raise a patient's anxiety to levels which they are not yet ready to tolerate, causing them to want to stop the therapy. Behavior therapy itself should not be blamed for this, however, and this only emphasizes why sufferers should be careful consumers, seeking out experienced clinicians. If you are just beginning behavioral therapy and are feeling extremely anxious and agitated and cannot seem to make a start, it would probably be wise to turn to the use of medications. If you cannot wait for your antidepressant to begin working or haven't found the right one yet, it would, in this case, justify the use of antianxiety medications in addition, just to be able to get started. These can be withdrawn as you make enough progress to feel that your anxiety can be managed without them. Remember that these particular medications are not meant to be a substitute for treatment, but a temporary tool to assist you in responding to your treatment.

KNOWING WHEN YOU NEED THERAPY

There is no real indicator as to how serious your OCSD has to get before you need therapy. My recommendation would be that by the time you have begun to notice it, it is probably already an established problem that needs to be faced. Unfortunately, many people don't seek help until the symptoms have begun to seriously affect their functioning. This can be due either to fears of revealing the illness and being labeled "crazy," to procrastination, or simply because of denial. Also, there are some uninformed therapists out there who tell patients that their symptoms are not serious enough to require behavioral treatment, much less medication. I suggest that you do not wait until the problem becomes severe, since you'll only have that much more work to do once you finally get started. The best time is now. Don't lose years waiting for the "right" time; there is no such thing.

RECOVERY WITH BEHAVIORAL THERAPY ALONE

It is possible for some people to recover using behavioral therapy alone, but not everyone. My experience has been that those with mild to moderate cases of OCSDs have the best chance. In all honesty, I have only seen a few who were seriously ill with an OCSD succeed at recovering without medication. This is not to say that it is impossible, just less likely. If a patient wishes to try therapy without medication, it has always been my policy to give them a chance, but I always reserve the right to recommend it later on if I see that they are not succeeding.

There is still much stigma attached to taking psychiatric medications, and this, together with a kind of perfectionism, is one cause of reluctance on the part of some people. They believe that only those who are "crazy" take medications. Using drugs would only confirm that something is "genuinely" wrong with them, forcing them to face their situation. Some also believe that if they cannot recover strictly on their own, it means they are somehow weak or lacking in some type of moral fiber, and that their recovery will be imperfect and less genuine. I do not see these as valid reasons for avoiding medication. It should not be a moral issue or a test of your "fitness." It is a matter of practicality.

Others avoid medication out of fear. Some of those with OCD are suggestible and always scanning their world for the possibility of harm. They have exaggerated and phobic ideas about medication, and worry that it may cause them some permanent harm or change their brains in some way, either now or in the future. They sometimes read drug books or package inserts and imagine that they will experience every listed side effect, no matter how rare. We all know that every course of action in life has risks. However, the risks involved in taking OCD medications are very small and harm is extremely unlikely, unless they are being wrongly prescribed or misused. There is no evidence that they can cause long-term harm. A variation on this type of fear is the idea on the part of the sufferer that by taking medication, "something" will be taking place in their brain and body that they cannot "control." They worry that they will feel or think things that are somehow not natural to them and that they will dislike. This is, of course, totally false. An exaggerated need for control is common in nervous individuals. If it keeps a person from getting needed help, then it is no longer control, it is a state of being "trapped." I like to point out that something has already happened which is causing a lack of control at times. What we are trying to do is to actually give back control.

Obviously, it is always more desirable not to have to take medication if possible. A better reason for not starting medication at first would be because you may wish to see if you can recover without it. If drugs were used from the start, you would be denied the opportunity to find this out.

COMPULSIONS, OBSESSIONS, AND BEHAVIORAL THERAPY

While not enough controlled studies of large groups have been conducted to scientifically verify whether behavioral therapy works better for compulsions than for obsessions, it has been my experience, and the experience of other professionals in this field, that obsessions can be helped as easily as compulsions with behavioral treatment. The idea of the untreatability of obsessions has unfortunately kept many obsessive individuals from seeking behavioral treatment, and also kept many therapists from using this effective method.

One of the main reasons for this mistaken belief is that most of the original behavioral treatment studies focused on compulsions. This was probably because these behaviors were easier for researchers to observe and record. Keeping track of mental events is more difficult. It was much simpler to track hand washes or double checks than thoughts. Researchers also may have believed, incorrectly, that you could not expose sufferers to obsessive thoughts the way you can to physical situations. Working with compulsions alone made for "neater" studies; however, it also caused researchers to neglect studying the treatment of obsessions.

Based on this lack of evidence about treating obsessive thoughts, many writers have gone beyond the fact that it was simply a poorly studied area and wrongly concluded that compulsions were easier to treat. Because of these reasons, there has been a failure on the part of many practitioners and researchers to properly apply the methods they have used for years to treat compulsions only. Other less effective methods were used to treat obsessions and as these were mostly useless, they also caused researchers and clinicians to wrongly conclude that the symptoms were untreatable. These older methods included such things as "thought stopping" (saying the word "STOP!" strongly to yourself in your mind every time you get an obsession while snapping a rubber band worn around your wrist); relaxation techniques (listening to tapes which guide you through body relaxation to calm your anxiety); distraction techniques, or just trying to help the sufferer reason their thoughts out logically (which can't be done since obsessions are not the result of a logical thought process and any new conclusions would be canceled out by the obsessive doubt within a short time).

Although Exposure and Response Prevention techniques have been around for over thirty years, they still do not seem to be widely known or understood. Even those who currently use them for compulsions sometimes have difficulty understanding how they can also be used to treat mental events, such as obsessions, which are not observable. There seems to be the idea that you can't get someone to stop doing something that cannot be witnessed or physically prevented. The goal in treating obsessions, however, is obviously not physical restraint. The goal here instead is to build tolerance to the thoughts and thereby reduce or even remove the anxiety. Through exposure and confrontational methods, the sufferer gradually builds up habituation to the thoughts. They learn to accept the presence of the thoughts, even if they don't like them. Sufferers can also learn that everyone occasionally gets unpleasant intrusive thoughts and that they should not be regarded as catastrophic. In addition, by reducing the anxiety that the thoughts cause, they learn that they do not have to respond or act on them in any way. Facing the thoughts, or leaving them alone as necessary, allows them to subside as quickly as they are ever going to. Because trying to act on them typically does not work, the sufferer's stress increases, and the thoughts and the anxiety they produce only increase as well.

As mentioned earlier in this chapter, a new approach to treating obsessions via the use of cognitive therapy is currently being studied in Europe. It teaches sufferers to challenge their notions of risk and responsibility and to see the lack of logic both in their obsessive thoughts, as well as in their reactions to them. It may also prove to be an important tool when used together with behavioral techniques.

More research clearly needs to be done to demonstrate the treatability of obsessions. There are several small-scale studies of behavioral treatment, which have been done in Great Britain by Dr. Paul Salkovskis and others. Their findings have been positive and point the way to the use of E&RP to treat obsessional thoughts. In the meantime, we should continue to use what obviously works.

ONLY COMMITMENT BRINGS SUCCESS

There are people for whom behavior therapy doesn't work. In my experience, there have been those who were not totally committed to getting well for one of a variety of reasons, and who either could not get started or dropped out after a short time. It wasn't that behavior therapy wouldn't work. It was just that for one reason or another, they were not able to make it work for them. Their reasons included the following:

- They truly did not believe in their ability to recover.
- They feared that the therapy would worsen their symptoms, since they would have to face what they had been avoiding.
- They feared that they would not be up to handling the responsibilities that would face them if they recovered.
- They had grown too comfortable in the discomfort of their illness lifestyles and did not wish to go through the changes and effort involved in recovering.
- They genuinely required medication to be able to get started with the therapy due to the seriousness of their symptoms, but for mistaken or fearful reasons would not use the drugs to help themselves.

- They felt their entire situation was unfair, believing that since they did not ask for their illness, they should not have to do anything to recover from it—that it should somehow be taken from them by God, fate, etc.
- They had a low tolerance for frustration, and if they could not recover easily, immediately, and with little or no work, they were not interested.
- They were also suffering from a severe and treatment resistant depression that prevented them from getting started with therapy because they lacked the energy and drive.
- Stress from other areas of their lives, such as their jobs, marriages, or families, kept symptoms at a very high level, preventing them from seeing the initial success they needed to make a good start, or if they did start to maintain it.
- Their expectations for recovery were so high that when they weren't "cured" immediately, they were overcome by their own frustration and decided that they simply couldn't do it.
- They had come to incorrectly believe that their illness was the result of their being "bad" people and that they "deserved" to be ill as some sort of punishment they had earned, even if they couldn't say why.
- They suffered from morbid obsessions and impulsions and believed that their fear was the only thing keeping them from doing what their morbid obsessive thoughts suggested (see chapter 8, Morbid Impulsions). They therefore believed it was better to remain fearful and inhibited, rather than risk letting go and causing a catastrophe.
- They denied the seriousness of their problem, or worse yet, they denied that they had any problem at all, because they would not face the fact that something could be wrong with them. They could not accept that their judgment was faulty and didn't work. They believed their real goal was finding a way to "perfect" their symptoms and still have a normal life.

I believe that anyone willing to risk frustration and difficulty, and who has the motivation to recover, can succeed at behavior therapy. It can be difficult at times, but it is certainly not "too difficult." The growing number of those who have recovered is proof of this.

USING MEDICATION WITH BEHAVIORAL THERAPY

Generally speaking, medication can contribute to a positive outcome along with behavioral therapy. Studies have shown that medication and behavioral therapy together have produced better and longer lasting results than either one alone. Medication should not be regarded as an end in itself. There are no quick fixes for OCSDs and drugs are no "magic bullet." They should instead be thought of as a tool to assist a person in meeting the demands of behavioral therapy. Often, patients will tell me that they are nervous at the thought of taking psychoactive medications and would rather try to do behavioral therapy alone. After making certain they have all the facts about medication, I most often say that I have no objection to this. If they genuinely think they can do it without medication, they deserve a chance to give it a try. If I believe they are not making progress, I may then recommend that they be realistic and consider medication. I remind them that taking medication is not a one-way street. If they do not like the way they feel while taking it, they can always stop. There are no permanent side effects.

My own observation has been that those most likely to recover without the use of medications have compulsions as their greatest problems, and do not appear to have an extremely strong belief in some catastrophe occurring if they don't perform them. Some sufferers have performed compulsions for so long that they cannot remember why they started. They would just feel uneasy or nervous if they didn't perform them. As a group, those who are troubled more strongly by vivid and seemingly believable obsessions seem to be more in need of medication. The degree of belief in the obsessions seems to be what makes the difference here.

One reason why it is beneficial to begin medication immediately upon going to see a behavioral therapist is that it takes most antidepressant medications a few weeks to begin working. Since it takes several visits to gather and organize the information necessary to begin the therapy, the start of the medication's effects and the assignment of the first therapeutic tasks can usually be made to coincide. This can make for a good beginning. Interrupting therapy later on due to lack of progress, and then waiting several weeks for a medication to start working, can lead to a lot of lost time and momentum.

BEHAVIORAL THERAPY CAN HELP BIOLOGICAL PROBLEMS

It should be remembered that OCSDs are both biological and behavioral disorders. Obviously, you cannot predict or prevent the obsessive thoughts or impulsive urges which simply pop into your mind; however, you are the one who determines how to respond when they occur. Remember, as mentioned earlier, that obsessions bring anxious responses, and compulsions are designed to relieve that anxiety. Obsessions are involuntary and come to mind automatically. Rituals and other compulsions are voluntarily created by the sufferer as a way of dealing with these abnormal thoughts. While it is true that some obsessive thoughts will go so far as to tell the sufferer what specific compulsive act to perform, they cannot rob a person of their free will. How else can we explain the fact that many do learn to resist and permanently stop performing their compulsions and go on to recover?

Recent studies of PET scans, which, in the form of computerized colored pictures, show how the brain metabolizes radioactively tagged glucose, have also added some insight into the possible biological effects of behavioral therapy on the brain. The scans, which were done both before and after behavior therapy for classic OCD, appeared to indicate changes in which the metabolic activity of sufferer's brains shifted in a more normal direction. Future studies will hopefully go further in providing information about the relationship of behavioral change to changes in brain activity and chemistry.

Given the fact that the brain is an organ with both electrical and chemical activity, it is possible to speculate (as did the PET scan researchers) that changes in behavior would have to be recorded within it in terms of new and changed electrical and chemical activity. Furthermore, it would also logically follow that the changes brought about by behavior therapy, in terms of an individual's symptoms, would therefore appear as changes in the brain in some way. Those who recover and stay recovered may possibly have brought about important changes in the workings of their own brain. We can only guess at this time how permanent these changes might be.

In any case, the results speak for themselves and common sense would indicate that behavioral therapy is worthwhile, despite the biological origins of OCSDs.

~ *Self-Help for OCSDs*

~ *It is part of the cure to wish to be cured.*
—*Seneca*

Most powerful is he who has himself in his own power.
—*Seneca*

The only place where success comes before work is a dictionary.
—*Vidal Sassoon*

*I*t is possible to treat your own OCD, but why would you prefer a self-help approach to treatment by a professional? I ask this question to get you to take a realistic look at your own reasons and motivation and to help you to be clear in your own mind as to what you are about to do. There are several fairly obvious reasons for pursuing self-help:

- Therapy may be beyond your means financially. The weekly expense may be too great, and you don't have health care coverage for it.

- A qualified psychologist or psychiatrist may not be available locally. There are many areas in the country where someone with an OCSD would have to travel four or five hours or more to even get a consultation.

- You may live in a small town and worry about your privacy, even though your local professional is ethically bound to confidentiality.
- You may be very independent and mostly prefer to do things for yourself.

This is not to say that self-help is better or worse than professional treatment. Each may be right for different people, but how do you tell which is right for you?

The actual things you must do are usually rather obvious, direct and not very mysterious, although they are not necessarily easy. Changing yourself never is. Realistically, there can be a number of obstacles on the path to self-help. Human beings, by nature, don't love hard work and tend to avoid things that are uncomfortable or difficult. That is, we are often somewhat lazy and have a low tolerance for frustration and discomfort. To set out alone to face your worst obsessions or your most stubborn compulsions will take persistence, a high tolerance for frustration and discomfort, self-discipline, and the ability to finish what you start. If you really know yourself well enough to believe that these qualities don't come easily to you, you will probably do better working with a trained therapist.

A second issue in self-help may be the level of belief which you attach to your obsessive thoughts. This belief can be very strong for some and as mentioned earlier, those in this category are referred to as "overvalued ideators." (Chances are that people with an extremely high degree of belief will not engage in any treatment and probably won't even want to read this book.) The stronger the belief, the more unshakable the conviction that catastrophe, guilt, or strong discomfort awaits if you don't carry out your compulsions correctly. (For those with TTM, skin picking, or nail biting, substitute "urge" for belief.) If you possess even a small amount of doubt that your beliefs are true, there is at least something there to build on, but self-help may still not be for you. The persistent coaching and the logical challenges that someone skilled in treating OCSDs can give may be essential for your recovery.

A third issue that could affect helping yourself is whether or not you live in a supportive environment. If you live alone, this may or may not be a problem. Some people do very well on their own and can motivate themselves, while others feel more comfortable having someone else to motivate them. Sometimes, just the presence of someone else can discourage you from acting abnormally. The presence of others, while helpful, can work both ways, however. An environment in which there is fighting, arguing, and other types of friction (especially if it is aimed at you, the sufferer) is one which will definitely not help you get well. Other family member's problems may also have a negative effect on you. The stress of these family or living situation problems may be enough to aggravate your symptoms to the point where it will be extremely difficult to get well there. Those you live with may have built up anger and resentment toward you and your disorder over the years. Let's face it—they are only human, they have their limits, and living with someone going through the agonies of an OCSD can be a real strain. Their lives may also have been limited and controlled by your disorder, and the skepticism and negativity they express toward you may be difficult to take, while trying to overcome your own doubts about your ability to recover. Conversely, those close to you may make misguided but well-meaning efforts to help you via nagging, pressuring, or making sarcastic remarks, in a misguided effort to "cure" you.

As another type of potential obstacle, you may find it difficult to separate from the involvement that may have already developed from others taking part in your symptoms. Family and friends will have to work hard to resist answering questions or helping to perform well established rituals and doing anything that your symptoms have made too difficult for you to do alone. These habits are often as difficult for them to break as the habits of an OCSD itself, and if not controlled, can be a strong force pulling you backward in the direction of your illness.

If you are going to go it alone, self-motivation is really the key. It is crucial to see getting well as your own responsibility. This is because only you can make yourself do what must finally be done—no one else can do this for you. This is true whether or not you have a therapist. Having to regularly report to someone and to have the advantage of their coaching and encouragement, as well as their experience and creativity in attacking difficult symptoms, can often mean the difference between success and quitting if you are not really able to get yourself started. Even with help, you must still be willing to do your best. The road to recovery does not always run in a straight line. There will be inevitable slipups and reverses, and at times it will be difficult to keep from perfectionistically labeling yourself a "failure." Having someone there to help you accept your lapses and setbacks as a part of the process can be crucial.

If your disorder is extremely severe or you have been disabled for a long time, you might benefit from the services of a trained professional. It can be very difficult to stand back and look realistically at fears which seem real and in which you have a high degree of belief. Also, the doubts surrounding them can be particularly torturous. Having someone point out when you are being unrealistic or extreme in what you are avoiding can be a great help. A therapist can be an important reference point for regaining touch with the world of the average person, sometimes just by modeling for you what they themselves would do in a given situation.

One other factor that might prove to be an obstacle to self-help would be the presence of depression. Approximately 60 percent of those diagnosed with classic OCD suffer from depression. Dr. Gary Christensen (1995) found that 52 percent of those suffering from TTM were also found to suffer from depression. In the case of BDD, Dr. Katharine Phillips found depression in 59 percent of sufferers. Where depression is present, it must be treated for one to be successful in overcoming any other disorders. This is because depression can cause serious negativity and is usually accompanied by such a lack of energy and drive, that those who suffer from it often cannot see that any change is possible or move themselves to accomplish very much. This is also true when a sufferer is in treatment with a professional. Depression may be the result of a reaction to having your disorder, or it may be a separate biological condition. Whatever the cause, if your depressed mood is serious, then you will probably need to seek out treatment for it before you can tackle your OCSD.

The number of years you have had your symptoms may not necessarily be a factor in keeping you from recovery. The old saying about not being able to "teach old dogs new tricks" doesn't always apply. I have seen people who have had symptoms as long as sixty years or more make full recoveries that are as solid as those who have only suffered for a short period of time.

This is not to say that only those who are supposedly "weak" in some way, or who lack any of the desirable qualities mentioned above, go to therapists. Many do have the necessary self-help skills but prefer to work with someone else anyway, because they do not wish to "reinvent the wheel" and would rather get started quickly and do it without all the guesswork. As a rule, it may be more rapid and efficient to work under the guidance of an experienced person. Not everyone can make the type of effort that self-help requires.

SELF-HELP FOR OCD

If you do wish to start a program of self-help, and have considered the above issues, I recommend the following steps as a way of organizing your efforts. A more detailed explanation of each step will follow.

1. Make a complete and detailed listing, categorizing all your symptoms.

2. Determine whether OCD is really your problem.

3. Using your list of symptoms, create a hierarchy, in which you order them on the basis of the anxiety they would cause you if you were to confront them.

4. Beginning with the lower end of the hierarchy, create homework assignments aimed at accomplishing realistic goals for yourself which are designed to get you to face the obsessions, while resisting the compulsions. Learn to track your anxiety through each step of the process.

5. Review your homework performance on both a daily and a weekly basis, remembering to credit yourself for your successes and to learn from your errors. Replace older assignments as their goals are accomplished and carry over the ones that will take more time and effort. Keep working your way up the hierarchy.

6. Continue to repeat Step 5 until you have reached and accomplished the top rated items on your hierarchy. You are now entering the recovery phase.

7. Implement the steps for Relapse Prevention, and work on your self-maintenance. This will be your ongoing task.

Step 1. List and Categorize Your Symptoms

An OCD Symptom Checklist has been provided in appendix A for two purposes. The first is to help you list and identify your symptoms to assist you in determining whether you have OCD (Step 2), and if you do, to see within what category your symptoms may fall. Seeing all your symptoms laid out by category will also be helpful in giving you an overview of the problem in order to help you accept it. Remember though, that whether you have only one symptom or many really doesn't determine whether or not you have OCD, or whether it is mild or serious. You can be severely ill with only one main symptom or only mildly ill with many different ones.

The second purpose is to give you a list to help organize what you will want to explain to a professional caregiver, even if you only go for a consultation. Showing it to them will certainly make it a lot simpler for them to understand what you are experiencing. The information the checklist will contain about past symptoms will also be informative to them as to how your problem has evolved over time. Don't forget—this is one of the most misunderstood and misdiagnosed disorders. Because OCD is so complex and takes on so many different forms, many practitioners may be prone to overlook your symptoms or not see them as relating to OCD. The checklist is probably complete enough to include most OC symptoms. One other benefit of this list is that it can tell you something about the professional to whom you show it. If they do not seem to understand what it is all about or simply dismiss it without serious consideration, my advice is to think about finding a more concerned and informed helper (see chapter 13).

It is highly important, as mentioned earlier, to differentiate between obsessions and compulsions, as this understanding is crucial when determining how to deal with each type of symptom. The checklist can help you do this, as it is also divided into two major sections: obsessions first, and then compulsions. An important point worth mentioning here is the issue of some sufferers believing that they are "Pure Obsessionals" (also known as "Pure O"). It is actually rather uncommon to have obsessions without compulsions. This term was mistakenly coined several years ago, and I believe that the concept it represents is a potentially harmful one. A compulsion is basically anything mental or physical that you may do to relieve the anxiety resulting from obsessions. The truth is that many sufferers either fail to recognize many of their own behaviors as compulsions or mistake mental compulsions for obsessions. The concept of being purely obsessional may therefore be harmful because compulsions will either be treated as obsessions or not treated at all. It defies common sense to believe that sufferers can experience the types of odd thoughts that are characteristic of OCD and not do anything about them. Whenever a sufferer tells me that they are a "Pure O," I like to question them carefully about this. I have yet to run across anyone who actually belongs in this so-called category.

Try not to be perfectionistic in filling out your checklist—the number ratings are only rough guides. Don't worry about filling out the same symptoms in more than one category, as some of them do overlap. If your family can be helpful, they might be able to assist you in filling out the list, especially when it comes to remembering past symptoms from childhood.

You may find it more difficult to be objective about your symptoms. This may be especially true if you have had OCD since you were a child, have had a high degree of belief in the content of the obsessive thoughts, or if those obsessive doubts are so strong and so wide ranging that they cause you even to doubt that your obsessions are obsessions. In more difficult situations such as these where insight is low, it might be wise to have at least one professional consultation with a practitioner who specializes in OCD. Should you then be diagnosed with OCD and still find yourself having great difficulty comprehending it through the fog of your doubts or the strength of your fearful ideas, it might be wise to switch from self-help to professional help if possible.

Step 2. Determine Whether OCD Really Is Your Problem

Determining whether or not you have OCD may be a more difficult task for some than it appears. Many who simply read the official DSM criteria (see appendix C) for their disorder, or hear about the stories of others, can consider the information and say "That's me!" Checkers, hoarders, counters, washers, and hair pullers can often identify themselves without much difficulty, as their problem behaviors may be spotted easily. Years ago, many sufferers I knew were able to identify themselves after reading *The Boy Who Wouldn't Stop Washing* by Dr. Judith Rapoport, which was the first popular book on the subject. Hopefully, this book and the checklist you fill out will show you enough of the many sides of OCD so that you will be able to find examples of symptoms similar to your own and to identify the types of symptoms you have (see chapters 8 and 9). People who may find it more difficult to see that they have OCD would include many of those who belong to the subgroups where insight is generally a problem. These subgroups include anorexia and bulimia and BDD. If you have checked off some of the symptoms and still have difficulty accepting that OCD is your problem, seek out a professional to discuss it with. In fact, if you are finding any particular difficulty with this step, at least go for a professional consultation. Just be sure that it is with someone who is well versed in OCSDs.

Step 3. Create a Hierarchy

Creating a symptom hierarchy is the next step. This provides the basic framework for making up your actual step-by-step approach to resisting and eliminating your compulsions, while at the same time confronting your obsessions. A hierarchy is a listing of as many situations as you can think of that can cause you the particular anxiety that results from your symptoms. In reality you should only aim to make it as complete as is practical, trying to make it perfect would only be compulsive. It is also an opportunity for rating all these situations to give an accurate picture of how much each of them bothers you. Beyond this, a hierarchy is a way of specifying what your goals for recovery will be.

A goal is some type of desired result toward which a person may apply particular efforts. It is something you should be able to specify and measure, in order to determine whether or not you have eventually achieved it. Be aware that in order to eventually call yourself recovered, you will have to do *all* the items on your hierarchy. Some of you may be asking why, especially if you have items on your list that might be a bit difficult for the average person. There are several reasons why:

1. In order to stay recovered it will be necessary to reach a level of wellness that you can maintain. If there are situations that you still cannot tolerate, they could possibly push you into a relapse.

2. You may have to build yourself up to be a bit more tolerant and stronger than the average person, because your fears are greater to begin with.

3. People you know may look at your list and tell you that even they would find a particular item difficult, but don't use this as an excuse not to do it. Most people have certain things that bother them, but unless they have OCD or BDD they will not have as many as you, nor will that fear or worry hamper their lives. They can have more leeway to

double-check or avoid things, for instance, while you will not be allowed to check the same thing even once or avoid it. It won't get them into the same kind of trouble.

There will be both costs and benefits involved in working your way through your hierarchy. Consider the benefits to be gained from doing the things on your list, and whether or not you feel the costs will be worth it. Let's face it, looking at that list of tasks can be intimidating at first. If you definitely feel it won't be worth it, perhaps you are not ready to make the commitment. If you are simply unsure, my suggestion is to press ahead anyway and at least give it a try.

Assign numbers to the situations you have listed, rating them anywhere from 0 to 100, depending on how much anxiety they would cause you if you were to stay with them and not do what you usually do to avoid or cancel them out. A 0 rating would represent your feeling no anxiety whatsoever, while 100 would indicate the highest level possible for you. (These numbers are commonly referred to as SUDS levels or Subjective Units of Discomfort.) Some therapists prefer to work with 0 to 10 ratings, however, I recommend using a 100-point scale, as it allows for a finer distinction between situations. There is no absolute way of rating anxiety-provoking situations. You just give them whatever rating seems right for you. You can always change them later if you discover that you misjudged them. Try to include as many of the following that can stimulate obsessive thoughts and urges to do compulsions:

- Locations you can go where obsessive thoughts can be made to occur—both around the house, at work, and in the community.
- Books, magazines, or newspaper articles you can read to bring up subjects you obsess about. Pictures or photos can also help.
- TV shows, videos, or movies which contain scenes or have subjects relating to your obsessions.
- Objects you can touch, resist touching, or be near which will raise your anxiety.
- Items which can be purchased or borrowed and carried on you or kept around the house, for the purpose of facing fears.
- People you can be around, whose age, presence, lifestyle, or actions lead to anxiety.
- Things you can throw or give away which will raise your anxiety. Conversely, things that you can resist bringing home which you may have the urge to save.

- Activities you can perform, which your obsessions tell you are wrong or improper, but which average people around you seem able to do without difficulty. Conversely, activities which your obsessions tell you must be done, that you can resist or neglect to do, and which the average person seems not to have to do either.
- Doing things at specific feared times or dates.
- Words, phrases, or numbers you can write, say, look at, or listen to that will bother you.
- Arrangements of objects or possessions you can disarrange or mess up.
- Accounts of certain events or memories that can stimulate obsessive thoughts.
- Mental images that you can create and then focus upon.

Some people's hierarchies contain a fairly wide spread of a large number of items that range from low through medium to high, giving them many steps by which they can work their way up the list. Other people's hierarchies may contain fewer items but all highly rated, forcing them to start right from the beginning with steps that are very anxiety provoking. While those in the latter category have their work cut out for them, it is still possible to create half steps even within these types of hierarchies.

- Don't just list situations in which you touch contaminated objects directly—include situations where you touch things that have touched the contaminated objects. Also use these secondary items on your list to create steps in which you touch them to other things.
- Make up graduated steps with limited contact time in feared situations. Make contact very brief at first. Even a few seconds or minutes may be sufficient to get started.
- Create steps in which you watch others who would be willing to help model the things you fear to do.

In order to clarify what a typical hierarchy consists of, I have provided some sample hierarchies below.

Sample hierarchy for contamination obsessions:
SUDS

10	Touching the tops of my own shoes
20	Touching a garbage can at home

30   Touching a doorknob
30   Touching elevator buttons
35   Touching a public waste can
50   Drinking from a public water fountain
50   Trying on a coat in a department store
55   Touching the sidewalk
60   Sitting on a public bench
60   Sitting in a hospital waiting room
70   Touching a stairway handrail in public
75   Handling dirty laundry belonging to family members
80   Touching the soles of my shoes
80   Touching the tread of a car tire
80   Trying on gloves in a department store
80   Touching bathroom taps at home
85   Touching toilet flush lever at home
90   Touching toilet seat at home
95   Touching bathroom floor near toilet at home
100   Touching anything in a public bathroom(doorknobs, water taps, flush levers, stall doors, etc.)

Sample hierarchy for hoarding compulsions:
SUDS

25   Throwing away a Kleenex from my pocket without first examining it
30   Throwing out an old greeting card
35   Throwing away a business card
40   Throwing out a newspaper
45   Seeing an interesting piece of paper in the street and not picking it up
50   Throwing away an old newspaper clipping containing interesting information
55   Throwing away the box and wrappings an appliance came in
60   Throwing out a plastic container and lid
60   Throwing out a paper bag without checking inside it
60   Throwing away an empty glass jar and lid
65   Emptying a wastebasket into the garbage without examining the contents
75   Throwing out a week's worth of newspapers
80   Throwing out a newspaper without having read it
85   Putting the garbage in the can without first checking inside the bag
90   Discarding junk mail without opening or reading it
95   Vacuuming the house without checking the floor while doing it, then throwing out the vacuum cleaner bag without checking

100　Throwing away an old nonworking appliance that was being saved to be repaired some day

Sample hierarchy for morbid impulsions to harm others:
SUDS

30　Seeing the word "kill"
40　Writing the word "kill"
45　Putting my hand against some fragile glassware in a department store
55　Looking at a knife or other pointed object on a table
65　Walking through town with a knife in my pocket or purse
75　Walking through town with a rock in my hand
80　Reading a book about a psychopathic killer
85　Reading a newspaper article about someone who went berserk and killed people in public
90　Walking through town with my hand on a knife in my pocket
90　Putting my hands around my dog's neck
95　Standing next to a child
95　Handling knives in a store with other customers standing nearby
95　Standing on a busy street corner behind other people with a lot of traffic going by
100　Sitting in a diner with my hand on the utensils while talking to a waitress
100　Standing behind someone near the edge of a train platform while a train is coming into the station
100　Driving my car down a busy street crowded with pedestrians
100　Lying in bed next to my spouse with a knife on the night table

Although the above hierarchies are only partial, you can see that an attempt was made to include many common everyday situations that would put the sufferer in contact with their fears. In your hierarchy, try to also include situations that are not so common but are particular or special to you. When making up the list, it is often helpful to think back to difficult situations you have previously experienced, or those you still experience on a regular basis. Because each person is unique, hierarchies cannot be "canned" but must be tailor-made in each case. Everyone's hierarchy will be different, even those of people with similar fears. Use the form provided here to create your own hierarchy.

What all hierarchies have in common is that they represent all the specific tasks you will need to accomplish to reach your goal: RECOVERY. Looking over all the things you will have to do can feel overwhelming. In order to increase your motivation at this point, it might also be helpful to create a list of the benefits

Fig. 3.1 ∽ Hierarchy Worksheet

SUDS Rating (0–100)	Thoughts or situations that cause anxiety

you will gain if you reach your goal. Try to state the benefits positively. Such a list for a washer might look like this:

1. I will feel calm and relaxed a lot more of the time.

2. I will be able to touch my favorite possessions whenever I want to.

3. The skin on my hands will look and feel normal.

4. I will be free to bring things into my home whenever I want to.

5. It will be possible to touch people, shake hands, and hug and kiss the people I love. This will enable me to date and find a relationship.

6. I will have the freedom to take the types of jobs I have always avoided.

7. I will feel like a normal human being.

Put this list where you can see it several times a day. Keep reviewing it and looking at it often. Once you have completed this step, you are now ready to actually begin confronting your symptoms.

Step 4. Begin Assigning Yourself Homework

You have now arrived at the most important step of the process. You are actually going to start facing the things you have been avoiding, while resisting the behaviors you have habitually used to relieve your anxiety. While things like distraction and telling yourself that it is only a symptom may have helped you at times, there is no substitute for turning and staring your fear in the eye and facing it down. I like to tell my patients that the worst day of the actual therapy is the day before it begins. You will find that your worst imagined fears of what facing your OCD will be like will never come true. Your mind is capable of dreaming up far worse terrors than can ever really happen in any behavioral therapy. After all, if it were that bad, how could all those recovered sufferers have gone through it and gotten well? As I have said earlier, it is hard to do, but it is not too hard. It is important to understand that obsessive thoughts are essentially a bluff. As my patients like to say, "OCD lies to you." They are nonsense thoughts, no matter how real they may seem. They really don't have any power over you, other than the power you give them. When you confront them, you discover that they really can't make anything actually happen, nor can they control your behavior. By clinging to compulsions, you fall into the trap of believing that they help relieve your anxiety. While they may help you to feel less anxious for a brief time, they will always fail you in the long run. In reality, you have probably felt anxious most of the days you have had your disorder. Compulsions help keep the whole system going and guarantee that you will experience the anxiety again and again. They may look like a solution to you, but they are really the problem. By resisting compulsions, you will feel increased anxiety, but it will only last temporarily. It really does come to an end, although perhaps not immediately. Weigh the discomfort of what you are about to do against the total discomfort you have suffered over the previous months or years and will continue to feel if you don't face your problem. Don't tell yourself you cannot stand this new anxiety. How does a temporary kind of discomfort stack up against long-term unending discomfort? As one of my patients once said, "If you have to suffer, suffer with a purpose." Think back on situations where you were forced to face your fears and did so successfully. How were you able to survive them? Did the anxiety grip you for weeks afterward, or did it go away sooner than you expected? What do the answers to these questions tell you?

If contamination is your problem, you may find yourself saying, "But how can I dirty everything? Suppose it doesn't work, or I change my mind, how will I ever get things clean again?" To you, I would suggest that you think of recovery as decontaminating your life of OCD, rather than having to contaminate your home and belongings.

Whatever your symptoms keep this in mind: you need to accept that you will never be able to keep and perfect your symptoms and live a normal life as well. Many have tried and failed. If you want to reach the goal of becoming an average person, then you have to do what average people do. This also means accepting the normal amounts of risk present in everyday living. Risk is an essential part of life and if you are to live fully, you need to realize that you cannot eliminate it. Risk is such a normal part of life that without it, you eliminate your ability to function. You cannot create a risk-free world for yourself because you cannot control everyone and everything in it. Actually, all you can ever really hope to have control over is yourself. You can try to be compulsively safe and live risk free or you can be well—you cannot have it both ways.

Try to think of yourself as a scientist conducting experiments to see whether your theories of disaster are correct. You probably don't stay in the feared situations long enough to get any useful evidence about this. As a result, you may have come to believe instead, in a superstitious way, that the compulsions you did protected yourself or others. By facing the anxiety, you will now be receiving powerful new information which will not fit in with the old, causing you to start radically revising your thinking about what once seemed dangerous. This response will then result in your finally letting go of the old beliefs that were based on the doubtful information that the OCD was feeding you. This is a far more effective way to defeat your disorder than by simply telling yourself that there is nothing to fear, as some therapies would have you do. In her book, *When Things Fall Apart,* the Buddhist nun Pema Chödrön explains it very simply:

Fear is a natural reaction to moving closer to the truth. If we commit ourselves to staying right where we are, then our experience becomes very vivid. Things become very clear when there is nowhere to escape. . . . No one ever tells us to stop running away from fear. . . . The trick is to keep exploring and not bail out, even when we find out that something is not what we thought. That's what we are going to discover again and again and again. Nothing is what we thought.

Learning to be there in the present moment and to stop trying to escape and avoid are the crucial elements. In reality, there is no escape. You can't run away from thoughts that are being generated inside your own head. They must be faced if you are to succeed. It is a kind of a paradox. The more you try to avoid the fear, the more fear you will have. The opposite, however, is also true.

It will also help this process if you can find ways of challenging how you think about what you are avoiding. An example of how this can work is illustrated by two phrases I give my patients who fear contamination and believe that they can create clean worlds for themselves: (1) "When everything is contaminated, nothing is contaminated," and (2) "Everything touches everything." These phrases are difficult for patients to understand at first, but as they move through the therapy process, it all starts to make sense.

Try not to procrastinate about starting your program. Remember that TV ad that is always telling you to "Just do it?" You must let go and take the risk if you want to recover. In fact, you need to change your whole approach to risk taking. It is the number one issue in classic OCD and BDD. It is important to accept the fact that, as someone with OCD or BDD, your ability to determine risk is faulty when you apply it to certain areas of your life. Try to see taking risks as opportunities to work toward your recovery. If you set a date for starting too far in the future, you may allow other things to creep in and interfere, and you'll never get around to it. It is best to start sooner than you'd like. Also, don't set up too many conditions for when will be the "right time" for you to begin changing. There is no "perfect" time. The right time is whenever you start, but sooner is better. Looked at another way, you could say that by already having made a commitment to change, you have already started the change process.

You may find that your compulsivity makes it difficult for you to break out of your rigid schedules to find time to get started. Or your doubt and perfectionism may cause you to be unable to make decisions or set priorities. There can be no more important priority than getting started. Fight that urge to get distracted by all the little things that have prevented you from getting your life and your time organized. They are part of the disorder. Accept the anxiety and get going!

Begin with the lower level items on your list. I usually start my patients with items that rate about a 20 or a 25. Give yourself about four items at this level and make them your homework for the first week. You can take on a slightly larger number of assignments in future weeks. About six to eight separate assignments will be your eventual goal. Remember that if an assignment doesn't make you anxious, it isn't working. If you are feeling confident and wish to try more later on, feel free, but avoid pressuring yourself to do so at first. Try to remember that this is a process, and that behavioral change means gradual change. Also, don't be tempted to take on items which are too far ahead of you at this stage. Impatience can push you to be too ambitious, and you can end up giving yourself an anxiety attack. When you run out of items at the starting level, move on to the things you rated at 30 and 35.

Try to make the assignments things that you will do at least on a daily basis, rather than things you will do only once in the week ahead. The more you expose yourself to what you fear, the quicker and more completely you will become habituated. The goal is to build up your tolerance and to learn to take risks. Obviously, some things can only be done at particular times, such as when you are taking on symptoms that occur at work or in places you only find yourself on infrequent occasions. When assignments involve touching things that are contaminated or cause bad luck, try to do them several times daily or regularly carry contaminated or unlucky materials on you. The main thing is to try to make your contact with the feared item or situation as constant as possible and to stay with it. I have had a few people who had to work for several weeks on a particular symptom before it was mastered.

As you do each item, allow enough time for habituation to work and tolerance to build. Don't rush through things just to get them over with. In some cases, your fear will go away almost immediately, as if a spell were broken. In other cases, you will have to stay with certain situations longer—an hour, several hours, or even extended and repeated contacts over several days, before the anxiety begins to drop. A few people may even require weeks. Everyone is different. Even if you don't habituate as quickly as you'd like, don't give up. Time is on your side if you stay with the anxiety and trust the method. The anxiety must eventually give way under the sheer weight of practice. For example, in approaching something that seems contaminated, you might have to sit with your hands on the object for an hour or more. Try to keep track of your anxiety as you do these things. If you can do so without being compulsive about it, monitor your own SUDS level about every five minutes. It will help you to feel more like the scientific researcher you need to be. Also, watching your anxiety drop can be very motivating. It may go up further at first, but as you wait, you may well find it going down after a while. When it drops below 30, you can say you have habituated to it. There will be some things you can do while performing other daily activities, while others you will have to totally concentrate on and do nothing else that might distract you from the anxiety. Remember to review the previous week's assignments occasionally as a refresher and verify that you have maintained your habituation.

Start using audiotaped self-exposure from the beginning. It is one of the most effective methods for overcoming obsessions. As I mentioned earlier, obsessions are paradoxical. The surest way to have an obsessive thought is to try to not think about it. The opposite is also true. The more you listen to it, the less will be your reaction. I give my patients the motto—"If you want to think about it less, think about it more." Tapes are a very efficient way of listening to the same dislikable thought over and over. I tell them that the way to tell that they are overcoming an obsession is when their tape is boring them. The tapes you make can be about two to three minutes in length. I generally assign patients to write two-page compositions that they then use as scripts for tapes of this length. Reading from a script can often be easier than trying to invent things off the top of your head. Some people favor the use of tape loops but an ordinary cassette is fine. A small portable tape recorder is best and earphones can help with privacy. Listen to the tapes about six to eight times per day and spread them out over time. Begin by making the first tapes very general and mild, in terms of the anxiety they can produce. You can talk "around" the feared subject at first. The overall idea is to play up your doubts. Tell yourself that the harm or threat to yourself or others could possibly have happened or will happen, but that you cannot be sure. You also want to be certain to add that if you are in trouble, it cannot be avoided and the worst will happen. As a variation on this, if you worry about past harm to yourself or others, you can, in later stages, tell yourself directly that it did happen or that you definitely did it (if this will make you anxious).

For instance, if you have fears of becoming ill, your first tape might be about how much illness there is in the world, how bacteria and viruses are everywhere, and how easy it is to get ill. You can next move on to saying on the tape that you might become ill. Later tapes could be targeted even closer to your feared catastrophe, talking about how you will contract a disease due to some careless thing you did, and how you cannot escape from it. The last tapes in the series might focus on how you will now die because of the illness.

Another example would be the case of someone with morbid thoughts about harming others. Early tapes could speak about how there are people known as psychopaths who harm and kill others impulsively and how we don't always know who they are. Later tapes might suggest that you could possibly be a psychopath because of the thoughts you are having. Finally, your last tapes could say that you definitely are a psychopathic murderer, will soon go berserk, and will do all the horrible things your thoughts suggest.

The main principle here, as you can see, is to start very generally and then make tapes more specific by gradually including more feared material. In this way, the tapes should work their way up your hierarchy.

Try as much as possible to relate the material you are putting in your tape to your other behavioral assignments. For instance, if you are working on not checking your stove or other appliances, make up a series of tapes telling yourself progressively that your house is in greater and greater danger of burning down due to your carelessness. A very important point is that you should not go on to make a new tape until you can rate your SUDS level with the current tape below 30. Most people take from one to two weeks to habituate to a tape. The number of tapes you will have to make in a series differs from person to person. I find that about six to eight tapes per subject is average.

Be careful not to fight or "undo" the effect of your tapes by "talking back" to them mentally, disputing them, or telling yourself you didn't really mean what you were saying when you made them. One of the worst things you can do is to try to argue with your obsessive thoughts. In fact, in between listening to your current tape (or if you don't have a tape recorder to work with), when the thoughts occur, make strong efforts to agree with them, telling yourself that they are definitely all true, will eventually come true, or represent your own real wishes. Do this as often as possible for maximum effect, but also remember to ease into this gradually. If you are using tapes, do this only after you have been listening to them for several weeks. Be certain that when you listen to a tape you are doing nothing else at the time. Give it your full attention and don't let yourself be distracted by other activities. Deliberately letting your mind wander while listening can be just another way of avoiding exposure.

Another type of tape that can also be helpful is something I call a "coaching" tape. These tapes are similar to the list of positive benefits mentioned in Step 3. Record yourself giving an encouraging message, reminding yourself why it is important to resist your compulsions and face your obsessions. Mention all the positive reasons for persisting and moving ahead. These tapes are best used when you need a boost or are having a tough time getting yourself to do an assignment. They should only be about three to five minutes in length. Listening to one will have a further benefit of interrupting the flow of behaviors that lead to compulsive acts.

Watch out for other little "tricks" that you may be tempted to play on yourself when it comes to facing homework assignments. One frequently seen among those who suffer from contamination fears is when they assign themselves to resist washing. They do resist but also make sure not to touch anything that would make them want to wash. I call this "obeying the letter, but not the spirit of the law." Another way in which people can fool themselves is by correctly resisting washing in a particular situation, but then deliberately engaging in some other activity immediately afterward where they are allowing themselves to wash, such as washing the dishes or bathing their child. They may actually believe that they really are following their program. Be careful not to trick yourself when you reduce your checking ritual to just one check. Your single check may sound average, but it may still go on a whole lot longer and be done much more carefully than most people's. If this is the case, it must be considered abnormal. In general, your best bet is to eliminate checking altogether. It is a futile activity. The information you will get from checking either won't "stick" for more than a little while or may even raise further doubts, leading to an even stronger urge to check. Remember that when it comes to checking, "the more you check, the less you know."

As mentioned earlier, if you find that you cannot do something in a whole step, don't treat it as a tragedy. Try approaching it in half steps instead. An example would be someone with contamination obsessions fearing to touch something. If touching the object directly is too difficult at first, touch a tissue to the feared object and then handle the tissue. With hoarding, if you can't throw out a whole bag of trash you have been saving, throw out one or two items at a time. If the problem involves encountering an obsession that is very frightening, try confronting a milder or watered-down version of it.

As a way of overcoming rituals and compulsive habits, try rearranging your environment or daily routines as a way of distracting yourself or making yourself more conscious of behaviors which have become very automatic. It is a well-known phenomenon in OCSDs that many sufferers do better with symptoms while on vacation. This is probably because there are many cues and signals in their everyday world that are habitually associated with performing compulsions or impulsions. When those with OCSDs leave home, they are suddenly freed from these cues and have fewer symptoms. If they were to stay long enough in their new environment, however, the symptoms and cues would eventually be reestablished. While you may not be able to go on a continual vacation as a way of helping yourself, you can do things like rearrange the furniture, change the order in which you do familiar activities, perform everyday activities in different parts of your home, sit in a different chair, sleep on the other side of the bed, enter or leave your house through different doorways, drive different routes in your car, etc. A person with a dressing ritual may get dressed in a different order, or someone with checking compulsions may take a different path through the house or put things they check in new locations. Posting signs or notes in strategic places can be another way of changing your environment. Post-it notes reminding you of what you are supposed to do can be useful for this. You can also easily remove them when others come to your home. One further thing you can do with these notes is to write fear-provoking messages on them and then put them in all sorts of places where you will eventually run across them by accident, which will be even more challenging.

Don't let self-consciousness keep you from doing homework assignments that can only be carried out in public places. I have found that people really aren't as aware of you as you think. They have their own business to worry about and will not constantly have their eyes on you. Also, if you act like you belong somewhere and act as if you know what you are doing, it is very unlikely that anyone will question you or stare at you. Even if they do look—so what? They most likely won't have a clue as to what you are doing.

The following is a selection of suggestions that may give you ideas for creating behavioral homework assignments for yourself. In the case of superstitiously feared words, numbers, or phrases, some good techniques would be to write them twenty-five times per day, say them frequently, post them on signs around the house (Post-it pads are also good for this), write them on T-shirts and wear them at home, put them on pillow cases you will sleep on, draw them on mirrors, write them on your hand (or on a piece of tape put on your hand, to make them removable), write them on pieces of paper and put them in your shoes and pillowcase, or work them into conversations. When you turn off your television, leave it tuned to a station number you dislike. Perform different small activities a bad number of times. Buy quantities of things that are the same as the disliked number. Make purchases that add up to the bad number. Look at license plates that have the bad number on them. Dial phone numbers that have the disliked number in them. Go into buildings that have the bad number as their address. If a disliked number appears on a clock, don't stop all activities to wait until the time changes. When reading books and newspapers be sure to finish on pages with feared numbers. Create a series of graduated audiotapes spelling out how you have broken the rules, how bad luck will surely happen, and how there is no undoing things. A good technique for magical thinkers is to write feared phrases, words, or numbers on money you are going to spend— once you have given it away you can't undo it. I have even had some female patients with number fears go so far as to write the words or numbers on their nails and then apply polish over them, sealing them in.

If you suffer from morbid obsessions and fear hurting others either on purpose or accidentally, be certain to place yourself in the situations you fear. Do not avoid touching or being very near others, handling pointed or sharp objects in their presence, driving near where they are standing, or preparing food for them. In fact, you should go out of your way to do these things. Carrying sharp objects in your pockets or purse that could be used as weapons when you go out in public will also contribute to the desired effect. Gradually increase whatever you fear doing around others. If you have saved lists detailing past events where you might have harmed others and you read them compulsively to check if or how these things really happened, throw them all out. Resist going back to check if you have harmed anyone. Fight the urge to call or question others, even if you have the opportunity to do so. In particular, do not call the police to find out if an accident, injury, or death has been reported. Don't allow yourself to keep reviewing past situations in your mind, to determine just what it was you did or didn't do. Read books or watch videos about people who have committed murders or sex crimes and tell yourself you are just like them. Make a series of audiotapes for self-exposure, gradually building up the idea that you really are a psychopathic murderer and enjoy committing crimes. Above all, do not argue with your thoughts or try to analyze them. Every time they occur, tell yourself they are all true, and that the feared events actually happened.

Where fear of contamination is the problem, the goal is to gradually maximize contact with feared objects, people, or substances. Try to find ways to bring home feared items or things that have touched them. Do not maintain separate clean or dirty zones within your home or workspace. Eliminate those clean rooms or areas. Wear the same clothing all day and do not change them when you come home. Do not wash keys, change, or jewelry at these times. Allow others into your home, workplace, or car. Don't make them wash, take off their shoes, or change their clothes. Shake hands with others. Do not avoid people who look unclean or unwell to you. Walk near them, touch things you have seen them touch. Give change to panhandlers. If things fall on the floor or on the ground outside, don't wash or discard them. Keep them and use them. Don't clean new clothing before wearing it for the first time. Resist the urge to wash or clean groceries when you bring them home. Sit on public benches and drink from public fountains. Open doors in public places with your hands. Touch mailbox handles, and let your hands touch waste cans when you throw things away in public. Visit hospital waiting areas. Sit there and read magazines, drink from fountains, and use the public phones. Have something to eat in their coffee shop. Work on using public restrooms. These can be among the most challenging places. Flush toilets with your hand. Don't use paper to touch faucets or light switches. Open stall doors and entry doors with your hands. Make up a series of audiotapes in which you remind yourself of all the dirty, filthy, and infectious things you have come into contact with, how you and/or others will now surely become ill and eventually die as a result.

As far as decontamination via handwashing and showering is concerned, there are several important techniques you will find helpful. Get rid of all antibacterial soaps, alcohol wipes, and anything else you use to clean your hands or body with, other than bar soap. Get rid of all your disinfectants. In the average home, there is no need to disinfect anything. Eliminate the use of paper towels to dry yourself. Use an ordinary towel, and change it only once per week. As far as actual washing itself is concerned, you can take one of two routes. The first is the more moderate approach. The goal of this approach is to limit handwashing to very specific situations, such as after using the toilet, handling raw meat, eggs, or fish, or changing a baby's diaper. In no case should handwashes take longer than 10 to 12 seconds, nor should hands be washed more than once per time. Showering should be limited to ten minutes in length and to once per day. It should be done first thing in the morning in order to not immediately wash off the previous day's supposed contamination. The second approach is much stricter and should be used if you find yourself too inclined to cheat by washing more frequently or for longer than recommended. It is similar to the approach that has been used in intensive behavioral therapy programs and involves not showering or hand washing for five days at a stretch, and then allowing yourself a single 10- to 12-minute shower at the end of this interval. This should be done for four of these five-day cycles. The advantage of this method is that it eliminates all the guesswork and temptation by taking you away from washing altogether. When you then resume more frequent washing on a moderate schedule, it will seem sufficient by comparison. It may also bring about quicker results than the moderate approach.

For compulsive hoarding, it is very important to have specific guidelines. All newspapers, magazines, and greeting cards must be discarded or put in the recycling bin immediately after they have been read. All mail must be read and sorted immediately upon bringing it into the house. Junk mail must be discarded immediately. When it comes to shoes and clothing, I give patients my "Three Year Rule." If an article of clothing or a pair of shoes has not been worn in the last three years, it must be thrown out or given to charity. If you have not used it within that span of time, you don't really need it. All other clothing must be put away in closets or drawers. Broken or worn out appliances and other belongings must go right into the trash. Forget about fixing them. As far as other people's trash is concerned, you must forbid yourself to bring home items others have discarded. Don't even stop to look. Clothes and toys from your distant childhood must also be thrown out or given away. It is extremely important to be very strict and honest with yourself and not let sentimentality get in the way. When you are drowning in a sea of junk or excess possessions, you can't afford it.

In the case of ordering and arranging things perfectly or symmetrically, the solution is obvious. Mess up the order, and disarrange things as much as possible. Move pieces of furniture out of line with each other. Make pictures crooked. Randomly arrange things that have been sorted by color, size, or alphabetically. If you must keep your possessions in perfect condition, stop cleaning or protecting them. Take them out of protective wrapping or packing. Use them frequently. Allow others to use them or lend them to others. If possible, put smudges of dirt on them or allow them to get dusty. If you are a compulsive house cleaner, stop vacuuming for several weeks. Leave pieces of crumpled paper on the floor and dirty dishes on the table and in the sink. Leave your clothes lying around on the furniture. Don't make your bed. Pull out your sofa cushions in different directions. In all cases, be sure to look at these disordered and imperfect things as much as possible, in order to maximize your exposure.

Moral or religious scrupulosity can be somewhat tricky to work on. In the case of the former, you will have to commit a variety of minor infractions that will seem very serious to you, but that would not trouble the average person in the slightest. This could involve such things as telling small white lies, dropping pieces of paper on the ground to create litter, eating a grape in the supermarket without paying for it, or moving a piece of merchandise in a store to the wrong shelf. When it comes to religious scrupulosity, it may be advisable to consult with a member of your clergy before making up your own assignments, but be very certain that they have an understanding of this type of OCD. Unless they do, it is possible that they could only make things worse by giving you the wrong advice. They can advise you about where you are being excessive in your observances, and to what level you can properly reduce them. Homework can be based on these cutbacks. You can then make up audiotapes telling yourself that they are really mistaken, that you are now offending your deity, and that you will be punished or penalized in some way as a result.

Some useful assignments for BDD might include going out in public without your usual makeup or camouflage. You might go out for only a little while or stay close to home at first, and then attempt to lengthen your trips. If going out in daylight or being under bright lighting is a problem, be sure to include doing these as you move up your hierarchy. Later on, you could also graduate to wearing clothing or makeup that accentuates the defect about which you are anxious, or deliberately do things to make it more obvious to others. An example of this would be smiling and showing your teeth to others, if you fear there is something wrong with the way they look. Another would be wearing short sleeved shirts and shorts, if you believe there is something wrong with the way your skin looks. It can also be helpful to collect pictures of those whose appearance is similar to the way you fear yours looks, if possible. You can mark up photographs of yourself, altering them to accentuate and exaggerate your bothersome feature or body part. This has actually become much easier to do lately, through the use of computer photo retouching programs. Posting signs around the house which remind you of your defect can also contribute to creating an atmosphere of exposure. Making audio tapes telling yourself all about just how bad you look will further add effectiveness to your efforts.

When working on compulsions that make everyday activities take excessive amounts of time, such as long handwashes or showers or compulsively slow behavior, the use of a timer can be invaluable. It can be something as simple as a wristwatch or a digital timer or stopwatch. It will be extremely helpful for you to keep track of the time you are spending, since it is easy to get so preoccupied that you lose all sense of time passing. Tracking your progress will also be easier. A timer that buzzes or rings may be necessary if you are inclined to not pay attention otherwise. When cutting down time spent on compulsions over a period of days or weeks, remember to set realistic daily goals to avoid feeling demoralized. One further note about the use of timers: they can also be helpful as training tools for those who compulsively check and recheck their own decisions, making the process take forever. When making a decision, try setting the timer for thirty seconds, or one minute, and make that your deadline for settling on an answer.

Make these exercises as much a part of your life as possible. The ultimate aim is total immersion. Try not to be dependent on others to get you to do your work. It is your responsibility. It is not up to them to nag or remind you. It is up to you to remind yourself. Also, don't do your therapy simply to please someone else in your life. Do it for yourself because if they do not show enthusiasm or encourage you, or are skeptical about past tries, you will quickly run out of motivation. In the beginning, it is not uncommon for those close to you to be skeptical. Remember that they may have seen you try unsuccessfully before or heard you promise to improve and then not follow through. It may be difficult for them to be enthusiastic, as they may fear being disappointed again. Your actions will convince them in the long run, even if they may not do so in the short run.

This would also be a good time to try disconnecting family and friends from your symptoms. Even though it may be further up on your hierarchy, you will be doing yourself a lot of good by getting them out of your rituals, not letting them touch or do things for you that make you anxious, and stopping them from answering your questions. Knowing that others will no longer participate in your symptoms will be a great help in resisting them. Be very clear about telling family and friends that you do not wish them to do things related to your illness anymore. Instruct them in how to give you gentle reminders if you should slip and fall back to your old ways. If you find it too tempting at times to resist asking questions, or sometimes forget not to, it will be helpful to tell those you usually question to answer you by saying, "I don't know, what do *you* think?" If this still doesn't always work to get you to stop, you can have them take the next step and give you an answer you really don't want to hear. This usually does the trick. Emphasize that they must not be swayed by your pleading, tears, or promises that this request is "different" or the absolute "last one" you will ever make. Don't try to trick them into "helping" you, as you will only be hurting yourself. Remind yourself to not feel angry when they refuse—they are only trying to be helpful and are only doing what you asked. When you finally come to accept that no one will answer a question or carry out your instructions, you will stop asking. People tend not to keep up activities that have no reward. By separating others from your illness, you will probably be taking your greatest single step forward.

Something known as modeling is important also. I have frequently demonstrated behaviors for fearful patients by doing the assigned activity myself. If you can avoid making it a way of double checking, see if you can get a cooperative family member or friend to do first what you fear. Another alternative would be to go out in public and watch others doing what you fear to try. Seeing them do it can give you confidence and take away some of the hesitation. Try not to tell yourself that they are only able to do it because they are ignorant of the supposed dangers. Remember, it is important to accept that because of the OCD, your judgment of certain things is poor. It doesn't give you reliable information. You haven't been able to correctly figure out the risks or process the information. It is very important to ask yourself, "What would the average person be able to do in a situation like this?" (We define average here, as what the majority of people do.) Let the answer to this question be your guide. The average person must always be your compass. If you don't know or have forgotten what the average person does, ask someone you trust. Take a poll of average people you can ask or at least observe others around you.

Consistency is very important. You must work on your homework each and every day. Your disorder is with you every day. Don't tell yourself you are too busy or that other chores are more important. That is procrastinating. You were never too busy to find the time to obsess or perform rituals when you felt anxious. Constantly remind yourself of what you must do. Start each day by looking over your homework and asking yourself, "What is my goal today?" Write your homework down and post it on your refrigerator or somewhere you will see it regularly. Make copies and post them in several other places too. If your memory is bad (and you are not afraid of ink), write it on the back of your hand or put it on a card in your pocket. Antidepressants can sometimes hamper your short-term memory (see chapter 4), so if you are taking them, more frequent homework reminders may be necessary.

As you work your way up your hierarchy over time, you will notice an interesting effect. The items at the top of the list begin to look less frightening than when you first made it up. They seem to slide to lower levels as other items below them drop off the bottom of the scale. By the time you are working on items at the 70 or 80 level, the things that you originally rated at the 100 level will suddenly seem much easier to face.

There are several possible pitfalls to watch out for as you move up your hierarchy. As some people gradually improve, they begin to raise their standards for what they expect from themselves. The more they are able to do, the more self-critical they become. The result is that they give themselves the impression that they are not improving. Sometimes, as you get rid of certain symptoms, others you haven't yet worked on may suddenly seem worse simply by way of comparison. As you overcome your major symptom(s), other minor ones may sometimes seem worse temporarily because you now have the time to pay attention to them. Don't suddenly start thinking that you have somehow substituted brand new symptoms and will therefore never recover. Shift your efforts to these other symptoms and keep working, and they too will eventually be overcome.

Remember that behavioral change is gradual change. This process is going to take time. Some of your problem behaviors will fall away in a short time, and others will prove to be more stubborn. Don't let setbacks throw you. Expect them. They are a normal part of the process. The road to recovery is rarely smooth or in a straight line. No one accomplishes anything important without having some obstacles to overcome. Do you suppose that if you tried to learn any new skill, such as how to play tennis, how to draw, or how to drive, that you would immediately begin to do it like an expert without ever making a mistake? Don't lose sight of the fact that mistakes are integral to the learning process. Sometimes we learn the most from them. Rather than looking on them as failures, try to use the information you can get from them to improve your efforts.

It is very common to slip up or fall back on a familiar habit. Everyone who undertakes this process has their ups and downs. If this happens, it does not mean that you cannot recover. It means that you are just like everyone else. Who said it would be easy? Persistence is everything when you are trying to change. Don't forget that a lapse is not a relapse. Making one mistake or even a few doesn't mean that you have gone back to square one. Remember that square one was where you were before you even decided to work at recovering. To go back there, you would have to have forgotten everything you had learned up to the point of the lapse. You don't ever have to like lapses or setbacks, but you will have to accept them as a fact of life when it comes to change. Even several slipups cannot prevent your recovery if you just keep on working at it. If you do make a mistake, try to contain it, learn what you can from it, and try to get back on track as quickly as possible. Fortunately, this is one of those processes where you can always start again. If you wash off that contamination, recontaminate yourself immediately. If you checked something out of habit when you weren't supposed to, find a way to remind yourself the next time. If you forget and perform a ritual, either reverse it or repeat whatever made you want to do it in the first place. If you saved something you shouldn't have, throw it out now. If you arranged or organized things, mess them up immediately.

Just don't give up. You can only fail to succeed by not trying. Even an attempt to try to do something still represents an important change for you. It is something you would not have done in the past, and it signifies that the belief in your particular catastrophe must have weakened at least somewhat. Life holds no guarantees that you will succeed every single time you try something, but if you don't even try, we can guarantee that you won't reach your goal. Don't focus solely on your mistakes and dwell on them to the exclusion of everything else, as perfectionists are prone to do. Focus instead on the things you have been able to accomplish and the ways in which you have improved. Remember to stick to rating your behavior only—not yourself. Your behavior can be bad, disappointing, or undesirable, without you, yourself, being totally bad or a failure. After all, if you go on to change your behavior, how can it then be said that you are no good or a failure? You are an ordinary mistake-making human being trying to accomplish an important change one step at a time.

Don't make the mistake of comparing yourself to those who don't suffer from your disorder. This is not a fair comparison. Of course, they can do things you can't, because they aren't working to overcome the problems you have to face. A better comparison would be to look at the way you were at your worst, versus the way you are now that you have made some progress. Back then, could you have done some of the things you are doing now?

One further note: remember to allow time for new behaviors to become spontaneous and natural. Obviously, you may be acting more deliberately at first, since you will have to think about each new thing you are doing. With repeated rehearsals, new behavior becomes automatic like many things you do every day without thinking.

Step 5. Review Your Homework Regularly

Make sure to review your progress each day. Remember to praise your successful efforts and to try to understand situations in which you were not successful. Don't be harshly self-critical, instead learn from your mistakes by taking a problem-solving approach to them, rather than a self-critical one. Whatever you were unable to do today, you can resolve to accomplish tomorrow. There will always be another chance to start over. On the other hand, don't gloss over assignments that seem easy at first. It is tempting to do things that seem easy just once and conclude that you are forever finished with them. Sometimes an assignment that is done several times can suddenly become more anxiety provoking with repetition. Do each assignment for at least a week, and then, if it still does not cause anxiety, go ahead and discontinue it.

Because of the nature of OCD, it is sometimes possible to doubt whether you are working hard enough on your assignments. This concern can then lead to trying to get well "perfectly" and developing a lot of anxiety over your homework. It may also lead to either doing too much or things that are more extreme than would be necessary to recover. If you find yourself continually obsessed with this, it may be necessary to be deliberately less strict in doing your homework and to do it less perfectly than you would like. You walk a fine line with this kind of thinking. It might even be necessary to let yourself slip a little now and then to fight the perfectionism. You may have to seek professional help if this kind of perfectionism becomes too much of an obstacle to your recovery.

Try also to make a weekly review of your efforts. If at the end of a week, you can truly say that you have faithfully completed a particular assignment, and you can further say that your SUDS level while doing it is now a 30 or less, you may drop the assignment. It should now be replaced with a new one. If, on the other hand, you did not perform it as often as you should have, or it is still causing you to feel a moderate or higher level of anxiety, say above a 30 level, keep it on your list and continue to work on it. This is true for exposure tapes as well. Sometimes it is helpful to review old assignments to make sure that you are still on the right track.

Step 6. Working Through Your Hierarchy

Now that you have begun to do daily assignments, are reviewing them regularly, and are giving yourself new ones on a weekly basis as necessary, you have established a rhythm and a forward momentum. The goal now is to consistently work your way completely through your hierarchy. After the first few weeks, you should be able to get a sense of how it is going. Persistently facing your difficult situations and thoughts without acting compulsively is going to lead to your symptoms gradually dropping away. Your belief in your own effectiveness should keep increasing as you move along. If you have some setbacks to overcome, you should be able to see that these are only temporary and cannot ultimately block your progress. (See the next section on "Relapse Prevention.")

You are now at a critical point. Watch out for starting to slow down the pace when you have partially recovered. There is a danger of complacency and procrastination setting in once you are beginning to feel more comfortable. You may be tempted to settle for only a partial recovery, thinking that "things are better than they were, so why jeopardize what I have gained," or "I feel somewhat better, so why not stop here? I may not have to do those really difficult things at the top of my list after all. I wasn't really looking forward to facing them anyway." In order to get into recovery and stay there, you need to do all the items on your hierarchy and finish what you have started. Untreated symptoms leave openings for the OCD to reinstate itself in your life. Even if it doesn't happen right away, the odds are that it will happen eventually. If you can still justify doing a few compulsions, what makes you think that you will not soon be able to justify doing more? As long as you maintain the old habits of dealing with your anxiety in compulsive ways, the fact is that you still actively have OCD despite your improvement. Recovering from OCD is not like a card game where you can drop out and simply walk away with your winnings. OCD is a complex disorder and it is possible to relapse.

One further note here. It is even more important to confront your symptoms when you are feeling "good" than when you are suffering with them. It greatly helps to increase your self-confidence and strengthens your risk-taking abilities when you can take a chance when you feel well. Trying to maintain that "good" feeling is really a trap. If you find yourself feeling too anxious to take such a risk, you had better ask yourself just how well you actually are. In order to be truly free, you must be willing and able to think dislikable thoughts and confront your fears at any time, not just when your back is to the wall. Remember, being well means being able to make choices and take risks.

Step 7. The Recovery Period and Relapse Prevention

Recovery is a journey, not a destination. Think of it as a work in progress. There is no graduation. It is true that you have achieved a certain level of freedom from your symptoms and regained (or even just gained) the ability to function normally in the everyday world, for which you deserve tremendous credit. This is not the end of the story—it is actually a beginning. You will see the phrase "in recovery" used in a number of places in this book. This is to remind you that it is also something that you can fall "out" of. It would be wonderful if you could simply lose your symptoms the way you are finally cured of a cold, but you must remember that OCD is a chronic problem. While actively working through the first six steps of your therapy, you have been responsible for resisting compulsions and facing obsessions on a daily basis. When in recovery, you may not be working as intensively each day on a large group of symptoms. However, there are still things you are responsible for that you must do to preserve your wellness on an ongoing basis. This may not only include avoiding or effectively handling the old problem habits you have worked on, but may also mean changes in the way you live and work.

RELAPSE PREVENTION

In 1985, Marlatt and Gordon, two researchers in the field of alcohol abuse treatment, coined the term "relapse prevention." This term referred to a series of four steps that they outlined as a way for alcoholics to remain abstinent and in recovery. I believe that these steps are universally applicable for maintaining any kind of a recovery, and they should be considered the last stage of your self-help efforts. These steps are as follows:

1. Know your "hot spots"
2. Prepare for setbacks
3. Act immediately on setbacks
4. Live a balanced life

Step 1. Know Your "Hot Spots"

Knowing your "hot spots" is the first crucial factor in maintaining your recovery. This term refers to those situations in which you will be most likely to have an obsessive thought occur which could then possibly lead to doing a compulsion. Having prepared a hierarchy at the beginning of your program and then progressing through it, you will already have a good working knowledge of what things are most likely to set you off and what your potential may be in reacting to them. The old saying "forewarned is forearmed" comes to mind here. With your new awareness, you will now be able to anticipate problems before they occur and prepare yourself to meet them. By heightening your awareness and keeping your defenses up, you may well be able to head off a problem before it becomes serious. For those with OCD and BDD, the hot spots would probably include the items that were highest on your hierarchy. For those with TTM, skin picking, and nail biting, it would be times, places, moods, or situations where you feel the greatest urges to pull, scratch, pick, or bite. Because giving in to symptoms is actually a choice that a person makes, all those in recovery need to prepare before entering these hot spots.

Performing a compulsion or an impulsion is often not a single behavior, but a whole chain of behaviors leading to an undesirable conclusion. Each link becomes an increasingly strong signal for the next link to begin. Because there will be fewer accumulated signals, behavioral chains are easier to break if you interrupt them in their earlier stages. It is important to be aware of the existence of these chains, particularly how they start, so that they can be broken more easily. You need to see your compulsive behaviors as a series of steps, each leading to the next, drawing you in deeper and deeper. An example of such a chain might be:

1. Seeing an unclean-looking person on the street

2. Avoiding walking near them

3. Having thoughts that you may now be contaminated

4. Avoiding touching yourself or any of your belongings

5. Dropping all other plans and immediately heading home

6. Undressing and throwing your clothes in the wash

7. Washing your hands repetitively

8. Putting on clean clothes

Obviously, after the first step, our person in recovery should have reminded himself that he was not supposed to avoid the unwashed looking individual and should have exposed himself to the thought that he would now contract a fatal illness and die. Had he broken the chain at this starting point and stayed with the anxiety until it subsided, he would have strengthened his tolerance and been able to overcome the desire to fall back.

Preparing yourself verbally in advance of a situation which you can anticipate is another important technique. Let us suppose that in the past, going to a particular location or entering a particular situation caused you to have fearful obsessions. If, now in your recovered state, you find yourself having to go to such a place again, you could do several things in advance. If you're about to enter a potentially tricky situation, try a "Self-alerting Statement" such as one of the following:

"Okay, get ready, here it comes"

"This is the challenge I have been training for"

"Remember to resist"

"This will be a good opportunity to practice"

"This will be uncomfortable, but not dangerous"

"I've handled this before—I can handle it again"

"Keep your eyes open"

"Expect the unexpected"

There is also another variety we could refer to as "Instructional Statements." Some examples might be:

"Take the risk"

"Face the fear"

"Just do it"

"Stay with the fear—it will pass"

"Let go and live"

"If I want to get well, I have to do it"

"I don't like this, but I can stand it"

"To think about it less, think about it more"

"When everything is contaminated, nothing is contaminated"

"I don't do this any more"

"I can't choose whether or not I may get a symptom, but I can choose how
    to react to it"

Another good technique to use ahead of time would be what we call an "Imaginal Rehearsal." To prepare for an approaching hot spot, use your imagination to visualize yourself actually going through the situation, and acting appropriately by facing the anxiety and tolerating it. As a part of this rehearsal, you should concentrate on what specific techniques you plan to use and imagine yourself carrying them out successfully. If possible, sit quietly somewhere, breathe deeply, close your eyes, and concentrate on walking yourself through the scene and behaving as an average person.

Step 2. Prepare for Setbacks

The most important fact to remember about setbacks (or what some people call lapses) is that they are a normal part of the process of any behavioral change and that they will occur. Now and then you will make the wrong choice. It is not a matter of "if," but a matter of "when." In order to maintain your recovery you will need to realistically prepare for them similar to the way people practice fire drills. Even those who have made the best recoveries can have setbacks once in a while, and therefore these instructions are for everyone. One special note: this does not mean that you should tell yourself, "Compulsions and impulsions are inevitable, so why bother resisting anyway?"

The first step in preparing for a setback is understanding the difference between it and a relapse, just as you had to do when you were in the earlier phases of working on your symptoms. A setback is not a relapse. It is neither a total breakdown of your wellness nor is it a failure of willpower. Taking a step back in the direction of your symptoms is nowhere near the same as going all the way back to square one. In OCSDs it is possible to have setbacks involving only one of several possible symptoms or in some areas of your symptoms but not others. In such cases, it is not logical to demoralize yourself by believing that you have "totally" regressed. Going further, we can even say that a relapse is not the end either. You can always learn from your mistakes and start over again.

Looked at in a different framework, a setback can be viewed as a valuable learning experience. You can choose to regard it as an opportunity to get important practice and to rehearse your skills. It can show you that certain areas of your OCD need your attention and effort and act as a reminder that recovery is a state that must be actively maintained. It also points out to you that your efforts have in some way been inadequate. What it is not saying is that you or your ability to handle such things are inadequate, either now or in the future.

It is crucial to understand how setbacks happen to people. Generally, there is a background of contributing factors such as a buildup of stress of some kind or a triggering event. Unfortunately, we human beings tend to regress under pressure. This means that we fall back on old ineffective behaviors in order to cope.

Because these old strategies don't work, they probably only add further stress and actually worsen things. These old behavior patterns and ways of thinking were probably rehearsed hundreds or even thousands of times and have become overlearned. They easily occur to you when you are under stress because they can be activated with little or no thought or hesitation. The older, more rehearsed behavior can overcome a new behavior because there isn't time to think. This is why it was pointed out in the last section that it is important for you to be able to anticipate your "hot spots."

Step 3. Act Immediately on Setbacks

To recover from OCD and to stay recovered, it is important for you to accept that you are responsible for how you manage yourself, rather than acting help-lessly and blaming problems on "the illness" by saying such things as "I couldn't help myself." There are effective behavioral and cognitive tools that you now possess should you choose to use them. Remember that you always have a choice, no matter how difficult the situation. No one can take better care of you than you yourself. The goal is, and always will be, for you to become and remain your own therapist, seeing what needs to be done and assigning yourself the appropriate homework.

In terms of what to do behaviorally, the solution is obvious. If you have come this far, you know what you should be doing, even if you choose not to do it. It is almost always possible to recontaminate yourself, think the unlucky magical thought, bring back the doubt, etc. As some of my patients who attend AA say, "You can always start your day over." Even if you have missed a chance to reex-pose yourself to the fear this time, you can prepare for the next time or even arrange a next time. If your doubts are such that you are unsure as to whether this is truly an OC situation and requires a response, give yourself the benefit of the doubt (so to speak) and treat it as one anyway.

Beyond selecting the appropriate behavioral response, you must act with speed. Don't allow days or even hours to pass before you decide to do something about it. This will only allow further obsessions and compulsions to creep in during the interim, causing the setback to escalate. Do something immediately so that the situation is contained and confined to a limited level.

The cognitive response should not be ignored here either. It is a crucial tool which will help you to create your own internal support system at this difficult moment. Failure to use it is probably the greatest single cause of setbacks turn-ing into relapses. What you tell yourself will determine what you do next. The cognitive therapy work of Dr. Aaron T. Beck has outlined some of the common types of distortions people are likely to make in their thinking, which can lead to emotional and behavioral disturbance. It might be helpful to outline some of these for you, to help you avoid making these common errors. Dr. Beck's list is somewhat longer than the following, as I have only included the ones I believe are pertinent to setback and relapse situations.

Overgeneralizing. Telling yourself that one lapse or setback indicates that a total relapse is occurring, and that rather than it being a single event, it is a sign of total defeat or a pattern of never-ending failure. A typical overgeneralization would be, "Since I have had setbacks and problems in the past, I will always continue to have them just as seriously in the future."

Selective filtering. This involves selecting a particular negative event or detail and focusing on it alone. An example would be where you might concentrate only on a single slipup or lapse and totally ignore all your previous achievements.

Black-and-white thinking. You see yourself either as a total success or else a total failure, with nothing in between. All lapses are viewed as total relapses.

Catastrophizing. If you think in this distorted way, you will tend to blow your setbacks all out of proportion in a depressed and despairing way. You may tell yourself that this was the worst possible thing that could have happened to you, and that it will only lead to further "horrible" and "terrible" consequences.

I believe that the illogic of these distortions and the potential they have to harm your recovery are self-evident. If any or all of them do not seem to you to be distorted, you might consider either reading some of the books on cognitive therapy listed in appendix D or seeing a cognitive therapist.

Step 4. Live a Balanced Life

The more nonfunctional your life has been prior to your recovery, the more balancing will be required to undo the damage caused by the OCD. Those of you whose OCD began later in life will have more normal years to look back on and will have an image of what you need to restore. Those of you who have been ill since your early years may have little idea of what it feels like to live as others do. Life with your illness may have made you housebound with few outside contacts. Sleeping all day as an escape may have become a way of life. You may never have held a job, gone on a date, or lived on your own. The goal will be to restructure your life around something besides your illness. You can't keep living the same way you did as an ill person and expect to be a well person.

A normal life is made up of a variety of ingredients. I believe these include:

- Having a social life and relating to others around you
- Having intimate relationships and close personal friendships
- Being productively employed
- Getting enough sleep on a normal day/night schedule
- Eating a nutritionally balanced diet
- Getting sufficient exercise
- Seeing health professionals for appropriate regular checkups and taking care of health problems as they arise.

As a part of all these goals, it is important that you learn to live less rigidly overall. Some of those with OCSDs have come to live in strict overcontrolled patterns that don't vary from day to day or year to year. Getting well means recovering (or discovering) the ability to make choices about how to live. Give yourself a chance to change your daily routines of socializing, dressing, bathing, eating, etc. Although you may not realize it, you create an OC environment all around yourself through the way you live and think. Changing your basic mindset and introducing flexibility and variety into your life will help to change this environment and make it less likely that you will let yourself slide back.

The scope of this book does not allow me to go into detail about how all these may be accomplished. The goal here is to just make you aware of what is appropriate. If your life has been severely impaired, you may need professional help.

When we talk about living a balanced life, we also mean balancing your expectations for your postrecovery existence. You will have to learn to overcome your need for perfectionism and your need for certainty. Life even without the pain of OCD will never be "perfect." Everyday life will still have its share of stress, responsibilities, and disappointments. Being in a state of recovery doesn't mean that life will suddenly be trouble free for you. It does mean having the freedom to participate in the same imperfect world as your fellow human beings (who, of course, are also imperfect). As they like to say in AA (whose wisdom I am always fond of quoting), "The world doesn't get better, you get better." However, it also means that you will be free to be spontaneous, to strive, to take risks like others, to be able to experience successes and failures and take the credit or the responsibility for both. You will be able to live as an actor rather than as a reactor, making things happen rather than waiting for things to happen to you. You may also now have to work on feelings of bitterness about having had your disorder. Remember that life is not going to pay you back. Becoming depressed and angry now that you can see what you have been missing out on will only serve to deprive you further. Cognitive therapy and something similar to grief counseling can be of help with this (see chapter 7).

SELF-HELP STEPS FOR BDD

Self-help steps for BDD are practically identical to those for OCD. Individuals must expose themselves gradually to stronger doses of what they fear in terms of their appearance and at the same time resist the urge to carry out compulsive activities that they believe will relieve their anxiety.

The biggest issue in treating your own BDD involves the power of your degree of belief. Don't forget that in fighting your BDD, you are most likely coming up against an extremely strong thought process that has less room for doubt than most other forms of OCD. Many with BDD may find that simply accepting that they have BDD is the main obstacle to recovery, rather than any of the therapy activities they may have to carry out. Because of this, self-help for BDD may be somewhat more challenging than for other disorders within the OC Spectrum. Over the years, you may have built up elaborate webs of justifications and confirmations as to why you definitely have something wrong with your body, why everyone else is mistaken, and why your preoccupation is necessary. Most of your thoughts may be telling you that it is real, but what you must focus on is what this preoccupation is doing to you. People with real body problems or defects and who do not have BDD do not pursue treatment to the point of ruining their lives, nor do they meet with the same kind of widespread disbelief from others that you do.

Medication is a very important option here, so don't forget to consider it. Under the right circumstances, it can do a lot to weaken your belief in the thoughts, making self-help an easier prospect. I believe that medication has a vital role to play in overcoming BDD and that you will have a much greater chance of recovering if you include it in your self-help program.

If you are able to summon up enough disbelief in your obsessive thoughts to try to tackle them, they can be approached in the same ways outlined above in the OCD self-help section. Listing all the body defects that bother you is a good way to start. Making a hierarchy of all the situations that cause anxiety would come next and is a very important step.

As already mentioned, there are numerous ways to expose yourself to the thoughts about the defect for the purpose of habituating to the anxiety it causes. Audio-taped exposure is probably one of the best methods. Tell yourself via the tape, in gradually increasing doses, how ugly your "defect" looks, how you will never be able to correct it, how noticeable it is to other people, and finally, how others will look down on you and reject you for it. Whenever you do get the unwanted thought, be sure to tell yourself that the defect is real and that you really look terrible.

If you fear to see your defect, then making yourself inspect it is another good technique. I often have patients collect and look at pictures of people who either have or don't have the defect (whichever causes them more anxiety). Using Post-it notes to put up signs (especially on mirrors) reminding yourself about the defect is another approach. In addition, you can write daily about the "awfulness" of the defect, or simply jot down its name many times on a sheet of paper several times per day. Additionally, you can carry out any activities that would highlight or point up the defect to yourself or others if possible, such as dressing to accentuate it or show it off, resisting any kind of cover-up you typically use, or conversely, using makeup to accentuate it.

I instructed one patient who obsessed about bags under her eyes to use dark eyeshadow (a mix of brown and purple) to create realistic looking bags, which she then had to look at in the mirror and eventually keep on when going out of the house. I have also had patients create fake blemishes on their faces and lines on their skin. Another technique would be to draw facial defects on photographs of yourself and hang them where they can frequently be seen. Finally, as mentioned, you can make an effort to go where others will see you. If being with others who know you creates more anxiety, then be sure to be around these people as much as possible.

Don't look for instant results. I have found that those with BDD seem to take longer to habituate to their fears about themselves than those with classic OCD. It may take many repetitions of the various types of exposure before you see your anxiety begin to subside, so don't get discouraged. Another point to keep in mind is that those with BDD are often seen to obsess about different body parts at different times. If you begin to see a new concern starting up just as you are getting over your original one, don't be alarmed. Just keep working in the same manner with your new thoughts. As you become more skillful at facing what you fear, you will be able to resist acting out on the new obsessions.

The compulsions that must be resisted in BDD are rather universal among sufferers and they must be approached the same as any type of compulsion. Behaviors to work at resisting would include:

- checking or measuring the body part(s) directly or in the mirror (if this relieves your anxiety)
- avoiding looking at the defect(s) (if *not* looking prevents anxiety)
- getting others to inspect the body part and/or comment on it (or conversely, resisting the temptation to ask others to comment on your appearance if this bothers you)

- questioning others about your appearance or subtly maneuvering them into conversations about it to check their reactions
- going for medical or dental consultations to confirm if a defect exists
- going for medical, surgical, or dental procedures to correct the defect
- dressing in special ways to cover particular body parts or wearing loose or baggy clothes
- combing or setting hair in special ways (to cover what are perceived as thinning spots) or using special hair thickening products
- wearing special makeup (by both men and women) to cover blemishes or marks or to make features look larger or smaller
- picking at or squeezing blemishes
- avoiding social situations or refusing to be seen in public by others when you feel your defect is noticeable.
- not undressing or going without makeup in front of the person you are intimate with
- covering body parts you dislike with your hand or showing only one side or profile to others
- trying not to open your mouth wide because you believe your teeth look unsightly
- wearing glasses to cover defects you believe are around your eyes

Maintenance and relapse prevention issues are essentially the same as for those with classic OCD and TTM. Staying well is the obvious long-term goal and must be kept in mind on an ongoing basis. What this means is giving yourself permission not to have a perfect appearance, and learning to free yourself from what you imagine to be the criticism of others.

SELF-HELP FOR TTM

The self-help program described earlier in chapter 2 outlines the basic approach to therapy for TTM. I advise that you read it first, as it will give you a pretty clear idea of what you must do. Therapy for TTM is different from the type used to treat OCD and BDD. Unlike those with the other two disorders, you will not have to face frightening or doubtful obsessions. You will, however, as in the other two disorders, have to become aware of and resist urges to behave compulsively and to break well-practiced habits.

Self-help steps for TTM are as follows:

1. Destigmatizing yourself
2. Building or strengthening an awareness of the disorder
3. Self-relaxation training (the full-length method)
4. Diaphragmatic breathing training
5. Self-relaxation training (the brief method)
6. Competing response training
7. Assembling steps 4, 5, and 6
8. Augmenting your HRT
9. Weekly review and self-evaluation
10. Maintenance and relapse prevention

Step 1. Destigmatizing Yourself

The most important first step you can take in approaching your problem with TTM is by facing your feelings about it and yourself. I put this step before any of the actual behavioral work because if you cannot begin to come to grips with your feelings about the whole situation, it will be very difficult to find the motivation to see this task through to the end. There are numerous TTM sufferers who don't just dislike the symptoms—they dislike themselves. TTM is not as easy to conceal as other types of OCSDs generally are. It is not a "hidden" problem. Being bald, having large patches of hair missing, or having no eyelashes or eyebrows makes a rather public display. For this reason, I believe that TTM sufferers, as a group, probably suffer from greater stigmatization than those with other disorders.

There are many with TTM who have lived their whole lives feeling humiliated and abnormal as if they were social outcasts. They have either labeled themselves as such or have been encouraged to think about themselves in this way by misguided or cruel family members or acquaintances. I know of many cases where sufferers, as children, were punished, threatened, or severely criticized for their inability to stop pulling. There are also many adults who avoid social and work situations because of the fear of what others might think or say. For those of you with really serious hair pulling who have lived in a continual state of near baldness or without eyebrows or eyelashes and have had to live secret lives using wigs, makeup, hats etc., it is not hard to see how easily you could have become stigmatized.

Start by facing the facts. This is a biologically based problem. You did not ask for it, and you didn't cause it. It's not your fault! For a good deal of the time you have had it you probably didn't even know what it was. Having TTM doesn't mean that you are crazy. It doesn't happen to people who are somehow weaker than others or who are less deserving of decent lives. You are more than the sum total of the number of hairs on your body. If others in your society choose to judge you in that way, that is because of their ignorance and is no reflection on you. TTM is, in a way, only a problem because society places a value on having hair.

I see destigmatizing yourself as a two-stage process. Working on this may even have to come before the behavioral treatment. Learning to separate yourself as a human being from your behavior is the crucial first step. The main tool in accomplishing this is cognitive therapy (for a more complete description, see chapter 2). One of the things it teaches is that giving yourself an all-over rating as a "bad" person or a "loser," simply because of certain dislikable aspects of your behavior, is faulty and illogical reasoning. We are all imperfect as human beings, and it is safe to say that we all have our own behaviors that we dislike. These aspects of ourselves do not make us "bad" as people simply because we rate them as bad. There are just too many sides to each of us for one all-encompassing rating to mean anything. Behaviors can be changed and replaced with more desirable ones. Once we change them, can we say that we are now transformed into "good" human beings? If so, how were we able to change if we were once so "bad"? It is easy to see how little sense this makes. It is important to begin to look at these issues logically as you start to face the disorder. By casting off the stigma, I have actually seen individuals get rid of their wigs, hats, and other disguises prior to even starting therapy. They decided that if others didn't like the way they looked, it was their problem. Those who see themselves simply as abnormal or "crazy" will become convinced that they are just too imperfect and weak to be able to recover and may not feel motivated to try very hard or even try at all. They may even go further and believe that as imperfect humans they are not even entitled to a recovery. All they accomplish is to make themselves depressed—giving themselves symptoms because of their symptoms.

Once you have accomplished this first task, you are ready for the next. This involves accepting the hair puller within yourself and that it will always be a part of you in some way. Accepting does not mean liking, nor does it mean giving it power over who you think you are. It also means not hating it, as this would bring the risk of also hating yourself as well. Some have actually chosen to embrace it, using its intensity as a kind of internal barometer to tell them whether they are living balanced lives.

I don't believe that this brief discussion will settle the issue for you and it would probably take another book just to give this issue the space it deserves. I therefore suggest that you read *Overcoming the Rating Game* by Paul Hauck (see the book list in appendix D). I generally recommend this book to patients who are having a hard time accepting themselves due to their symptoms, and who feel inferior, weak, or unentitled to a recovery. It is probably the best discussion of how to accept yourself unconditionally that I have yet encountered.

Step 2. Building or Strengthening an Awareness of the Disorder

As mentioned earlier, there seem to be three different groups of TTM sufferers: those whose pulling is preceded by an urge, those who do it automatically, and those who do both. Automatic pullers generally seem to have very little awareness of the circumstances and the steps that commonly lead to their pulling. When asked to give details about when, where, and how and why they pull, they often just shrug their shoulders and admit that they really don't know.

A good way to begin this step is by filling out the TTM questionnaire in appendix B. If you can complete it, it will give you an overview of your problem behaviors. If you can't, then it will show you how much you have yet to learn about it. You cannot change behaviors you cannot anticipate or identify.

After finishing this, you are ready to begin filling out a daily record of your hair pulling behaviors. It is very important that this be done diligently from this point onward. It must be done each and every day there is something to record. A sample sheet is provided here for you to make copies of. Even if you do not use this particular form, you need to record:

1. When the episodes occurred
2. How long they lasted
3. How many hairs were pulled at each episode
4. How strong the urge to pull was (rated on a scale from 0 to 100)
5. Where the episode occurred (if in the house, specify the room, or if at work, specify the location)
6. What activity you were involved in at the time
7. What you were feeling emotionally and physically before, during, and after the episode

I would recommend filling out these sheets daily for two weeks before going on to Step 3, to establish a baseline for your pulling behaviors before any actual treatment steps are introduced. This record will then give you a basis for comparison so you can measure your own improvement. Obviously, if you do not have any symptoms on a particular day, there is no need to fill out a sheet. I

Day _____ Name _____

Fig. 3.2 ∿ Hair Pulling Recording Sheet

	Time	Duration	Urge to pull 0–100	# pulled	Activity	Place	Feelings at the time
AM							
PM							

Behavioral observations:

would also recommend that you fill out a sheet in the case of episodes where you catch yourself merely running your fingers through your hair, touching, twirling, or tugging at it. These are often preludes to hair pulling and will also need to be controlled. Look through your collected recordkeeping sheets and see if you can list below the following information:

The locations where you are most likely to be when you pull:
1.
2.
3.
4.
5.
6.

The times of day you are most likely to be in the locations where you are most prone to pulling (match the numbers of the times with the numbers of the locations above):

A.M.   P.M.
1.
2.
3.
4.
5.
6.

The activities, physical positions, or situations in which you feel the most tempted to pull:

1.
2.
3.
4.
5.
6.

The moods which seem to be most connected with your pulling:

1.

2.

3.

4.

5.

6.

The physical sensations which seem to be most connected with your pulling (these would include physical sensations such as itching, tingling, or burning that seem to bring on pulling episodes, as well as the satisfying sensations that pulling gives you):

1.

2.

3.

4.

5.

6.

You are also looking for something that goes beyond the information on the sheets themselves. Your goal is to uncover the sequence of events and sensations that lead to pulling and also keep it going. Pulling is usually the result of a whole chain of smaller behaviors that have become habits. Each link in the chain acts as a signal for the next one to begin and leads directly to it. A typical chain might look something like this:

1. Coming home from a hard day at work or school
2. Walking to the family room
3. Sitting down in your favorite comfortable chair
4. Turning on the TV and tuning it to your favorite show
5. Leaning to one side with your head resting in your hand
6. Running your fingers across your scalp
7. Feeling a hair that is "different"
8. Tugging on the hair
9. Pulling the hair out

After you have gathered two weeks worth or more of information about your pulling, see if you can use it to discover and list one or more of your own typical chains. You will probably have several. See if you can list one of your chains in the spaces provided below (you may not need all the spaces):

1.

2.

3.

4.

5.

6.

7.

8.

9.

(You may want to go on to list the steps of other chains as you identify them. It is recommended that you do.)

Understanding how these chains work will help your efforts in two ways. The first is that you will be better able to predict in advance when a pulling episode may take place. This will enable you to prepare yourself to use the Habit Reversal Training (HRT) before you actually need it. The second is that you will be able to make changes in your routine or your environment that will serve to break up the chains. Usually, steps that come later in a chain serve as more powerful signals for pulling than ones that come earlier. The goal is to break a chain early in the sequence so it will be easier for you to resist. There are some tips listed in Step 7, which suggest some ways in which you can modify your routine and your environment.

While self-monitoring, you may find out that your increased awareness may lead to less pulling. This result may only last a short time. However, for some people it may have a more lasting effect.

Step 3. Self-Relaxation Training (the full-length method)

If you are going to face and oppose a stubborn and often automatic type of habit about which you have strong negative feelings, it will be very important to be able to center yourself and concentrate on what you have to do. Accomplishing this involves learning to relax yourself physically and mentally. In addition, you are fighting a habit that may have a rather soothing effect when you are overstimulated and stressed. Pulling can be very relaxing because it allows you to focus totally on the experience of removing hairs while shutting out all other outside stimuli. Unfortunately, one of the reasons it is hard to stop is because of this immediately rewarding feeling of pleasurable relaxation or relief from stress and tension. Clearly, we cannot take this away unless we have something to replace it with.

To do all this, we must bring on something known as "the relaxation response." Your central nervous system is divided into two halves. One is known as the sympathetic nervous system. It is responsible for activating and turning up nervous system activity. The other is known as the parasympathetic nervous system, and its function is just the opposite—it turns things down and quiets you when you are activated. Normally, these systems turn on and off without our help. It is this second parasympathetic response which you will try to learn to deliberately bring on at will.

There are many approaches to self-relaxation. There are some who practice meditation or listen to music or sounds of nature, but for our purposes we will use what is known as progressive muscle relaxation. This is a clinical approach to relaxation that has been around for over fifty years and is preferred as a part of the HRT approach. There are two main approaches to progressive muscle relaxation. One type has you tighten and then relax various muscle groups. The other has you simply try to relax and let go of the tension in different muscle groups without the tightening. I favor the second approach because I have found that some people seem to have difficulty in relaxing a muscle once they have tightened it or are already too tense in some areas of their bodies.

I have given you a script below which you (or someone you know with a nice relaxing speaking voice) may read onto a cassette tape and which you can then use to relax yourself. When recording the tape, speak slowly and calmly. If you find that it does not meet your purposes, you are certainly free to make up your own or to purchase one of the many types of relaxation tapes commercially available. The one below takes about twenty minutes to do. Whichever one you use, try to follow these guidelines while doing the exercise:

1. Sit in a comfortable chair. Don't lie down. The goal is to learn to relax, not fall asleep.

2. Wear comfortable loose clothing.

3. Do not cross your arms or legs during the exercise.

4. Wait for about an hour after eating to practice, so that you will not feel sleepy.

5. Do not try to do any other activities at the same time.

6. Refrain from using caffeine for two hours before starting.

7. Arrange to not be interrupted in any way for the duration. It is not possible to stop in the middle and then pick up again where you left off.

8. Do not practice at bedtime unless you are also using it to help you sleep. If you do, also practice it earlier in the day as part of your HRT program.

9. While it is not required, listening to your relaxation tape through a pair of headphones is recommended. It helps shut out distracting sounds.

Relaxation Script

To begin your relaxation, first place yourself in a comfortable position, uncross your arms and legs, and if you are wearing any tight or uncomfortable clothes, either remove them or loosen them at this time. To start, close your eyes, take a deep breath, hold it a moment, and let it out. Take another deep breath, hold it a moment, and let it out. Take a third deep breath, hold it a moment, and let it out. I'd like you now to imagine in your mind's eye a switchboard. There is a long row of switches and each switch is connected to a different area of the body. As we turn off each switch, we are going to shut off the muscle tension to that particular area of the body.

Concentrate now on the area of your feet. Imagine that you are shutting off the switch that controls the muscle tension in your feet. As you turn off this switch, much as you would shut off a light switch, imagine that the tension in your feet is something like a liquid, and it is running away from your feet, out through your toes and away from your body. As this liquid muscle tension is leaving your body, your feet are left feeling very limp and loose and heavy, almost as if you are unable to move them. They are very comfortable with all the tension gone out of them now. Let us move on to the next area. Imagine that you are shutting off the switch that controls your lower legs. I'd like you to turn that switch off now and imagine all the muscle tension from your knees downward draining toward the feet and leaving the body through the toes. The muscles of the lower legs are getting more and more limp and loose with a heavy and very comfortable feeling. The next area will be the upper part of your legs, from where the legs join the body down to the knee. Now shut off the switch as you would turn off a light and as you do so, you will feel that muscle tension draining downward from the upper legs to the lower legs to the feet and away from your body through the toes.

The muscle tension is leaving and now the entire area of both legs is feeling limp and loose and comfortable and relaxed, with a slightly heavy feeling as if you could not move them. The next switch that you will turn off controls the area from the waist downward. So now turn this switch off and as you do so, you will allow yourself to feel the muscle tension flowing from the lower part of your body down through your legs to your feet and out through your toes. From the waist downward now, the muscle tension is draining away and in its place is a feeling of relaxation and a limp, heavy feeling.

The next area that we will move on to is the area of the stomach. As you shut off the switch to the stomach muscles, the tension drains away leaving the muscles of the stomach loose and limp and relaxed. The muscle tension drains downward through the legs to the feet and leaves the body through the toes. This will leave the stomach muscles feeling very loose and limp. The next area will be the chest and as you shut off the switch that controls the muscle tension in the chest muscles you will begin to feel tension draining away like the liquid we talked about. It drains downward through the legs to the feet and out through the toes. The muscles of your chest feel loose, heavy, and relaxed. You may even begin to feel your upper body slump a little bit.

The next switch we come to controls the muscles of the lower back. As you turn this switch off, the muscles of the lower back release their tension and the tension drains downward through the body, through the legs to the feet and away through the toes. The lower back muscles feel very comfortable, loose, limp, and a little heavy as they release their tension. We move next to the upper back where you shut off the switch. The muscle tension again leaves the upper back down through the lower back to the legs where it leaves the body through the toes. As you release your grip on the muscles of the upper back, they will give up their tension and begin to feel heavy and relaxed and droopy. You are feeling very comfortable now. We move next to an important area. This is the area of the shoulders, and as we shut off the switch, I'd like you to concentrate a little more carefully now on releasing the muscle tension in your shoulders. As you begin to feel your shoulders feeling heavy and limp, the tension drains away through the body, through the legs to the feet where it leaves the body through the toes. Your shoulders are feeling much more relaxed now as you release all the tension there.

We move next to the neck. As you shut the switch off, the muscle tension from the neck drains down through the body to the legs, to the feet, and away through the toes. The muscles of the neck feel pliable, loose, and very comfortable, and your head may even begin to feel as if it is droop- ing a bit to the side. The next area is the area of the back of the head and the scalp. As you shut off the switch to this area, you will begin to feel the muscle tension releasing itself, flowing down through your body, to the legs and the feet where it leaves through the toes. You will feel the muscles of the scalp relaxing. They feel comfortable and pliable as they release their tension.

The next area is a very important area. This is the forehead and again I'd like you to concentrate a little harder on this area. As you concen- trate on this area and you shut off the switch to the forehead, you will feel the muscle tension draining away down through the body, through the legs, to the feet, and out through the toes. The muscles of the fore- head feel loose and limp and as they sag a bit you may even feel your eyes droop slightly as we concentrate extra hard on releasing the grip on those muscles. The next area is the area of the face and we shut off the switch now to the muscles of the face and release the muscle tension there. The muscle tension drains down through the body, to the legs, and to the feet, where it exits through the toes. As the muscles of the face lose their tension, you may feel your eyes beginning to droop a bit, your mouth may sag slightly, your cheeks relax and droop. The muscles of the face feel very comfortable and relaxed and very pliable.

Now we move to the last area of muscle tension and this is the area of the arms and the hands. As we shut off the switch to those areas, we begin with the upper arms as far as the elbow, and as we shut off that switch we feel the upper arms begin to sag and droop a little as the muscle tension flows downward to the hands now and exits through the fingers. As the muscle tension leaves the upper arms, they will begin feeling droopy and heavy as if you could hardly move them. The next area to move on to is the area of the forearms and as you shut off the switch to the forearms, we will allow the muscle tension to drain down through the hands where it leaves the body through the fingers. The muscle tension is now draining away from the forearms leaving them loose and limp, very heavy, and comfortable. Now we move to the last area which is the area of the hands. We will allow the muscle tension in the hands to release and exit through the fingers and leave the body, leaving the hands and the fingers feeling very heavy and relaxed as if you could not move them. They are very free of tension and as we do this, the last bits of tension drain away through the body leaving the body feeling very limp and loose, heavy, and very comfortable. Much

*more comfortable than you have felt in a long, long time. As we continue
to do this, I would like you to focus on any areas of tension that are now
left in the body itself. If you feel any other areas of tension remaining, I'd
like you to now release those areas of tension and allow them to run out
either through the fingers or the toes. I'd like you to concentrate extra
carefully on these areas now as any last bits of tension are draining
away, leaving the body feeling very comfortable, limp, and relaxed.*

*Now we'll move on to the next step which will help you to greatly
increase the amount of relaxation you are feeling. I am going to count
backward from twenty to zero, and as I count you will count silently
along with each number. As we count down, you will feel yourself
sinking deeper and deeper into relaxation. Your relaxation will
increase with each number we count. I will begin counting. 20 . . . 19. . .
18. . . 17 . . . 16. . . 15 . . . 14 . . . 13 . . . 12 . . . 11 . . . 10 . . . 9 . . . 8 . . . 7
. . . 6 . . . 5 . . . 4 . . . 3 . . . 2 . . . 1 . . . 0. And now you are many more
times relaxed than you were at the beginning of our count. You're feeling very peaceful and calm and relaxed. Much more relaxed than
you've felt for a long time. Each time you do this the amount of relaxation you feel will increase as you become better and better at relaxing
yourself, because you control your own level of relaxation.*

*Now we're going to move on to a further step. What I'd like you to do
now in your mind's eye is to imagine the most beautiful and safe and
comfortable place you can think of. I'd like you to take a sort of short
vacation in your mind. A place where you feel very safe and comfortable, a place that is extremely beautiful, the most beautiful place you
can think of. A place where you would like to be right now. This will be
your favorite place of relaxation and peace. I would like you to not just
imagine that you are looking in on it, but I would like you to imagine
now that you are in the midst of this beautiful and comfortable place,
and that you are feeling and sensing all the feelings and sensations that
are there. If the sun is shining, I'd like you to imagine the feeling of the
sun on your skin. If the breeze is blowing, I'd like you to feel the breeze
brushing against your face. I'd like you to smell whatever scents there
are in the air. As you look out in all directions from where you are, you
will see everything there is to see and hear all the sounds there are to
hear. I'd like you to place yourself there with your entire being and be
there as fully as you possibly can right now . . . Now I'm going to give
you a period of time to be in this place and I'd like you to fully imagine
yourself there now. Concentrate on how peaceful and calm and relaxed
and safe you feel there. . . .*

[Leave a one minute-long blank spot in your tape right here.]

At this point you may do one of several things. First, you may just sit visualizing your scene in this state of relaxation until the tape runs out or as long afterward as you wish. Or second, if you have things to do, I'll be counting backward shortly from 5 to 1 and as I do, you will open your eyes. You will feel extremely refreshed and full of energy as if you had a full night's sleep, and all the tiredness and tension will have been left behind, and you will be able to do whatever it is you have to do with full concentration. Your third choice is that you may wish to go to sleep at the end of this tape. You will be able to turn the tape off and lie down and have a relaxing night's sleep, and you will fall asleep as easily as you wish. The choice is up to you at this point. Remember, as you do this, you will become better and better at it, and you will find it easier to relax each time. Now I will begin to count. 5, 4, 3, 2, 1.

Try to practice your relaxation exercise at least once daily. If you are not used to deliberately relaxing yourself, you may find it difficult at first. This is a common occurrence when acquiring any new skill. One thing that many people find difficult to do is to empty their minds of thoughts about the day's events or other issues. Don't try to suppress them while you are relaxing yourself. Try instead to acknowledge their presence and let them slip by you. Accept that they are there, but do not feel that you have to do anything about them or concentrate on them. If it doesn't happen immediately, don't give up. It will happen for you eventually. Another experience for those new to relaxation is an unexpected feeling of nervousness and tension when doing the exercise at first. This is sometimes seen in those who are normally very physically tense and who tend to experience relaxation as something strange and out of the ordinary. Do this exercise for one week before going on to Step 4, and continue for a second week as you practice the next step.

Step 4. Diaphragmatic Breathing Training

Since we all come equipped to breathe automatically, it may seem a little strange now to be instructed how to do it. Actually, there are many ways of breathing, not all of them helpful. Along with being able to relax your body and mind, breathing from the diaphragm will be a necessary skill in centering yourself as part of HRT. Singers and those who practice yoga are quite familiar with breathing in this way. Breathing has also been an important component of meditation, a centuries-old technique for centering and focusing oneself. In his book *The Miracle of Mindfulness*, Thich Nhat Hahn, a Buddhist monk, tells us that "breathing is a natural and extremely effective tool which can prevent dispersion. Whenever your mind becomes scattered, use your breath as a means to take hold of your mind again."

The diaphragm is a sheet of muscle which seals off your lung cavity from your abdominal cavity. As you breathe, its regular movements up and down change the pressure in the chest cavity. Its downward movement increases the volume of your chest cavity and causes your lungs to fill with air by lowering the pressure in the space around the lungs, making you inhale. When the diaphragm moves up it causes the lungs to deflate by making the chest cavity volume smaller. This increases pressure on your lungs and makes you exhale. We are usually only aware of the movements of the diaphragm when it has spasms, causing us to have hiccups. By learning to concentrate on helping the diaphragm move up and down more strongly and evenly, you help yourself to take deeper and more regular breaths. This helps to relax you by increasing the amount of oxygen in your blood, and gives you a feeling of being more centered within yourself, increasing your ability to concentrate on directing your energies at a desired task. Deep breathing has long been known as one way to control feelings of anxiety and tension.

Doing all this is not as difficult as it might seem. It mostly takes concentration at first. The way to begin is to sit or lie down in a quiet and comfortable spot, placing both hands lightly upon your stomach, with your little fingers just above your navel. As you inhale, try to push your stomach outward against your hands, lifting them upward, while keeping your chest from moving. Try to visualize yourself filling your lungs to the very bottom with air. Hold this breath for the count of two, and then try to pull your stomach back in while exhaling through your nose. The goal is to empty your lungs as completely as possible. Keep them empty for a two-count, and then begin the cycle again. As you do this, try to keep your full attention on your breathing and focus on the movement of your diaphragm. If you still have trouble getting the feel of this, try lying on your back, and instead, place a book on your stomach, and try to make the book go up and down as you inhale and exhale. When you have more of a feel for breathing this way, you can switch to doing it sitting up. I recommend practicing this for five minutes, three times a day. After practicing this along with, but separately from, your self-relaxation for a week, you should be able to do it with much less effort and conscious thought. You will soon be combining it with your relaxation exercise. If you wish to get a step ahead at this point (although it is not required), you may try using it right at the beginning of the relaxation tape, where it instructs you to take a deep breath.

Step 5. Self-Relaxation Training (the brief method)

By now you will have been practicing self-relaxation for about two weeks and diaphragmatic breathing for one. The purpose of the twenty-minute exercise was to help teach you to relax your body and to simply learn what it feels like to relax in that way. Because HRT must be a brief, portable response that you can quickly bring into play, it is obvious that you will not be able to perform the full twenty-minute relaxation exercise as part of it. What you will now move on to will be a shortened version of our relaxation exercise that will last about a minute and a half. As with the longer exercise, I am giving you the script for the shorter one that you can read onto your own tape. It is as follows:

Brief Relaxation Exercise

I'd like you to begin by closing your eyes and taking several deep breaths. Try to visualize the word RELAX *in your mind as if it were on a billboard. As you focus on this word, I would like you to feel the muscle tension draining out of your body from the top to the bottom. Try to feel an allover sense of relaxation. As you keep seeing this word* RELAX *in your mind, I would like you to also begin counting backward from 10 to 0 to deepen your relaxation. Let's begin counting slowly, 10, 9, 8, 7, 6, 5, 4, 3, 2, 1, 0. You are now much more deeply relaxed and the tension is gone. Just keep thinking of the word* RELAX. *Every time you think of this special word, you will be able to drop quickly into a very calm and peaceful state.* RELAX.

The same rules apply for practicing the brief exercise as were used for the long version. Try practicing your brief exercise at least six times per day over the next week. During this time, you will also be practicing your diaphragmatic breathing. You may continue using the longer version for other purposes if you choose; however, we will not be using it any further as a formal part of your HRT.

Step 6. Competing Response Training

This is quite simple to learn and will not require much practice either. Along with using your brief relaxation exercise and your diaphragmatic breathing to relax and center yourself, you will need to learn to do something else with your hands. It must be something that is incompatible with pulling your hair and that will eventually help to strengthen the opposing muscles needed to resist reaching for whatever area of your body you pull from.

Simply described, it involves clenching the hands, bending your arms at the elbow to a 90-degree position, and pressing your forearms against your waist while tensing all muscles from the elbows downward.

Step 7. Assembling Steps 4, 5, and 6

Now that you have taught yourself the three basic parts of HRT—relaxation, breathing, and the competing muscle response—it is time to put them all together and use them to help stop your hair pulling. The overall goal of HRT is to relax and center yourself, while activating a group of muscles that will oppose the physical movements you use when you pull your hair.

When you get the urge to pull, you will need to do the following:

1. Begin breathing from the diaphragm and after about fifteen seconds, do the brief relaxation exercise.

2. At the end of the brief relaxation exercise, bend your arm at the elbow, placing your forearm against your waist, and clench your fingers to make a fist. Your fists should rest at about belt buckle level. Tense the muscles of your hands and forearms. Hold your arm in this position for the next three minutes.

3. If at the end of these three minutes the urge is still strong, repeat the cycle.

4. Keep repeating as necessary.

5. You must practice your HRT in all cases, whether you manage to do it before you actually start pulling, interrupt pulling while in progress, or have already pulled. That is, do it before, during, or after.

I believe that HRT should be regularly practiced on a daily basis, whether it is immediately needed or not. I usually advise patients to practice their HRT a total of six times per day. These six times would include both the times it is actually needed for habit control, as well as whatever number is needed to make up the total. For instance, if you had to use your HRT exercise three times to prevent yourself from pulling your hair, you would need to do three HRT drills at other times during the day for a total of six sessions.

Remember that your self-recording continues throughout your therapy. At the point where you begin to practice your HRT on a daily basis, you will have to switch over to a slightly different type of recording sheet.

You will no longer need to record the number of hairs pulled (the focus is off that now), but you will have to record how often you practiced your HRT, and whether you used it before, during, or after a pulling episode.

Those using HRT usually find themselves going through several phases before they reach their goal. In the first phase, they tend to only catch themselves "after" they have already finished or nearly finished pulling. This is to be

Fig. 3.3 ∾ Habit Reversal Training Recording Sheet

Day _____ Name _____

Time	Duration	Place	Urge to pull/pick (0–100)	Activity at the time	Feelings at the time	Did you use HRT? Did it work? Before, during, or after?
AM						
PM						

Behavioral observations:

expected at first and is quite normal. However, it is the trickiest phase because it is so easy to get discouraged. It will therefore be vital to stubbornly practice your HRT. The goal is to make this new behavior as automatic as possible. It may seem at times that you will never remember to do it before you pull, so don't expect instant results. Remember how many times you have practiced pulling your hair. It may take weeks to really get the hang of it.

In the second phase, you will gradually start to record more "durings." You will find yourself occasionally cutting off episodes sooner and therefore pulling fewer hairs at a time. As you persist, this should gradually improve. Don't forget to give yourself credit for your "durings."

Finally, you will find yourself entering the third phase as you begin to achieve some "befores," cutting off pulling episodes before they begin. As with the previous two phases, don't look for instant change. It might take as much as several months to reach this point. Remember to keep your focus on your greater goal of changing your behavior, rather than whether you are a total success each day. Just take it one episode at a time and you will eventually reach your goal. Don't become impatient if it takes a while, the time will go by anyway. Continue to keep filling out your recording sheets, only now, on the new ones, be sure to mark down whether you did your HRT before, during, or after, and eliminate recording the number of hairs pulled.

One important way to help yourself reach your goal is not to judge your success in terms of whether or not you have pulled any hairs. You will need to accept that on the way to mastering HRT you will still pull hair at times. If whether or not you have pulled a hair becomes your measure of success, you will probably give up before reaching your goal. No one gains a new skill without having occasional lapses. This is a process, and it is a common mistake during such training to say to yourself, "Why bother resisting if I have one bad episode and pull out all the hairs that grew back? What's the use of all that work if I'm going back to square one?" Sometimes a strong habit can be mistaken for something that controls you. It can fool you into thinking you are powerless. If you believe you can't do it, then you probably won't try very hard. It is far more helpful for you to focus instead on how regularly you are using your HRT, whether it is before, during, or after a pulling episode. Keep reminding yourself of how much you want to stop pulling. Remember that "square one" was back where you weren't trying at all. Many who have felt powerless in the past tend to downplay their successes, saying, "How much of a success could it be if a failure like me could do it?" Even when you are trying unsuccessfully, you are still doing something different and this is a step up. Try not to see your lapses as totally negative. View them as learning experiences and try to use the information you can gain from them to help sharpen your behavioral tools.

One other thing to expect and to watch out for is the point at which the novelty of HRT wears off. Most behavioral techniques work well at first because they are new and interesting. Eventually, they become routine and may even feel like a bit of a burden. This is where some people feel as if they will never be able to use the HRT without thinking. They may start to feel frustrated, saying to themselves, "It's too hard," and want to give up. In order to avoid this, it is important to expect this feeling and see it for what it is when it happens—a temporary problem. Stay with your HRT and you will pass through this phase.

You should be able to practice your HRT even when you are around others, since it is possible to do it without attracting attention. If you are someone who gets urges to pull when other people are around, you will have to learn to relax with your eyes open. Using some subtle deep breathing may be your best bet. Gripping the arms of a chair or an object such as a pen or book can substitute for the usual competing muscle response. Another situation where you can adapt the technique is while you are driving a car. In this case, grip the steering wheel or gearshift lever with your hand instead of making a fist, and again, use your diaphragmatic breathing.

Step 8. Augmenting Your HRT

It is very important to mention here that strict reliance on HRT alone will probably not get the job done. TTM is, as we have said, a complex disorder with many different inputs. According to pioneering TTM theorist Dr. Charles Mansueto, these various inputs must be identified and targeted if treatment is to be successful (see chapter 1). This means that a multicomponent treatment will be necessary. Because there are so many different types of inputs that may affect each sufferer in different combinations, it is advisable for each individual to put together their own particular package of different techniques to augment their HRT. A list of many of these techniques follows. They have been arranged according to different types of inputs that may affect your pulling. Some may be helpful to you, and some may not. Feel free to pick and choose from among them. They will help you to eliminate or modify many of the links in the chains of behavior that can lead to pulling episodes as mentioned in Step 2.

Stimulation Replacements

Pulling can be a reaction to understimulation, such as when you are bored or inactive. Find other ways to get stimulation when you feel that urge to pull.

- Brush your hair or massage your scalp when you get the urge to pull. This may also satisfy those who experience itching or tingling sensations prior to pulling.

- Try brushing or massaging your dog or cat (just be careful that this doesn't lead to a new kind of pulling).
- Find other things to do with your hands such as knitting, crocheting, needlepoint, or sewing.
- Playing with Silly Putty as a way of keeping the fingers stimulated and occupied.
- Handle a foam ball, a Koosh Ball, a hand exerciser, a piece of velvet, or very fine sandpaper to satisfy the need to stimulate your sense of touch.
- Those who like to bite the roots of hairs or swallow hairs sometimes find the stimulation they need by eating sesame seeds or cracking sunflower or pumpkin seeds with their teeth and then chewing them.
- Eat strong mint candies as another way of stimulating the mouth.

Stimulation Reducers

In addition to your relaxation work, try to find other ways to soothe and calm yourself at the end of a busy day or in times of stress.

- Try taking up yoga or meditation.
- Set up a regular exercise routine for yourself. Exercise can be a tension reducer.
- Try taking a warm relaxing bath.
- Listen to a favorite piece of calming music.
- Use any other activity that you find pleasurable and relaxing.

Habit Blockers

Those things that interfere with performing your habit can get you to pay attention and also physically prevent the behavior from being carried out.

- Throw out any and all implements you use for pulling. If you use your fingernails, cut them short.
- Apply long acrylic nails over your real nails to make it difficult to grasp individual hairs.
- Wear white cotton waiter's gloves when you go to bed or in other high-risk situations. These inexpensive gloves are available at most restau-

rant supply stores and are sold in bundles. Unlike other types of gloves, they are made of loosely woven cotton and will not cause your hands to sweat. They can help prevent pulling and will also help to get your attention if you are an automatic puller. Some therapists advocate the use of the small rubber finger covers sold in business supply stores. Most sufferers dislike these because they tend to make your fingers hot and uncomfortable. The use of gloves and similar items should not be regarded as a long-term solution, just a temporary aid.

- At bedtime, wear a disposable hairnet of the type used by those who work in food preparation or in dust-free work environments. While this cannot actually prevent you from pulling, it can act as a reminder. It is also cooler for your scalp than wearing a hat to bed.

- Put a Band-Aid or tape over the ends of your thumbs and other fingers.

- Use hair spray, mousse, or hair gel to stiffen and change the texture of your hair. It may make pulling unsatisfying and dislikable by blocking the tactile stimulation you usually get. This is good for the head or eyebrows.

- Try wetting your hair or applying a conditioner. This can change the feel of it and make it seem unsuitable to pull.

Changing Your Environment And Routines

Changing your environment or your behavior within it can be very helpful in breaking the chain of cues and signals that contribute to the start of pulling episodes.

- Break up daily routines and the order in which you do them, using the information you have gathered on your record keeping sheets to spot the ones that usually lead to pulling.

- Move your furniture to new locations within rooms, cover mirrors, lower the lights that illuminate mirrors, or use lower wattage bulbs, etc.

- Try standing further back from the mirror when fixing your hair, or try doing it without using a mirror at all, if possible.

- Spend less time in the bathroom (if this is a high-risk zone). Leave as soon as you have finished what you went in there to do.

- Spend less time alone during periods of the day where there is a greater risk of pulling.

- Try not to sit on chairs or sofas that make it easy for you to rest your arm in such a way that your hand is placed in a position to pull. Stay away from the arms on your sofa. If other seating is not available, try sitting in a different position or even sit on the floor.

- Switch reading, work, and TV activities to different locations, if possible, to places that have not become associated with pulling. Try studying in the library.

- If you only pull when alone, try to be around others at high-risk times.

- Avoid combining high-risk activities as this can only multiply temptations. If you seem to do a lot of pulling in bed or when watching the TV, try not to watch TV in bed. If you have a tendency to pull while in bed, transfer all activities you do there (besides sleeping) to other locations.

- When all else fails, get out of the house for a while. Run some errands or visit a friend. This may give the urge time to pass.

Reminders and Attention-Getters

These techniques can be especially helpful where pulling is more the automatic type.

- Stick notes on mirrors, telephones, the TV, and by any other locations where you usually find yourself getting the urge to pull. Use the list you made earlier in this chapter. (Post-it notes are good for this.) You can also change the way you use your environment.

- Post lists of the times, places, and activities where symptoms are most likely to occur, to heighten your awareness. Make these lists large and write them in bold letters. Use the lists you made earlier in this chapter as the source for this information.

- Post a list of all the difficulties that hair pulling has caused you. This is known as an "Aggravation List." Print it in large, easy to read letters. Put it where you can see it clearly every day. If possible, post it in those locations where you are most likely to pull. Be sure to review it several times per day. Try to commit it to memory.

- Save the hairs you have pulled on a daily basis in separate envelopes with the date and number pulled written on the outside. This is strong medicine and can be very arresting and attention getting and can heighten your awareness if denial is a problem. Just knowing you will have to do this can get some people to pull less. On the other hand, if you tend to find this too depressing and upsetting, it may not be for you.

- Post photographs of yourself, which were taken before your problem began.

Belief Enhancements

- Self-statements are an important technique. Work up a list of statements that really get you thinking or that motivate you to try your hardest. Try using them whenever you get the urge to pull and need something extra. See the OCD self-help section for a list of some suggested statements.
- If you belong to a support group, call another member for some encouragement when the going gets tough. Talk out all the reasons not to pull and why you know you are going to succeed.
- Read a book that you find inspirational or that helps you to focus (providing that reading is not a high-risk activity for you).
- Post inspirational sayings or phrases prominently, particularly in high-risk areas.

There is one type of aid I would caution you about. Some people find it helpful to use various kinds of objects to actually pull or pick at, as a kind of replacement for pulling their own hair. They pull hair or fibers from stuffed animals, dolls, fake fur swatches, fuzzy clothing, etc. They carry these items around with them and take them out and pull at them whenever they get the urge. I believe that when you use aids of this type, you have not really gotten as far away from the problem as you need to. In order to truly recover, something essential has to change. When you don't change things very much, you maintain your pulling potential and the habits connected with pulling. To quote a saying I have heard Christina Pearson (the founder of the Trichotillomania Learning Center) use frequently: "The goal is transformation—not substitution." If you feel you absolutely have to have something to do with your hands or mouth at certain times, that is fine. There is nothing wrong with redirecting yourself. My advice is to try to find substitutes such as those in the list just above, which won't leave you teetering on the brink.

Step 9. Weekly Review and Self-Evaluation

Using your recordkeeping sheets, you will be able to periodically review your progress. Try to limit these reviews to about once a week, and try to avoid using these sheets to make yourself feel badly about your progress. It would be better to concentrate on using your HRT for each incident rather than constantly asking yourself whether you are a success or not. Reviewing too often can cause you to magnify a "bad day" into a pattern of total failure. Don't forget that you are in this for the long haul, not just a few days. Try not to be too critical of your efforts and don't confuse yourself with your behavior. You yourself can do badly without being "bad" or a failure. You can only fail when you don't try. Even then you haven't really failed, because you can always start over again. While you may have had your symptoms a long time and probably feel as if you can't tolerate them a moment longer, the goal is to keep your morale up so you can stick with it.

As part of your review, try to uncritically stand back and observe what you are doing and see how it can be improved. See if there are situations where you need to pay more attention to yourself. If you need to use one of the additional techniques listed in the previous section, do so at this time.

One different kind of problem to watch out for here is the illogical belief that if you allow yourself to work your hardest and it doesn't help, you will have nothing else to feel hopeful about. This actually keeps some people from putting out their best efforts. I like to answer this by reminding people that if they don't try their hardest, they may not recover and will end up feeling hopeless anyway. Some people will also not allow themselves to use medications for the same reason—not using them always leaves open an avenue of hope.

While we are on the subject of medication, let us suppose that after about eight weeks of work that you are not making any real progress at all. By this, I mean that you are still finding the urge to pull too difficult to resist and are still only using your HRT after you have finished pulling. It is at this point that you may wish to reconsider the possibility of medication if you are not already taking any. While it may not be your first choice as a treatment, it may be a necessary tool to aid your progress. Turning to medication doesn't make you a weakling or someone without any willpower. It is probable that some people's TTM is more strongly biochemical. Practically speaking, your overall goal is to stop pulling, and therefore you should do whatever you need to. Some may worry about never being able to get off medication once having started it and becoming dependent on it. Don't forget that you will still have to practice your HRT, even though you are taking medication, and will have that to fall back on. Also, once you have recovered, it may be possible for you to get off the medication or at least reduce it. Having to stay on medication may never be preferable, but it will always beat pulling. Those who are already on a medication, but not getting a good result (or any result) after six to eight weeks, may want to discuss the matter with their physician. A higher dose or a switch to another medication may be in order. For a further discussion of the issues surrounding medication, see chapter 4.

One question that is frequently on the minds of those who are beginning to get new hair growth is whether all the hair in those spots that have been bare will grow back in. Most often, it will, however, in certain severe cases where pulling has been constant over many years, hair may not totally fill in. Hair follicles may become scarred to the point where hairs will no longer grow. Also, some new hairs may grow in differently colored, due to the pigment cells having been damaged by previous pulling.

One further warning to keep in mind when your hair begins to grow back in is to try not to admire this new growth too often or touch the new hairs. This can possibly lead to renewed pulling, as new hairs feel bristly or "different" and may cause some itching sensations which can be very tempting. The goal is to minimize involvement with your hair.

Step 10. Maintenance and Relapse Prevention

Maintenance and relapse prevention issues for TTM are, in most ways, similar to those for classic OCD. Refer to the OCD relapse prevention section earlier in this chapter.

Specific maintenance goals particular to TTM are:

1. To accept and never forget that you have a chronic problem that will always need looking after in some way.

2. To continue to use your HRT as necessary, practicing it occasionally to keep it fresh.

3. To accept the occasional slipup or lapse, no matter what.

4. To not let your slipups hurt your morale or your desire to stay on track.

These goals are straightforward and simple, even if they aren't always easy. All of them require practice. The more you do it, the more automatic they will become and the less you will have to make a conscious effort. I strongly recommend that you still practice your HRT six times a day, even on days when you have no urge to pull.

SELF-HELP FOR SKIN PICKING AND NAIL BITING

Working on treating skin picking or nail biting problems is identical to the program for TTM. You can substitute skin picking or nail biting for hair pulling. Adapt all instructions as necessary. The only difference will be that you will start off with the Skin Picking/Nail Biting Recording Sheet provided at the end of this chapter. When you actually begin the HRT, you may use the same sheet provided for TTM.

Some additional tips for skin pickers:

- Make a point of visiting a dermatologist before you start your treatment. Taking care of any real acne problem you have will help things, as you will then have fewer blemishes you will be tempted to pick. Developing proper skin hygiene will have to be a continuing goal.

- Throw away any needles, pins, toothpicks, and any other pointed objects you use for skin picking. If you switch over to using other objects, throw them away too. This also includes such things as magnifying or specially lighted mirrors that may be used to help spot skin irregularities.

- Throw away any type of cover makeup you have been using to hide blemishes or the effects of picking. Knowing that there will be a visible consequence for picking may act as a deterrent.

Some additional tips for nail biters:

- Whenever you find a rough or jagged spot on a nail or have just created one through biting, file it smooth immediately. Carry a nail file and nail clippers on you at all times for this purpose. You may want to manicure your nails regularly.

- Women may want to keep their nails polished at all times and should touch up any nicks or chips that may tempt you to peel, pick, and finally, bite. Keeping your nails looking nice may be an incentive to leave them alone. Acrylic nails may also be a help.

- Use hand lotion around your fingers, cuticles, and other dry or rough spots on your hands to keep skin smooth and less likely to peel or flake, thus keeping down the temptation to bite or pick.

- Try to become aware of such habits as sitting with your hands near your mouth or resting your chin in your hand. The closeness of your fingers to your mouth may increase the likelihood that you will bite.

Day _____ Name _____

Fig. 3.4 ∿ Skin Picking, Nail Biting Recording Sheet

Time	Urge to pick (0–100)	Implements used	Duration	Activity at the time	Place	Feelings at the time
A M						
P M						

Behavioral observations:

FOUR

Getting Proper Medical Treatment

Medicine can cure only curable diseases.
—*Chinese proverb*

The best treatments for OCSDs at this time, and the best overall results in treating OCSDs, are obtained from a combination of medication and behavioral therapy. In the case of classic OCD, studies have shown that both together bring better and more long lasting results than either one alone. This may one day be shown to be true for the other OCSDs as well.

At present, there is no medical test for any OCSD. There are psychological tests that can point to its presence, but these are far from perfect and certainly not conclusive. No one should be diagnosed merely on the basis of a few tests. A detailed history and a good in-depth clinical interview by a well-trained professional should always be a part of the process of reaching a diagnosis. One method that can contribute to the diagnosing of an OCSD may involve sending a patient home with recordkeeping sheets, to have them keep track of their behavior over selected periods of time, to be able to learn exactly what is happening in their lives on a daily basis.

Many people have asked about the recent studies that have mapped the brains of those with classic OCD using Positron Emission Tomography (PET) scans. They ask why these scans cannot now be used as a diagnostic tool, since they do show some differences between the brains of those with OCD and those without. The answer to this is that while it is true the scans do show differences, it is still not exactly clear what these differences represent, and whether they are true markers particular only to classic OCD. In addition, it is also unknown at this time whether the observed differences were present before the onset of the OCD, or whether they were the result of it. Many more such scans need to be done, and the information they give us must be studied in much greater depth before we can use them in any valid and reliable way (assuming we ever can). It should also be noted that they are extremely expensive.

Another test which people ask about involves the measurement of levels of serotonin, a brain messenger chemical. A problem in the brain's use of serotonin is believed to be the main cause of classic OCD and possibly the other OCSDs as well (see chapter 12). Those who are aware of this problem want to know if their levels of this chemical can diagnose their OCSD. These levels can be measured in two different ways—by levels in the blood, and by levels in the spinal fluid. There are a number of studies of serotonin blood levels, but they have not been particularly helpful in contributing to our knowledge, since the findings do not seem to agree. It also appears that blood serotonin levels do not correspond to levels found in the brain. Spinal fluid, which bathes the brain and spinal cord, can only be obtained via a lumbar puncture, also called a spinal tap, a somewhat uncomfortable procedure. It has been studied by a number of different researchers, but unfortunately, the findings have been unclear. Serotonin levels can be affected by a variety of factors, not all of which are predictable. It is not even certain whether serotonin levels found in spinal fluid drawn from the base of the spine are representative of serotonin levels in the same fluid at the level of the brain. It has also not been established whether actual serotonin levels correspond to the presence or severity of OCD. This is, therefore, not a reliable test, and while it may still be used as a research tool, it would not be recommended for making a diagnosis of an OCSD at this time.

MEDICATION AS PART OF TREATMENT

When medication should be included as a part of treatment can be a difficult question to answer. Probably the best response would to be to say that you may try medication if you feel you need something extra, because the anxieties or urges are strong enough to prevent you from following through with treatment. If your symptoms are mild, you may well be able to overcome them without medication.

Medication can lower levels of obsessions and reduce the urge to do compulsions or impulsions, even if it cannot always take away all your symptoms. It should definitely be considered under the following circumstances:

1. You find your compulsions almost irresistible and do them constantly.
2. Your everyday life is severely limited.

3. You have been housebound due to the disorder or are mostly unable to function at times.

4. Your anxiety is so high and so constant that you find it unmanageable at times.

5. You have pulled out a great deal of hair from your scalp or other parts of your body and find the urge to do so overwhelming.

6. Your nails are so severely bitten as to cause constant pain, bleeding, and infection.

7. You are extremely depressed and cannot find the motivation or energy to participate in therapy.

Remember that medication by itself should not be regarded as a complete treatment. It reduces symptoms and can improve your mood. It should be seen as a tool to help your therapy be more effective.

MEDICATIONS USED TO TREAT OCSDs

The medications most commonly and widely used to treat OCD, BDD, and TTM come under the general heading of antidepressants. Most of the antidepressants commonly used to treat OCSDs currently fall into two main categories: Serotonin Reuptake Inhibitors (SRIs), which includes a subgroup known as Tricyclic antidepressants (TCAs), and Serotonin Specific Reuptake Inhibitors (SSRIs). There are also some newer medications that do not fall into any specific category.

What all these medications have in common is that they affect the brain's use of the chemical serotonin in one of several ways. Their main effect is to make serotonin more available at key sites in the brain where OCSD symptoms are generated. (For a more detailed discussion of these processes, see chapter 12).

TCAs have been used in the treatment of OCD and its related disorders since the last half of the 1960s. Only one of them, Anafranil (clomipramine), has been widely used in OCD treatment. Anafranil works by blocking the reuptake of serotonin; however, it also blocks the reuptake of norepinephrine, another neurotransmitter chemical. Another TCA, Tofranil, was more widely used prior to the release of Anafranil in 1989 but is rarely used these days. Although there are a number of other TCAs, Anafranil is really the only viable choice, as it is the only one that has been found to reduce OC symptoms effectively. It should also be mentioned that two newer drugs Effexor (venlafaxine) and Remeron (mirtazapine), while not classified as TCAs, also block the reuptake of serotonin and norepinephrine.

SSRIs are a somewhat newer family of antidepressants and have been available for research use in the United States since the mid-1980s. The major developments in the field of antidepressants have centered on this group in recent years, and there are five drugs (listed below) under this heading which are of use in treating OCSDs. The drugs in this category are quite potent in specifically blocking the reuptake of serotonin. They are not believed to work on any other brain neurotransmitters, hence their name. They tend to have fewer side effects than the older TCAs and are therefore better tolerated.

Technically speaking, of all the drugs now used to treat classic OCD, only Anafranil (clomipramine), Prozac (fluoxetine), Luvox (fluvoxamine), Zoloft (sertraline), and Paxil (paroxetine) have specifically been approved by the Food and Drug Administration (FDA) for this type of use at this writing. However, the others are currently being tested for eventual approval in treating OCSDs, and it is common knowledge that many physicians regularly use them to treat OC disorders. The depression that accompanies many cases of OCD would probably justify their use anyway. The other drugs are all in varying stages of the testing required before they can be officially approved for use in treating OCD. Their approval for this purpose will no doubt be forthcoming in the near future. It should be noted that at this time, there are no drugs specifically approved for the treatment of BDD, TTM, skin picking, or nail biting. They are, however, treated with the same medications used in the treatment of classic OCD.

Both of these groups of drugs block the reuptake of the neurotransmitter serotonin (see chapter 12, "Serotonergic Theory of OCD"). The SSRIs work in this way strictly on serotonin. The TCAs are believed to also work at blocking the reuptake of the neurotransmitter norepinephrine, giving them a somewhat broader scope of action on brain chemistry. The fact that both groups work to relieve the symptoms of OCD in different individuals may be indicative that there are several biological inputs into the disorder. The main drugs in use for OCSDs as of this writing are grouped as follows:

Table 4.1 ᛰ OCSD Drugs	Manufacturer	Maximum FDA Recommended Dosage	Half Life* (hours)
Tricyclic Antidepressants (TCAs) or (SRIs)			
Anafranil (clomipramine)	CibaGeneva	250 mg	32
Serotonin Specific Reuptake Inhibitors (SSRIs)			
Prozac (fluoxetine)	Dista/Eli Lilly	80 mg	87
Zoloft (sertraline)	Roerig/Pfizer	200 mg	26

Paxil (paroxetine)	SmithKline Beecham	60 mg	21
Luvox (fluvoxamine)	Upjohn/Solvay	300 mg	16
Celexa (citalopram)	Forest Laboratories	60 mg	33

Unclassified Antidepressants

Effexor (venlafaxine)	Wyeth-Ayerst	375 mg	5
Serzone (nefazadone)	Bristol Meyers/Squibb	600 mg	5
Remeron (mirtazapine)	Organon	60 mg	40

Antipsychotics

Haldol (haloperidol)	Ortho-McNeil Pharmaceuticals	40 mg	n/a
Orap (pimozide)	Gate Pharmaceuticals	10 mg	55
Risperdal (risperidone)	Janssen Pharmaceuticals	16 mg	24
Zyprexa (olanzapine)	Eli Lilly	20 mg	30
Seroquel (quetiapine fumarate)	Zeneca Pharmaceuticals	800 mg	6

* Half life refers to the point at which blood levels of the medication have dropped to one-half of the highest level reached.

All of the above medications are currently available in American pharmacies or hospitals. It should be noted that there is an intravenous form of Anafranil not currently approved for general use, which is still being tested experimentally at certain hospitals around the country. It has been shown to be helpful to many who did not respond to the oral form of Anafranil, but it is unclear if it will ever be approved for general use. There are always numerous other experimental medications being tested at any given time. You must investigate whether or not you qualify for one of the programs. You may be able to find their distributors by calling the manufacturer or the OC Foundation (see chapter 13).

When an individual's OCD is treated with one of the above drugs, we refer to this as monodrug therapy. Hopefully, one drug will be enough, but in cases where single drugs alone do not seem to remedy a person's symptoms, a physician who is skilled in the pharmacological treatment of OCD will usually move on to using two or more drugs in combination. This is known as polypharmacy or more commonly, "drug augmentation." In drug augmentation, a second drug is given which will increase blood levels of the first drug or combine with it to produce a more potent overall effect. In the past, polypharmacy was thought to be hazardous and an approach to be avoided. We now know that in some cases where we cannot produce adequate levels of the primary drug without risking overdosage, this combination usage is acceptable. Currently, we see this approach practiced routinely among physicians who have kept up with the latest methods.

Sometimes you will hear of disorders that do not respond to standard monodrug therapies referred to as "treatment resistant." Don't let this unfortunate term scare you. It does not mean that you cannot be treated. It is quite rare for someone to have no response to any of the numerous medications we have today. It does mean that you will probably have to take two or more medications simultaneously, and that finding the right ones may take more time and expertise. The following augmentation combinations are among those commonly used when single drug approaches do not seem to do the job.

Anafranil. Known generically as clomipramine. Can be combined with any of the SSRIs (Prozac, Zoloft, Paxil, Celexa, or Luvox). Some caution should be exercised in combining it with the SSRIs, particularly with Prozac, as elevated blood levels of TCAs have been reported. Anafranil is also likely to cause numerous uncomfortable side effects, including dry mouth, constipation, low blood pressure, fatigue, and decreased sex drive.

BuSpar. A nonaddictive antianxiety medication with the generic name buspirone. It has few side effects (fatigue being the most common) and is often the first drug used for augmentation. Can be combined with Anafranil or any of the SSRIs. It can also be combined as a third drug with any of the Anafranil and SSRI combinations or with an antidepressant and Lithium combination. Although one study claims that it does not work, my own observation is that it seems to work for 25 to 50 percent of those who use it. More studies of this medication in combination with others need to be conducted.

Lithium. This is a mood-regulating drug most commonly known for its use in treating manic depression (now known as "bipolar disorder") or major depression. It can be combined with Anafranil or any of the SSRIs, as well as with BuSpar as a third drug. It may be of particular value for those who also suffer from recurrent bouts of major depression, mood swings, or agitation along with their OCD. If you take more than a certain amount daily, a regular blood test may be required to check that blood levels are not too high, although it is not often taken in doses large enough to warrant this. Also, there are some reports of Lithium alone being helpful in some cases of TTM.

Orap. An antipsychotic drug with the generic name pimozide. It can be combined with Anafranil or any of the SSRIs. *(Should be used with care as it can cause an irre-*

versible neurological side effect known as tardive dyskinesia. This would be one of the last drugs to try as an augmenting agent.) It has been used to treat Tourette's Syndrome, and it may be of particular help where tics, twitches, or touching rituals are present. It may sometimes help as a secondary drug for TTM.

Haldol. An antipsychotic drug with the generic name haloperidol. It can be combined with Anafranil, or any of the SSRIs. The same cautions apply to Haldol as to Orap. As with Orap, it has been used to treat Tourette's Syndrome, and may be of particular help if you have tics, twitches, or touching rituals. It may also be helpful as a secondary drug for TTM.

Risperdal. The first of the newer generation of antipsychotic drugs with the generic name risperidone. It is generally used together with SSRIs for the same purposes (treating TTM and TS) as any of the older antipsychotic drugs (Haldol or Orap). This drug has a lower incidence of tardive dyskinesia than the older drugs.

Zyprexa. One of the newer antipsychotic drugs with the generic name olanzapine. It can be used together with an SSRI for the same purposes (treating TTM or TS) as Haldol or Orap. It is also less likely to cause tardive dyskinesia than these two drugs.

Seroquel. Another of the newer antipsychotic drugs with the generic name quetiapine fumarate. It is used in the same way as Risperdal or Zyprexa and also carries a lower risk of tardive dyskinesia.

Visken. A beta blocker whose generic name is pindolol. It is usually used to treat high blood pressure or angina. It also has the ability to cause the release of serotonin in the brain. There are reports of its being effective as an augmenting drug, particularly when depression is also present. It has also been reported to shorten the time it takes to get an initial response from an antidepressant when both are started together.

Another class of antidepressants, Monoamine Oxidase Inhibitors (MAOIs), are occasionally (although rarely) used for OCD. MAOIs may be used when TCAs and SSRIs have failed to produce results. They are also known for their effect on panic attacks. This class of medications is not considered to be a first line treatment for OCD. As of the present time, we have no controlled studies of the use of MAOIs in the treatment of OCD. Taking MAOIs involves many dietary restrictions, otherwise serious side effects such as a surge of extremely high blood pressure may result. *One important note about MAOIs: they should never be combined with a TCA, an SSRI, or BuSpar.* A condition called "Serotonergic Syndrome" can result, causing many serious side effects such as tremors, restlessness, muscle twitches, excessive perspiration, shivering, or even more seriously, leading to death by cardiovascular collapse. It is generally recommended that you wait about two weeks between stopping TCAs, SSRIs, or BuSpar and starting an MAOI. An exception is in the case where someone is switching from Prozac to an MAOI, where a wait of five weeks is generally recommended. On a related note, there is a growing body of case reports which suggest that SSRIs should not be combined with each other either, due to the possibility of Serotonergic Syndrome.

The newest class of antipsychotic drugs has been showing some promise in helping certain cases of OCD. This group includes the drugs Risperdal (risperidone), Zyprexa (olanzapine), and Seroquel (quetiapine fumarate). While these medications were developed as antipsychotic agents designed to affect dopamine levels in the brain, they also have an effect on serotonin. There are many fewer side effects and risks associated with these drugs than with other drugs used to treat schizophrenia. Compared to older antipsychotic drugs, they apparently have a much lower risk of causing tardive dyskinesia, a particularly unpleasant neuromuscular side effect that is irreversible. There are reports of their successful use in treating OCD, BDD, and other somatization disorders when combined with SSRIs. Because they are serotonin blockers, as opposed to being serotonin reuptake blockers, they may not be appropriate for many cases of classic OCD but may possibly be better for those with lower insight, as well as BDD, where the thoughts can be so strong as to resemble delusions at times. (Problems with insight in OCD are on a continuum with some having more, and some having less.)In cases where I have seen them used for classic OCD and BDD, they seem to have had variable effects of causing feelings of agitation and worsening the symptoms in some, while they have helped others greatly. There are also reports of the effectiveness of these medications in treating TTM and Tourette's Syndrome. In the case of TTM, they are usually given together with any of the SSRIs.

While we are on the subject of antipsychotic medications, I would like to mention here that they constitute a group of drugs which over the years has been the most misprescribed for those with classic OCD. Older drugs such as Thorazene, Mellaril, Stelazine, and Navane were, and in some cases still are, prescribed as a main treatment by physicians who mistake people's obsessions and odd compulsions for schizophrenia. The result has been heavily sedated sufferers who are still unable to function. Unless there is a very specific reason for taking any of these medications, they are not to be considered the first drugs of choice for your OCSD. (Please note that in cases of extreme anxiety and agitation that cannot be controlled by milder antianxiety medications, these drugs are sometimes used along with OCD medications. This type of use is considered appropriate.)

A few notes specifically about the pharmacological treatment of TTM would be worthwhile. While it can be treated in many cases with the same antidepressant medications mentioned above, there are a few differences that are important to be aware of. One is that for some with TTM, it is not unusual for a medication to prove effective for a number of weeks or months and then stop working for no apparent reason. This can also be seen occasionally when treating OCD. As mentioned above, augmentation with Lithium or one of the newer antipsychotics may be of benefit in such cases. I have personally observed this approach to be helpful.

Another important note about treating TTM is that there is some speculation that different types of pulling may respond better to different groups of medications. Those who pull deliberately in a more perfectionistic OC manner may do better using those antidepressants that work best with classic OCD. Those whose pulling is more automatic, and stimulated by physical sensations or sudden urges which more resemble tics, may do better on SSRIs together with those drugs used to treat Tourette's Syndrome (such as the newer antipsychotics). This has actually proven to be true in a number of these cases that I have seen. These were cases where an SSRI alone either did not produce results or stopped working after several weeks. This theory needs to be researched further and is an intriguing idea.

There are also reports of the successful use of the opiate-blocking medication Trexan (naltrexone). This medication has been used to treat addictions, and it is theorized that for some, it blocks the pleasurable sensations that accompany hair pulling. With no satisfying payoff, this would then lead to a decreased urge to pull. Trexan has also been used to augment SSRIs in some cases.

It should be mentioned here that when a particular drug is not helping, it may not be the fault of the drug, and it may not be necessary to add a second or third drug. I have seen a lot of individuals needlessly give up on drugs that could have helped them. When discussing their previous treatment history, they tell their subsequent physicians that a particular drug has already been tried and didn't work. Unfortunately, some physicians take such reports at face value and never investigate that particular drug again. The following possibilities should always be checked first, before assuming that what you are taking or have taken in the past will not work for you:

1. Did you take the drug for a long enough period of time? Some individuals are slow responders and may take as long as twelve or even sixteen weeks to show signs of effectiveness. Physicians and patients sometimes give up too quickly after only a few weeks.

2. Did you take a large enough dose? Your physician may not have prescribed the maximum dose for the drug, even though you were tolerat-

ing it. For reasons that are not clear, some physicians are reluctant to prescribe the highest allowable dosages of particular medications.

3. Did you take the medication as directed? If you skipped days or even weeks, or did not take the full dose, it is easy to see why the drug may not have worked. These medications require a steady (and sometimes increasing) buildup over a number of weeks, or they will not produce a therapeutic effect.

4. Did your physician build up your dose too quickly? Too rapid an increase in dosage can sometimes bring on strong side effects which otherwise might not have happened. This can cause individuals to abandon drugs that might have helped them.

5. Did your physician initially start you on too much medication, causing you to experience serious side effects? Too high an initial dose can cause side effects that would not normally have occurred. There are also some individuals who are extremely drug sensitive and don't do very well even on standard starter dosages. Older patients may also have difficulty tolerating ordinary dosage levels. Those who have such sensitivities are forced to give up when strong side effects appear, but would actually have done well had they started and stayed on an extremely small dosage and built up very slowly in very small increases. (*Note*: The use of available liquid forms of Prozac and Paxil can be particularly helpful to those who need to be able to take smaller doses than can be gotten from pills or capsules. These liquid drugs can even be diluted by a pharmacist with a simple sugar syrup to enable you to take a microdose as small as 1 or 2 mg.)

There are some physicians who prescribe amounts that exceed the recommended maximum dosages. Some may try to do this when the standard maximum dose hasn't produced results. Generally speaking, there are enough different drugs that if a particular one is not working for you, it is probably advisable that you be switched to another, rather than having your dosage raised to these levels. On the other hand, there may be a particular justification for taking this approach if

• you are on the maximum dose of the only available medication that has been shown to work at least somewhat for you;

• you are having no particular side effects;

• a blood test reveals that its levels in your blood are still too low for it to be effective. There are case reports of this having been done successfully, and I am also personally aware of several successful treatments of this type. When a higher-than-recommended dosage is given, it should only be done with great care and only by a qualified psychiatrist.

PRESCRIBING MEDICATION FOR OCSDs

Any legally licensed physician can prescribe any medication that has been approved by the FDA. There are some sufferers who go to their family physicians for prescriptions for psychiatric medications in order to save the expense of seeing a psychiatrist. Unfortunately, nonpsychiatrist physicians tend to have little or no knowledge about OCSDs or how to properly administer treatment for them. I have seen numerous OCSD sufferers receive inadequate treatment at the hands of well-meaning family physicians. It takes much training and expertise to be able to treat disorders as specialized as OCSDs, particularly where drug combinations are necessary. It also requires careful monitoring to guard against problems involving side effects. Seeing someone without the necessary expertise can prove to be a false economy, wasting both your time and money. If you have no trained psychiatrist nearby, then you may have no choice. If your only option is to work with your family doctor, at least see that he or she consults with a psychiatrist with experience in treating OCSDs and reads up on the subject.

GETTING STARTED WITH MEDICATION

When you show up for your first visit with a physician, there are several important points to be aware of. They will most likely begin by taking a medical history, as well as a history of your disorder. At this time, be sure to inform them of any medical conditions you may have in addition to your OCSD, and any medications (of any type) that you are currently taking. It will also be extremely important for you to give them a listing of all previous medications you have taken for your OCSD, as well as the dosages you took, how long you took them for, how effective each of them was, and any side effects you experienced. Your best bet is to write all this down before you go, so that you do not have to take up valuable time trying to recall this information.

Beware of physicians who tell you that you require whole batteries of expensive tests before you can start taking a medication. If you suffer from any form of heart disease, it is appropriate that you have an EKG and blood testing. It is also appropriate to have your blood tested if you suffer from liver disease. Other than such tests as these, there are no special lab tests that are required before you can take any of the medications commonly prescribed for OCSDs.

MEDICATIONS: EVERYTHING WORKS FOR SOMEBODY, NOTHING WORKS FOR EVERYBODY

When comparing the various medications used to treat OCSDs, it really isn't possible to say which one is best. It is really a question of which one is best for you. Just because one has worked well for someone you know, there is no guarantee that it will do the same in your case. Everyone's particular brain chemistry is like a fingerprint—similar to that of others, but also different in its own special way. There may be various reasons to start with a particular medication as opposed to some other. This would have to be determined medically. For instance, when an OCSD patient is also reporting a serious sleep problem such as insomnia, or feelings of agitation, drugs such as Anafranil or Zoloft might be prescribed for their sedating properties, instead of other commonly used medications less likely to have such effects. Conversely, if a patient has experienced a great deal of fatigue or drowsiness, the physician might prescribe one of the more activating SSRIs instead. A particular drug might also be selected for you to avoid a specific side effect known to be associated with that drug. For instance, if you have a tendency toward problems with hypotension (low blood pressure), your physician might not choose Anafranil for you and would perhaps start you on a different medication not known to lower blood pressure.

Other accompanying problems or side effects may also determine which drug is best for you to take or may indicate a need for a second drug as well. No one likes to take more medication than necessary, but in some cases it may be unavoidable. Lithium, Neurontin, or Depakote might be a necessary accompaniment if you also suffer from serious biological depression. If you have problems with tics or touching rituals, Orap, Haldol, Risperdal, Seroquel, or Zyprexa might be necessary. If you suffer from bipolar disorder (manic depression), it might be best for you to only take antidepressants with great care and expert supervision, to avoid causing you a manic episode.

THE BEST MEDICATION FOR YOU

There is no way to determine in advance which medication is best for you. There are currently no pretests whatsoever for the medications used to treat OCSDs, although we may be able to do this in the future. Aside from a physician's educated guess, there is no reliable guide other than actually taking the medication. As mentioned above, your physician may pick one for a particularly helpful property or to avoid the possibility of a side effect that would be particularly undesirable for you, but there is no "best" drug.

It should be said here that finding the most effective drug can sometimes be a time-consuming and frustrating experience. For some, the first drug is the right one, but for others it may take several tries. It is done by trial and error and is a little like playing the lottery. Much patience is required in such cases. The reason it may take time is because the antidepressant drugs used to treat OCD are not drugs that work as rapidly as the drugs for anxiety, such as Valium, Xanax, or Klonopin. They must build up slowly in your system over a period of several weeks. Results are not usually noticeable before about three weeks and can sometimes take as long as twelve or even sixteen weeks in certain cases. I have actually witnessed a handful of cases where patients reported noticeable improvement the day after starting their medication, but such cases are very rare. Remember, too, that when switching from one drug to another, it is usually advisable to wait one or two weeks after stopping the first drug and before starting the second drug, to avoid a possible interaction. This can also add time to the process.

Obviously, if you try a particular medication and prove to be allergic to it, or suffer serious side effects within the first few days, your physician will certainly discontinue it. The majority of people on antidepressant drugs, however, will only experience some minor side effects that in most cases are simply annoying. Of these types of side effects, most will subside within the first few weeks if you are willing to wait them out. Some people I have seen have unfortunately stopped taking their medications after only a few days or a week, not wishing to have any side effects, or thinking that these would never go away. The result of such actions has sadly, I believe, caused many of them to miss out on a drug that would have actually helped them had they only waited a few days or weeks longer.

A general approach to working your way through the medication maze is shown in Figure 4.1. One word of advice here. As you work your way through the various medications, always be sure to keep careful records of which ones you have taken, how long you were on them, the various dosages, any side effects, and what your response was to them. If you should change physicians or seek a second opinion, this information will prove to be extremely valuable.

HOW TO TELL WHEN MEDICATION IS WORKING

Medications for OCSDs do not work instantly. The newer types may begin to show results within two to three weeks. The older ones, such as Anafranil, may take six weeks to begin showing any change. If you are someone who tends to respond only to higher doses, this may take even longer. Usually, if you have reached the maximum dose of an antidepressant and been at that level for at least three weeks without result, it is probable that it will not work for you. The

Fig. 4.1 ∿ Steps in the Pharmacological Treatment of OCSDs

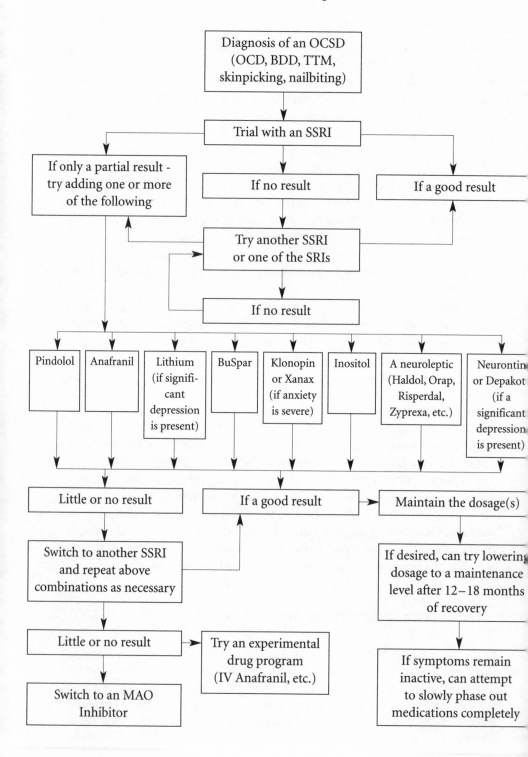

same is true if you cannot tolerate the maximum dose but have gone as high as is possible for you.

It is not always easy to tell at first if a medication is working, since the effect can be very subtle. Most people can sense that something different is happening but cannot always say what it is. Often they will deny it is the medication. They will notice periods of time passing without the occurrence of symptoms but may only notice this after the fact. As time goes by, these periods will get longer and they find themselves gradually being better able to push thoughts out of their heads or to resist compulsions or impulsions.

LONG-TERM MEDICATION AND SIDE EFFECTS

The issue of side effects can be very tricky and particularly so for those with classic OCD or BDD. So many sufferers lives are strongly oriented around not taking risks that they cannot easily think about or discuss the subject without a great deal of nervousness and negative anticipation. They will usually read the entire package insert that comes with a drug and worry that they will suffer every serious side effect listed there. As usual, they will overestimate the *probability* of any risks involved and confuse it with the *possibility*. This attempt to control all of life's possible risks has probably kept many with OCD from using medications that would have helped them. The question they most often ask is, "How do I know they won't discover some long-term danger thirty years from now?" My answer is that using this kind of reasoning, you could not take *any* drug of *any* type that has not been around for at least thirty years. This would then eliminate practically all modern medications.

Medications should always be used with care and only when necessary. As far as can be determined from the available research, there do not appear to be any long-term side effects or harmful biological changes associated with antidepressant medications. When used in children, there is no evidence that they affect their growth or development. As a group, antidepressants have a very good track record for safety. Anafranil has been around for over thirty years and has not shown any long-term problems. All the other drugs are tested extensively on thousands of individuals over years under the strict supervision of the FDA. I have known people who have taken them for over a dozen years with no ill effects. As mentioned previously, most side effects tend to show up and also subside within the first few weeks. Many other types of side effects will also dwindle over a period of months, as a person's body becomes more acclimatized to the presence of the drug.

There are only three instances where I have observed potentially harmful reactions to antidepressant medications. The first is where physicians greatly exceeded the maximum recommended dosage limits in an attempt to get a treatment response from a drug that was not working. A second instance I have observed is where patients who developed side effects of increased nervousness or jitteriness were raised to higher doses of their medication instead of having their dosages decreased or discontinued as would have been proper. Apparently, their physicians thought this reaction was merely due to insufficient medication rather than a side effect. As a result, the nervousness and jitteriness turned to even more serious agitation, sleeplessness, and high anxiety. Discontinuation or decrease of the medication eliminated this reaction in all such cases.

The third instance involves patients who suffered allergic reactions to their medication. In all cases, this seems to have resulted only in rashes on the forearms or upper body. However, since the physicians were unsure of what was causing the rash, they did not discontinue the medications immediately and the rashes became fairly severe in a few cases. While these were not dangerous situations, it was rather uncomfortable for the patients. Also, allergic reactions do sometimes have the potential to become serious and should not be taken lightly. With the discontinuation of the medication, all cases of the rashes disappeared within several days. I have heard that in some cases the allergic reaction may be to dyes in the pills rather than the medication itself; however, I haven't seen much information about how common this actually is.

One other issue that deserves to be mentioned here is that of drug interactions. Always be sure to check with your physician and pharmacist if you take any other medications for other problems. Not all medications can be taken together at the same time. Two drugs in particular, Seldane and Hismanal, should not be taken together with certain antidepressants, particularly Luvox or Serzone. A harmful interaction may result.

Many with OCD will have to face the prospect of having to take medication indefinitely. Each time they try to stop, the symptoms creep back within a few weeks. There are several studies that verify this happens in the majority of cases. In spite of this recurrence of symptoms, there is nothing wrong with trying to see if you can manage without medication periodically. I see nothing wrong with such attempts, and neither do the psychiatrists I work with. My guess would be, however, that if you have already tried several times without success, the odds are that you cannot do without the medication and need it to remain in recovery.

There appears to be a small group of individuals who only experience occasional bouts of OC problems, with periods of remission lasting months or years in between. These people seem to have to take medication during these symptomatic periods only, stopping when the problem has passed.

OCSDs, MEDICATION, AND PREGNANCY

Generally speaking, it is recommended that pregnant women not take most medications. Because drug researchers cannot ethically test medications on pregnant women, we have very little reliable information about the effects of antidepressants on unborn children. There are some scattered case reports of Prozac being used after the first trimester of pregnancy without causing harm. A recent large-scale study conducted at the University of California at San Diego indicated on the one hand, that the babies of women who took Prozac during the first trimester of pregnancy showed no greater levels of problems than those whose mothers had not. On the other hand, this same study also indicated that babies of women who took Prozac throughout pregnancy were more likely to be born prematurely, be more jittery at birth, and have respiratory problems. Full-term babies born to mothers in this group were also shown to be smaller at birth. Beyond these studies, I am not aware of any long-term follow-up studies being done with the children of pregnant Prozac users to see if problems turn up at a later point in their development. If you read the package inserts that come with medications, you will also see reports of problems occurring at birth following the use of TCAs.

I am aware that some physicians have felt obligated to use some of these medications in cases where their pregnant OCSD patients were feeling tremendously agitated or even suicidal, but these were desperate measures. Until we have a greater body of case reports and follow-ups, it would probably be best to avoid the use of antidepressants during pregnancy, unless your physician considers it an absolute necessity. Even then, it usually is not recommended to begin medication until midway into the second trimester.

This can create a dilemma for women with OCSDs who wish to have children, but don't think they can manage without their medications. The period of time it may take to get pregnant plus the nine months of pregnancy can add up to two or more years (in some cases) without the benefit of medications. This period can even be longer if the mother chooses to breast-feed, as OCSD medications or their breakdown products can be excreted in breast milk. These are cases where behavioral therapy can make an important difference. Having other tools with which to face symptoms is of the greatest importance in such situations. I have had several patients who were in recovery come back for regular behavioral refresher sessions after having given up their medications to have a child. Before deciding whether or not to have a child, or finding a physician who will feel comfortable prescribing for you under such circumstances, it would be wise to first give behavioral therapy a try.

SIDE EFFECTS AND WHAT CAN BE
DONE ABOUT THEM

All the drugs used to treat OC Spectrum disorders have the potential to produce side effects. More than a few people with classic OCD and BDD are quite fearful of any type of risk and can be difficult to treat with medications because they read drug package inserts and books about drugs and worry that they will get every side effect listed. Such fears are exaggerated as the majority of people taking these medications experience only minor side effects, some get none, and not everyone gets the same ones. Reactions to medications are entirely individualistic, and there is no predicting whether you will have any or if they will be serious. Furthermore, the presence of side effects may have nothing to do with whether or not a particular drug is effective for you. I have seen some individuals who had to stop taking medications that were helping them due to these problems. Side effects can range from extremely minor tolerable reactions, to more serious ones that would prevent you from taking the medication altogether.

Side effects tend to be similar within families of drugs. Tricyclic antidepressants such as Anafranil are known for having the most side effects overall. The most typical side effects in this group would include dry mouth, constipation, excessive perspiration, blurred vision, lowered blood pressure (orthostatic hypotension), sedation or fatigue, urinary retention, increased appetite accompanied by weight gain, or sexual dysfunction (delayed ejaculation in men, inability to have an orgasm in women, decreased sex drive in both men and women).

SSRIs (Prozac, Zoloft, Paxil, Luvox, etc.) have somewhat fewer side effects than the tricyclics. They include nausea, headaches, insomnia, increased feelings of nervousness or agitation, fatigue, sexual dysfunction (the same as those seen in TCAs), diarrhea, or tremors (usually seen in the hands).

The most basic general approach to dealing with side effects is to discuss the possibility of lowering the dosage with your physician. Some individuals are extremely sensitive to medications. In such cases, it is sometimes a good strategy to drop the person to the lowest possible dosage, stay there for a few weeks, and then only increase the dose by the smallest possible unit over much longer periods of time than usual. I have seen some adults do very well on dosages appropriate for children. Unfortunately, some physicians will take a person off an otherwise effective medication before considering a much smaller dosage.

It should be noted that many of the side effects that occur with antidepressants are only temporary. In many cases, they tend to pass after the first three to four weeks as your system adapts to the presence of the drug. If side effects are serious, you should, of course, report them immediately to your physician. If they are merely annoying or only a bit uncomfortable, it would be best to still report them to your physician, and under his or her guidance, try to stick with the medication to see if the side effects pass within the first few weeks. In any event, always consult with your physician if in doubt about side effects. Unfortunately, many with classic OCD or BDD are among those who have stopped taking medication which would otherwise have helped them had they waited only a few weeks.

One word of caution here. The following information is not meant to be an absolutely complete rundown of all possible side effects, nor should you use it to make a decision on whether or not to take a particular medication.

As far as the treatment of specific side effects is concerned, I have listed various approaches that have been shown to help. REMEMBER: *this information is not meant to be a substitute for the advice of a trained physician.* It is given here solely as a possible basis for discussion with the person treating you medically. Speak to your doctor if you have any questions whatsoever.

Sedation or Fatigue

Because serotonin helps regulate the cycles of sleep and waking, this is a fairly common side effect, especially with the tricyclics, which act in some ways similar to antihistamines. Most often, it begins about the time you start taking the medication and tapers off after about two to three weeks. It may recur for a few days each time you increase your dosage. If it does not decrease, but you have to remain on the medication (having tried the others), there are several strategies to try. The first, and simplest, is to ask about taking your full dosage in the evening, between dinner and bedtime. Hopefully, the fatigue will peak while you are already asleep. The exact time will have to be determined by experimenting. If you are trying this and still feel tired, the second strategy is to use caffeine, especially during the earlier part of the day when fatigue is likely to be more of a problem. Should coffee or colas be unable to do the job, the third possibility would be to have your physician combine your antidepressant with a stimulant drug such as Ritalin (methylphenidate), Cylert (pemoline), Adderall, or Dexedrine. If you are taking Anafranil, these drugs may also have the added advantage of acting as augmenting agents: that is, they may boost the blood levels of this drug by interfering in its metabolism. This effect, however, can also be a problem, and the use of these drugs together must be done with care. Taking a stimulant with Anafranil may enable you to get by with lower dosages of the antidepressant, or at least help you get more out of the amount you are taking. One word of caution, all stimulants, including caffeine, carry the risk of increasing anxiety and jitteriness and the possible worsening of obsessions, and so should be used carefully. One further option that may be of help is the addition of the antidepressant Wellbutrin. It seems to have an energizing effect on some individuals, can relieve feelings of depression not helped by the primary antidepressant, and may even reduce other side effects as well. As with the stimulants, there is some risk of increased anxiety and jitteriness. A new development in treating fatigue may be Provigil which is a stimulant drug recently approved for the treatment of narcolepsy. It can apparently relieve fatigue without causing increased anxiety and jitteriness. I have seen it help in several cases but it is not yet in widespread use, and requires further study.

Dry Mouth

This is a particularly common side effect seen mostly with tricyclics. While not a harmful side effect in itself, constant dry mouth can lead to an increase in cavities, as there is little or no saliva with which the mouth may periodically rinse itself. Regular tooth brushing, dental checkups, and other forms of essential dental hygiene are especially important to prevent these decay problems. The use of sugarless gum or sucking candies can be helpful. Also, a 1 percent solution of Pilocarpine used as a mouth rinse three to four times daily can stimulate salivation. The drug Bethanacol (uricholine) taken daily may have the same effect. Finally, some patients have used artificial saliva preparations, such as Glandosane, but their benefits are temporary and they must be used several times daily.

Constipation

The two most obvious solutions, and the ones most often suggested, are to drink more water and to alter your diet so that it contains more fiber. The latter solution would include eating more foods containing bran and other natural roughage. Additionally, the use of prune juice may be helpful. If these solutions are insufficient, ask your physician about the use of such stool softeners as Metamucil or Colace. The use of stimulating laxatives such as milk of magnesia or Senekot on a regular basis is usually not recommended because of their long-term effects on the functioning of your intestines. Some of those using the vitamin Inositol as an augmenting agent along with their antidepressant have reported that its tendency to cause diarrhea actually counteracted the constipation their antidepressant was causing.

Diarrhea

Sometimes, an increase in intestinal motility due to your medication can lead to this problem. Generally, drinking apple juice or eating apples (both of which contain pectin) or taking absorptives such as Kaopectate can be helpful. Avoiding caffeine may also help in such circumstances. It is recommended that you stay away from the regular use of prescription drugs such as Lomotil to treat this side effect. They are not meant for more than occasional use. One further solution I have encountered would be the addition of a very small amount of Anafranil to your other medications, as its side effect of producing constipation may balance things out.

Lowered Blood Pressure

Also known as orthostatic hypotension, this side effect can lead to feelings of dizziness, especially when changing position too rapidly. It is sometimes seen in those taking tricyclics. I have seen this in particular with patients who had already shown tendencies toward low blood pressure before ever taking medication. First and foremost, remember to move slowly when getting up out of bed or going from a kneeling to a standing position. This side effect can be particularly dangerous for the elderly, as their circulation tends to be poorer, and the dizziness it produces can lead to falls and bone fractures. If you are already taking medication for a hypertension problem, you will need to be closely monitored by your physician. If you do experience this side effect, it is probably best to switch to some other medication, if at all possible.

Urinary Retention

This side effect can range from very mild to severe. Not only can it cause discomfort, but it can also lead to urinary infections and other bladder problems if not treated. The most common approach to remedying this side effect is through the use of the prescription drug Bethanacol (uricholine), a cholinergic agent, taken daily. If severe enough, the usual response is to discontinue the medication.

Headaches

These appear to be a common side effect and may be quite frequent and regular. It is probably best to begin treating them with such over-the-counter remedies as aspirin, Tylenol, or Motrin. If these do not prove helpful, physicians will sometimes resort to treating them with beta blockers, particularly Inderal.

Sexual Dysfunction

Of all the side effects, this one can be the most annoying and frustrating, although probably the least physically harmful. I have seen more people switch medications or even stop taking them because of this. It manifests itself in women as a loss of interest in sex or as an inability to have an orgasm. It can affect men in several different ways, such as causing them to have a decreased sex drive, difficulty in having or maintaining an erection (impotence), or in causing a delay or loss of orgasm. The most obvious way of dealing with this is to try switching to another antidepressant, in the hope of finding one that does not do this to you. Serzone and Celexa are two particular medications that are less likely to cause these problems. One technique for helping these problems, which does not involve medication, is via the use of a vibrator to increase sexual stimulation. Another nondrug approach involves taking a "holiday" from your drug on weekends. This method needs to be carefully monitored by your physician and may not be for everyone due to the fluctuation in blood levels of your medication. This is particularly so for those on medications with short half lives such as Paxil. Be sure to consult with your physician before making any changes of this type. Several medications have also been used to treat these problems, with varying degrees of success depending on the individual. Those found to be most effective would include Periactin (cyproheptadine), a serotonin antagonist, which is taken daily; Bethanacol (uricholine), taken one to two hours before engaging in sex; Yocon (yohimbine), which can sometimes help with impotence and orgasmic difficulties (this medication can also cause overstimulation and jitteriness); Symmetrel (amantidine hydrochloride); Permax (pergolide); and Parlodel (bromocryptine). Another medication I have seen to be particularly effective for this side effect is Wellbutrin (bupropion). It is an antidepressant not typically used to treat OCSDs but which can be taken together with other antidepressants. There are also reports of the successful use of stimulants such as Ritalin and Dexedrine. Such drugs should always be used carefully. Some individuals find that stimulants increase feelings of anxiety and jitteriness. Two further possibilities that have been reported to work would be BuSpar and the antidepressant Remeron. The latter drug should be used carefully, as it can be quite sedating at lower doses. One helpful new development is an oral medication for impotence in men called Viagra. It seems to help relieve the side effect of impotence in men. Contrary to what some people believe, it does not appear to increase sex drive. A growing body of evidence indicates that it may also be helpful to women. Another potentially helpful medication that is currently in testing is Vasomax, which is said to be similar to Viagra. A version of this drug, Vasofem, is also being developed for women. There are a number of other medications currently in development, and these may also give us further options in treating sexual side effects. A nonprescription remedy currently under investigation is a naturally occurring compound that comes by way of Chinese medicine, Gingko Biloba. This compound is extracted from the leaves of the Gingko tree. It is not clear, at this time, whether long-term use may produce side effects. While there are case reports of its effectiveness in daily doses of up to 420 mg, no controlled studies have been done yet, so it is too soon to tell if it will be truly useful.

Tremors

Hand tremors may not only occur with the antidepressants used to treat OCD, but are also seen to result from the use of Lithium, an augmenting drug that can be taken with them. This side effect is largely treated with drugs known as beta-blockers, particularly Inderal. Should the Inderal cause fatigue or a depressed mood, a switch to some other beta-blocker is usually recommended. I have also heard of using small amounts of drugs known as benzodiazepenes, such as Valium or Xanax. However, these are habit forming and therefore only to be used as a last resort.

Increased Appetite and Weight Gain

If you notice a sudden increase in the amount you are eating and the fact that your weight seems to be increasing, and that these side effects are coincidental with starting on your antidepressant, it is probably because of the drug. A strong appetite for sweets and carbohydrates is often seen. The best solutions here are the age-old ones of watching what you eat and getting more exercise. Try to find low calorie alternatives to help satisfy your appetite. Make sure to consult your physician if you are considering the use of any type of weight loss drug, product, or diet to be certain that it will not interfere with the action of your medication or cause an adverse reaction. If you are diligent, it is possible to control this side effect.

Feelings of Nervousness and Agitation

This side effect is sometimes seen in those using SSRIs. It may not be easy to immediately spot this side effect when you are already suffering from anxiety and nervousness. However, you will sense that when it is caused by the medication, it has a different quality. In many cases, it may subside within a few weeks. In general, the thing not to do is to raise your medication dose when you are feeling this way, as this may only increase these feelings. Obviously, if you are taking any stimulant drugs, the antidepressant Wellbutrin, or large amounts of caffeine via coffee or colas together with your SSRI, you might want to lower or eliminate them before assuming that the SSRI is the culprit. If it is determined that the problem is due to your SSRI, a strategy some physicians use is to drop your dosage to a much lower level, wait about two weeks, and then begin to raise it again much more slowly and by much smaller amounts. If this side effect still does not subside after slowly being returned to your previous dosage level, the best course may be to switch to another medication. If this is not possible because it is also the only drug that has lowered your symptoms, you might ask your physician about the possibility of taking an anti-anxiety medication in the benzodiazepene family, such as Klonopin (clonazepam), which some say can be helpful with OC symptoms as well. Another possible approach would be to combine a small amount of Anafranil with your SSRI to take advantage of that drug's sedating effects.

Insomnia

This side effect is most frequently seen in those taking SSRIs and may sometimes be accompanied by the restlessness and agitation mentioned above. Because it can affect your therapy and ability to cope in general, this is a side effect that should not be allowed to continue for a long period of time. The simplest approach, and the one which should be tried first, would be to ask your physician if you can take the medication with breakfast, in order to allow the peak blood level to occur during your waking hours, possibly allowing you to feel less stimulated at bedtime. Should this not help, another solution may be for your physician to add a small amount of Anafranil to your SSRI, taken some time in the evening after dinner, to encourage drowsiness. Another solution, if you cannot tolerate Anafranil, would be for your physician to prescribe a small amount of the antidepressant Desyrel (trazadone), taken about an hour before bedtime. This drug is known for its ability to cause drowsiness, although one possible drawback is that some people have also been known to experience a hung over feeling the next morning. It is considered wiser to use the above antidepressants rather than some type of prescription sleeping pill or an antianxiety drug such as Xanax (alprazolam). Prescription sleep medications lose their effectiveness after daily use over a few weeks and related drugs such as Xanax are benzodiazepenes and therefore addictive. The antidepressants don't have either drawback. It is also not considered good practice to regularly indulge in over-the-counter sleep aids, most of which are essentially preparations of Benadryl (diphenhydramine). A nonbenzodiazepene sleep aid, Ambien (zolpidem), has also proven to be helpful.

Blurred Vision

The effects of the medication on the muscles of the eye usually cause this problem. If reducing your medication dosages doesn't help, either a 1 percent solution of Pilocarpine eye drops used several times a day, or Bethanacol taken orally on a daily basis, may prove helpful. This is another side effect that sometimes clears up by itself. In any case, be certain to get regular eye examinations should you experience any changes in your vision, and don't forget to report it to your psychiatrist as well.

Excessive Perspiration

While not harmful, this is an annoying, uncomfortable, and embarrassing side effect. Over-the-counter antiperspirants can help with underarm perspiration; however, they cannot be used on other areas of your body. One prescription antiperspirant I have heard of is called Drysol, but again, it is only for underarm use. Aside from lowering your medication dose or changing medications, there are not many good solutions for this problem.

Memory Problems

A number of people who take antidepressants have reported problems with their short-term memory. It is not always clear that it is the fault of the drug. For one thing, a certain amount of forgetting is normal. Some sufferers tend to obsessively magnify normal forgetfulness to the point where they think they have a more serious problem. In addition, being preoccupied with frequent obsessions can interfere with your concentration and thus your ability to remember. Those who really are affected in this way by medication describe it as being absentminded in ways they did not recall before they took the drug. Some also report a problem known as "word loss," in which they often find themselves unable to come up with the correct word while in the middle of a sentence and feel as if it is just on the tip of their tongue. These problems are not known to be permanent and will tend to last only as long as you are on the specific medication causing it. My own observation has been that if you discontinue the medication, your memory returns to its former levels. There is no treatment for this side effect, and if it becomes serious enough to cause you difficulty in everyday functioning (which it rarely does), the only answer is to discontinue the drug and try another. Some people who are unable to change drugs compensate for it by being better organized and by simply writing things down that they cannot afford to forget.

Increased Dream Activity

This is an extremely common side effect with many patients reporting vivid, colorful, and more active dreams. There is no harm or danger in this, although it can be disconcerting to those not expecting it. Some even report being more physically active in their sleep. There is no particular treatment for this, other than just knowing what it is and that it is harmless, if surprising at times. The main thing is not to become anxious about it.

OCSD MEDICATIONS AND ADDICTION

This is a matter of concern to many sufferers, especially those who have a history of abusing alcohol or legal or illegal drugs. Antidepressant medications, the drugs most commonly used to treat OCD, are not classified as controlled substances. They produce no cravings, nor does stopping them result in physical withdrawal, although there can be some chemical rebound effects if high dosages are stopped abruptly.

Some of the medications used to treat symptoms of anxiety and which are given along with these drugs can, however, be addictive. I am thinking particularly of a family of drugs known as benzodiazepenes. This group includes Ativan (lorazepam), Xanax (alprazolam), Valium (diazepam), and Klonopin (clonazepam). These particular drugs should only be taken with a good deal of supervision and only when absolutely necessary. With proper therapy and help from other medications, it is hoped that you would not have to take such dependency-producing medications for long periods of time. I have often seen that they can be helpful at the beginning of therapy, where the antidepressants have not yet started to work, and where behavior therapy is still in the planning stages. An anxious and agitated new patient will be much better able to concentrate on starting therapy if these symptoms can be brought under control quickly. Later on, however, when the main approaches to treatment have begun to work, these medications can often be phased out.

Unfortunately, I have seen cases where patients were needlessly maintained on antianxiety drugs for years at a time, with no periodic review as to their necessity. The drugs became a substitute for any type of first-line treatment and resulted in the person becoming totally dependent on them in order to function. This should be viewed differently from the long-term use of antidepressants which, while they are being taken, correct the actual biochemical problem and reduce symptoms, as opposed to just keeping down anxiety levels while the symptoms persist.

For those who require relief from anxiety but wish to avoid the benzodiazepenes for various reasons, there are some alternatives. One is the nonaddictive antianxiety medication BuSpar. Another is the beta-blocker Inderal, a medication that has been commonly used over the years to treat tremors and stage fright in musicians and actors. Your physician will be able to determine if one of these is appropriate for you.

Special Note: please be advised that if you are on one of the benzodiazepene family of medications mentioned above, do not take yourself off of it suddenly without your physician's knowledge or advice, as there can be serious consequences in some cases. Always consult your physician before making changes in any of your medications.

GETTING WELL USING MEDICATION ALONE

About one-third of those who rely on medications alone get good to excellent results, although even in these cases, enough symptoms still remain so that these people cannot actually call themselves recovered. Another third see moderate results, and the remaining third get results ranging from low levels of relief to no result whatsoever. This is not to say that no one can get complete symptom relief from medications. I have seen a number of cases over the years, but they are more the exception than the rule. Remember that medications for OCD only relieve symptoms, they are not a cure. Using medications alone is risky because you might have to go off them for reasons of health, side effects, pregnancy, or if they just stop working (see the next section). Several studies have demonstrated that when individuals discontinue their medications (even those who have been taking them for long periods), the rate of relapse is high and the return of symptoms is rapid. Studies suggest that relapse rates in such cases can be greater than 90 percent. Also, it appears that even those getting good results from medications alone can sometimes relapse if they are under high stress.

I have seen too many people become somewhat improved on medication and then hesitate about going for therapy. Their reasoning is something like this, "I feel better now than I did, and I can sort of function, so why rock the boat by facing my fears further? After all, the therapy might make me more anxious again and I might go back to the way I was before I started the medication."

The best general advice is to use behavior therapy together with medication. With behavior therapy training, you will always have something to fall back on, no matter what is happening with the drugs you are taking. You cannot get worse for having undergone the therapy—only stronger and more self-reliant. Although it is helpful, medication teaches you nothing about managing your anxiety or changing your philosophy of risk taking in life. It also cannot help you recover the missing pieces of your life and patch up your relationships, something that therapy can help. The research literature shows better and longer lasting results for those using both treatments, compared with those who only used either one alone. Medication should be regarded as a tool to help you do the behavioral therapy.

OCSD MEDICATIONS CAN OCCASIONALLY STOP WORKING

Over the years, I have seen some individuals whose antidepressant medication seemed to gradually stop working for no apparent reason. Fortunately, this seems to have been limited to only a few people. In most cases, an increase in dosage, a switch to another medication, or the addition of an augmenting drug seemed to solve the problem, and the change meant uninterrupted effectiveness. I have heard specific reports of Visken, Ritalin, or one of the newer antipsychotics being used as augmenting agents for this purpose. In some instances, taking a break from the medication for several weeks and then starting it up again may also work. While hearing about such happenings can cause anxiety among those people who seem to have obtained relief from only one particular medication, I would again like to repeat that this is a rather unusual thing to have happen. One does not build up tolerances to antidepressant medications, so why they occasionally stop working is unknown at the present time.

TTM may represent a different case. With this particular disorder, it is more common to hear reports of individuals where various medications repeatedly ceased to work. There is no certainty about this, and it should not keep you from using medication. Those with TTM who have experienced this setback should not feel hopeless, since many of the strategies mentioned above have been shown to work just as effectively as for those with OCD. At the same time, it makes a strong case for using behavioral therapy (Habit Reversal Training) as well.

One other case in which medication can sometimes seem to stop working may be if a person is under extreme life stress. In these cases, the medication can be temporarily overwhelmed. With counseling to help deal with the stress, or if the stress is the type that subsides on its own, the medication will usually resume working again. Again, this makes a good case for getting therapy in addition to medication, to help you become more stress resistant.

IF MEDICATIONS DON'T WORK

If standard OCSD medications don't seem to help, and you are certain that they have been correctly administered, you have several options. One, mentioned a few sections earlier, would be to make sure you have tried the various augmentation strategies in which medications are combined. Sometimes the combination of two medications will work even where neither has worked alone. If this doesn't help, you could move on to try a combination of three medications. Granted, this is a lot of medication to take, and no one would argue that this course of action is the most desirable, but if your own particular chemistry makes you a complicated person to medicate, there may be few other drug options. If you have failed to get results due to extreme drug sensitivity, it may be that trying some of your previous medications again, in microdoses, may be the answer (see above section "Medications Used to Treat OCSDs").

A second consideration is whether or not you have tried behavioral therapy. It can add considerably to your efforts and if no medications work for you, this alone can still help you to greatly reduce your anxiety, while getting your behavior under control. Also, don't assume that because you were told you had behavior therapy that it is safe to assume that you did actually receive it. Make certain that it was Exposure and Response Prevention (for classic OCD and BDD), or Habit Reversal Training (for TTM, skin picking, or nail biting), that it was done for an appropriate length of time, and that it was directed by a qualified practitioner.

A third option you could investigate might be to check to see if there are any experimental drug programs in your area. I know that some people get nervous about trying medications that are still being tested. The fact is, however, I have had quite a number of patients improve with the drugs they received in programs like these. Remember, many drugs that are still experimental in this country have actually been used effectively for many years in Europe. This information is not difficult to obtain. The medication you receive is free, and in some programs, if you improve while on it, you may be able to keep getting it at no charge until it is actually approved for release to consumers. At the same time, you will be making a valuable contribution to the treatment of OCD.

Drug studies generally fall into two categories. The first type of program is called an "open label study," and you are simply given the experimental drug either for a fixed period of a number of weeks or indefinitely, if it is helping you. Another type of experimental program conducted is known as a "double-blind study." In studies of this type, you may either receive the actual drug, or be given what is known as a placebo or inert substance. In either case, the drug you are taking is not revealed to you. This is done in order to test whether the experimental drug truly has an effect, or whether participants are improving simply because they believe they are on something effective (this is, of course, known as the "placebo effect"). Even the physicians administering the drugs are not told which one you are actually getting so that they cannot influence your reaction. If you are given a placebo first, rather than the drug being tested, you will be given the actual drug afterward and vice versa. Some double-blind studies will allow you to continue to take the medication after you have finished, if it has helped you. The OC Foundation is a good source of information about where these programs are being conducted. You might also try to contact the drug manufacturers or the National Institute of Mental Health.

If you have tried these suggestions but are still looking for further relief, another option would be to import a medication, an antidepressant from Great Britain or Canada that is not on the FDA's banned list. European pharmacies that are willing to cooperate in doing this can easily be located on the Internet. I know this sounds a bit extreme, but it is currently legal, provided you are under a physician's care, have a legitimate prescription for it, and have it shipped to your physician who will then dispense it to you. Some physicians might be reluctant to do this, but you may find one who will if you ask around. In any case, don't give up. New medications and combinations are constantly being discovered or developed. Two recent discoveries that are typical of this come to mind. For example, I recently read a report of a small-scale study by Dr. William A. Hewlett of Vanderbilt University in which a drug (Ondansetron), previously only used to treat nausea in cancer patients, was shown to be effective in reducing the symptoms of OCD in three of eight patients. There are also some recent case reports indicating that the analgesic Ultram (tramadol) may be of use. While such findings may not help everyone, there may be a number of sufferers for whom other medications were ineffective, and who may now be helped by one of these medications.

There is one further option. There has recently been a revival in the use of neurosurgery for those whose OCD has failed to respond to any treatment whatsoever. This is a rather tricky subject to discuss without a great deal of emotion and distaste because of the many well-known past abuses in the use of brain surgery to treat mental disorders. Years ago, neurosurgery, particularly the prefrontal lobotomy, was used to alarming and reckless excess. It was conducted wholesale, with little care for the well-being of patients, and used for conditions where it was totally inappropriate and even criminal. It was also done on a rather large scale, and many of the victims whose brains were irreversibly damaged remain as permanent residents of state hospitals. There are currently four forms of neurosurgery being performed to treat OCD. They are anterior cingulotomy, subcaudate tractotomy, limbic leucotomy, and anterior capsulotomy.

What all these procedures have in common is that they are designed to interrupt the nerve pathways that run between the frontal areas and either the striatum or the thalamus. In the anterior cingulotomy (currently the more common type of procedure used in the U.S.) and limbic leucotomy, two small holes are made in the skull, thin electric probes are inserted, one on each side of the brain, and the tips are heated, destroying tiny areas of tissue believed to be the site of the OC processing problems. A study conducted by Dr. Michael Jenike and others estimated the success rate of the anterior cingulotomy at about 25 percent to 30 percent of treatment resistant cases being significantly improved. The subcaudate tractotomy involves the use of two thin radioactive rods, again, inserted on either side of the brain. There are actually two types of capsulotomies. One involves the insertion of two probes with electrically heated tips, similar to the procedures mentioned above. The other type is known as a gamma capsulotomy and uses a device called the Leksell Gamma Knife, which is not a knife at all, but which uses a beam of tightly focused gamma rays to destroy a tiny area of brain tissue about 1 mm in diameter. It is not an invasive technique, in that it does not require the opening of the skull. These surgeries are not without possible side effects, which can include hemorrhage, seizures, increased fatigue, apathy, and poor memory.

To prevent its indiscriminate use, no one can just walk in and get this treatment. Very strict requirements must be met for someone to qualify for it, and all candidates are carefully screened. Hospitals that offer this treatment usually insist that you meet something like the following criteria (these may vary a bit from center to center):

1. You must have had your illness for longer than five years.

2. Your disorder must be an extremely severe one, almost completely limiting your ability to function (i.e., being housebound, unable to work or care for yourself, etc.).

3. You must have systematically tried all available treatment options for a minimum of five years without result or have had to discontinue pharmacological treatment due to side effects.

4. You must be between the ages of twenty and sixty-five.

5. There must be no other complicating brain problem or history of substance abuse.

Even those meeting these criteria will be hospitalized for several weeks to try some renewed intensive treatment just to be even more certain that nothing was left out. Risks must be spelled out to patients in detail and in advance, and informed consent must be obtained. Obviously, this is, and should only be, considered a treatment of last resort. Its use should only be contemplated in an extremely desperate case, where all treatments have failed and suicide is almost certain if some relief is not found. Treatments that cause irreversible changes in a person's brain should never be regarded casually. The success rate of these treatments seems to average about 40 percent when you look over the various studies, and then results may only be partial. There may also be irreversible physical aftereffects. After surgical treatment, behavioral therapy is recommended as a follow-up. Medication is usually still necessary after the surgery and for some it may work better than before. It is still unclear to researchers exactly why and how neurosurgery works for OCD. Much more remains to be known about this type of treatment.

DISCONTINUING MEDICATION ONCE SYMPTOMS IMPROVE

One of the first questions people ask when they begin taking medications for their OCSDs is, "How long will I have to be on this?" Whether or not you will be able to eventually discontinue your medication is something to be determined on an individual basis. Based on my clinical experience, I believe this is best accomplished by making no changes in medication levels until a twelve- to eighteen-month period of recovery has elapsed. It is recommended first to have a good span of time in which life has normalized and your new healthier habits have taken hold. At this point, your physician can provide a schedule for gradually reducing the medications. As they are reduced, individuals should carefully monitor themselves for signs of returning symptoms. If symptoms come back strongly, patients are usually advised to bring the dosage back up to its previous level. If symptoms do not seem to return, then the dosage can continue to be gradually reduced until it is eliminated. Medications can always be restarted at a later date should symptoms return.

Even if you are unsuccessful at tapering off your dosage and are facing the prospect of having to stay on medication indefinitely, this isn't cause to feel disappointed or depressed. True, on a practical level, medication taken regularly can be a big expense. On an emotional level, there are some who feel stigmatized at having to take a psychiatric medication on a daily basis and thus are never able to put the disorder out of their minds. I would remind you that there are far worse prospects. Not too many years ago there were no commonly available medications for OCSDs, and there were many individuals whose desperation would have made them grateful to have any effective medication to relieve their suffering. Some were willing to spend any amount and travel anywhere to get it, so the idea of people with numerous medications to choose from worrying about how to stop taking them might seem a little ironic nowadays. Taking several pills each day would seem like a small price to pay for having a normal life and being able to function. Let me further remind you of the one alternative to discontinuation. By managing your symptoms through the use of behavior therapy, you may be able at least to reduce your medication to a lower maintenance level, even if you cannot eliminate it entirely. One other note: as mentioned in an earlier section, some individuals may not have to stay on medications for the long term. They only seem to get bouts of symptoms periodically or when they are under some particular stress. These people may find themselves taking the medications for only a few months a year or every few years. This type of intermittent OCSD, however, is probably more the exception than the rule.

ELECTROSHOCK THERAPY

Electroshock therapy, or more technically, Electroconvulsive Therapy (ECT), is not considered to be a treatment for OCD. It is most commonly used as a treatment of last resort for severe cases of major depression, where medications have not produced any improvement and suicide is a possibility. I have encountered many individuals who were wrongly treated with ECT for classic OCD, and I have never met anyone whose symptoms were helped by it. ECT can at least result in temporary memory loss, and there are those who allege that it can cause subtle types of brain problems, although this has not been experimentally verified.

SPECIAL DIETS OR SUPPLEMENTS

To my knowledge, there are no special diets that have been conclusively shown to be scientifically effective in directly relieving the symptoms of OCD. There are some who believe that their symptoms are the result of the lack of serotonin, the chief neurotransmitter implicated in the disorder; however, this has not been proven to be true. The only real dietary recommendation I am aware of would be to decrease or discontinue the use of caffeine, as it is a stimulant, and as such can contribute to feelings of anxiety in some sufferers.

The story on supplements has been a bit more interesting. It has been suggested by some researchers over the years that large doses of the amino acid L-Tryptophan can be helpful in treating OCD, as this compound is known to be the chemical precursor (or raw material) of serotonin, the chief neurotransmitter implicated in the disorder. Overall results of testing L-Tryptophan have been mixed. That is, there are several studies which suggested that it may, in fact, help to alleviate the symptoms of OCD; however, there are also studies which showed it to be ineffective. There are other studies which showed it to be hazardous if taken together with antidepressant medications, causing what is known as Serotonergic Syndrome. Discussions of this compound are mostly theoretical at this time. The FDA has banned L-Tryptophan in recent years as its manufacture was found to be faulty, causing a syndrome called Eosinophilia Myalgia, which resulted in a number of serious and even fatal hematological reactions. Even if it should make its return to the market, it still has not been properly tested under controlled scientific study for OCD. Claims about its usefulness are therefore not verified at this time. L-Tryptophan can be obtained with a doctor's prescription, although I have not seen it widely used for many years. One further note on this subject, there is currently being marketed a substance known as 5-HTP, which is what the body converts L-Tryptophan to, before converting it to serotonin. It is claimed that 5-HTP does not cause the same problems as L-Tryptophan, as it is derived from a completely different source. While I have heard some reports of its being helpful, there is not much available information at this time concerning possible side effects, other than that it is known to cause drowsiness and is usually taken at bedtime. As far as dosage is concerned, it is said that a dosage of between 100 and 300 mg per day is the effective range. This has yet to be verified by research. Also, it should not be taken together with prescription antidepressants, as Serotonergic Syndrome may result. There are many unanswered questions about this supplement, and more needs to be known about it before its use can be recommended.

Much more promising is the use of one of the B vitamins, Inositol. While this vitamin has been known since the early 1970s to have an effect on anxiety and depression, it was never thoroughly studied. More recent well-designed studies have shown it to be effective in the treatment of classic OCD, depression, and anxiety. While these studies are small, the results are impressive, and Inositol is being used either alone or to augment antidepressant medications for those who have not seen good results. Informally, I have also seen Inositol produce some results when used to treat TTM. Large amounts of the vitamin are required: up to 18 grams of Inositol in powdered form were taken daily in the studies, however, overdosage does not appear to be a problem, as this is a water soluble vitamin and does not build up high levels in your body tissues. In the research, adult participants took three, 6-gram doses dissolved in juice each day over a period of six weeks. Improvement was seen as long as participants took the Inositol. Few, if any, side effects were reported. Among these have been diarrhea and gas, which are temporary in many cases. Larger and better-controlled studies of Inositol still need to be conducted. Recently, I have seen Inositol work in several cases of TTM. In one of these cases, it was even more successful when combined with 100 mg of 5-HTP. On a practical note, those I know who have taken Inositol successfully seem to tolerate it better when they gradually build up to their highest dosage level over a period of about six weeks. They usually start with 4 grams per day, divided into two doses. Eventually, at higher doses, it is taken three times per day. It does not appear that everyone needs to take 18 grams per day as was done experimentally. I have seen some adults report improvement on as little as 2 grams per day. In cases where Inositol has been given to children, smaller doses amounting to one-half of adult levels or less (depending on the child's weight and age) have also seemed to work well and are probably necessary due to their having a smaller body mass. I have also heard that caffeine can deplete the body of Inositol, so if you do try it, it may be wise to cut your intake of beverages containing it. One caution concerning Inositol is that it can interfere with the action of Lithium if you are already taking that drug. As with any therapeutic treatments, always be sure to get professional advice before using Inositol or any other compound yourself.

Many claims have been made for the ability of various herbal remedies to treat OCSDs. With one possible exception, there is no evidence that any of these claims are true. That exception is St. John's Wort. This herbally derived medication has been used for years to treat depression in European countries. The active ingredient is known as hypericin, and appears to inhibit the reuptake of serotonin in a manner similar to SSRIs. Thus far, there has been only one published open-label study. In this study, St. John's Wort was shown to produce significant positive changes in the symptoms of seven participants with classic OCD. While it only a small study, the results were interesting. Subjects took 450 mg. of St. John's Wort with a strength of .03 percent hypericin twice daily for nine weeks. This remedy bears further study, and may prove to be another compound available to help OCSD sufferers.

There have also been certain disreputable practitioners claiming that OCD is the result of allergies, body-wide yeast infections, nutritional deficiencies, inner ear problems, etc. I have also had patients go off their prescribed medications in order to try untested herbal remedies or homeopathic medicines. All of these people had setbacks which lasted until they got back on their prescribed medications again. One word on nonprescription treatments you may hear about: do not be misled by claims that natural or herbal compounds are somehow superior to prescription drugs, or better for you, simply because they are natural. Your body cannot tell the difference between a manufactured chemical and one from a natural source. Any compound which alters your brain or body chemistry should be considered a drug. St. John's Wort is a good example of this. People who offer this kind of treatment without proper testing do not deserve your attention. Their work is unscientific and shoddy and their claims cannot be substantiated by any real data. Their evidence usually amounts to their own claims to having seen their treatment work or a few unverified testimonials. They promise rapid, simple cures. In actuality, they separate a lot of desperate individuals from their hard-earned money, and leave them nothing to show for it. The finest scientific minds are still puzzling over OCSDs, so beware of anyone who claims to "know it all" or to have found "the magic bullet." As the old saying goes, "If it sounds too good to be true, it probably is."

WHEN YOU CAN'T AFFORD MEDICATION

Medication for the treatment of OCSDs can be expensive, running to quite a few dollars per day for those on higher doses or drug combinations. This is fine for those with the financial resources or low cost drug plans, but not so good for sufferers with modest incomes or those who are disabled by their disorder. One way around this is to establish a relationship with a compassionate physician who is willing to supply you with some of the free samples that the drug company salespeople frequently give away. This may get you by; however, if you need a large daily dose over a long period of time, it may not be feasible.

Another alternative is to turn to one of the assistance programs which most of the drug companies maintain for the benefit of those who cannot otherwise afford their products. In order to be accepted you and your physician will have to fill out applications, and you may have to submit financial information, proving that your income and savings are below a certain level. If you are accepted into one of these programs, they will either send free medication directly to your physician to be dispensed to you, or they will send a voucher that your physician will give you together with a prescription to take to your drug store. The voucher will then be accepted as payment.

Your physician can obtain a comprehensive listing of these assistance programs from The Pharmaceutical Research and Manufacturers Association. Have your doctor call (202) 835-3450 to have a copy sent to them. You or your physician can then call these programs to find out how to apply. Here is a list of some of these programs:

Celexa:	Forest Pharmaceutical Company Indigent Patient Program	(800) 678-1605 (physician's line)
Effexor:	Wyeth-Ayerst Labs	(800) 568-9936 (physician's line)
Luvox:	Solvay Patient Assistance Program	(800) 788-9277
Paxil:	SmithKline Paxil Access To Care Program	(800) 546-0420 (patient's line) (215) 751-5722 (physician's line)
Prozac:	Lily Cares Program	(800) 545-6962
Zoloft:	Pfizer Prescription Assistance	(800) 646-4455

~ OCSDs and Children

The joys of parents are secret, and so are their griefs and fears.
—Francis Bacon

We cannot form children on our own concepts; we must take them
and love them as God gives them to us.
—Goethe

People of all ages can develop OCSDs. Most studies conducted to
determine when they can start have focused on classic OCD, and
they generally agree that the average age of onset for OCD seems
to fall somewhere between nineteen and a half and twenty-two years of
age. These numbers may not be entirely accurate. It may actually begin
earlier than this, due to its being unrecognized by children and parents
alike. I have had a large number of patients who claim that they have had
symptoms from as early as they can remember—around the age of two
or three. Figures from the National Institute of Mental Health (NIMH)
tell us that 9.7 percent of the sufferers have classic OCD by ages five to
ten, that 20.8 percent have it by ages ten to fifteen, and 41.9 percent by
ages fifteen to twenty. Among children, more males have classic OCD
than females. However, females seem to catch up by adulthood, when the
overall ratio of adult males to adult females becomes equal. Additionally,
there are studies that suggest that the highest occurrence of the onset of
symptoms among children is around the age of seven to eight.

The ages at which the other OCSDs begin have yet to be studied adequately and remain unknown at this time. Most of the children I have

treated for TTM seem to have started somewhere between the ages of seven and twelve. The earliest reported age I have heard for the onset of TTM was in an infant of about eighteen months.

RECOGNIZING OCSDs IN CHILDREN

If you think your child has some form of OCSD, you may want to consult a therapist for an official diagnosis. This is a task that should not be difficult for a well trained professional but can be very difficult for a parent, teacher, or anyone else inexperienced in recognizing OCSDs. Pediatricians, as a group, often prove to be unhelpful, telling parents such things as, "Your child will grow out of it," or, "Let's wait and see." Sadly, they have not been trained to spot these disorders and seldom know what questions to ask. What complicates the matter is that children can often behave superstitiously, tend to perseverate in doing certain routine things in the same way each day, do favorite things repetitiously, and can have unusual fears. While there is always a risk of overdiagnosing and mislabeling normal behavior, OCD is probably more likely to be overlooked in children. Let us not forget that for roughly 31 percent of those with classic OCD, it begins at some time before the age of fifteen. This works out to about one in every two hundred schoolchildren.

The following factors are among those that complicate our ability to diagnose children:

1. OCSDs can be very hidden problems, and children can be quite secretive about their thoughts and feelings. Often, they will not volunteer information unless asked, and many times they are not.

2. Children, especially the very young, often do not have the insight or the expressive abilities to realize or let us know that they are having a problem until it begins to seriously affect them.

3. Sometimes these behaviors can be difficult to diagnose as young ones normally tend to be superstitious about certain things and may have many little rituals for getting through the day.

4. Adolescents are extremely image conscious and will frequently refuse to admit that they are having difficulties, even when these difficulties are both obvious and severe. Pressing them to admit it usually brings an angry response.

5. Parents, understandably, often have a tendency to deny that anything may be seriously wrong with their child. No one wants to believe that they no longer have that "perfect" child they thought they had.

6. Obsessions, as purely mental events, cannot be observed in children or anyone else. Compulsions can often be difficult to spot as well. Unless they are very repetitive, particularly bizarre, or attract attention in some other way, they may go unnoticed. Many children will only do them when they are alone so as not to attract attention.

7. There actually are times when children are articulate enough to tell us that something is wrong, but unfortunately, we frequently do not take the time to listen to what they have to say about themselves. We either make assumptions about their behavior without any evidence or discount what they are trying to communicate as "childish."

8. Many professionals who treat children are not properly trained to spot OCSDs. Frequently, a few simple questions, had they been asked, would have revealed a disorder. Where symptoms are obvious, they often pass them off as something that the child will "grow out of."

There are certain signs and symptoms which are particular to OCSDs, and which are not a part of normal development in children. They are not difficult to spot if you know what to look for. (Please note that the following indicators may be signs of other types of problems as well. They are only presented here as general guidelines.)

One of the most important general signs is the way the suspected problem appears to be affecting your child's ability to function. A child's functioning in school or social situations with friends or family is frequently a good barometer of how serious a problem may be, particularly if there has been a recent noticeable change. Socially, look for withdrawal from situations that were formerly enjoyable or at least tolerated. Also, look for fears of doing anything new or different. In school, look for the following: a marked drop in grades; inattention in class; forgetfulness or great upset about assignments; avoidance of particular class activities in which they used to participate; great difficulty in making up their minds when answering questions in class or on tests; excessive questioning of the teacher; unusual slowness or perfectionism in carrying out assigned tasks; and the use of illness and other excuses to avoid attending school. They may be extremely preoccupied with their thoughts, and poor classroom attention and concentration have often been mistaken in the past for the presence of attention deficit disorder. In addition, with children who are having obsessions about being perfect, you may also see a lot of anxiety about doing assignments perfectly, erasing mistakes until there are holes in the paper, or ripping up written work and starting all over each time an error is made.

The presence of constant worry and avoidance can often be an indicator of frightening obsessive thoughts. Children who have these thoughts may appear agitated or tense at times or be given to anger or tears more easily than in the past. Your child may show a strong reluctance to take part in everyday activities or to go somewhere, in a way that is far out of proportion to any discomfort that you might normally expect. They may refuse to give reasons, may make up reasons, or give reasons that don't seem to make sense.

The presence of unusual or very strong and specific fears may also be an indicator. While it is true that all children may have odd fears, those connected with classic OCD have a different quality and are less typical than what would be considered normal. The extreme washing, cleaning, and clothes changing seen in contamination compulsions are good examples of behavior not usually seen in children. One contamination fear seen in children is the belief that siblings or other family members are "dirty" or unclean in some way, must be avoided, and that anything they touch must either be washed or thrown away. Another frequently seen fear is that of choking or vomiting. Such fears are usually accompanied by a refusal to eat solid foods and persistent worries about getting stomachaches or feeling nauseous. It is normal for children sometimes to worry about losing their parents or having harm come to their family. However, children with classic OCD go much further, by constantly warning them, keeping track of their whereabouts, and requiring continual reassurance that they will all be safe. Exaggerated and frequent fears of prowlers or burglars breaking into their home and harming the family can also be seen. Again, while such fears are normal to children, the degree to which children with classic OCD become preoccupied goes far beyond what is commonly seen. Parents observing these OC fears frequently ask themselves, "Why would my child even think of such things?" Some fear driven symptoms can be very subtle. One child had been taken to several urologists because he reported so many urges to urinate. No one ever really bothered to ask him why. When he was finally questioned, what actually emerged was that he obsessed about having an accident and would go to the bathroom frequently as a way of double checking if he actually had to urinate.

The frequent performance of repetitive or ritualistic behaviors, some of which may be rather strange in nature, are often the way that classic OCD is first spotted in children. These should not be mistaken for the normal rituals of childhood. Some children's games, rhymes, and songs are performed repetitiously, and some must be done according to exact rules, otherwise they must be started all over again. These only resemble OCD in a superficial way. There is no doubt or fear connected with the performance of these kinds of normal activities. Also, the level of upset that a child with OCD experiences if a ritual is disrupted or prevented is much greater. In children with classic OCD, it is common to see elaborate bedtime or saying goodbye rituals which are long, drawn out, and repetitious. They may have to follow an exact series of steps that will have to be started over from the beginning if a mistake is made on anyone's part.

Counting aloud while doing certain activities or having to say certain repetitious phrases or sentences at special times (although not during games) may also be seen. Nonverbal rituals such as touching or arranging objects in special ways or having to walk or step in particular ways can also be a part of classic OCD. Be certain if your child is very young, that he or she isn't simply playing a game in such cases.

Hair pulling and nail biting may also be seen in the very young. There is one type of hair pulling which emerges around the age of five, but which only lasts a few months and then subsides. If your child suddenly seems to be lacking eyebrows or eyelashes, or you begin to notice thinning patches of hair or bald spots or severely bitten nails, you can be pretty certain you are not simply dealing with a "nervous habit." Because of their visibility, TTM, skin picking, and nail biting can be somewhat easier to spot in children than some of the other OCSDs. Also, you may be able to actually observe a child in the act of pulling hair or biting their nails. Secondary signs may include excessive time spent in front of mirrors and a lot of touching or twirling of hair with the fingers. While nail biting is not unusual in children, you may see it done to a much more damaging extent in a child with an OCSD. Painful, bleeding fingertips are common. The biting of cuticles and the skin on fingers and hands can also be a part of this. You may also see little rituals with the bitten nails or pulled hairs or find that the child is making a collection of them. Toenails can be treated similarly.

Extreme doubt and repetitive questioning are frequent markers for classic OCD. Your child may ask the same question dozens of times and in many different ways, never seeming to be able to grasp the answer. Their need for reassurance can seem endless. A favorite topic for obsessive children is to ask over and over if they, their parents, their relatives, or even their pets are going to be "all right." The opposite may also be present, as they continually question whether they may have done something wrong or harmed someone else. When not questioning others, children may engage in constant checking in order to reassure themselves. Another sign of this doubt is difficulty in making even the smallest decisions. Deciding what clothes to wear to school or what to order at the fast food restaurant can be agonizing for OC children. Their indecision can often be a cause of lateness and is almost always a cause of parental anger.

Your child's need to strongly and unreasonably control others and their environment may sometimes mean more than that you simply have a willful child. The things they insist on tend not to be average, and the strength of their insistence and the emotion behind it can be very powerful. There are stages of development around the age of two to three years, where children must have certain items in the home kept in special spots or do not allow furniture or other things to be rearranged, but this is not considered normal in older children. It is not unusual for children with perfectionistic or magical types of symptoms to have to arrange items in special orders, to make them symmetrical, to line things up, or to clean marks or smudges off walls or appliances. They tend to try to keep their rooms especially perfect and their possessions pristine. Their rooms will usually be made off-limits to other family members, and they themselves may even have difficulty entering due to a fear of dirtying things or messing them up in some way. Family members may also be asked to participate in rituals, to say or not say certain things, or to move, straighten, or arrange things at the child's request. They may also be asked to go or not go to certain places. Failure of family members to cooperate may bring a flood of tears or a temper tantrum.

The presence of tics may be a warning sign for the presence of OCD in a child. Tics are most prevalent in those classic OCD sufferers whose symptoms began in childhood. In many cases, the tics preceded the OCD. As many as 50 percent of those with classic OCD may also have motor tics or twitches. These body tics alone would not qualify as Tourette's Syndrome for which vocal tics (blurting out, grunting, swallowing, barking, yelping, cursing, coughing, sniffing, throat clearing, clicking, etc.) must also be present. A number of my patients have reported the presence of tics in childhood that disappeared as they matured. Some tics can be easily mistaken for other things, such as the case of an eight-year-old boy who sniffed continually and was taken to several allergists with no result. It ultimately turned out that the sniffing was actually a type of tic that the child had an urge to perform. As often happens, no one had ever thought to ask the child the obvious question as to why he needed to do it. If tics are noticed, professional diagnosis may be necessary to determine whether you are dealing with a motor or vocal tic disorder or Tourette's. OCD should not be immediately ruled out in such cases either. Compulsive touching or movement rituals can sometimes look like motor tics but are intentionally done for magical reasons and so would be considered OCD. Children with these may also have to walk in certain ways or step on certain spots on the floor.

Perfectionism may be seen as a part of any of the above symptoms and generally plays a large role in OCSDs. Children can often see things as extremes in their thinking and can believe that things must be perfect or else they are no good at all. Perfectionism may also be a response to the serious doubts that are central to classic OCD. If such doubt can be a torture to an adult who has better reasoning capacities, imagine what the experience must be like for your child. Children with TTM may be seen to behave perfectionistically, pulling particular hairs that seem different or don't look or feel right to make their appearance perfect.

Symptoms of problems like facial skin picking and BDD are more likely to be seen in adolescents rather than in younger children. Look for an adolescent spending excessive time in front of the mirror, refusing to go out in public, using clothing or makeup as camouflage, or asking numerous questions about their appearance. In the case of skin picking, look for the obvious skin damage it causes. The types of sores or bleeding caused by this compulsion go far beyond ordinary teenage acne.

In addition to some of the symptoms mentioned above, children seem to experience the same broad range of symptoms that adults do. These symptoms do not usually seem to depend on the child's age either. I have seen children as young as four who experienced morbid sexual thoughts, as well as five-year-old hand washers.

The variety of symptoms that can be observed in one child can be found in Bruce's description of what he lived through as a child and adolescent.

Bruce's Story

∿ *"Taboo," the ultimate word that comes to mind when I think of my intrusive thoughts. I thought of having homosexual relations; incest with all of my relatives; and the most horrifying murder scenes. I thought of hurting myself and others too. I never actually followed through with these intrusive thoughts, but I did actually believe I was going to. I started to believe I was a homosexual and perverted monster. As a child, I didn't know what to think. As an adolescent, I still didn't fully understand.*

Some of the rituals I did throughout my childhood and adolescence included touching things more than once. I switched the light switch on and off at least a hundred times. I would check under my bed every night. I checked the zipper on my pants to see if it was open. I always checked the back of my jacket in order to see if anybody had put a sticker on it. I was very paranoid and felt very insecure. I also washed my hands more than needed.

The reason I did these rituals was to satisfy my intrusive thoughts. If I thought my dog was going to be killed, then I would touch my left fingers together three times and then touch both sets together, then I would switch to my right hand and so on and so forth. This ritual lasted for about fifteen minutes and was very secretive. But if I accidentally touched something else during this ritual, then I would have to do the whole ritual over. I could sometimes spend about forty-five minutes on one ritual. I am still not sure why I chose to do things three times instead of picking an even number, and I still am not certain why I did many of these rituals. Sometimes I did these rituals out of habit and other times I did them so my thoughts would not come true. I suppose it was a superstitious sort of thing.

This section would not be complete without this parent's experience with her son's serious illness, which is typical in a number of ways.

Bobby's Story

~ *As I crawled around on the floor searching for the lost Lego block I realized I was actually* PRAYING *to find it. "No big deal," I thought, but then I'd been there before, and all too many times. We had two older children and though there had been an occasional crisis over a lost toy, we could usually work it out by distraction or substitution when the search failed. Not with this child. We* HAD *to find it. Incidents such as this made me aware very early that Bobby could not manage to "let a thought go."*

I suppose Bobby's first symptoms of OCD were manifest before he was two years old, though for some time we only recognized his habits as being interesting. His play always focused around a single interest with no variation. Bobby's first obsessive interest that we noticed was his playing with music tapes and records. He wore out several cassette tape recorders before he was six years old, then moved on to a consuming interest in baseball cards.

The intensity of Bobby's world increased as he entered school. He was always fearful of the future and needed to depend on routines for some security. Even sleep does not relieve his anxiety as he has always awakened once or more during each night to ask for comfort in some way.

It was during Bobby's ninth year of life that his first really troublesome obsessions began to take form. In the summer after completing the fourth grade, he spent many hours sitting on the couch worrying that something horrible that he could not control would take over his body and compel him to do things that he did not wish to do. He had a relentless fear that he would someday become addicted to illegal drugs. No amount of parental assurance made a difference. He would think up many solutions to this problem, only to abandon them soon after. He once had us hide his money from him so that when the time came that he would be compelled to buy drugs, he would not have access to any money. This "solution" relieved him for about five minutes. The ruminations brought depression and less ability than ever to deal with any stress. Our first request for help was from our family doctor. He listened well and prescribed BuSpar to help relieve his anxieties. We saw no effect. Every new beginning and ending causes some sort of stress for anyone, so the beginning of fifth grade caused problems that led us to take Bobby to a hospital for psychological evaluation. They listened and referred us to a psychologist for therapy.

There was no particular diagnosis given and after six weeks of weekly sessions (talking about relationships and drawing pictures), Bobby and I agreed that this was not a help. It was the following summer that the depression became so severe that Bobby repeatedly expressed his wish to "just get out of this life."

I chose a child psychiatrist in a university town. On our first visit, I handed the doctor an outline of Bobby's behavior. She read the notes, asked my husband and me a few questions, and said, "Your son has Obsessive-Compulsive Disorder." We admitted Bobby to a psychiatric hospital that day and canceled Amtrak and hotel reservations we had made for a planned vacation the next week. Bobby entered the hospital willingly, no more fearful or anxious than he already was. We met with a social worker who said words that I had never heard before. "Your son has a mental illness." I tried these words out with my own voice, "My son has a mental illness," and for the first time began to comprehend what it was that we were struggling so hard to overcome. I found that to treat an illness, we must first name it and come to accept it. We then better understood Bobby's need to repeat certain words many times, sometimes silently, yet almost constantly some days. We had some insight into his pattern of changing TV channels, always turning the dial to numbers that went down numerically because to go up would indicate getting "high" (as if on drugs).

CHILDHOOD OCSDs AND STREP INFECTIONS

Over the last few years, a growing body of research suggests that certain children may be susceptible to having classic OCD and tic disorders triggered by strep throat infections. There are also some possible indications of a link to TTM as well. This may sound unbelievable at first, however, these children are currently being identified and treated at such a distinguished facility as the NIMH. Although I, myself, was a bit skeptical on first hearing about this, I have since helped to identify a number of children within my own practice.

Strep apparently leads to the onset of classic OCD and tics through an autoimmune reaction, in which the antibodies produced by the child to combat streptococcus bacteria attack particular areas of the child's brain. This syndrome is known as PANDAS, which stands for Pediatric Autoimmune Neuropsychiatric Disorders Associated with Streptococcal infections. This process is thought to be similar to rheumatic fever, which is also an autoimmune disease, and seen to occur in children ranging in age from three to puberty. PANDAS is actually believed to be a variant of rheumatic fever. There is also some speculation that PANDAS may actually be brought about through an underlying genetic predisposition. Some guidelines have been established to better aid in diagnosing possible cases of PANDAS. These include

- having symptoms of classic OCD and/or a tic disorder.
- onset of symptoms between the ages of three and puberty.
- symptoms which wax and wane in severity.
- the presence of a strep infection as evidenced by positive throat culture (group A B-hemolytic strep) and/or high levels of antistreptococcal antibody titer (indicated through anti-DNAase B and antistreptococcal titer blood tests).

A very important sign of PANDAS is the suddenness of the onset of OC symptoms or tics. Parents can often give an exact date when symptoms began. I have made it a routine practice, when seeing a child for the first time, to ask if the child has had a history of repeated strep infections, if the onset of their symptoms was sudden, and if the current symptoms appeared to follow a recent strep infection. Where PANDAS is present, you will see positive results from the tests for titers and/or a positive throat culture when symptoms are worse. These tests may show negative results when symptoms are fewer and milder. Ideally, testing should be done when symptoms are worse, which they will be a few days or weeks following a strep infection. I have recently begun to wonder whether all children being brought in for treatment of OCSDs or tics ought to be given a routine screening for strep. Perhaps this eventually will be recommended.

At first, treatment for PANDAS involved the long-term administration of antibiotics. While this would often show results within ten days, the safety of taking these drugs over long periods of time is now being questioned. Aside from this, it is still recommended that this group of children be treated with a full course of antibiotics whenever an episode of strep occurs. Other treatments that are still being tested include plasmapheresis (filtering of the antibodies from the child's blood), and immunoglobulin given intravenously. A number of the children I have identified received treatment with antibiotics, and a number of them did so well that only a little follow-up behavioral therapy was required. They were spared lengthy therapy or having to take any psychiatric medications. Of these, a few have come back for brush-up sessions, following recurrences of strep, but overall have done well. Further information about diagnosis and treatment can be obtained from NIMH or the OC Foundation (see chapter 13 for addresses and phone numbers). If you seek information about this syndrome from your pediatrician, don't be surprised if they haven't heard about it.

PANDAS is still not very well known. Perhaps you can help educate them and this, in turn, will lead to some other child getting help.

COMING TO TERMS WITH YOUR CHILD'S DISORDER

Speaking as both a clinical psychologist and the parent of a special needs child, I can appreciate how easy it is for professionals to sit there and give others advice on how to step back and be objective about your child's disorder. I know that it took me a lot of work to accept my own son's difficulties. I think that I can at least share with you some of the things I have learned over the years.

Professionals will often start out by telling you not to become disturbed or upset at your child's symptoms, but I will not do this. Such feelings are a natural reaction and a measure of your protectiveness toward your children, especially when you see them behaving uncontrollably and doing unusual things that other people's children are not doing. It is also natural to feel your child's pain. If you didn't feel distress, what would motivate you to get help for them?

Feeling distressed is where you begin, but it is not where you should stay. It is a place to move beyond. This is accomplished by recognizing these feelings and then getting them out in the open by talking to those who are close to you. It is important that you see your reactions as normal and to work toward accepting that these problems really exist, are chronic, and will not simply go away on their own. I found that going through this phase of things was very difficult, and that I could hardly discuss the matter with anyone without becoming extremely sad and upset. As I discovered, the more you talk about the pain, the more it subsides. It is a grieving process, where you are working through mourning the loss of that *perfect* child you thought you were going to have (see chapter 7). Eventually, you will come to the point where you can discuss it without as much pain, even though there will always be a place deep inside where some still exists. I believe that this is what we call acceptance.

When you have reached this step, it is important to avoid a particular trap. Resist the temptation to blame yourself or indulge in needless hours of soul-searching to discover what it was you did that was wrong. In the past, psychoanalytic theory encouraged this type of thinking by placing blame on parenting and development. This caused a lot of pointless suffering and self-recrimination. The scientific evidence has discredited these theories and tells us that OCSDs are actually neurobiological disorders that are most likely genetically based (see chapter 12). This means you did not cause your child's problem. Even if you have handled it badly in the past, there is still no point in blaming yourself. No one starts out prepared to handle these things perfectly. In truth, you will never handle them perfectly. No one does. This is because there are no per-fect parents, and raising a child with an OCSD can be extremely stressful. To learn to do better takes time, and mistakes are inevitable. Sometimes you must first do the wrong things in order to discover for yourself that they don't work. In this way, you eventually find out what the right things are. The main thing is that you keep educating yourself and learn from your mistakes. It is fine to regret making mistakes, but it is unproductive and illogical to keep flogging yourself because of them.

Do not blame your child either. This is also senseless. They did not suddenly develop this disorder to deliberately make your life miserable. Imagining that there are bad motives behind their behavior is an easy mistake to make. Some parents I have met actually think that their child is trying to punish them. What child would be capable of thinking up such a thing? Children with OCSDs are victims of their own genetics and no more responsible for their disorder than if they had asthma or diabetes. Don't anger yourself at them because they cannot always be in good control of themselves. You can be misled by the fact that they can appear to control their behaviors some of the time. Children with OCSDs are able to delay or postpone symptoms at times when they absolutely have no choice. Also, OCSDs can wax and wane. It is okay to set realistic limits for your child but do it in a firm and caring way, rather than making it seem that you are punishing them. Put the anger and the blame aside. It will only create a gulf between you and your child that will be difficult to cross, if it ever does get crossed. Your child may not have been angry with you before but may become so, as they sense your anger and rejection.

If your child is in treatment, learn to curb your impatience. It is true that they are responsible for helping themselves, but they don't have to be ready or mature enough for the job just because you say they must be. One of the keys to understanding child psychology is readiness. Children will only do things when they have grown to the point where they can do them.

As a parent and a psychologist, I suggest that you do not treat your child's disorder as some shameful and horrifying secret, which will put an indelible blot on your family and cause others to shun your child as if he or she carried the plague. This is your beloved child we are talking about—not someone to be ashamed of or to apologize to others for. This is how your child was given to you. If you take this negative view of your child, you risk convincing them to think about themselves in this way as well. A good part of the work I must do as a psychologist involves destigmatizing my patients. They often feel that they cannot be helped and do not deserve to recover. Feeling like an unworthy and inferior human being will make your child's recovery that much more difficult.

Do not concern yourself with what others will think about your child. As Roy C. of OC Anonymous likes to say, it is none of your business. If you worry about how it will reflect on you, then you are thinking selfishly. In any case, you cannot control what others think. Anyone who rejects you or your child based on the presence of a disorder is someone whose opinion is worthless anyway. I tell people that my son is *my perfect child*. Every child is a complete person in their own right, with strengths and weaknesses just like any other human being. Try not to lose sight of the person behind the disorder. They are more than a mere collection of symptoms and just as worthy of love and respect as any other individual. Just keep accepting them, listening to them, loving them, and supporting their efforts to do better. If you have done this, then you have done a lot.

EXPLAINING THE DISORDER TO A CHILD

A lot of how you explain the disorder depends on the child. Some children, even young ones, are extremely bright and perceptive and can be told the facts. This is also true of older children and adolescents. What level of information you wish to give them concerning genetics, brain chemistry, and the power of habit will have to be tailored to their ability to understand. Just make sure that you educate yourself adequately, so that the information you give them is accurate.

There is one way in which you should not be misled by a child's intelligence and understanding. Whatever a child's age or intelligence, they must still be reassured that they are not bad or crazy, and that you do not love or accept them any less because of it. They must also be told that it is not their fault, nor is it anybody else's fault. Make a point of telling them that you understand that they are suffering, and that you will be with them the whole way until they are feeling better, just as you would with any problem.

Many children will be struck by the fact that it is "unfair" that they should have this, when their friends do not. While it may not be terribly reassuring, it should be stressed to them that many other people have similar problems and that they are not alone. You may have to get a bit philosophical at this point about the fact that many things in life are unfair but must be faced anyway. Fairness really has nothing to do with it. These things just happen to people. It may be helpful to point out to them others who are familiar to them who also have disabilities or difficulties to deal with. They may wish to know if they will always have their problem. Let them know that there is help, and if they are willing to work, they can learn to control it, so that it does not control their life or bother them any more. Expect that they may have to go through periods of denial, anger, and sadness as they learn to accept the fact that they really do have a problem. Achieving this acceptance will take time.

TREATMENT FOR THE CHILD WITH OCD

To make sure your child gets the proper kind of help, I will outline in this section the way I handle typical cases. Other therapists may not follow the same pattern; however, it will at least give you an idea of what to expect.

Preadolescent Children

I have often found that children under the ages of ten or eleven require therapy to be handled in a somewhat different way from adults. We still utilize behavior therapy in the form of either Exposure and Response Prevention (for OCD or BDD) or Habit Reversal Training (for TTM, skin picking, or nail biting), whichever is appropriate. However, the way in which we get them to take part in it is where the difference lies. Let's face it, confronting your fears means discomfort and hard work, neither of which is usually easy to get children to accept. The therapy is not instantly rewarding in the short run, and young children do not tend to be long-range thinkers. They cannot be forced into therapy, and it should not be made into a test of wills. What I try to do, instead, is to make the building of motivation a part of the therapy and to make getting well as rewarding as possible.

I do this by using a system of what is known technically among behavioral psychologists as "contingency management." That is, I try to reward the desirable therapy-related behaviors and try to deny any type of reward or payoff for the undesirable compulsive behaviors. This is actually an old and proven technique in helping parents manage their children's behavior, adapted for the treatment of OCSDs. The important point here is that in therapy we do not resort to punishment, force, shame, nagging, or coercion. We do try to make it immediately rewarding for the children to follow their course of therapy, in order to compete with the immediate rewards of doing compulsions.

I have never seen a child successfully threatened or punished out of their OCSD, but I have seen many miserable children and families come for therapy after having failed at such an approach. If your child had some other chronic disorder such as diabetes, you would not threaten or punish them. I strongly believe that positive systems based on rewarding good behavior are superior to those based on punishment. There is a limit to how much you can restrict your child's life and take things away as a means of controlling them. You will only encourage defiance and your child will soon realize that you really are limited in the amount of control you have over them. Punishment will make your child cleverer at avoiding punishment. Another effect can be to make your child angry and thus more resistant to change. They may also become more secretive about their symptoms out of a fear of punishment. They will simply go underground with their thoughts and behaviors. The use of reward is clearly the more humane and logical approach.

I believe that parents and caregivers should be involved in a young child's therapy as much as possible, since parents control so much of a child's daily existence. Unless there is a lot of family disturbance, the child will usually not object to you sitting in on at least some sessions, especially at first. They may even request that you be there. Parental cooperation is also essential in obtaining a complete history and background of the problem and the family. It is also essential to find out whether you have generally been good managers of your child's behavior prior to the beginning of their symptoms. It may be necessary for you to learn to improve your parenting skills at the same time your child is learning to manage symptoms, if they are to succeed. There is one further point in favor of parental involvement. Young children like to get a therapist's approval and will sometimes fib about how well they are progressing and how many therapeutic assignments they are doing. As a way of preventing this, it is best for family members to meet periodically with the therapist, either for a few minutes at the end of each session or for longer, every few visits.

Adolescents

In the case of older children, it may actually be better for parents to be less involved. Adolescents tend to be very self-conscious and usually prefer to be more independent about their treatment. Unless family members are very involved in the symptoms, or the adolescent in question is very immature or irresponsible, it is better for them to learn how to deal with symptoms on their own within the therapy. Family members may still have to be there for the initial history taking, but once therapy gets under way, it may be best for them to bow out. There is one case where occasional meetings with family may be necessary. Some older children will try to appear to be better than they really are due to their image consciousness. They will play down their symptoms, and once therapy has begun, may even lie about how much better they are doing. It may be necessary to get periodic progress reports from family members in such a situation.

Unless a child is very aware of the problem and motivated to get help, I prefer to meet with just the parents first. I do this to be able to ask the types of questions about the child, the symptoms, and previous treatment(s) that would be somewhat tricky if they were present. Also, parents tend to speak more candidly at such sessions. If therapy has not yet been discussed with the child, we also review various ways you can bring up the subject, which may vary depending upon the child's age, level of maturity, and how motivated they are.

At a first session with a child, I like to begin by asking them if they know why they are seeing me and who I am. This usually serves as a good takeoff point to begin explaining the therapy and the disorder to the child. I try to judge their level of motivation and to explain why treatment is necessary. I also give them a pep talk and tell them that I believe they are up to the task of beating their problem. It is very important to teach the child that they are not "crazy," weird, or bad. It is best to explain that their problem behaviors, no matter how strange, are some not very good ways they have used their imagination to come up with to make themselves feel less nervous, but that there are better ways that they can learn instead. Generally, if these things can be accomplished, and if I can get the child to begin even talking in small ways about the symptoms and the pain they cause, I consider it a successful start.

At subsequent sessions, I go on to interview both the parents and the child in detail. Questionnaires regarding the child's early history and current life are sent home, as well as behavioral recordkeeping sheets, to be filled out by the parent or the child, if they are old enough. The first few sessions are spent learning as much about the family, the child, and the child's symptoms as possible. Not only is what they say taken into account, but also the way they behave together as a group is closely observed. An attempt is made on my part to create a working relationship with the child and to describe it to them as a partnership. Whatever the child's age, I find it is important to show them that I understand what they are going through and that I accept it without judging them.

In the next step I create, as with the adults, a hierarchy of anxiety-producing situations that take in all the different problem behaviors and thoughts. I try to put them in order according to how much anxiety they will cause and how difficult they would be for the child to face. Children usually find this part interesting and somewhat challenging to do.

Young Children and Immature Adolescents

This next section on the behavioral use of rewards is aimed at younger children under the age of ten or immature adolescents. If you are dealing with an older child or a more mature adolescent who is very motivated to get well, you may skip this part.

At this point, if we are dealing with a young or unmotivated child, we begin to institute our behavioral management program. The first step is to create a "reward menu." This involves having your child and you put together a group of about a dozen desirable rewards. This can be fun to do, and your child's enthusiasm can really be stoked at this point. Your child is told that they may select one item from the list if they turn in a week's worth of good performance on their behavioral homework. Items on the menu can include such things as a small collectible toy, a favorite meal or dessert, new video game software, a chance to rent or go to a desirable movie, staying up a little later to watch a television program, receiving a favorite audio tape or CD, lunch with a parent at a favorite eating place, having a parent play a favorite game the child enjoys, going to an arcade, etc. Each menu is tailored to a particular child's tastes and doesn't always have to involve spending a lot of money. For older children and less mature adolescents, money will be a better reward than some type of prize. This makes the reward seem less childish and as an added benefit can also teach them to manage money.

After the rewards have been set up, I show the child a weekly chart (see Fig. 5.1) on which the behaviors they need to work on will be listed. It is divided into seven sections horizontally and five sections vertically.

From here I go on to actually assign homework by writing on the chart the behaviors we wish the child to perform. It is generally desirable to let the child select the behaviors they will work on. This gives them a feeling of control over the process and helps to get cooperation. The behavioral requirements for winning rewards are made somewhat easier at first, to give the child a better chance to win something, to feel successful, and to get a taste of how the system works. For instance, they may only have to get a particular assignment right for five out of the seven days of the week. The bar can be raised after the first few weeks. They are instructed to post the chart and the reward menu side by side in a prominent location that they will see frequently, such as on the refrigerator. The child, with your help, fills in or checks off the boxes at the end of each day. At the end of the week, if all requirements as listed on the chart have been met, the child is then allowed to select their reward. A lot of verbal praise should accompany this. Making it a little ceremony would not be a bad idea either. We try to keep things as positive as possible and to work at the child's pace. You are advised to avoid reminding, nagging, or criticizing your child about the homework, because we wish them to become responsible for managing their own symptoms. These children will have to learn to do this the rest of their lives if they are to live normally as recovered persons. If your child only does the homework because of your reminders, they will have learned nothing. Your child is told that the homework will be their responsibility alone, and that if they do as requested, they will earn something they really want. It is stressed that we are treating them more like grownups, because the responsibility is theirs.

With younger children who are having problems with symptoms in school, it may be necessary to get daily or weekly teacher reports so that you can verify if your child did the behavioral homework there. You should also request that the teachers not nag, criticize, or publicly embarrass your child because of the symptoms. (See the last section on Children with OCSDs and School for more on this subject.)

Charts are brought to each weekly therapy session for review. The child must be given strong praise for successes by the therapist at these sessions. Encour-

Fig. 5.1 ~ Special Homework Sheet for Children

Special Homework Sheet for _____

for the week of _____

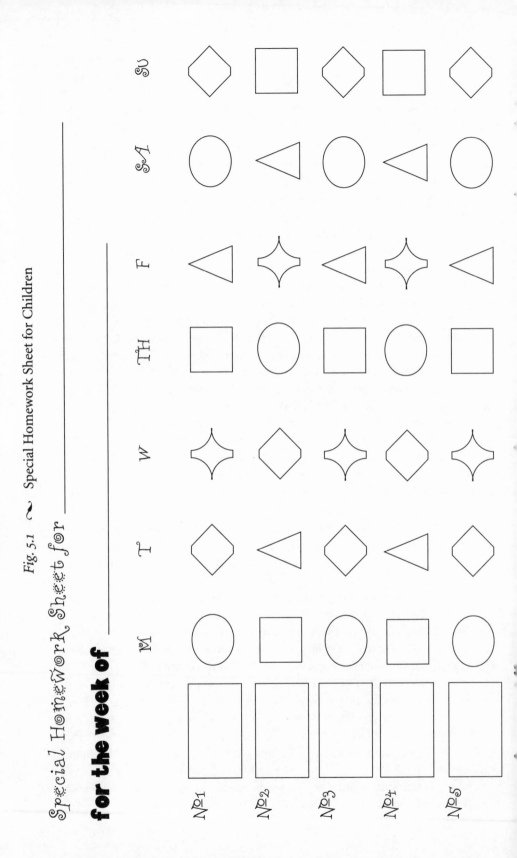

agement, rather than criticism, is used where performance has not been as good as desired. You are also encouraged to give praise. This is especially important if your child has received much criticism for their symptoms in the past. It is important to never let your child feel as though they are a failure if they are having a difficult time. They must be shown that there is always another chance to get it right. Persistence must always be encouraged. It is also good for their motivation to remember to ask them how they enjoyed the prize they earned and to spend time discussing it.

One further advantage of this behavioral management system is that much later, when the child is recovered, household chores and responsibilities can be substituted for behavioral homework and also rewarded. It can become a framework for teaching your child desirable and positive behaviors in other areas of their lives.

No matter what the age of your child, you may find that your behavior must also change along with that of your child. You may be instructed in how to gently refuse to answer obsessive questions, how to ease your way out of helping with rituals, and how to stop rewarding compulsive behaviors with attention, either positive or negative. You must learn to ignore the undesirable behaviors once treatment begins in order to give your child a chance to recognize and work on them. Your old reactions involving anger, ridicule, or punishment must be suppressed. A trained therapist can be extremely helpful in advising you about how to do these things, and you should not hesitate to ask their advice.

Parents need to be reminded that behavioral change is gradual change, and a lot of patience is called for. Keep in mind that if your child could just stop, they would do so. Family members sometimes become impatient when they see the child starting to improve, and can start pressuring the child to hurry up and change all their other behaviors at the same time. It is important to keep in mind that individuals, both children and adults, get well at their own pace. Setbacks are common and should even be considered normal on the way to recovery, and you, as parents, need to learn not to become anxious or pessimistic when your child occasionally takes a step backward. This type of negative thinking can be communicated to your child and can sabotage the therapy. Your approval is a powerful reward, just as your disapproval can be devastating. Use these powers wisely. Praise your child for what they are able to do. Don't criticize them for what they aren't able to do yet.

It is important to communicate to your child a sense that you believe in them and their essential underlying wellness and ability to recover, no matter what. Gradually, they will then come to believe in themselves. You must never forget to let your child know that even if you don't always approve of inappropriate behavior caused by the disorder, you still love him or her unconditionally, because they are your child. The goal is to help your child feel like someone who matters and is worthy of love and caring despite their disorder. You want to let them know that they are really "a person who also happens to have OCD" (to paraphrase Patricia Perkins-Doyle, the president of the OC Foundation).

Be certain to read the section on "Relapse Prevention" in chapter 3 so that you will be aware enough of these issues to be able to assist your child in staying well. Along with helping them to be realistic about staying recovered, you may want to see about making changes in your family life. For many families, having a child with an OCSD has meant living limited lives, not going out as a family, or socializing very much. If this has happened to your family, you will have to learn to stop living as if your child is still unwell.

I have included here one family's story of their daughter's struggle with OCD, as I believe it exemplifies the experience of many families.

Carol's Story

～ On a chilly November evening in 1985 I heard a vague whisper. "Mom ... Mom." My daughter was summoning me to her bedroom. Carol was fourteen at the time. I could hear distress in her voice, and frankly I was somewhat puzzled. Her day had been uneventful and filled with fun and laughter with school projects. "Mom, all these thoughts keep going through my mind." Carol's eyes had become a blanket of tears. "I think of murder or washing my hands. I don't mean it! I don't deserve to live!" Her voice trailed off into a whimper. My husband's and my first thoughts were of a teenage crisis or depression. With mixed feelings we contacted a trusted family friend who was a school psychologist. His counseling session with Carol revealed a very "normal" stage, amounting to a preoccupation with sexual matters and boys. "Nothing to be concerned about," he said. Two to three months of therapy revealed no clue concerning OCD. Carol voluntarily stopped therapy and she appeared to return to being a vivacious kid on the block.

Over the next three years, Carol's development did not appear to be out of the ordinary. We did notice some preoccupation with "squeaky" clean shower taking, neatness with the family newspapers, "gross" facial pimples, and concern over touching children. There were the occasional emotional outbursts over end tables being out of place and these episodes gave me a bizarre feeling, but I dismissed Carol's behavior as "growing" pains. It was in the spring of Carol's senior year of high school when OCD made its full-scale debut into our family. "Mom, I know that I have this terrible thing. I heard about it in health class. I will never live it down!" "What thing?" I queried. "A disorder, I'm a crazy person. How can I live with myself?" I reassured her that she wasn't crazy. Soon after, during a stay away from home, I received a concerned phone call from my husband that Carol had lapsed into a depression and would not attend school. "Senior year blues," I pondered, which prompted a referral to a psychiatric social worker. The depression persisted in spite of psychotherapy sessions, with more hand washing than ever before. Another referral to a psychiatrist. In distress, I relayed an account of apologizing over the smallest mistake, washing already clean hands, and spending more time in her bedroom. The doctor carefully listened over the phone and felt that Carol's problem sounded like Obsessive-Compulsive disorder. The repeated "I'm sorry's," trips to the bathroom for another round of hand washing or washing everything in sight, or the fear of touching or harming others were red flags for this often baffling biomedical disorder.

Our first trip to the doctor was like opening a door. We had never heard of OCD even with both of us being professional people. My husband is a teacher and I am a nurse. In very simple terms, the doctor educated us. Carol was put on a controlled dose of Prozac combined with psychotherapy and over a period of four to six weeks her symptoms abated. She made it off to college in the fall. She became her "old self." All during this family crisis, my husband and I attended a local OCD support group for sufferers and family members. We had written away for information from the OC Foundation leading us to a group with a qualified therapist. With much reading and footwork behind us, Carol suffered a major relapse after two years of college. She tried going off the Prozac, which is a big gamble for most OCD sufferers. Again, it was another round of psychotherapy and medication combined. This time, however, behavior modification was started in earnest. There were day-to-day goals and homework assignments. Carol had to gradually face people and situations that she feared the most. She had to learn that nothing terrible was going to happen and that resisting the compulsive urges was the order of the day. She could have dirty hands or touch children she feared she would harm, and it was "O.K."

When dealing with a young college girl on medication, it can be a roller coaster ride. "I'll bet I'm the only one on campus with this thing. Do I really have to take medication? Can I drink? What will my friends say?" We reassured Carol that medication was a "must," and she eventually realized that she was not the only one in the universe with these problems. Often the scenario was, "Mom, Dad, I can't go on. I want to give up. . . put me away. . . I have suffered enough." I felt like a swimming coach for the English Channel crossing. She had to cross her own channel of self-doubt or else "drown" in despair. Through repeated persistence in therapy and beginning with small tasks such as doing laundry and then moving on to holding down a part-time job, she recovered enough to study abroad and complete four years of college.

Carol is now a blossoming young woman, full of life and fun. She is attending graduate school and is a truly remarkable gal who has beaten the odds. There are days when her confidence is low, but she pursues a self-help program nearby. Her illness is under control. Many questions still tug at her soul. "Will my boyfriend love me for who I am? Should I marry? Can I have a family? What about a career?" These are very difficult issues for her, more so than for most other young adults. The answers are, yes, with early intervention, medication, and ongoing support programs.

As parents, we have to learn to "let go" because Carol must wage her own battle for independence. It is often easier to protect the OCD sufferer from pain by enabling him or her to keep destructive rituals. This is a mistake because pain is necessary for growth.

Carol's story really doesn't have an ending. Every day presents the challenge of looking at Carol's problem in terms of "not being crazy," but taking charge of her life.

TREATING CHILDREN: TTM, SKIN PICKING, AND NAIL BITING

Generally speaking, you will encounter many of the same issues in a child with TTM that you see in children with other OCSDs. Their reactions to the disorder run the gamut from wanting and accepting help, to getting upset at the mention of it, to even getting angry and denying there is a problem when confronted.

It is extremely important that you not become agitated and depressed about your child's appearance. This can only serve to frighten and stigmatize your child and make them feel defective and unlovable. We do not wish to communicate to them that the only thing that is really important about them is their appearance. It is also not a very good demonstration of how to solve a problem. Try to remind yourself that while your child's appearance may be different from that of other children, their problem is not life threatening, and that help is available. Try not to lose your perspective. Look around you, and you will see that there are many worse things that can happen to your child. Work at learning to stop feeling ashamed, worrying about what others will think about you or your child when you go out in public. This is still your wonderful child, no matter what others may think. As Roy C., the founder of OC Anonymous has stated, "What others think of me is none of my business." This also applies to what they think of your child and his or her appearance.

Unlike some of the other OCSDs, TTM is a rather public problem, noticeable to other children. This sometimes makes the child sufferer a target for teasing and ridicule. This is especially true if your child is over eight or nine years old.

Very young children may often be indifferent to their own symptoms until they begin to develop more social awareness. A child who has become the object of teasing will need sympathy and advice in how to cope with it. Although some children can put on a brave face and act as if they don't care, it is likely that they are hurting inside. Some children may be comfortable in explaining that they have a problem habit that makes them pull out their hair, while others will prefer to simply say that it is a skin disease or an ailment that has caused the hair loss.

In treatment, younger children may be difficult to motivate at times. This is because, as just mentioned, they are not particularly troubled by the hair loss, enjoy the pulling, and find resisting pulling to be hard work and not immediately rewarding. At times, the hair loss may seem a lot more troubling to you than to them. As in the treatment of classic OCD, a system of rewards may have to be used in order to create some motivation. On the other hand, your child may be one of those who can be encouraged to see it as a challenge and who also finds your parental attention and approval enough of a reward. If rewards and encouragement do not work, however, you may just have to accept that your child is not yet ready to work on this problem. It doesn't mean that they never will be. It just means that they aren't ready right now. They don't always have to want what you want when you want them to. Try to resist becoming impatient or pressuring them in any way, as the stress this will cause can only lead to increased pulling. In treating children, readiness is everything, and this means that they do not necessarily have to be ready when you say so.

If your child is younger than eight or nine, the formal Habit Reversal Training (HRT) approach (fully described in chapter 3) may be too complicated. Simply rewarding them to resist may work the best, since what we are asking them to do is not in itself rewarding. To accomplish the delivery of this reward, it is important to have them chart their own desirable behaviors on a special sheet each day. In this way, they can then receive a reward for progress weekly, based on whether the chart indicates they have met their goals. Goals are kept modest, at first, to build feelings of success and to give them an opportunity to sample rewards and get a taste for earning them. Such an approach will be the most helpful for this age group. It keeps them focused on what they must do and allows them to see their own progress. It also provides you with an opportunity to give a further verbal reward and some encouragement as they fill out their chart and again, when you give them their material reward.

If your younger child has a competitive spirit, trying to create the feeling of a contest with the problem can be helpful. Give the problem a silly name and try to get them to see it as a tricky opponent that tries to outsmart them. This may create enough interest and challenge to get them to do the work necessary to fight the behavior, much as if they are playing a video game for points. Another strategy would be to characterize the disorder as a neighborhood bully who is trying to push them around and tell them what they can and can't do. Like all bullies, it proves to not really be so tough when finally stood up to.

Adolescents and teenagers can react in a number of ways. Unlike very young children, most are bothered so much by what the symptoms do to their appearance, that they will work willingly to overcome the behavior. Their social self-consciousness, so typical of this age group, can work in their favor. They tend to be motivated and hardworking. Rewards and prizes will be unnecessary and may even seem babyish to this group. Some, unfortunately, have an opposite reaction. They won't discuss it or hear of it. They won't read information or agree to go for help. Inside, they may be hurting and humiliated, but on the outside, they may try to act indifferently or put on a show of angry defiance. Your best bet, in such a case, is not to make it a test of wills. They may come around at a later date, but even if they don't, you cannot force them to help themselves. It is hard enough work even when they are willing. If you can get them to at least go to a local support group (if there is one), this may be a powerful convincer. Otherwise, all you can do is obtain some reading matter from one of the foundations and leave it where they can find it. Let them know you are willing to listen or get them help at any time. My own policy toward children who will not take part in therapy is to respect their choice. It is best to let them be, but be sure to tell them that the door is always open and that they are welcome to come for help at any time. Besides this, all you can do is hope for the best. I know it hurts to see your child suffer when they could be helped, but this is one of those things you must be patient about and even sadly accept.

If your child does go for therapy, your role will also be a difficult one, but for different reasons. You will have to learn to stand back and let them do what they must. It will be very unhelpful if you nag, spy, criticize, or check on whether or not they have done their homework. It is also not your job to constantly be on the lookout to see if you can catch them pulling. The goal is for them to learn to deal with the problem independently and to eventually become their own therapist. After all, they will have to cope with it themselves throughout their lives. Making them independent in terms of helping themselves is the ultimate goal. You will frequently be tempted to comment if you see them doing something you know they shouldn't be doing. Resist the temptation. You may also be tempted to tell them where they went wrong if they backslide. Again, try to resist. Allow the therapist, who is not emotionally involved, to make these comments and to give pointers. If, in the past, your involvement has included angry scenes, criticism, or punishment, it is even more important for you to keep your distance. You may want the therapist to help you, if you find you cannot resist.

Your other job will be to give support and encouragement to your child. Try to help keep their morale up and be encouraging. Tell them that if they keep working, they will have a greater chance of success than if they do nothing. Don't remind them of past failures or pressure them to succeed because "This is costing me money," or "You're looking even worse than ever." Try to avoid frequent comments about their hair, skin, or nails. Pressure and stress will only backfire by leading to more pulling, picking, or biting.

If your child is a skin picker and has either created a skin problem or is reacting to a real acne problem, a visit to an informed dermatologist will be very helpful. At least you will be able to eliminate that part of the problem that can be handled medically. Clearer skin may also be less tempting to pick at and the dermatologist can explain to your child how squeezing and picking can only worsen the original skin problem rather than help it. Sometimes a little education can go a long way.

Small hand toys that can provide tactile stimulation can be helpful for younger children. Possibly even more than adults, children tend to be active and fidgety and really do need something else to do with their hands. Such toys could include foam balls, Silly Putty, pieces of velvet or fine sandpaper, or anything small, textured, or squeezable.

The use of medications in children is something that must be considered carefully. Guidelines would be similar to those for children with classic OCD (see next section). While there is no evidence that the standard medications for TTM are harmful to children, it is always preferable not to have to use them if possible. Children should at least be given a chance to try behavioral therapy alone first. Medication should be considered if

- HRT has been in full use for about eight weeks with no noticeable result.
- the child has been working hard, but feels that the urge to pull/pick/ bite really is irresistible.
- the child shows little or no interest in participating in behavioral therapy due to their age or immaturity.

A child psychiatrist with expertise in treating these disorders should monitor any course of drug therapy, if possible. Pediatricians and family physicians just don't have the training. Medication should be introduced at the lowest possible dose and increased very slowly. Generally, the same medications used to treat classic OCD are also useful in treating these disorders (see chapter 4 for information on medications).

MEDICATIONS USED TO TREAT CHILDREN

Medication does have a role to play in treating children with OCSDs, but it is not something that should simply be rushed into. I am not at all opposed to its use, but there are some important issues to consider. My own approach is to begin with behavioral therapy alone, to first see whether or not the use of medication can be avoided. I particularly believe in taking this approach with children under the age of ten or eleven, and there are several reasons why. The first is that when handled properly, children can become motivated enough about behavior therapy to not need medication, and I have seen excellent results and recoveries in quite a few cases where medication was not used. Even if they should experience some setbacks or new symptoms in the years to come and do go on to use medication, the children have had a positive therapy experience. They have also acquired tools that allow them to face their anxieties in other ways that go beyond merely taking pills and have been able to put off taking medications for a further period of time.

Another reason I do not immediately rush to refer children for medication is that parents are often leery of drugs. Most parents are rightfully concerned at the prospect of putting a child on psychoactive medication. The discovery that their child has a chronic neurobiological disorder has already been one unpleasant and upsetting event for them, and the idea of medication is another. When drugs are not just prescribed automatically and behavioral alternatives are considered first, parents tend to feel better about their use when they themselves can see that it may be a necessity. Finally, children may tend to regard medications as a magic pill, and once they are taking it, may be inclined to stop working on behavioral changes, which now seem too difficult in comparison.

If medications are to be used, it is very important to adopt a realistic attitude toward them. Medication rarely provides complete relief and should instead be regarded as a tool to enable the child to succeed at behavioral therapy. Finding the right drug is not a precise procedure. It may involve a lot of trial and error. You may have to go through trials with several medications until the right one is found. An adequate trial can last as long as twelve weeks or more.

Many parents are fearful of possible serious consequences which would result from having their child take a psychiatric medication. There is simply no clinical evidence that the medications used to treat OCSDs can have a negative effect on a child's growth or development. It is true, however, that children are subject to the same side effects as adults. (See chapter 4 for further information on medications and side effects.) In the children with whom I have worked, the effects on sleep or wakefulness have been the most noticeable. One is fatigue, which can cause difficulties in staying awake and paying attention, and another is insomnia that can bring about the same result by preventing children from

getting enough sleep. Conversely, restlessness and feelings of agitation sometimes caused by certain medications can also be disturbing to parents and children alike.

Another side effect that can be especially obnoxious to children is weight
gain. It can be rather upsetting to a child who has always been slim or of normal
weight to suddenly become heavier or even overweight. This can, as we know,
lead to social problems for children and adolescents, adding to the bad feelings
they may already have about themselves. Fortunately, this side effect can be controlled through the proper management of diet and exercise.

One side effect, which I have observed several times among my young
patients on Tricyclic antidepressants (TCAs) (chiefly Anafranil), is a difficulty in
urinating. This can become serious enough that in a minority of cases the children were almost unable to urinate without the immediate use of a second drug,
Bethanacol (Uricholine). Needless to say, they were not kept on the TCA for
long. Dry mouth can lead to an increased number of cavities, and more frequent dental care is warranted.

Let me repeat that even in view of the above, I am not opposed to the use of
medication in children. There are cases which are severe enough that its use is
essential to a successful recovery. Despite the side effects mentioned here, there
are presently enough different medications to choose from, increasing the
chances of finding one which will be well tolerated. Also, not everyone who uses
these drugs gets side effects. If these do occur, there are more options for treating them these days.

I will refer a child for medication under the following circumstances: if
behavioral therapy has been pursued strongly with the child's cooperation for a
period of several months without strong results; if the child is simply uncooper-
ative with behavioral therapy, despite the best efforts to motivate him or her, but
is agreeable to medication; if the child would like to cooperate but appears to be
suffering from a biologically based depression along with the OCD that is preventing them from taking an active part in therapy; if the child is motivated and
has made improvements through therapy, but finds the pressure of the symptoms so strong that it is still a daily struggle to function normally.

As far as which medications can be used, it would appear that children can generally tolerate the same medications as adults. While exact guidelines have yet to be
established for children, their dosages tend to be much lower than those for adults,
and those for some drugs are often based on body weight. For instance, the generally accepted guideline for Anafranil is a dosage of 3 mg per kilogram of body
weight in a child. Increases are generally made in the smallest possible increments
and are probably best when spaced far apart. The development of liquid versions of
such antidepressants as Prozac and Paxil have made the use of tiny doses a lot simpler. It should be noted that adolescents sometimes tolerate antidepressants better

than older adults and do not necessarily require smaller doses. The use of these medications in very young children has not been extensively studied. As stated, prescribing medications should be left to a qualified practitioner.

Should parents be flatly opposed to the use of medications, or should the child be highly sensitive to almost any medication, then behavioral therapy alone will be the best option. It is a good option, and children can be motivated, even if they do not seem so at first (see the previous sections in this chapter on treating children with behavioral therapy).

One further note about the use of medications by children. If a child does end up taking medication throughout childhood and into their adolescent growth years, it would be a good idea to keep track of the size of their doses relative to their size and weight as they change. I have encountered several situations where children who had been doing well on medication suddenly took a turn for the worse after going through several growth spurts. While it was thought that their medication had stopped working, they had actually outgrown their childhood medication levels.

HOSPITALIZING A CHILD

Placing a child in a hospital for psychiatric treatment is not a step to be taken lightly. Luckily, it is an issue that comes up infrequently. In my opinion, it should only be done if a child is in some way a danger to themselves or others, or is so out of control with their symptoms that they cannot be successfully treated on an outpatient basis. Severe depression, extreme agitation, compulsions that endanger a child's health or life, and suicidal urges are the most frequent reasons to hospitalize. Unfortunately, most hospitals can only offer you medication, as they lack behavioral therapy services. Also, most hospital stays tend to be brief, due to the current state of insurance coverage. While there are several longer-term treatment facilities for adults, there is an almost complete lack of residential OCSD treatment programs for children.

The pros of hospitalization include the following:

+ it can protect a child's life and health or the life or health of another;
+ it can give a child a break from an environment that may be stimulating their symptoms or that is stressful for them;
+ it can give a physician a chance to get the child's medications adjusted under controlled conditions;
+ it can give their family a badly needed break from a serious and stressful situation;

+ it can give a behavioral therapist (if the hospital has one on staff) the opportunity to work in an intensive way with the child, free of other distractions, and in a completely controlled environment.

The cons are:

− going into a psychiatric ward can, itself, be extremely stigmatizing and stressful for a child, particularly if they have never been away from home or in a hospital before;

− it can be a dead-end if the hospital doesn't have staff that is trained in the treatment of an OCSD;

− it can be ruinously expensive if you don't have insurance coverage.

Hospitalization should not be used as punishment for a child whose behavior is simply difficult or oppositional. It should be regarded as a measure of last resort when all attempts at outpatient treatment have failed.

CHILDREN WITH OCSDs AND SCHOOL

If the OCSD is not affecting your child's schoolwork and is not making them conspicuous to their classmates, there is probably no need to tell school personnel about it. If, on the other hand, the disorder is affecting your child's ability to go to class, perform work in school or complete homework, or is drawing a lot of attention to them, then it is essential you discuss it with the teachers, guidance counselors and school psychologists. They will probably mention it to you anyway.

Some ways in which OCSDs can adversely affect schoolwork and class performance would include:

• not wanting to go to school for fear of being teased by others for their odd behaviors or appearance problems due to missing hair.

• habitual lateness in getting to school because of indecision in selecting clothing, having to perform numerous rituals for getting dressed, washing, eating, or leaving the house.

• poor attention and concentration due to the distraction caused by constant obsessional thoughts, hair pulling, or nail biting.

• slowness in doing written work resulting from perfectionism, which may lead to repeated checking, overly careful erasing, or having to start over from the beginning if any errors are actually found by the child.

- slowness in carrying out reading assignments due to compulsive reread-ing.

- problems in completing tests because of indecision, double-checking answers for mistakes, rewriting answers, rereading questions, perfec-tionistic erasing, or having to form numbers or letters perfectly. High levels of anxiety due to other symptoms can also hamper test perfor-mance.

- incomplete note taking due to poor concentration, rechecking, and rewriting.

- disruption of lessons due to repetitive compulsive questioning.

- difficulty in getting around school due to numerous walking, looking, or touching rituals.

- getting stuck in school restrooms due to repetitive hand washing, or conversely, not being able to use school restrooms due to contamina-tion fears.

- reluctance to go to school due to superstitious fears of harm coming to their family, or of their possessions being moved or contaminated while they are away.

- reluctance to go to school due to fears of coming into contact with con-taminated locations or people there.

You may find that school professionals know little about OCSDs. This is not unusual, as most do not, and unfortunately this may also be true of your school psychologist. It will be up to you to educate all of them. If your child is seeing a trained therapist, you can enlist that person to help you by speaking to school personnel. Perhaps they can even teach an in-service course there, if they are expert enough. The OC Foundation now has a set of videotapes produced, specifically, to instruct educators about OCD and its effects on school perfor-mance. It would also be helpful to provide pamphlets obtainable from the OC Foundation or the Trichotillomania Learning Center (see chapter 13). You might also give them a copy of this book.

If your child's symptoms are serious enough to prevent them from going to school, you will have to arrange for home tutoring until treatment is far enough along and your child is recovered enough to return. Unfortunately, not all schools are willing to provide this type of help, and you may have to strongly press your case with those who administer special education for your district. You would be well advised to learn about the laws governing your child's right to an education, and it might even be necessary to contact a parent advocate and an attorney.

If your child is well enough to go to class, but symptoms do make it difficult, it will help considerably to mobilize school staff to assist your child. Teachers can be encouraged to help keep your child's stress levels down by not making demands that cannot be met because of the OCSD. Extra time may be needed for assignments or tests. Telling the child to "Stop doing that" and "You're not trying hard enough" are not acceptable ways for them to handle this. Neither is punishing or belittling the child to get them to control their own behavior. Drawing attention to your child's behavior in front of the class is also unacceptable. There can be absolutely no tolerance for such actions on a teacher's part. It may also be necessary for the school to provide a quiet refuge in the nurse's or psychologist's office, should anxiety become too high. In the case of TTM, if hair loss is very noticeable, your child may wish to wear a hat or scarf in school and may need special permission to do so. Children with TTM who wear wigs or hair pieces may also need permission to be excused from physical education to avoid exposure. Teachers may have to instruct other class members not to ridicule or embarrass your child.

If your child is taking medication that may make them tired or a bit drowsy at first, be certain to notify the teacher and the school nurse. Usually, this is only a temporary problem that passes within a few days or weeks. If it doesn't, be sure to notify your physician, who may either lower the dosage or switch to another medication.

Do try to strongly encourage your child to go to school if at all possible. The stigma of having to stay home and explain an absence to other children may create a great deal of stress. Also, the structure of going to school daily will be helpful. Too much free time at home can lead to increased symptoms.

Try to be sympathetic and supportive. If your child has been a good student and has lower grades for a time, try not to be too critical. Sometimes just going to school at all can be considered a real accomplishment. Remember that the work can always be made up. Never forget that stress means increased symptoms. While it is true that some children may take advantage of having the disorder to avoid their responsibilities, this is not true of all children. Don't simply assume that your child is using their symptoms in this way. Should this be true, however, some firmness will be helpful. Consult with your child's therapist to get the best advice on how this should be dealt with. No one can be forced to learn, so this needs to be handled carefully.

In some cases, your child's treatment may have to be coordinated with the classroom teacher. This is usually reserved for children in the primary grades, where symptoms may also be occurring in school. Older children will not want any of their teachers to know and this should be respected whenever possible. Where behavioral assignments are given to your child to carry out in school, the teacher may need to be made aware of them in order to be able to report on whether or not they were done. Teachers can also give important information about progress in class. Their reports are crucial if your child is keeping a chart and is being rewarded for progress, for example, verifying that behavioral homework was actually done, or that your child participated in certain activities. Teacher reports can be made daily or weekly as needed. Be sure that you advise the teacher (or have your therapist do so) that you are trying to build responsibility in your child and to please not nag the child to complete therapy assignments. Teachers should be asked to be supportive but not critical if the child is having difficulty with the behavioral homework in school.

One caution about teacher reports. While teachers do try to be helpful, there may be a tendency on the part of some to go a bit too far and start labeling most things your child does as compulsive. Don't always take their word over your child's, but try to get a balanced picture, if possible. Some teachers will also try to do some amateur therapy on their own once they are made aware of the problem. While they surely mean well, they should be discouraged from doing this without consulting anyone. Always listen to what they have to contribute, but make it clear that the assigning of behavioral homework should not be undertaken without the consultation of the parent and the child's therapist. Have the teacher and therapist communicate periodically to ensure good coordination of treatment. Your child's teacher can be a valuable ally, so be diplomatic and do everything possible to get their help and fullest cooperation.

~ OCSDs and the Other People in Your Life

One can't help many, but many can help one.
—Bridge, Cheshire proverbs

What a tragedy is help where it harms what it supports!
—Publius Syrus

Fear is a feeling that is stronger than love.
—Pliny the Younger

O CSDs enter the lives of families and friends like uninvited guests. They arrive without warning, and the hosts are rarely prepared. When this happens, we can see a wide range of reactions on the part of family members and friends. The type of reaction probably depends on a number of factors, including:

- the health of relationships and specific attitudes toward the sufferer before the start of the disorder. Obviously, if you did not get along well before, the OCSD will not improve things.

- the attitude of your significant others toward illness in general. If your family and friends see this as a weakness rather than an illness, you can expect little help or sympathy.

- the presence of OCSDs in your family or significant others. If others in your life have problems themselves, they may be more likely to understand how you feel and to show empathy. However, you may find that their problems leave them little in the way of time or resources to offer you.

- other stressors that can limit the time or interest family and friends will have for your problems.

- the degree to which your symptoms intrude upon the lives of those around you, and the amount of control you have established over their lives. It is likely that the more your symptoms have made life difficult for others, the more resentment they may feel toward you. Whether you are to be blamed for the illness will not even be the issue. Remember that they are only human and unless they are especially sensitive and forgiving, it could take them a long time to be able to forgive your illness, and the effect it may have had on them.

- the degree to which you have become self-absorbed due to the disorder and alienated others in your life. OCSDs sufferers can become self-centered, inwardly focused, and withdrawn from the lives and needs of others. For instance, I have heard many spouses say that their husband or wife seems to be living in their own little OC world. When they try to initiate a conversation, the sufferer's mind is elsewhere and they seem not to have any spare time or energy to devote to others. Friends and family, in reaction, may withdraw from the sufferer and leave him or her further isolated.

- the degree of responsibility that you take toward managing your symptoms. The more independent you are, the more sympathy you can expect from those around you.

- the role the OCSD may have come to play in the family structure, and the purposes it has come to serve. Other people may need a "scapegoat" to justify their own problems or lack of harmony. Your disorder may serve as a useful distraction from other family difficulties, or they may need you to remain at home as a disabled person to keep them company or take care of them.

THE PEOPLE CLOSE TO YOU:
HELP OR HINDRANCE

In order to help, it is important that family members and friends accept the existence of the disorder. There are some individuals who cope with unpleasant realities by ignoring them or denying their existence in the hope that they will go away. This type of denial has prevented many sufferers, especially children, from being allowed to get the help they badly need. I can recall one mother who, on hearing that her young son had OCD, hastily retreated from my office, never to return, saying, "I just can't believe it. It's not true." When it is impossible to ignore symptoms in a child or an adult, they may be minimized or explained away as being nervous habits, laziness, childish behavior, or attempts to get attention or get even. No one likes to think that someone close to them has a serious problem, but the existence of OCSDs cannot be denied or ignored. Whether you like it or not, they are there and a part of the sufferer.

If or when the existence of the disorder has been accepted, family and others would do well to educate themselves about OCSDs. This is absolutely vital and can be accomplished through books, videotapes, or pamphlets on the subject obtainable through the OC Foundation, the Trichotillomania Learning Center, the OC Information Center, or by attending lectures or support groups that are open to family and friends. (See chapter 13 and appendix D.)

Overcoming personal feelings of guilt is another way in which family members and friends can help. Such feelings can lead to indulging sufferers in inappropriate ways, giving the types of misguided support that keep them unwell and dependent. For parents, it is important to understand that even if they may have passed an OCSD genetically (assuming that the genetic transmission theory is true), they are not responsible for the sufferer's behavior, and they are not responsible for, nor can they control, the sufferer's success in or acceptance of treatment. Family members may come to recognize that they helped create a home environment of rigidity and perfectionism, or which may have been dysfunctional in some other way and which contributed to the disorder. In such a case, it is also important to realize that they did the best they could and were products of their own experiences and upbringing.

Family members and friends can be helpful by being gently encouraging when it comes to getting help, but they must also remember that acceptance of the disorder or successful treatment are something that can never be forced on an individual. For instance, it is perfectly acceptable to obtain literature about OCSDs and give it to a sufferer. It is wrong to try to force or coerce them into reading it. It is also acceptable to suggest gently once or twice that it would be in the person's best interest to seek help and that such help exists. It is a bad idea to nag. It is also wrong to try to force or drag someone bodily to a therapist's office or support group, or to threaten or blackmail them into getting help. People treated this way seldom, if ever, do well in therapy. Getting well can be a difficult task, even when a sufferer is motivated. The possibility of becoming overinvolved in the sufferer's recovery is another hazard that must be guarded against. It is just as detrimental in its own way as becoming overinvolved in the disorder itself and helping a sufferer to carry out rituals. It must be kept in mind that recovering is primarily the sufferer's responsibility.

Everyone involved would do better to join together to oppose the disorder rather than each other. It is good for family and friends to show faith in the person's ability to get well, even if the sufferer does not always have such faith. It is clearly very wrong (and even childish) to ridicule, taunt, laugh at symptoms, or describe a person as incurably "crazy." Having an OCSD is a humiliating enough experience, without anyone else adding to it. Remember that the disorder is only one facet of who the sufferer is and not their complete identity. Try to see the person behind the symptoms. If family and friends are unable to be sympathetic to the sufferer and cannot see that person, it is best for them to keep their distance and say nothing. If they cannot curb their involvement in the disorder, perhaps some counseling might be in order or at least a visit to an OCD family member's group.

Once a sufferer is in therapy, family members would do well to show support for the person's efforts by recognizing any improvements (but not overdoing it), gently encouraging them to go further, sympathizing with their setbacks, and openly acknowledging the difficulty of what they are trying to do. This produces the best results. There should be no checking to see if they are following treatment, or reminders or fighting about doing therapy homework, or telling them they will never get well if they have the occasional lapse or setback (which is quite normal in treatment). This is overinvolvement. I try to teach family and friends that those with an OCSD must learn to responsibly take care of themselves entirely free of help from others if they are to ultimately live recovered, independent, adult lives. Independence is the goal. If a sufferer merely does homework because someone else made them do it, or because a family member reminded them, then they have lost a valuable opportunity to learn to care for themselves, and nothing will have been gained. Children must also be guided toward this goal of independence. Those with an OCSD must ultimately become their own therapists if they expect to stay well.

Family members must also be patient with a sufferer's rate of progress, because they often have a tendency to pressure patients who are just starting to improve. They begin to see a little progress and want to know why more of the behaviors cannot be changed right away. As I have said elsewhere in this book, behavioral change is gradual change. Everyone progresses at his or her own pace. Even among people who are making good progress, some symptoms hang on stubbornly. Family members must learn to be satisfied with whatever the sufferer is able to accomplish comfortably. Constantly watching the sufferer like a hawk waiting to pounce on every behavior that looks like a compulsion is a very bad idea. Pressure will only lead to upsetting and angry confrontations, and this type of stress will surely lead to a setback rather than to progress. Such lapses are "potholes" on the road to recovery. No one learns new skills or changes him or herself without making mistakes. They are a normal part of the learning process. The sufferer in treatment needs unconditional support.

Another way in which family and friends can help during treatment is to learn how to stop participating in the patient's symptoms. This is often best done with the help of the therapist. By the time many individuals have come for treatment, they, their families, and their friends, have usually established patterns where family members take part in rituals like double checking, washing or cleaning, or touching things, changing clothes, giving reassurances, or answering endless questions. They may have to make decisions for the sufferer and also carry out everyday personal and household chores that would normally be the sufferer's responsibility. These types of short-term "fixes" really don't help. Worse yet, they may even help the sufferer to function well enough to feel that they really don't have to get help or change at all. For the therapy to succeed, family members will also have to change and withdraw from these activities. This can be done either gradually or rapidly, in a sort of "cold turkey" approach. In my experience, the patient usually prefers a gradual withdrawal, while family members prefer the quick approach. I believe that each individual must find the way that works best for them. You cannot take a "one-size-fits-all" approach to treatment. I typically see patients make their greatest and quickest gains of the entire therapy process when family involvement with symptoms is eliminated. This is best done at the beginning of the therapy rather than at the end. I would not recommend that families try to carry out such a disengagement without the help of an experienced therapist. A practitioner with the proper training can explain its necessity to the sufferer and set the pace for change, so that it is not viewed as some kind of punishment. They can also instruct family members in what to say to the sufferer, when refusing to participate in the disorder. It is much better if such instructions come from the therapist, who is a neutral third party. Learning to say things like—"I'm sorry, but I'm only carrying out your therapist's instructions," or "I am helping you. I'm helping you to get well"—will go a lot further and get better results than an angry refusal or an insult. In this way, if the sufferer is unhappy with the family's lack of cooperation with their symptoms, they will have to discuss it with the therapist, rather than angering themselves at family members.

It must be expected that old habits die hard. Family members and friends typically forget to withdraw at first, and patients may continue trying to get this unhealthy aid either directly or by more subtle manipulations. As the days go by, however (often by the end of the second week after family involvement has been withdrawn), family members become better at remembering their instructions, and patients stop testing them when they finally see that it will do them no good.

Finally, it will help greatly if, as the recovery process begins, family and friends can forgive the sufferer for past happenings, and forgive themselves as well. There can be no benefit in making someone continually pay for past problem behaviors. People must live in the present. It may take time for friends and family to learn to trust the sufferer to manage themselves once again or even for the first time. The sufferer may also need to realize that they will have to work to win back the trust they may have lost during the illness and to be patient with those close to them. For the sufferer, showing concern once again for family and friends is a way to say, "I'm back." It will take work to move from the self-absorption of an OCSD to rejoining family life and friendships. All parties will need to forgive each other for the way they may have behaved due to the disorder and to make a new start.

IF THE OCSD SUFFERER REFUSES HELP

The long-term results of not getting treatment have not been studied scientifically. My experience has been that those who do not get help may end up in one of three categories, depending on the severity of their symptoms. In the first category are those with mild and unchanging symptoms. For this group, not getting help becomes a quality of life issue. These sufferers can function, but the disorder probably takes the edge off their quality of life. In the second category are those whose symptoms are more serious, but which also remain at a steady level. They can find themselves settling for a poor quality of life, in which symptoms are tolerated despite great pain and inconvenience. I call these people the "walking wounded."

In the third category are those people whose symptoms may start out mild but gradually increase and become more intense over time. For OCD and BDD sufferers in this group, life steadily deteriorates as they become caught in a vicious circle of avoidance. Such individuals often end up housebound and unable to care for themselves, living only on disability payments and the charity of friends and family members. These untreated adults who live with their parents follow an unhappy course. They hang around the house unproductively and are a burden to their families. They live in constant fear of what will happen if their parents die or become disabled. The parents, of course, worry about who will help their adult child when they are gone. These ill adults will eventually become totally dependent on the state if they are not able to recover: not a pleasant prospect.

Unfortunately, there is not much family or friends can do with an OCSD sufferer who shows no inclination to work at recovery or even go for help at all. Individuals have many reasons for not engaging in therapy. Some of the most common reasons for not seeking help are discussed in chapter 2, Only Commitment Brings Success, and this is by no means an exhaustive list. In general, most reluctant sufferers really want to recover; however, they want it on their own terms. They would like to get well, but don't want to feel anxious or uncomfortable, or have to confront their fears while doing so. Since this is not possible, they prefer to do nothing and stay as they are with their familiar discomforts. I often receive many anguished calls from family members asking, "How can I get this person to go for treatment? Every time I bring up the subject they get angry with me and won't talk about it." Another variation on this is, "I really think he/she needs help, but when I tell them I think they have a problem they totally deny it. They say that I'm exaggerating, and that they just have a few little problem habits that really aren't anyone's business." I even hear, "Is there some story we can make up to trick them into coming to your office?" Or, "Is there any way I can force them into therapy?" Or, even worse, "Do you think there is any way we can slip medication into their food without them knowing about it?"

When someone other than the prospective patient makes the initial phone call (children excluded), I tend to suspect a motivation problem. I typically ask, "Why are you calling me and not the person with the disorder?" In all fairness, some sufferers actually are motivated but are too shy, ill, or reluctant to get things started. Many times, unfortunately, the prospective patient has not been consulted, is unaware that the call has been placed at all, and would be very upset if they knew about it.

I think the biggest problem here is that family and friends find it difficult to accept that no one can *make* someone else recover. I tell patients that "We can't want you to get well more than you do." Getting well takes a lot of hard work, even when a person is motivated. When a person isn't motivated, it is obvious that little or nothing is going to happen. I have seen people dragged into therapy through the use of threats, anger, blackmail, guilt, and deception. If the person is not willing, it almost always ends badly. Therapy should be viewed as an opportunity for an individual to grow and change willingly, not some form of discipline or punishment to be forced on those with problems. If even a small spark of hope or motivation is actually there, it can sometimes be fanned into a flame with the right approach, but if it isn't, being pushed to get help only leaves the sufferer with a lasting bad feeling about therapy and therapists.

However much we wish for someone to recover, we must still respect their rights to choose as individuals, no matter how wrong we think their choices are. Significant others will say, "How can I just stand there and watch this person I care for go down the drain?" It is understandable when family and friends refuse to take "no" for an answer. It is extremely painful to watch a loved one go unaided through the agonies of a mental disorder. Friends and relatives feel a profound sense of helplessness and despair. They believe that the only reason the reluctant sufferer hasn't responded to pleas to get help is because they haven't explained things correctly or strongly enough, or that the sufferer simply didn't understand or is staying ill on purpose. They imagine that if they plead, explain, or apologize just one more time and show how much they care, the sufferer will finally hear and be moved to seek help. The odds are that this will not happen.

When this doesn't work, some people move on to the use of anger and punishment to get the person to recover. This is seen particularly in situations where it is felt that the sufferer is staying unwell on purpose, in order to get even for past wrongs and resentments. Most people react to being pushed by resisting or angrily pushing back. This approach will only lead the sufferer to back away even further from getting help. Another common outcome here is that the stress of such an approach can stimulate symptoms, and actually make them even worse.

Even where kinder and gentler approaches are tried, the result may still be the same if the sufferer is unwilling or unready. I have seen some extremely loving and caring families wait patiently for the sufferer to come around. They are afraid to confront the sufferer, and yet their lives are controlled by the sufferer's symptoms. Years go by and nothing changes, except that the family ceases to live their own lives, becomes more burned out, and parents grow older with an adult invalid on their hands in their later years.

Family and friends need to disengage from the ill person's symptoms and concentrate on living their own lives more fully. This is not a new idea and comes from the treatment of drug and alcohol addiction. Relationships where a functional person has given up important parts of their own life and assumed the running and supporting of the life of a nonfunctioning person are known as "codependent." What you end up with in such relationships are two nonfunctioning people.

Significant others need to stop enabling the sufferer and quit acting as if they are responsible (unless the sufferer is a child). To accomplish this they may need to get some professional advice, as this is quite difficult to do alone, especially after years of anger, guilt, and bad habits. There is no point in feeling resentful for having to get help on the sufferer's account. When others are involved in the symptoms, and in effect run a sufferer's life, then they actually have a problem themselves. Blaming the sufferer, or oneself, will not help anyone. A good counselor can help people disengage without feeling guilty, stop participating or assisting in rituals or other compulsions, and resist answering compulsive questions. If it is clear that the sufferer cannot and will not recover while being supported at home, they may have to move out or at least set a target date for doing so. The idea here is that if you cannot save them, at least you can save yourself. These last suggestions are probably the most difficult to consider or carry out. A therapist can help explain to the sufferer what is being done, without it appearing to be punishment. Sufferers may finally be willing to negotiate about getting help when they see that their supporters are serious and won't budge, but this cannot be relied upon. Further instruction in how to handle the sufferer's anger, resentment, and attempts at manipulation will also help. Most important, allow time to make this disengagement. It doesn't happen overnight. Remember that any behavioral change is gradual change.

An important exception to disengaging is when an individual is suicidal or making suicidal threats. This must *always* be taken seriously, and help must be sought *immediately*. Temporary psychiatric hospitalization is the best answer when suicide is a possibility. If the threat was serious, a life will have been saved. If it was only a manipulation meant to control others, it probably won't be tried again. Situations of this latter type, however, are relatively uncommon in those with OCSDs. One other important exception is where the sufferer's compulsions are posing some type of serious threat to their health. I recall one patient with contamination phobias, who had developed ulcers on his legs from standing at the sink and washing for many hours. As these were in serious danger of becoming gangrenous, hospitalization was judged to be a necessity for treating them, as well as his OCD. Other situations, where sufferers are starving themselves or using dangerous chemicals on their bodies, may also have to be dealt with in this way. I sometimes encounter desperate families seeking advice about how to involuntarily hospitalize someone who is reluctant to get treatment. I tell them that these are among the only justifications for involuntarily hospitalizing someone.

I would just like to make one further point about hospitalization. You can temporarily hospitalize someone to protect their life and health, but if you are seeking real treatment for their OCSD, you may have to take them to one of the specialized inpatient programs. Your ordinary local hospital probably won't be able to offer much beyond basic treatment with medications during a stay of a few days. Owing to the current state of health insurance coverage, it is unlikely that any more than a brief stay in your local hospital will be approved, in most cases. Extremely serious cases of OCSDs that cannot be treated on an outpatient basis will sometimes be able to get approval for more intensive inpatient treatment. Obtaining this approval may involve getting letters from specialists, as well as making a formal appeal to the insurance company. All this, of course, assumes that you have the sufferer's cooperation.

Your refusal to continue supporting the sufferer in their illness is not a guarantee that they will suddenly want to work at recovering. It is more of a guarantee that the people doing the supporting will have a life. It does happen at times that the sufferer cannot continue as they have in the past because the equilibrium of their illness system has been disturbed. It might even precipitate a move toward treatment when they finally see that there is no other acceptable option. I am always reminded in such situations of a quote from the psychologist Rollo May, who said, "People only change when it becomes too dangerous to stay the way they are."

There are many good books on codependency written for the friends and family of substance abusers. The disorder may be different, but the issues are the same. There is also *Obsessive-Compulsive Disorder: A Survival Guide for Family and Friends* by Roy C., a helpful book specifically written for families of those with OCD (see appendix D).

~ *Recovery and Acceptance*

A just man falleth seven times and riseth up again.
—*Proverbs 24:16*

It is not death that a man should fear, but he should fear never beginning to live.
—*Marcus Aurelius*

As far as we know, OCSDs are chronic and similar to such disorders as diabetes. This means that once one of these disorders has begun to emerge, it will most likely remain throughout your life. OCSDs are a potential you will always carry with you. In some rare cases, a person's symptoms may go away and not return, and I know this appears to have happened in a few individuals whose childhood OCSDs disappeared as they matured and did not return in adulthood. It is also not unusual to see temporary remissions in some individuals, where all symptoms seem to disappear (this should not be confused with the day-to-day or weekly ebb and flow of symptoms, which is common in OCSDs). These remissions may last from a few months to as long as ten years, as in one case I encountered. There is no clear explanation as to how or why this happens. Perhaps temporary positive shifts in brain chemistry or the ending of stressful conditions in a person's life are the cause. In any case, I counsel people not to count on this happening for them, in order to avoid the risk of disappointment. Remissions are more the exception than the rule. Those who hold on to the belief that OCSDs will just go away on their own, or that they will some day find a miracle cure, are only kidding themselves. This thinking can lead to procrastination and a failure to seek help.

When discussing OCSDs, we do not use the word "cure." To use the word "cure" is to say that you will *never* have another symptom again. There is no cure for OCD and its related disorders, but this does not mean that you cannot recover. By using all the therapeutic resources available to you at the present time, you should be able to reduce its effects and confine it to a very small part of your life and live as normally and productively as others.

Treatment, in the form of behavioral therapy, cognitive therapy, and medication, can help you as you have read in previous chapters. Through hard work and determination, the symptoms can be controlled or in some cases largely eliminated, and you can maintain a normal life. I tell my patients that getting well is 50 percent of the job, but that staying well is the other 50 percent. This is meant to remind them not to develop a false sense of security or let down their guard. Those who successfully get through treatment will always need to maintain their recovery, because such things as serious stress or the discontinuation of medication can sometimes lead to a relapse. I use the word "maintain," because recovery is not simply a state you achieve and are then no longer responsible for doing anything about. Recovery is an active process. It is probably even better to say "in recovery," rather than "recovered," because it is something you can fall "out" of if you do not maintain it.

RECOVERY AND RELAPSE

While it is crucial to be aware of the fact that you can relapse, it is preventable. At the risk of repeating myself, we do not apply the word "cure" to someone who has gone through a successful course of treatment, we say instead that they are "in recovery." Since OCD is a chronic problem, we cannot say that a person has ever "finished" their therapy. Doing so would be similar to people who have lost large amounts of weight, thinking in terms of being on a "diet." This would suggest that they are only making a temporary change and will later go back to their old ways. People who want to lose weight and keep it off permanently must change their old familiar eating patterns forever. As long as they maintain their new healthier patterns of eating and exercise, they will not return to their former situation. If they do not work to maintain themselves, they will, of course, return to their former weight level and poor physical condition.

So too, must those with OCSDs work to maintain their improvement, taking care to monitor themselves for signs of a return to old compulsive habits. A relapse often begins when you either deny that one is taking place, or rationalize to yourself that "It will be okay to do a compulsion just this once. How can it hurt?" or, "I'm in a hurry right now, and I haven't got time to do the correct thing. I simply can't afford to feel anxious right now and need instant relief," or "How can one compulsion hurt anyway? I can go back to doing the right thing tomorrow." Unfortunately, many sufferers can be procrastinators. They not only do not stop after that one time, but also may go on to excuse many other undesirable behaviors, despite their good intentions. This is not to say that a person in recovery must never have a lapse or a setback. You are only human and bound to make mistakes occasionally. Lapses are normal and should be prepared for. Let us just say that a person in recovery would do well to prevent what is preventable, and to work to get back on their program immediately after an episode of what could not be prevented.

Most studies looking at relapse prevention have been done with substance abusers, and the rate of occurrence of relapses in OCD has never really been studied in depth. Studies involving OCD have only looked at the results of discontinuing medication. It was found that almost all those whose only treatment consisted of medication were seen to relapse as a group, when they stopped taking it. Follow-ups to other studies of those who have successfully undergone behavioral therapy tend to show much lower rates of relapse months and even years later. If you have worked diligently at your therapy, have come out of it well trained, have had the techniques of relapse prevention properly explained to you, and have put them into practice daily, you will have minimized your chances of a relapse. For a discussion of the techniques of relapse prevention, see the second section in chapter 3 on self-help.

ACCEPTANCE

Up to this point, you have been reading about the nuts and bolts of changing and staying changed. While this technical information will be valuable to you, it may not, in itself, be enough for many of you. There is one further concept that I believe is extremely important to understand. In many ways, it may be the most important idea in this book, and it is "acceptance."

Even though the same information and sources of help are available to people with OCSDs, not everyone changes. Clearly, each person brings something different to situations where they must help themselves. It seems to me that many of those who do not do as well in therapy or recovery seem to be struggling with something else in addition to their disorders.

Years ago, psychoanalysts tended to label the lack of change in therapy as "resistance." It was judged that the person "needed" their neurotic symptoms in order to defend themselves from unacceptable impulses. Modern clinicians do not hold with this point of view. It is an easy thing to simply blame patients who did not do as well as we would hope. Currently, therapists view problems people have with change as a reflection of their illogical or distorted beliefs and philosophies. These beliefs prevent them from accepting the realities of their situations and doing the things they need to do to get well and stay well. The well-known "Serenity Prayer" nicely sums up much of what needs to be said on this subject.

The Serenity Prayer (1934)

> God, give us grace to accept with serenity
> The things that cannot be changed,
> Courage to change the things which should be changed,
> And the wisdom to distinguish the one from the other.
> —Reinhold Niebuhr (1892–1971)

Too often in the field of mental health, we become "obsessed" with the idea of change—changing our thoughts, behavior, relationships, etc. It seems that we sometimes regard ourselves more like appliances that need to have parts replaced, than the complex beings we are. One of the central dilemmas of therapy is this: *everything cannot be changed.*

The processes of treatment and recovery involve both *acceptance* and *change.* They are really interlocking concepts that help define each other. You cannot have one without the other. Unfortunately, the concept of change is often overemphasized at the expense of acceptance. This imbalance deprives sufferers of valuable tools that would aid in more complete recoveries. What I am advocating here is the reestablishment of this balance in OC treatment.

DEFINING ACCEPTANCE

In *Webster's New Collegiate Dictionary (Tenth Edition),* the word "accept" is defined as:

1.(a) to receive willingly . . . 2. to give admittance or approval to; 3.(a) to endure without protest or reaction; (b) to regard as proper, normal, or inevitable; (c) to recognize as true . . .

I have another useful definition applicable to OCSDs. It is a working definition that I believe is helpful for those pursuing a recovery. For our purposes, I define acceptance as a willingness to unconditionally undergo every part of the struggle for recovery, including negative feelings such as anxiety, and in spite of the possibility that setbacks and pain may result.

What I am trying to emphasize here is that acceptance means allowing yourself to take the chance to experience treatment and recovery as they are, which in itself is a risky business. Without being fully open to new experiences, change cannot happen. Please note that whatever definition you are using, acceptance doesn't necessarily mean "liking" something.

THE EFFECTS OF NONACCEPTANCE

The noted psychoanalyst Carl G. Jung said, "We cannot change anything unless we accept it." But what if we do not accept it? Nonacceptance creates problems because it creates paradoxes. By this, I mean that it causes sufferers to bring about the opposite of what they want. A good example can be seen in classic OCD, when the stress of struggling not to have obsessive thoughts creates more of them. Nonacceptance leads to misguided attempts to control what *cannot* be controlled and to avoid what *cannot* be avoided.

Some blocks to acceptance are:

Irrational demandingness. The willfulness and babyish insistence that we *must* get everything we want in life when we tell ourselves things like: "Getting well should be easy" or, "My disorder shouldn't exist."

Denial. "My disorder doesn't exist. There's really nothing wrong with me"

Distortion. "My disorder exists, but it doesn't really affect me or others."

Avoidance. "My disorder exists, but I just couldn't stand to face it or do anything that would make me uncomfortable."

Procrastination. "My disorder exists, but I'll deal with it later on when the time is right (or perfect) for me."

Perfectionism. A frequent accompaniment to classic OCD. The desire for this is probably a response to suffering from continual doubt. When everything is perfect, there is no room for doubt or risk. It leads to living a rigid, overcontrolled life, in which there is little or no tolerance for change, risk, difference, or anything being less than 100 percent. Many cannot accept that they no longer have the perfect life they thought they had.

Cultural Influences. Our can-do, "Just do it" culture, which teaches us that the sources of problems can simply be removed or modified, much as we solve mechanical problems. You are taught that you don't have to accept anything you don't like about yourself or your life, and that you can eliminate or avoid whatever you dislike at will, if only you use the right product. As part of our consumer-driven, self-enhancement culture, we are taught that we should never have to accept our imperfect selves as we are, or accept what we have, and should always continue to strive for some yet-to-be-attained, future level of perfection or ownership. Dissatisfaction and nonacceptance are what keep our consumer-oriented society going. If everyone were satisfied with their own image and what they owned, they wouldn't buy as many "things." I like to call this nonsensical advertising creation of the as-yet-unattained "perfect" life—THE BIG LIE—a king-sized irrational belief.

It is taught that in the "perfect life" there are no intrusive thoughts, sad events, problem habits, or failed efforts. This thinking prevents people from accepting the normal problems and imperfections of everyday life in recovery. Paradoxically, if you are going to live a full and complete life out there in the world, you need to accept the entire package life has to offer you, with all the accompanying pleasure and pain.

ACCEPTANCE, OCSDs, AND TREATMENT

Thoughts, and our reactions to them (or the resulting feelings), are not necessarily true reflections of the world beyond our own minds. They are simply something we experience on a mental level, or, as Recovery, Inc. says, "Feelings are not facts." The simple occurrence of obsessive thoughts or impulsive urges themselves does not have to result in a disturbance. It is the nonacceptance of thoughts, feelings, and impulses, or the unwinnable struggle to control them that is the real source of distress and suffering in OCSDs. Obsessive thoughts or impulsive urges do not necessarily have to become full-blown disorders. Most people's first responses to them tend to be ineffective. This is because of two factors. One is that our instincts tend to make us believe that all thoughts that occur in our heads are our own and should be taken seriously. The other is the misguided belief that we should somehow be able to control all our thoughts and urges. Intrusive thoughts, for instance, cannot be controlled, even in the average person. Given the nature of obsessions, and the way we seem to instinctively regard abnormal thoughts, it is not surprising that we choose to respond in fearful and extreme ways. Most people are not prepared to have or accept such repetitive mental events. However, this does not mean that they cannot learn to do better if they choose to do so.

You cannot necessarily change the fact that you have obsessive thoughts or impulsive urges. OCSDs are chronic problems that are probably genetic. You can, however, change your *beliefs* about them. Two important beliefs that must be changed are: (1) that you must respond to the thoughts or impulses or act on them, and that not doing so would mean taking an unacceptable risk or experiencing a serious discomfort, and (2) that there must be a quick and easy solution. In the case of obsessions, we are faced with a paradox. Studies have shown that attempts to suppress thoughts result in a rebound effect leading to more thoughts. To not think about something, you have to first think about it. Since struggling against the thoughts is impossible and therefore stressful, you only wind up with more distress in terms of depression (due to feeling helpless), anxiety, and more obsessions, as stress seems to stimulate their occurrence. So, paradoxically, your avoidance of anxiety only leads to more suffering. You perform compulsions to avoid the pain, which only leads to more pain.

In Recovery, Inc. they say, "Refuse to act on an obsession and it will die of inaction." Unfortunately, many sufferers do not do this and instead go for the quick fix—they act compulsively to reduce their anxiety because it works in the short run, even though it is defeating them in the long run. They never wait long enough to see what would actually happen if they simply stayed with their anxiety. Therefore, they neither learn the truth of the situation, nor do they build up any tolerance for the anxiety. What they do build up is a greater sensitivity to feeling anxious and a lot of bad habits. As a gentleman named John Clinton Collins once said, "There is often less danger in the things we fear than in the things we desire."

To further help yourself to achieve acceptance, it is important to resist the temptation to "hate" your OCSD. Quite a number of sufferers disturb themselves by hating their obsessive thoughts. Remember: since acceptance doesn't mean liking something, it also obviously cannot mean hating it either. Your disorder is not a thing to hate. It is a potential that lies within your own brain chemistry. It is a part of you, like it or not.

Another step toward acceptance for OCSD sufferers, is for them to learn to concentrate their efforts on living in the present, or, as they wisely say in AA, "One day at a time." Projecting catastrophes that may lie ahead, or "what-iffing," means that you are living in the future. Double checking on, or fearfully ruminating about previous events, means that you are living in the past. Much of classic OCD involves guilt about past events that cannot be changed, and worry about feared events in the future. Neither path represents living in reality, that is, in the here and now. Not living in the present moment can only bring unhappiness, since living in the here and now is the only thing you can really do successfully. The past is gone and cannot be changed, and the future is unknowable. You cannot live in the past or future and hope to be free of an OCSD. These two things are not compatible.

For classic OCD and BDD, not struggling desperately against obsessive thoughts or trying to get rid of them is the key. Instead, by changing your thinking about the thoughts in the present and accepting them, you can free yourself from the web of compulsions that control your life. It must be seen as a positively paradoxical situation that one must accept in order to bring about a change. Getting well means giving up the illusion of controlling what cannot be controlled (both the obsessions and the people and things in your environment), but *not* giving up real control itself (control over the way you regard the things that happen to you). Actually, too much rigid, compulsive control is just another way of being out of control. The French philosopher Descartes said that "the only thing we have power over in the universe is our own thoughts." While obsessive thoughts are the exception (as these are biochemically generated and not a part of your own real thought process), they can still be dealt with indirectly. So many people dread facing their fears because they anticipate that they will suffer. I often point out that they are already suffering and therefore have nothing to lose. As the French essayist Montaigne said, "A man who fears suffering is already suffering from what he fears."

Accepting the presence and existence of obsessive thoughts is the first step toward recovery. Behavior therapy in the form of Exposure and Response Prevention (for those with OCD and BDD) or Habit Reversal Training (for those with TTM, skin picking, or nail biting) is the second step. It represents the *change* part of the process. It is a way of confronting and experiencing the true consequences of not acting on your obsessive thoughts or impulses. By conducting your own private scientific experiment, you provide yourself with new information. What will actually happen if you touch that contaminated object, don't act on that superstitious thought, or resist pulling that hair? The new information will not fit comfortably with your old information, causing you to revise your present thinking. At the same time, you become desensitized to the experience of anxiety and discomfort in the present, and stop fearing that it may occur again in the future. That is, you come to accept the existence of the thoughts and urges. This can help you to also accept that you don't have to respond to obsessive thoughts or impulsive urges. As previously stated, classic OCD and BDD sufferers typically do not stay with their anxiety long enough to learn the truth of the matter. All that really happens is that you become anxious, and this will eventually pass after a period of time.

If you were able to step back and examine or listen to your mind and the thoughts it generated, it might sound like this: your *short-term thinking* might say, "I want to feel less anxious right now!" Your *long-term thinking*, on the other hand, might say, "I'd better not act on this fear because doing so on an ongoing basis is preventing me from functioning normally."

I know that I have been emphasizing the need to live in the present. This doesn't mean that you should be totally ignorant of both the short- and long-term consequences of your own actions. Living one day at a time does not mean that you should not be aware of the impact of what you are doing. To do otherwise is to be a totally impulsive human being.

The issue of acceptance is even involved when you go the route of taking medication for your disorder. I believe that for some, medication can be an important tool in treatment, and you must accept that it is not perfect (it may only eliminate part of your symptoms), and that you may not find the right one immediately. It may take many months and many fruitless attempts before you find one effective drug among the many we now have. You may also have to tolerate some side effects in order to get its benefits. This process takes a great deal of patience, and it is not miraculous.

Getting treatment for OCSDs does not promise you that you will never get another obsessive thought or impulsive urge again. These will recur from time to time. However, you will learn not to fear the presence of the thoughts or urges and how not to feel compelled to act on them. As mentioned earlier, not all our thoughts or urges can be controlled. Everyone gets unpleasant intrusive thoughts, but those with OCD and BDD cannot screen them as easily as others can, for a combination of biological and behavioral reasons. Everyone gets urges to pick or pull at themselves at times. Those with TTM, skin picking, or nail biting get them more frequently and intensely. Since it is normal for even non-OCSD sufferers to have unpleasant thoughts and grooming impulses, an OCSD sufferer who cannot accept this, and who has unrealistic expectations for what being well is like, can never feel recovered and will simply conclude that they are a failure. Treatment success should not be measured by the proportion of positive and negative thoughts and feelings you have, but by the extent to which you live your life in accordance with your values and experiences. This means not merely improved scores on clinical symptom rating scales, but also through involvement in pleasurable and enriching activities and relationships and in openness to new experiences. Many people learn to resist compulsions and impulsions and to accept obsessions. However, they still live their same old restricted lifestyles, lacking in spontaneity and challenge, much as though they were still ill. They therefore risk falling ill again.

THE FIVE ACCEPTANCES

So what do you need to accept to be able to successfully engage in the change program we call treatment, and then stay recovered?

1. Accept yourself.
2. Accept others.

3. Accept the illness and the nature of the illness.

4. Accept the nature of the task of therapy.

5. Accept the nature of the task of ongoing recovery.

Accept Yourself

The goal is unconditional self-acceptance. You are an ordinary fallible human being—neither good nor bad. As such, you cannot be rated in your entirety. Only your behavior is ratable as good or bad. You cannot rate yourself in your entirety because (and I draw here on the work of Dr. Paul Hauck and his excellent book, *Overcoming the Rating Game*):

- The *self* is many different properties including thoughts, deeds, physical appearance, etc.

- A single trait is not a whole person. People are complex beings made up of thousands of different traits. There are so many that you cannot be totally bad or totally good. It isn't possible to weigh or measure them all, and even if you could weigh the number of the good against the bad, how would you rate someone on these percentages? What can you make of someone who is 51 percent good and 49 percent bad? Doing badly doesn't make you totally bad, any more than doing good makes you totally good. Many of those with OCSDs tend to rate themselves badly on the basis of their disorder. Either others taught them this, or they concluded it on their own.

- Due to prejudices, how can we tell if each trait is good or bad in itself? Who would decide how to account for the cultural or personal prejudices of those doing the rating?

- People's traits change over time due to changes in their situations or the passage of time. We are not the same people at thirty that we were at fifteen.

- How do you compare the sum of all of one person's traits to the traits of another? Or even their single traits? Could you compare one person's main trait of being a hard worker to another person's thriftiness?

- To demand perfection of yourself is arrogance. It is like saying, "Those other losers out there can be imperfect, but not me. I'm capable of being better than the rest of them."

- If you can do badly at first, and then change for the better, did you go from being bad to being good? If this can change so easily, how can it mean anything that has any permanence? If doing bad made you totally bad for all time, there would be no such thing as recovery or rehabilitation. This is as foolish as saying that someone who is good can never be bad.

• While you cannot rate yourself, you can rate your behavior as good or bad in terms of your goals. If you simply rate yourself badly, and given the fact that you can't change yourself in your entirety, the only option you have left is to become depressed because you have backed yourself into a corner. The advantage here is that if you rate your behavior as bad, this still leaves you in a position to focus on the specific behavior that needs to be changed.

You are not the illness—it is something that you carry, but it is not your identity. To once again paraphrase Patricia Perkins-Doyle, president of the OC Foundation, you are a person who also happens to have OCD.

Reducing yourself to only one facet is a serious error. This type of thinking leads sufferers to become stigmatized and to look upon themselves as lower forms of life. Since the illness is only one facet of who you are, it cannot make you bad or less acceptable as a total human being (you can use this thought to help destigmatize yourself). It can only make your behavior less acceptable (and even that can be changed). Your illness was an accident of genetics and biology, and it is not your fault. You cannot be blamed for having it. You did not bring it on yourself. Therefore, because you cannot be anything other than imperfect, and can be neither totally good nor totally bad (because you are unratable), you have no choice but to accept yourself without conditions.

Accept Others

Other people are also fallible human beings, neither good nor bad. As such, they cannot be rated in their entirety either, only their behavior can be rated as good or bad. You cannot rationally demand perfection of them in their support of you or in their understanding of your symptoms. I have even seen other OC sufferers at support groups shake their heads in disbelief at someone else's symptoms and remark how crazy they sound. If this is the case, how can we expect those without the illness to understand? Accept that they will do the best they are able to, given who they are and what they have to work with.

You may not get the support and understanding of others for your illness. You are on your own. Other people don't have to do as you say or support your efforts if they do not choose to. There is no law that says they must. You can hope for it and desire it, but you cannot demand it. Or you may simply not have anyone in your life at the moment to give you such support. What do you do then, if you believe you cannot recover on your own? How do those without any outside support recover? There are many stories of those who have done just that. How is it possible? They learned to depend on their own inner resources.

You cannot expect others to live with your symptoms or support you, so that you can live for them indefinitely. No one "owes" you anything, and you are not entitled to reparation. Others have a right to their own lives free of your illness whether you like it or not. Our society has a specific attitude toward chronic illness: others will only be sympathetic to your condition if you appear to be making efforts to help yourself; otherwise, it will appear to them that you have brought your continued troubles on yourself through your own negligence or passivity (Note: *not* your original biological troubles, but your continued troubles). If it appears that you are just using others to support you in your illness, they will withdraw their support. Material support may be freely given by others if they choose to, but it is not a continuing right when you reach adulthood. When help is given to you in such a way that it enables you to live in a state of illness indefinitely, it is not help. We call it "codependency," and it is an unhealthy situation for all concerned.

Accept the Illness and the Nature of the Illness

Accept that you have an OCSD and that you will have unpleasant intrusive thoughts and repetitive compulsive or impulsive behaviors. Don't say, "I shouldn't have these symptoms. This shouldn't exist." You have an OCSD, and therefore, given the nature of OCSDs, you *should* have symptoms.

These are serious chronic illnesses with the potential to be debilitating. They are probably genetic, and currently, there is no way to reverse the problem. You will always walk around with a tendency within you toward the illness—even when you are recovered. I don't say this to discourage you— although there is no cure, there is recovery. There are people who do stop performing compulsions completely, and whose obsessions decline to near zero levels. By working hard, you will at least guarantee that you will come as close to this goal as is possible for you.

You will never "perfect" your symptoms. You cannot have it both ways: that is, keep the symptoms, get them to control things perfectly for you so you can live a risk-free life, and yet also have a normal life. This is an either/or situation. It's like the self-defeating alcoholic who wants to be a better alcoholic rather than a recovered one, and who thinks that there must be a way to drink two quarts of vodka a day and still live and function the way others do.

If you have classic OCD, your reasoning abilities in some areas may be out of focus. You probably are unable to clearly assess how risky certain things are, or how responsible you are for the well-being of others. Cognitive therapists have suggested that these are the chief features of this disorder. Whether or not this feature is cognitive or biological, it appears to be a reality. If others don't see things as being risky in the way that you do, it is not because they are ignorant. You are off track, not the rest of the world.

Accept the Nature of the Task of Therapy

You are alone with your illness. It is your responsibility to help yourself by relying on the advice of experts, and then doing the work of therapy. If you only do the work of therapy to keep others happy or just to get them off your back, you will not succeed. If you do it because someone is always there to push or remind or nag you, you will have learned nothing. The only exception is for the seriously ill who are just starting out. Even children need to learn to help themselves be independent of adult assistance, and in such cases, this help must be gradually phased out.

Therapy involves tasks which, to you, will seem like risks and almost impossible (especially at first). As mentioned before, you need to accept that you are not good at assessing risk. You must also accept that life entails a certain amount of risk which can never be eliminated. It is impossible to control the world external to yourself in order to eliminate that risk, and if you try, you also eliminate, along with it, your ability to function. Anything that is important to undertake in life involves risk. Therefore, if you are to accomplish anything that has meaning, some element of risk must be accepted. You must work hard and expend effort to recover (however hard as is necessary, and with whatever effort is required). Recovery will not come easily. You must confront your fears and urges in order to overcome them—they can no longer be avoided. The problem exists within you—it is not a problem stemming from your environment, nor can you eliminate all activities that might stimulate your symptoms.

As you confront your fears or urges, you will feel discomfort and anxiety, but as a patient of mine once stated, "If you have to suffer, suffer with a purpose." Some people try to eliminate this discomfort through the use of large amounts of anti-anxiety medications (to which they can become addicted) or worse yet, to alcohol or illegal drugs. However, it is only when you feel the anxiety that you can you say you are really following treatment, and that you are doing something to truly improve.

The therapy process takes time (however much it takes), and progress toward recovery does not proceed in a straight line. No one ever learns a new skill without making plenty of mistakes. There will be lapses and errors made at times, but things will work out if you persist. Knowing this about therapy should actually take the pressure off you and ease your stress, thereby avoiding this paradox:

if you make a mistake and tell yourself you are a failure, you will stop trying and never recover. Persistence is everything.

Great works are performed not by strength, but by perseverance.
—*Samuel Johnson* (famous OCD and Tourette's sufferer)

Perseverance is not a long race; it is many short races one after another.
—*Walter Elliott*

Accept the Nature of the Task of Ongoing Recovery

Recovery means that you have your symptoms under control and have begun functioning more fully again. Recovery takes work and is really a work in progress, not a final destination, but a daily journey. Each day you focus on your goals for only that day, living in the present.

A lapse or a slip is a temporary setback, and as they say in AA: "You can always start your day over." This does not mean that you are now all the way back to square one, just that you have taken a step in the wrong direction. Beware of all-or-nothing thinking, as in, "Because I slipped up, this proves I can never get well or stay well." Or, "This proves I'm too weak." Don't be taken in by the false concept of willpower, which is based on the idea that it is through some kind of weakness of character that you have your disorder.

There is yet another ongoing task of recovery that needs to be accepted. A person with an OCSD would do well to come to terms with having lost a portion of their lives and opportunities to the disorder. While much of this book is directed toward understanding symptoms and recovering from them, it is also important to raise the issue of how a sufferer can make sense of what has happened to them, and how they can go on living with the personal losses that an OCSD has inflicted. People have lost careers and relationships, not to mention decades of their lives that may have included their most productive years. Everyone who has lost parts of their lives cannot help but feel a sense of grief, and if left unresolved, this can cause problems for those beginning treatment or even those who are in recovery. There is clearly more to regaining a normal life and rejoining the everyday world than simply bringing one's symptoms under control through medication or behavioral therapy.

I try to impress on my patients that coming to terms with what they have lost in life is a lot like the process one must go through when mourning the death of someone close. In both cases, someone or something has been lost which cannot be returned to you. When a great loss has been suffered, healing the grief can only be achieved through the process of mourning. Suffering a loss means having had your life thrown out of balance. Mourning encompasses a period of time during which an individual regains that sense of equilibrium and achieves an adjustment to the fact of their loss. A sufferer's inability to start or complete this process can result in feelings of great sadness or depression. They may also feel anger toward the illness itself, toward those who may have misdiagnosed them or given them inadequate treatment, or even toward themselves for not having stood up to the symptoms. I endorse the 12-Step motto, "One day at a time." We cannot change the past, and we cannot totally predict or control the future. Those who limit their vision to only looking backward at their yesterdays will find that all it yields is remorse, bitterness, and regret. It will also deprive them of their present.

Where symptoms have been previously incapacitating, unresolved grief for a lost life can also make an individual in recovery feel like a perpetual outsider— detached and disconnected from the everyday world they were kept apart from for so long. So many people and possibilities have passed them by. In some, we see the loss of their ability to experience their own emotions and their emotional contact with others. It almost seems to have wasted away during the term of their illness.

The people who I have seen face their strongest fears and go on to make the best recoveries are those who have most effectively dealt with these issues. They were able to acknowledge what had happened to them but could still focus on the opportunities that recovery presented. They had their regrets but could also feel fortunate to have overcome their symptoms. Beyond this, they went on to concentrate their energies on creating new lives that did not revolve around OCSDs. I believe that all this is well exemplified by something that Erica had to say (see more of her story in the section on Grooming Impulsions in chapter 9):

Erica's Story

ᔪ *I do believe that realizing this is mostly a biochemical disorder in the brain proven by research, and not blaming family members or other people or yourself for this disease, is the first step in recovery. It is up to the person to do the best that he or she can to fight either by medication or behavioral therapy. I was raised in a family where all my needs were met, and it saddens me to see parents ask what they did to make a child suffer so. For me, having faith in God and using the terrible frustration that comes along with OCD gave me the energy for the perseverance of fighting it. I use the energy to say to myself, "I will fight this and not let it defeat me!" It is my goal someday to be able to speak about this disease to let other people know how much someone can suffer and that it is not their fault. I hope to be a success story someday, and in many ways I feel that I already am, as I look back over my life and see all of the things I have dealt with. I still am very much a happy person. I function effectively in relationships with people and am able to keep the responsibilities of being an adult. It is just a lot harder for an OCD person to get away from the anxiety and be able to fully relax and enjoy life to the extent it should be enjoyed.*

While some may be able to achieve this type of healing on their own, there are those who cannot seem to make a proper adjustment over time. There are various reasons why some find the task of mourning difficult. I believe that one of the main reasons is because of the lack of social support. J. William Worden, Ph.D. mentions this in his intelligent book *Grief Counseling and Grief Therapy* (2nd ed.): "Grief is really a social process and is best dealt with in a social setting in which people can support and reinforce each other in reaction to the loss." It is an important factor to be able to talk with others about your loss and to acknowledge and express the feelings you have about it in order to work through the grief. A loss due to a psychological disorder is not as easy to share with others as is the death of a loved one. It may mean revealing the existence of the disorder and risking rejection. Even when there are others to talk to, they may not take the loss seriously or may not even be willing to acknowledge that it happened. Support groups can help to fill this need. You may also need further and more specialized therapy, beyond that which was needed for your OCSD. Since you are dealing with loss, it would seem to follow that the best type of help would be similar to the grief counseling used with those who are bereaved. It is not surprising that the goals of grief therapy are also applicable to this type of situation.

- First, to accept the reality of the loss (getting past the disbelief that it really happened). Accepting that you do not have the perfect life you thought you had.

- Second, to work through the pain of the grief (getting past not allowing yourself to feel, so the pain doesn't have to be carried lifelong). It is brought out into the open, examined, and discharged. Talking to others helps. The more you talk, the more pain you give up, and the less the subject hurts each time it is raised.

- Third, to adjust to living a life without what has been lost, developing a new sense of self and of a world where such things can happen, and adapting to the loss and making the best of it.

- Fourth, to withdraw the emotional energy previously invested in the past, to reorganize, and to get on with life (to learn not to feel that your life somehow stopped permanently when the illness started). To realize that there is life after your disorder.

You know you have accomplished these tasks when you can finally think of your loss without the pain, experience the pleasures of life again, and when you can reinvest your emotions in life and living, adapt to new roles in the present, and work toward a new future. Life in the world of average people is imperfect and also has its share of doubts, fears, failures, and unpleasant thoughts. You, too, are imperfect, but at least you are free to make your own mistakes and to be spontaneous as you live in the present. You are now free to live in that same imperfect world that others do. As the AA slogan goes, "The world doesn't get better—you get better."

Once again, if you find that you are not able to properly mourn on your own and come to terms with the grief for what you have lost, get help with the process. To not do so is to risk further losses, either in terms of not being able to move ahead with your therapy or with establishing a postrecovery life for yourself.

Another practical issue related to accepting past losses is the need for rehabilitation in the present. There are those whose OCSD began to occur later in their lives and who have normal years to look back on. Their symptoms may have been mild to moderate, but they have generally been able to maintain average behavior in public and have kept up with everyday responsibilities. They generally look forward to regaining what they once had and can clearly visualize what a more normal life will be like for them in the future.

There are also those, however, whose OCSD began in early childhood, or whose symptoms have been extremely serious for many years. They may have lived reclusive or dysfunctional lives deprived of relationships or productive work, and organized and centered around trying to cope with their symptoms. If this sounds familiar, you may find yourself unable to imagine what life in recovery will be like, or how you will be able to cope with its numerous pressures and responsibilities when you are no longer controlled by the symptoms. Since all you may have to look back on is failure and rejection, everything to do with recovery may seem overwhelming. In some, the anxiety they feel when considering these questions can actually hold them back from trying to recover at all. Others may also look toward recovery with anxiety, but they are hopeful and determined enough to get well.

If you are someone without the experience of a significant period of normalcy, it is especially important that you be helped to prepare for life in the future. You may yet have ahead of you an education to begin or finish, a first date (or the first one in a long time), a first apartment, or a first real job. It is vital for you to understand that no one with any sense will suddenly throw you headfirst into everyday life, nor should you allow them to. Reentry can and should be a gradual process, tailored to whatever pace you can manage.

You might first need to be taught the basics, for example, learning not to sleep all day and stay up all night, which is a typical illness pattern. Starting out in some kind of day program or having job training to go to may help you, as it will give you a reason to get up and out. Next, social skills and assertiveness must be concentrated on to help you cope with the people you will meet. After attending a day program or job training, you could start working at volunteer jobs to gain confidence and the feeling of having structure in your life. Eventually, you can move on to paid part-time and then full-time work. If your illness kept you from completing your education, the pursuit of that high school or college diploma might precede looking for work.

On a different note, you may be one of the many with an OCSD who has long been disabled but has never applied for Social Security disability, simply because you did not believe that you qualified. There are some who may try to discourage you from applying for disability benefits, saying that you will become lazy and dependent on it and not go any further in life. Simply getting public assistance is not, in itself, a cause of laziness. To claim that it is, is insulting to many who are using it to aid in their recovery. I believe that anyone seriously wishing to find rehabilitation will not settle for a "life" on disability. Those who aren't serious would probably have found some other way out, in any case. Applying for disability benefits while working on rehabilitation can give you a needed headstart in terms of having some income. Qualifying for disability can also make you eligible for a wide array of publicly funded services. State and local agencies can often provide assistance in job training and educational opportunities. Disability payments can cover the cost of supportive living programs until you are able to provide it for yourself. As these agencies are usually not well acquainted with how to help persons suffering from OCSDs specifically, it is frequently helpful for a private practitioner/specialist (if you have one) to work with the state agencies on your behalf. Hopefully, there will one day be supportive living programs specifically for those with OCSDs.

EIGHT

Different Forms Obsessions Can Take

He that doubteth is damned.
—*Romans 14:23*

Doubts are more cruel than the worst of truths.
—*Molière*

Where there is no imagination, there is no horror.
—*Sir Arthur Conan Doyle*

robably the two largest overall categories of obsessions involve either thoughts of harm coming to the sufferer, or thoughts of the sufferer being involved in harm coming to someone else either deliberately or through negligence. Beyond these two major categories, I have created eight smaller subcategories for classifying obsessions. This is obviously not the only way that obsessions can be classified, but I believe this list takes in the major types and organizes them in a way that makes sense. They are as follows:

1. Morbid Obsessions About Sex or Harm

   • Aggressive Obsessions/Impulsions, Including Morbid Thoughts

   • Sexual Obsessions/Impulsions

2. Contamination Obsessions

3. Religious Obsessions

4. Obsessions of Harm, Danger, Loss, or Embarrassment

5. Superstitious or Magical Obsessions

6. Body-Focused Obsessions

7. Perfectionistic Obsessions

8. Neutral Obsessions

MORBID OBSESSIONS ABOUT SEX OR HARM

Obsessive thoughts and questions can often be about nasty and morbid subjects. Morbid obsessions can be about sex or wanting to hurt yourself or other people. For reasons we don't yet understand, some people's obsessive thoughts seem to latch onto whatever they may find the most repulsive or disgusting. Typically, those who have them do not have past histories of morbid preoccupations or behaviors. Morbid obsessive thoughts are especially hard to cope with because they are so foreign to the person. They mostly involve sinful, destructive and/or disgusting acts, wishes, impulses, or mind pictures. Morbid thoughts are a separate category by themselves and can be divided into those which are violent, those which are antisocial, and those which are sexual.

Aggressive Obsessions/Impulsions and Morbid Thoughts

This category takes in both aggressive and other antisocial thoughts (apart from those relating to sex). Aggressive thoughts involve ideas of either directly or indirectly bringing harm to others, either known to the obsessing person or strangers. The thoughts themselves are disgusting and horrifying to obsessive thinkers and seem not to be their own, but at the same time are persistent and remain in the person's thinking much of the time.

The kind of violent thoughts that have been reported to me include those where people see themselves hitting, stabbing, strangling, mutilating, or otherwise injuring their children, family members, strangers, pets, or even themselves. The thoughts suggest using sharp or pointed objects, such as knives, forks, scissors, pencils, pens, broken bottles, letter openers, power tools, or poison, their hands, or even their cars. I usually refer to these kinds of thoughts as "impulsions" because they represent a sudden urge to take action. Some sufferer's thoughts may involve pushing or throwing themselves or others into the paths of trains or cars, out of or into windows, or off balconies, buildings, or other high places. One patient frequently reported thoughts of ramming her car into a bridge abutment on the highway or steering it into the path of oncoming traffic. She also had thoughts at other times of running into pedestrians. Another patient, a teenage boy, had frequent thoughts about knifing or strangling his father when they stood next to each other in their kitchen. One middle-aged businessman feared sleeping next to his wife or driving alone with her in their car, as he feared he would get a sudden impulse to choke her to death or punch her into unconsciousness. His fear later grew to include anyone smaller and weaker that he felt he could easily overpower, such as children and elderly people, and he feared being alone with them. I have also seen many cases of mothers who experience repeated thoughts of acting violently toward their infants or small children. None of the people with these thoughts had ever behaved violently.

Sara describes what it was like to have thoughts like these.

Sara's Story

∾ *I was lying in bed, half awake and suddenly I had this terrifying image of myself stabbing my son. He was the most precious thing in my life and I could not imagine where this had come from. But what made it even more frightening was the intensity of the feeling associated with the image. I was so frightened, and I couldn't shake the feeling or the image no matter what I did. I had always been a very easy going, loving, and gentle person and this image was very foreign to me. Not only could I not shake the image, but the feelings both associated with the image and in response to it were very much out of proportion. I couldn't seem to get my emotions under control no matter how hard I tried. I did not have another image like that for several days, but the one I had experienced was always on my mind. When the second one happened, I began to wonder what kind of monster I really was. I knew I would die if anything happened to my son, but where had these thoughts come from? Was I really that kind of person? The only person I told at the time was my husband, and he thought I was overreacting and couldn't understand how I felt at all, although he knew I was hurting. Now I had the memory of two images to deal with, as well as the questions I had about myself and what kind of person or animal I really was.*

When I finally got the courage to tell my Dad, who had always been very supportive of me all my life and someone I could always go to for help, he said, "Don't think like that. Don't talk like that. I don't want to hear about it." And he walked out of the room and slammed the door. I was devastated! I was trying to tell him that I couldn't stop these thoughts, that they were frightening to me, and that I didn't know how to make it stop. At the time I was pregnant with my second son, for whom I had waited six years. However, this turmoil I was experiencing distracted me from the joy I felt in his upcoming arrival. All I could think about was the fear. Was I really crazy? Was I really a vicious person inside? How could I think such awful thoughts about my own child? I even told my obstetrician what was happening, and he was so uncomfortable that he never looked me in the eye. He was very patronizing and said, "Some women have some emotional problems while they are pregnant, don't worry." But this was more than the average emotionalism associated with pregnancy and I knew that. But I couldn't make anyone else understand.

I became very suicidal, as that seemed like my only way out of this and the only way I could guarantee that nothing would happen to my son. By this time, the thoughts and associated aggressive feelings were with me every waking moment, day and night. I was never free of them even for a moment. I was terrified to be alone with my son, so my mother spent all day every day with me until my husband got home. I would be so relieved when my son would go to school, because, as bizarre as it sounds, at least then I knew he was safe. I did not have the usual obvious rituals that most patients have, but what I did come to learn was that I had mental rituals instead. I was forever counting things and then dividing that number.

Allen's account portrays another experience of this type.

Allen's Story

～ *I got morbid obsessions about murdering my Mom and later on, I got thoughts of murdering anyone, that is, pushing people in front of subway trains. I dropped out of college after two-and-a-half years because my OCD was getting to be too much to handle. I got thoughts about murdering the person next to me. It was difficult to study or absorb what I read. There was one time thoughts raced into my head like a tape recorder on fast forward. This lasted about one week. I couldn't accept my thoughts. I'd see an airplane in the sky and would get a thought that I wanted it to blow up to see what it would look like. I even told myself that I wanted bad things to happen to friends. These thoughts were against my will, that is, being glad their car was stolen, etc. If I got any bad thought, I was convinced that I wanted to do it, such as wanting to see people murdered or tortured, thinking I wanted to jump off a bridge, rape women, and sexually harm my brother's kids. I could not come up with the strength to say "of course I don't want this." (I even told myself I wanted to be unhappy.)*

There are also less violent but also antisocial, thoughts that fall within this category. One woman reported thoughts of breaking the dishes and glassware on display every time she entered a department store, and she also frequently felt the urge to shout out obscene words there and in other public places. Some people even have thoughts about taking off their clothing or doing other antisocial things in public places. This sort of impulse is somewhat reminiscent of another related disorder, Tourette's Syndrome, which may be genetically linked to classic OCD. In Tourette's, if a sufferer thinks that they should not say or do something because it will be embarrassing to themselves or others, there may be a sudden urge to say or do that thing. Frequently, the Tourette's sufferer actually does do impulsive things. (In all fairness to Tourette's sufferers, it should be added here that the antisocial things they get the urge to do only represent one group of tics, don't involve hurting others, and are usually limited to such things as shouting obscenities or racial epithets, making noises, grabbing themselves, poking or pinching others, slapping, touching, or hitting themselves or others, teasing others, or touching hot or pointed things to cause minor injuries to themselves.)

Sexual Obsessions/Impulsions

Sexual obsessions have been known to center around such themes as having heterosexual or homosexual relations with one's own or other people's children, one's parents or relatives, animals, or even inanimate objects. Sometimes the thoughts even center around having sex with or thinking sexually about religious figures, such as saints, prophets, Jesus, the pope, etc. Sexual impulsions can involve thoughts that tell the sufferer to "go ahead" and do sexually inappropriate things such as exposing themselves to others, making suggestive remarks, or molesting others. Such thoughts, however, bear no real relation to the individual's true sexual desires or interests. Behaving in these ways would not be pleasurable or fascinating to them. A classic OCD sufferer would never do the things they think about, nor would they ever want to. An important point to add here is that individuals with these types of obsessions worry that the thoughts somehow reflect true "unconscious" wishes and desires. Their anxiety results in a desire for perfect certainty that they are not some type of pervert or deviant. This causes them to lose sight of the fact that it is quite normal for people to sometimes have unusual thoughts, impulses, or even fantasies about sex. One common theme involves thoughts and fantasies about having homosexual relations. Often, thoughts in this particular subcategory of sexual obsessions will only involve the repetitive question "How do I know I'm not a homosexual?"—a question which no amount of reasoning can remove. They may also have thoughts that tell them they are homosexual or will become homosexual.

Mental pictures of themselves committing homosexual acts can sometimes accompany these thoughts. The fact that the sufferer has never shown any homosexual tendencies or behaviors makes no difference in the face of these strong doubts. These types of obsessions do not appear to be strictly limited to heterosexuals. I have had homosexual patients troubled with obsessive thoughts about being straight. As with morbid impulsions, such thoughts do not result in the individual acting them out.

A Note About Acting Out Morbid Thoughts

Let me make it perfectly clear here that I have never seen or heard of someone with classic OCD ever acting out a morbid or sexual impulsion. One very important point to remember is that even though thoughts of violence and inappropriate behavior commonly occur in obsessions, there is no evidence that the mere presence of obsessions alone can cause a person to become a murderer, criminal, deviant, or change their sexual orientation. One point about aggressive thoughts should be made clear. There are some OC sufferers who do get angry, have fights, or get physical with family members or others. Anger at the disorder, interference with symptoms, and family problems have, in extreme cases, led to pushing, shoving, yelling, and even occasionally hitting. This is not the same, however, as the harmful acts that those with violent impulsions think about. Actually, in my own experience, those with such thoughts are the least likely of all groups of sufferers to engage in family fights. This is due to the timidity and doubt that the violent thoughts cause.

Many people who have these kinds of thoughts needlessly suffer strong guilt, fear, and shame, worrying whether these impulsions are things that they really wish to do. The strength of the thoughts and their persistence is often what confuses sufferers, as Tony related to me in his account.

Tony's Story

⁓ *My OCD symptoms consisted of moderately strong obsessions of a violent and harmful nature. I would realize, for instance, that when I picked up a knife, the intrusive thought would go through my brain that I would pick up that knife and kill or hurt somebody with it. I knew this was not possible and that I could never hurt somebody else, but the thoughts seemed so real, so agonizing, that it was almost impossible to distinguish whether or not they were reality.*

Those with these types of thoughts begin to wonder if they are sociopaths. Sociopaths are actually quite the opposite, experiencing no guilt at all about their antisocial behaviors. Classic OCD sufferers fear that under the right conditions, they will "snap" or "go berserk" and simply lose control. They ask themselves obsessively, "How do I know I won't go crazy and lose control?" Their thinking can become even more doubtful, causing them to ask "How do I know I haven't already done some of the things I think about?" Sometimes a sufferer will try to think their obsessive thoughts on purpose, in order to see how they will react, as a type of compulsive double checking. Even when the diagnosis of OCD is explained to them to help give them some perspective, the OCD can take an insidious twist and tell them, "Maybe I really don't have OCD, and therefore I will go berserk." The result is that they end up avoiding many public or private social situations, even to the point of becoming hermits, to avoid harming others. One man gave up eating in restaurants because he had impulsive thoughts about stabbing waiters and waitresses with the silverware. When he commuted to work by train, he had thoughts that urged him to push others into the path of oncoming trains while he waited on the platform, and so he made sure not to stand too close to others there. He also experienced a fear of driving, as it occurred to him that he could steer his car into the opposite lane of traffic and cause a collision. There is no proof, however, that such thoughts can "make" a person carry out aggressive acts or behave in antisocial ways. This man, for example, had never acted violently in his life, nor has he since the start of his thoughts several years ago. "What kind of person am I," he would ask me, "who would think of doing such things?" As usual, the problem here was really one of doubt. His greatest and most frightening doubt was, "Will I go berserk one day and really do the things I am thinking?" He never did, of course, but this question was enough to paralyze his life.

Another difficult aspect of morbid thoughts is illustrated by what sometimes happens when a sufferer reveals these thoughts. Those who do not understand OCD tend to take the thoughts seriously, often show alarm, and try to take some kind of action to protect the person from themselves or to protect others from the sufferer. This has led to some dreadful misunderstandings, where people have been wrongly hospitalized or reported to the police, simply for revealing the content of their thoughts to someone they thought they could trust. These types of experiences have, in some instances, prevented sufferers from seeking treatment, for fear of being misunderstood. They have also unfortunately added to the great isolation, doubt, anxiety, and guilt these people are already experiencing.

The doubtful fear of "letting loose" is also something that keeps people with morbid obsessions from seeking treatment. They wrongly believe that their fear of the thoughts is really the only thing keeping them from acting them out, and that if therapy ever removed the fear, there would then be nothing holding them back. They therefore hang on to their inhibitions and fears.

CONTAMINATION OBSESSIONS

Many of us are familiar with compulsive behaviors such as excessive hand washing or showering which some OCD sufferers use to decontaminate themselves
and thus relieve their anxiety. They are probably the best known symptoms of
OCD. Probably the most famous example of someone with this problem would
be Howard Hughes, the millionaire industrialist whose wealth enabled him to
physically isolate himself from everyone. His fears ultimately prevented him
from getting treatment for a medical condition that resulted in his death.

Less frequently discussed are the thoughts about being contaminated, which
drive the need for these compulsions. Even when compulsive washers are not
washing, they are frequently tortured by such thoughts. These could include
whether or not they need to check themselves for perfect cleanliness, whether or
not they just accidentally brushed against something that might have been contaminated, what that stain on their clothing could be, trying to remember who
was the last person to touch something, etc.

There seem to be few limits as to what kinds of things can be thought of as
"dirty" or "dangerous." It goes without saying that body secretions such as feces,
urine, semen, mucus, vomit, saliva, and blood top the list. So does anything having to do with toilets or bathrooms. Among the things I have seen patients walking around in constant fear of coming into contact with are such things as soap
(yes, soap), radioactivity, lead, asbestos, household cleansers, drain cleaners,
insecticides, greasy foods, spoiled foods, garbage receptacles, pets, birds, dead
animals, broken glass, hair, hairspray, newspapers, water faucets, oil, baby pow-
der, ink, sewer gratings, or manhole covers, etc.

As you can see from this list there are some that fear contamination from
things other than dirt, germs, or chemicals. These people are more bothered by
the idea that anything that simply "doesn't belong" may be on them or their
possessions. Such things include odors from foods, the foods themselves, grease,
or anything with a sticky texture. They can acknowledge that these things aren't
dangerous or harmful, just repulsive in some way.

Contamination thoughts obviously have no real basis in logic. Sufferers cannot seem to compare themselves to the average individuals around them to see
how their behaviors are excessive and unnecessary. They think that they, themselves, their homes, or their belongings can somehow be "perfectly" isolated
from the rest of the world and kept clean. I often try to explain how ultimately
"everything touches everything." It is true that some of the things they worry
about can in certain cases actually cause people to sicken or die. The odds of
these things happening, however, are nowhere near as likely to happen as sufferers imagine. Ironically, as they allow all their protected things to gradually
become contaminated in therapy, they are able to let go and accept that none of

their things are really contaminated. In fact, a motto I like to give patients is that "When everything is contaminated, nothing is contaminated."

Fears of contracting specific illnesses are widespread among those in this category. Cancer probably used to top the list but has been surpassed in recent years by AIDS. Herpes (both kinds) and other incurable illnesses such as rabies, Ebola virus, and Hanta Virus are also sometimes seen. Thoughts of these can be quite severe and extremely debilitating. Sufferers fear having cuts, going near anyone who looks unclean or unwell, or touching things in public places. They may have no fear of the consequences for themselves, but may fear giving the illness to others and then having to suffer feelings of guilt. Amanda gives us a good picture of what contamination obsessions can be like.

Amanda's Story

⌒ *I was sitting at the sink in the back of the beauty parlor waiting to get my hair washed. As I sat there, I thought of all the people that might also have sat at that sink that day to get their hair washed. I wondered if any of them had cuts or scratches on their necks or ears and could have left traces of their blood on the rim of that sink. I wondered if I put my head on that rim, that their blood would somehow get into my body and possibly infect me with the HIV virus. I tried to turn around and examine the sink, but it was a black sink, and I couldn't tell if any of the water droplets could possibly be bloody. As I sat there I gazed at my daughter who was sitting next to me and wondered if she could sense my anxiety. Then I was asked to get up so a man could get washed before me. He was young, and I imagined him as a person who slept with a lot of women and was probably HIV infected as a result of that. As the hairdresser washed his hair, I imagined that somehow some of his blood got onto the rim of that sink. When I went back to the sink I was very scared and nervous that maybe blood from that man would somehow get into my neck, pierced ears, or scalp. I tried to look over the sink again but couldn't see anything because of the black color. The girl finally came to wash my hair. She was also the manicurist and young. I imagined that maybe she would have a cut on her finger or hand from the manicure tools she had just used. She washed an old woman's hair first in the sink next to me. I was hoping that if she was bleeding, it would wash off in that other sink. When she washed my hair, she scrubbed and scratched my scalp for quite a long time. I wondered if she had HIV. I was very anxious and nervous that one of her fingers was bleeding into my scalp. I wondered if I had any openings on my scalp that would enable infected blood to enter my body. I wondered why she scrubbed for so long.*

Contamination can also have magical origins. Words, names, colors, and numbers connected with bad occurrences or possible "bad luck" can be seen to be as contaminating in their own way as dirt or germs. It is not unusual for sufferers to have one or more outfits hanging in their closets that can no longer be worn because they are associated with something unpleasant. Clothes worn to funerals are frequently singled out for such treatment. Sometimes, clothes that have "bad" numbers or names on them are also to be avoided.

Many of my patients have feared the names or mental images of people who were ill, disabled, or dead, as if such bad outcomes could somehow be magically transferred. One former patient used to get anxious on hearing such words as "blind," "crippled," "deaf," etc., thinking that these disabilities could happen to him. Others have come to fear the names of specific illnesses, such as cancer or schizophrenia. It is also quite common to believe that objects belonging to people with disabilities are somehow contaminated and must not be touched.

Contamination obsessions can also cross over religious as well as magical lines. Individuals can be tortured by fears that they have become tainted or contaminated by evil or the devil in some way. (See the next section Religious Obsessions.)

Compulsive decontamination activities (see chapter 9) could be compared to the tip of an iceberg, with the contamination obsessions as the bulk of the problem hidden below the surface. In the case of serious contamination obsessions, the decontamination behaviors can only buy a little time in which the sufferer doesn't have to doubtfully agonize.

RELIGIOUS OBSESSIONS

Religion is an area that is a prime target for obsessional thinking. There are so many possible ways to do something seriously wrong that can then be agonized about. There are enough faults, sins, and taboos to avoid and rules and commandments to worry about to fill a doubtful sufferer's lifetime. Sometimes a sufferer doesn't have to do anything in particular to feel guilty and irreligious. They merely have thoughts that tell them they are perhaps improperly observant and that God dislikes them. In Tony's account (part of which also appears in the section on Morbid Thoughts earlier in this chapter), he expresses what such thoughts were like for him.

Tony's Story

⌒ *In church, I was struck with the feeling that I was not "religious enough," even though I am a very devout Catholic. I would have thoughts that God was going to send me to hell when I died because I was not reli-*

gious enough or that God would destroy my life or my family because I wasn't very faithful and I would turn into a very sinful person someday.

Interestingly, the sufferer's religion doesn't always seem to make a difference. I have met people with such obsessions belonging to every major faith. I have even met individuals who obsessed about matters involving religions other than their own. Obsessions have an almost uncanny knack for picking up on exactly what will bother the individual the most. In the case of this group, it may be that an overly strong sense of religious belief and of right and wrong predisposes many to have obsessions of this type. Another odd aspect in the case of those with religious obsessions is that the degree of a person's faith or their attitude toward religion doesn't always seem to matter, as far as I have been able to observe. Those who have them appear to range from the most observant to those in whose life religion plays a very small part. Mike is one of those whose religious upbringing seems to have had some influence on his disorder.

Mike's Story

〜 *The obsessions/compulsions that I have can be classified as magical. Their primary focus is on religion and death. There have been times, while changing channels on the TV with my remote control, when I would have an obsession occur on a Catholic station. Thoughts of the devil came to my mind which led to my compulsions—changing the station back and forth three times in honor of the Father, Son, and Holy Ghost, or five times because it's a "safe" number or a number that will take the evil away. Another obsession is visualizing a loved one's name or face and seeing the word "death" or "die" after it. At this point, I would feel the magical compulsion to "undo" or make it "safe" for that individual by spelling their name in my mind and attaching the word "live" after their name. This act would tend to make the obsession better, in other words, correct it. It served as a means to protect the individual. Another example of my OCD is one which occurs when going to a funeral home to pay my last respects to the deceased. My obsessive thoughts can include seeing the words "devil," "Satan," and/or "hell" on the deceased's face. Also, thoughts of wishing the deceased person damnation to hell have occurred to me. After seeing these words and experiencing magical obsessions, I would feel compelled to look toward and then away from the deceased several times while trying to replace these evil words with good words. Believe me, the last thing I want to do is to wish bad things to happen to either living or deceased individuals. Some of my other obsessions include thinking of the devil when I see a religious picture or wishing bad things or death to happen to another person.*

This can lead to an intense feeling of guilt and the performance of my rituals—counting to five, spelling the words "live," "heaven," etc. These are only a few of my magical obsessions/compulsions that I continue to struggle against at this time. I am a Catholic and attended parochial school and I believe that religion has magnified my OCD. This occurs through the guilt it imposes when I experience my obsessions and I feel I have sinned. I do not mean to blame the Catholic religion, however, I believe that because I am vulnerable, the strictness of my faith can be overwhelming for me.

In one type of religious obsession, we see a similarity to the types of impulsions that can be observed in aggressive obsessions. The individual gets thoughts suggesting that they will act out and deliberately do blasphemous or sinful things. These can include ideas of shouting obscenities or blasphemies or acting otherwise inappropriately in a house of worship, in the presence of a religious or spiritual leader, or merely in a public place. They can also include thoughts of defacing Bibles or other holy books, misusing religious articles, or vandalizing houses of worship. One woman suffered intense impulsions telling her she should take off her clothes in church. She also had thoughts about shouting out curses during the sermon. Centuries ago, she would probably have been judged to be possessed.

The reverse of the above has to do with doubtful thoughts that one has possibly behaved in an irreligious manner without meaning to. One individual feared to go to church because he believed he might shout out obscenities while singing hymns and not know about it. He often agonized that he might have done so in the past and frequently questioned his wife and his minister about this.

I also include in this category the type of "hyper-religiosity" also known as "religious scrupulosity." I suppose a case could be made for putting this type of obsession in the "Perfectionistic Obsessions" category, but this does seem to be a subtype concerned only with the perfect practice of one's religion, whatever it is. In this type of obsession, being rather religious to begin with seems to not only be a prerequisite, but is also the preoccupation. Although a person's upbringing doesn't always contribute to their particular symptoms, this is a case where the connection can clearly be seen. As a part of having to be perfectly religious, sufferers are often doubtful about their level of faith and whether they love their deity enough. They view many ordinary situations as tests of their faith and engage in much compulsive self-denial as proof of their commitment. Allen seems to be caught up in this hyper-religiosity as his account indicates.

Allen's Story

∾ *I grew up Catholic and most of my obsessions centered around morality and issues of right and wrong and committing sin. I feared going to confession and felt I never confessed sins correctly, either I left sins out or confessed some sins I didn't do, because I thought something was wrong if I didn't have much to confess. I could not accept any thought that wasn't perfect or good. I felt I was wicked and God would punish me. I especially felt scared of sexual thoughts. I realize now that I had taken my religion too seriously. I tried to avoid all possible chances of committing sin. I felt I shouldn't be good at anything because I might become vain and that would be a sin. I could also show off, gain attention and that would be a sin. After awhile, I was afraid to give myself anything because I'd ask myself a question, "Which do I want more, my favorite TV show or God?" I felt I had to choose God and felt it was evil for me to want anything. I even gave away toys of mine which I liked because someone suggested it and I felt guilty for wanting them myself. Even at four years old I felt guilty for having my toys and not concentrating on those who had little. When I was about nine years old, I moved to Massachusetts and I started to doubt God's existence and kept saying my prayers over and over because I thought I didn't say them right. I became very fearful of my thoughts and started to doubt the existence of Christ. I would constantly ask my brother for reassurance as to whether I had committed a serious sin or not. I could not tell the difference between serious sin and minor sin. It was all serious to me.*

Catholic sufferers with severe religious doubts have been known to engage in excessive confessions. Unfortunately, confessing such thoughts to religious or spiritual leaders often gets an unenlightened response. This is because the person being confessed to is uninformed about OCD. I have had patients who were assigned to do penance and made to feel even guiltier about their obsessions when they finally got up the nerve to tell a member of their clergy about them. Others have been treated suspiciously afterward. As unlikely as it may sound, I have even had a patient who had the suggestion made to him that he was perhaps possessed.

One also finds some crossover between this category and morbid sexual obsessions. Perverse sexual thoughts begin to mix with religious themes for some sufferers, adding a new and even more disturbing dimension.

OBSESSIONS OF HARM, DANGER, LOSS, OR EMBARRASSMENT

Simply having thoughts about bad things happening to you or others can be considered obsessions. In fact, the majority of obsessions seem to revolve around thoughts of negative or bad things happening to the sufferer or to others with whom the sufferer has contact.

This category of obsessions might, at first, seem to be a sort of catchall, but the symptoms which make it up are actually all tied together by the possibility that some type of bad occurrence, including embarrassment, injury, and death, will either happen to the sufferer or to another person or else will be perpetrated by the sufferer on someone else. In the last case, the sufferer worries that they will cause the harm due to some kind of negligence or carelessness. It is this feature which separates the thoughts of harm in this category from those found under Aggressive Obsessions/Impulsions. Along with these thoughts usually comes a great sense of exaggerated responsibility, as well as a potential for overwhelming feelings of guilt. This has been referred to by some as "hyper-responsibility." There is a sort of "Murphy's Law" at work in their thinking. That is, if anything can possibly go wrong, it will occur to them, and they will obsess about it. (Contamination Obsessions could perhaps be placed in this category, but I have chosen not to include them here, as they make up a very large and complex group on their own, and it is more efficient and less confusing to deal with them separately.)

There is a wide range of possible negative happenings which sufferers in this category obsess about. One, which seems less harmless but can lead to many doubtful agonies, is the thought of having accidentally insulted or offended someone. This can not only apply to friends, relatives, and coworkers, but also to total strangers. Sufferers imagine that they may have said something offensive, used an insulting tone of voice, gestured rudely, or merely looked at someone in an unpleasant way. The outcome is viewed as one in which the "victim" is made to feel bad, and the obsessive "perpetrator" must feel embarrassed and guilty. Furthermore, the sufferer worries that their mistake (assuming they made one) will then cost them a friendship, a job, or a business client.

A related, but opposite sort of obsession is where a sufferer thinks that others may be looking at them and criticizing them in some way, leading to feelings of embarrassment. They will look around and wonder if the expressions on other people's faces mean that they are thinking in a critical way about the sufferer's behavior, looks, clothes, or even the way they are walking or eating. There may be some relationship here to what is known as social phobia, where individuals avoid doing many types of things in front of others for fear of criticism, and are constantly scanning others for reactions when they are in public places. I believe the difference here is that the OC sufferer is much more ruminative, constantly dwelling on such things even when they aren't in public settings.

One step up from these ideas are those which involve doubts about having cheated others or having been cheated. This also comes under the heading of what is known as "Scrupulosity." Because of their doubts, these sufferers go far beyond ordinary honesty. These doubtful thoughts typically occur when the sufferer is either buying, selling, trading, or competing for something. They fear that they have either taken too much change in stores when paying or have shortchanged someone when making change. They get doubtful thoughts that they may have negligently taken merchandise they didn't pay for or were given discounts they weren't entitled to. Conversely, if employed in a sales position, they may worry that they gave customers defective merchandise, wrong product information, or perhaps put the wrong item in the customer's bag. When a sufferer/customer is given a free sample of something, they may have obsessions about having taken more than they were entitled to. Test-taking can be problematical, due to fears of having somehow cheated or having taken some type of unfair advantage. Another area in which this obsession comes into play for some sufferers is when they are figuring out their income taxes. I have encountered sufferers who, due to their doubts, deliberately overpaid their taxes rather than risk cheating the government.

The reverse of the last group is also seen at times among those in this category, that is those with obsessions about having been cheated by others. This is different from paranoid thinking, where there is a belief that there are complicated and organized plots to harm the person. We have here the usual agonizing doubts, but instead of their revolving around a particular group of evildoers or plotters, they may apply to almost anyone the sufferer has dealings with. Frequently, when they purchase something they will ask themselves, "How do I know I actually got what I paid for?" or, "How can I be sure I wasn't overcharged?" A rather insidious obsession which belongs with this group, and which I have encountered several times over the years, is the idea that one's child was switched in the hospital following delivery and actually belongs to someone else. Recent media tales of such unusual occurrences have probably worsened these ideas for some sufferers.

A variation somewhat related to these obsessions about being cheated shows a different twist. I have run across several cases in which sufferers get repetitive thoughts that they are trapped in unsatisfactory jobs or relationships and are thus being cheated in this way. They look at their job or spouses, for instance, and doubtfully worry that they are in the wrong situation and would be happier doing something else in life or being married to someone else. They look at people in other professions and ask themselves if these others may be happier than they are. They may look at other men or women and get doubtful thoughts that these people are nicer or more attractive than their own spouses, and that they might be happier with them instead. The follow-up thoughts to this usually involve ideas that they must perhaps quit their jobs, or get divorced. This leads to even greater anxiety, since they aren't really unhappy and can't make up their minds about what to do next. Because we all question our lives at times or experience periodic problems or unhappiness, there is a lot of daily fuel for these kinds of thoughts in those who are prone to them.

A less specific version of this type of thought is where the sufferer obsesses about having to break up with their boy or girlfriend, or divorce their spouse, with the thought giving them no specific reason why. This can be particularly distressing to those who have happy relationships, since they then begin to ask themselves whether the thoughts could really mean that they are "unconsciously unhappy." "Why else," they ask themselves, "would I constantly think these thoughts if they weren't my real desire?" When they share these obsessions with their loved one, it usually only worsens the situation. It confirms the sufferer's worst doubts, since the other person, on constantly hearing this, may react emotionally and finally even threaten to leave.

Obsessions under this heading can also become philosophical. Some suffer obsessions about their own mortality and repetitively question, in what looks like some type of existential dilemma, what is the point of being alive, since they are just going to die and be forgotten eventually anyway. This type of thought can not only lead to feelings of anxiety, but also to feelings of depression and despair, as no amount of reassurance or philosophical explanation can really satisfy such questions. There are subtle differences between this type of obsession and the ruminations of depressed persons, and it would be very easy to confuse the two. These questions stubbornly repeat themselves, and they have a way of insidiously intruding during a sufferer's happier moments. There may also be repetitive compulsive attempts to answer these questions, which a depressed person wouldn't try. Other related philosophical obsessions may involve the purpose or nature of life, time, or the universe.

On a less philosophical level, there are those who have obsessions about having an illness, accident, or injury occurring to them or to someone they know. This bad happening, and how it will occur, may be something very specific, or it may simply center in a vague sort of way on something unlucky. One of the better-known obsessions in this category is where the sufferer gets frequent thoughts of having accidentally hit a pedestrian with their vehicle. Generally, such occurrences as hitting bumps or trash in the road, driving close to pedestrians, or sensing objects or movement in their peripheral vision can be enough to stimulate thoughts that the worst has happened. The thoughts tell them that they may have had a hit-and-run accident, and that in addition to suffering the horrible guilt of having taken the life of another human being, they may end up in prison. Another variation is seen among those who, when preparing food for others, worry that they may have accidentally poisoned the food in some way. This type of thinking is well illustrated in an account by Doreen.

Doreen's Story

  ⌒   *I can remember my first attack like it was yesterday. I had gone for a walk around the town and I took along a stick that I had picked up from somewhere. Halfway through the walk I decided that I no longer wanted to carry it so I threw it away. Suddenly, after getting home I just knew that my brother's high school class ring was attached to the stick and I had thrown it away. I thought about it and kept saying to myself, "Maybe it wasn't, maybe it was. I know it, I just know it," over and over. It was all I could think about. I was in a panic. I went back to get the stick because I thought this would make everything right. But it didn't. I worried about it over and over. I had to tell my mother what had happened. She asked me why had I taken the ring. I told her that I didn't take it. I just knew that it was on the stick. She went and looked for the ring and it was on the mantle where my brother had left it. In spite of this, I still knew that I had lost something valuable, I just didn't know what it was.*

I then turned into a washer. My hands had to be clean. All I had to do was wash them when I thought they were dirty. If I touched my mouth, I would have to wash my hands. I would think, "Did I wash my hands? I should wash them now because maybe I haven't." I would try not to touch people if I thought my hands were not clean, since I was afraid I would make them sick and they would die. When I went to church I would not want to shake hands with people. I remember one evening when I came home, my mother had made barbecued chicken and I reached in the pot and broke off a piece. How could I have made such a mistake? I believed that I had contaminated the entire pot. I thought I would make everyone sick if they ate it. Then there was the mushroom. I was walking behind the church near the woods when I saw a mushroom and I kicked it. The top broke off and I noticed that it was black inside. "Oh no," I thought, "it's poisonous and now the poison is in the air. What could I do? How could I stop the poison?" I decided to put the top back on the mushroom and that would stop the poison from getting into the air, but now I had touched it and now my hands were tainted with the poison. I had to wash them. I went to the side of the church where there was a water faucet and rinsed off my shoe very carefully so as not to spread any more poison. I washed my hands and then I thought that now the water supply would be contaminated and thousands of people would die. I worried that when I washed my hands that the contaminants were being let in the water supply and would not be filtered out. People would die and it would be my fault. What could I do? There was no way to stop it. I expected the morning news to say, "Thousands Die—Water Supply Tainted." It did not happen and I accepted that; nevertheless I didn't stop washing. The washing was replaced by checking. I would think that the water was still running after I washed my hands. It became much easier not to wash my hands instead of worrying about the running water. I was unable to tell anyone as I knew they would not understand. My mother said I would grow out of it.

I took an electronics class in high school in which we would etch circuit boards. I was afraid of the etching solution because it was poisonous. What if I got some on my skin and did not know it? Would it hurt me or someone I came in contact with? I would worry about leaving the boards in the solution too long, because it could completely dissolve them. I wondered, "What if I left the water running after rinsing the boards?" I tried to tell myself that it would run down the drain and if the drain was stopped up, it would run into a floor drain. I could not remember seeing a floor drain, but now I told myself it would run out the doors. But what if it wouldn't? I just knew the water was filling up the electronics lab and everything would be ruined. I even called the school because I did not want to worry all weekend. The office secretary told me that the teacher had probably checked it before leaving. This was not reassuring at all.

My first year of college was enjoyable. This did not last into my second year, as I knew that the time would come for me to look for a job. I applied at many of the local industries, however, my confidence was lacking. I was not convinced that I could do anything that I wanted. I did not even want to try. I went to work at a restaurant after graduating. After working there for a year and a half, I found a job as a drafter. I would prepare working drawings showing what type of glazing and metal would be used in buildings under construction. This did not worry me as much as washing the ink from my pens. I thought that the ink might poison the drinking water. I also took outrageous precautions with the cleaning solution for the drafting table which I still have today (four years later) because I worried about disposing of it safely. I now work at a pharmacy where I can find lots of things to worry about. When I first went for the job I asked the pharmacist if I would be working with the prescription medicine and he replied that it was someone else's responsibility. That was what I wanted to hear, but somehow I managed to get my hands into it anyway. After leaving work, I would spend hours thinking, "Did you give someone the wrong prescription?" I am very careful in checking the names, but I worry that if I did someone could die! One lady picked hers up before I could check the name. I worried that it could have been the wrong one. I checked the price against the computer on her last refill. It was the same, but someone else could have one with the same price. I asked myself, are you sure it was the right name? I'm not. What can I do? It's three in the morning, and if I call the pharmacist, what would I tell him? If I said I think I may have killed someone he would think I was crazy. Maybe I am crazy. Maybe this is what it's like. No free time in your mind, worrying all the time, always thinking, "What if?" Never able to be sure.

In obsessions about being harmed, there is a type of thought that is reminiscent of the old movie *Gaslight*. In the film, a villainous husband subtly changes and manipulates small things in his wife's environment to make her feel as if she is losing her mind and then he denies that anything is different. Similarly, in this category we see doubtful thoughts in which a sufferer will constantly notice numerous small things such as the placement of furniture or objects, or tiny scratches, marks, or dents on walls, possessions, or cars and wonder how they got there. Often, in their anxiety, they worry that others are doing this to make them crazy or to harass them in some way. The belief, in this case, is not as fixed as in paranoia, and those with this form of OCD do not generally see organized plots to harm them. Actually, when questioned, they cannot really say who is doing it or why. Unlike paranoids, who usually can tell you names and numerous details, their explanations are very vague.

Finally, in this category, are obsessive thoughts that look like the opposite of morbid impulsions. Whereas in the case of impulsions, a sufferer will get thoughts telling them to actually do something violent or antisocial, the individual in this category will merely have doubtful thoughts in which they worry that for some unexplained reason, they will somehow lose control and behave unacceptably. There is no thought here telling them "Why don't you do it?" They just fear that perhaps they will do something to feel guilty about and have to be punished for.

SUPERSTITIOUS OR MAGICAL OBSESSIONS

Many obsessions seem to have a sort of "magical" quality. As in other types of magic, they tend to connect things that, in the real world, do not have any direct connection. Many of those who obsess seem to almost believe that their thoughts have the power to undo or change events and to cause harm to themselves or others. Their thoughts sometimes seem to resemble common superstitions or religious practices, although they are by no means limited to these. Popular sources of fear, involving such things as the numbers 13 or 666 or stepping on cracks in the sidewalk, can often be involved. Events they worry about causing or avoiding can be catastrophic, such as the deaths or illnesses of themselves, relatives, or even public figures. They may feel much guilt connected with the idea of failing to protect others. One sufferer believed that if while thinking about a particular family member she happened to think simultaneously about a particular illness, or hear of someone with an illness, then the family member would get that illness and perhaps even die. The same could also be true for her at times.

There are those who have thoughts that if they are going to enjoy something or do things which they prefer, something bad will happen to them or someone close to them. It is as if there is a price to be paid each time they enjoy themselves. They fear eating their favorite foods, watching preferred TV shows, listening to music they enjoy, etc. Even if they believe they have eliminated all such preferred activities, the thoughts will pick new ones.

It is common to fear and avoid words that sound like other magically feared words. One person feared the word "ill" because it sounded like "kill" and that hearing this word would mean she would then somehow turn into a psychopathic killer and "have to" stab and kill someone. Numbers can also have magical connections. Many with classic OCD have "lucky" and "unlucky" numbers, not necessarily limited to the most popular ones. Often, even numbers are seen as "good," and odd numbers are seen as "bad."

BODY-FOCUSED OBSESSIONS

People can be obsessed with their own bodies or the way their bodies work. These types of obsessions may be limited to the person alone, or may have to do with their body image or some part of their body. I refer to these as body-focused obsessions. They may become extremely concerned and obsessed with body functions such as heart rate, bowel functions, ability to breathe, pain in some part of the body (such as a local pain in the foot), skin blemishes, or the fit or tightness of clothing. Many people obsess about how different parts of their bodies work, wondering endlessly and doubtfully about how their arms or hands move, how their heads turn, or how they are able to talk or even think, for example. The variety sometimes seems endless and so does the thought process.

Anorexics and bulimics are perhaps another subgroup in this category. Frequently, after they eat, they become obsessed about the normal relaxation of abdominal muscles and see themselves as instantly becoming fat. This, of course, leads them to take the extreme and compulsive actions of starving themselves, abusing laxatives, overexercising, or throwing up everything they have eaten to relieve their anxiety. Their general ability to judge their own body image and shape is also impaired by obsessive doubts, and they are tortured by the question, "How can I be sure I'm not fat?" They also tend to compulsively weigh themselves and double check their bodies for fat. Although anorexics may be looking in the mirror and seeing a person of normal weight, their doubt causes them to wonder if they are seeing a person who seems "fat." They deal with this doubt the way that many other obsessive-compulsives do—by resorting to perfectionism. By being "perfectly" thin and by "perfectly" controlling their food intake, they think they can then feel more certain in the face of the doubt. They set up "perfect" weights for themselves which they must maintain regardless of the consequences. After all, perfectionism leaves no room for doubt or the accompanying anxiety. Unfortunately, like others with OCD, they make the error of believing that this is a type of doubt that can be eradicated, not realizing that it is chronic and biochemically generated. No amount of compulsive starvation, deprivation, or vomiting is going to get rid of it or the anxiety it causes. Actually, as anorexics become more nutritionally deprived, their judgment, and therefore their doubt, probably become worse due to poorer body and brain functioning.

A further subcategory of bodily obsessions involves doubts about the way a certain part of one's body "looks," the way it functions, or the way it is shaped. In one particularly distressing form of this type of thought, the sufferer strongly believes that their body is disfigured, asymmetrical, deformed, or prematurely aging. This variant is known clinically as Body Dysmorphic Disorder (BDD). BDD has also been referred to as "imagined ugliness" and has become somewhat better known in recent years. (See Body Dysmorphic Disorder in chapter 1.) Individuals with BDD can suffer from extremely fixed beliefs about something being wrong with their bodies and spend great amounts of time obsessing about it, to what extent they have it, and what they may be able to do to hide, correct, or eliminate it. The degree of belief in the deformity or problem may be so powerful as to be almost delusional. It is frequently stronger than that seen in classic OCD. The supposed defect or deformity may either be completely undetectable to others, or else may be so minuscule, that others who are questioned about it by the sufferer cannot understand why it is being focused upon at all.

One of the hallmarks of BDD sufferers, as well as others in the body-focused obsession category, is the defensiveness they display when confronted with their disturbance. They will strongly deny any allegation that they have gone too far in the pursuit of correcting a condition that needed little or no correction in the first place. They work hard at constructing elaborate justifications for their beliefs and actions. They will often tell others that they just don't understand, or that the problem isn't very serious at the moment but has been or has the potential to be in the future. They may also claim that the reason others cannot see their defect is because they did not see the sufferer before the defect occurred.

Examples of the types of defects that those with BDD worry about would include beliefs that they have excessive facial hair or that their hair is thinning, that their nose is crooked or too large, that their legs are too heavy or too thin, that they have scars or marks on their faces, that their ears stick out, that their face is somehow ugly, that (in men) their penis is too small, that (in women) their breasts are too large or too small, that their buttocks are too large or protruding, that their mouth is too small or too large, that their skin is excessively wrinkled, scarred, or covered with acne, etc. Symmetry is an important issue here, too. They may believe that parts of either of the halves of their bodies don't match. Those with BDD can spend hours focusing on and studying the parts of themselves they obsess about directly, such as by using mirrors or questioning others endlessly, or indirectly, by subtly listening or fishing for comments about their appearance and reviewing them for clues. Conversely, they will go to great pains to avoid looking at, hearing about, or mentioning their supposed deformity in any way. There is often a great deal of concern about what others may be thinking or saying about their imperfection. Innocent stares or comments by others are prone to be interpreted as criticisms of their imagined problem. Great anxiety and depression usually results from their thoughts about it, in any case. Sufferers will often avoid socializing or going out in public, even to the point of becoming reclusive or housebound. Working around other people may be so anxiety provoking that many end up being unemployed. They seek to avoid the comments or even the gazes of others. Even something as innocuous as a "strange" look by another can send them into an anxious and disturbed state.

BDD sufferers will frequently consult plastic surgeons, cosmetic dentists, dermatologists, orthopedists, etc. They truly believe that if they simply "fix" or reshape the parts of their bodies which they obsess about, all their problems will be instantly solved. I have known numbers of BDD sufferers who have gone for plastic surgery to fix noses, ears, chins, cheeks, necks, eyelids, breasts, buttocks, etc. They go for reshaping, implants, dermabrasion, collagen injections, or liposuction, to name only a few procedures. Expensive and unnecessary cosmetic dental work is also seen among those with BDD. Surgeons and dentists are often reluctant to operate but have been cajoled by a patient or sometimes even the patient's therapist, who may mistakenly believe that the surgical correction will be the solution to their client's obsessive preoccupation. Typically, once the postoperative healing process has finished, and the area has returned to normal, the sufferer will return to feeling dissatisfied and thinking obsessively about the corrected part of their body as they did before. To their way of thinking, nothing will have changed. Even where the results seem satisfactory to them, some BDD suffers will move on to becoming preoccupied with some other feature or area of their body.

Even in some cases where no correction has taken place, sufferers will shift their preoccupation over time, demonstrating that it really has nothing to do with that particular feature of themselves. They usually find it difficult to grasp this insight. Arlene's story gives us a good picture of the experience of BDD. In her particular case, it was actually surgery that touched things off.

Arlene's Story

ᑐ *I developed Body Dysmorphic Disorder after having cosmetic surgery done on my eyes. Before having the procedure done, I was merely dissatisfied with my eyes in an ordinary sort of way. My choice to go ahead with the surgery was not a well-thought-out decision and I regretted it soon after it was done. Along with my regrets came the all consuming obsessive thoughts and compulsions regarding how my eyes had turned out. The obsessive thoughts were constant. "I ruined my eyes. My eyes look abnormal. I look so different." Every moment of the day was either spent thinking about my eyes, looking at other people's eyes, looking in mirrors, looking at photos of myself and my family, looking at people's eyes in magazine pictures or questioning my husband about how my eyes had turned out. When talking to people, I could barely concentrate on the conversation because I fixated on their eyes. I would be in the middle of a task, even at work, and I would HAVE to go see what I looked like. I even found myself seeking my reflection in such items as our toaster! During this time, I wavered from working obsessively (to keep myself occupied) to being so depressed that I would sleep for fourteen hours straight. At this time, I also obtained five consultations from different cosmetic surgeons with regard to how my eyes had turned out. Finally, after several months of this, I went to a local psychiatrist who was rather insensitive to my distress. I spent a whole year in psychotherapy with him which did nothing to alleviate the problem. In fact, the time I spent with him was demeaning. He did prescribe medication for me though, which helped a great deal. Gradually though, I began to fear the very same objects I had at first sought out. Mirrors, eyes, and photos began to frighten me. I began to have severe panic attacks and to bang my head on things in an attempt to rid myself of the obsessive thoughts. My husband had to put all our mirrors and photographs in the attic. Leaving the house became a monumental chore for me. It was at this point that I began to do research on my own to find more appropriate professional help. I did not want to go on like this!*

Some with BDD may also seek to make more minor changes or alterations to themselves. This could include such behaviors as repeatedly cutting their hair because it somehow never looks "perfect" or symmetrical, picking at, or squeezing the smallest pimples or blemishes to perfectly clear the skin of what they have magnified into a "major" case of cystic acne. The irony in this is that people usually end up making their skin look far worse than if they had left it alone. Their picking and cutting leads to frequent swelling, infections, and scars. It should be noted here that this type of activity should not be confused with compulsive skin picking, which is done more to satisfy an urge in the same way individuals with TTM pull hair.

Other strategies used by BDD sufferers can include the wearing of loose or camouflaging clothing, covering the disliked feature with a hand when in the presence of others, or staying away from brightly lit places.

PERFECTIONISTIC OBSESSIONS

There are elements of perfectionism to be seen in many aspects of OCD. In this particular group of obsessions, the focus is on doubts of whether one has thought or acted perfectly. This group differs from other groups of thoughts, such as magical, mental rituals, or mental double checking, where the perfectionism is a means of preventing dire consequences to oneself or others. This is not to say that these particular obsessions are not accompanied by anxiety. There is a need here for closure, completion and order, and this need is so strong that sufferers can become extremely nervous and overwrought when it appears that it may not be achieved. In most cases, these individuals cannot specifically say what the consequence will be if their area of focus is not perfect. In fact, it is often not clear why they have singled out a particular area for perfection.

As in other areas of OCD, the fact that human beings and their thought processes are not and cannot be perfect sets the sufferer up in a vicious circle. The more they worry about whether certain things are perfect or not, the more anxious they become and the more confused and imperfect their thinking becomes. One patient obsessed about having to be able to visualize the city he lived in as a perfect square grid, where all the streets would be symmetrical and the street numbers would be identical at parallel points in the grid. There was no particular direct consequence to his not being able to think of his city in this way; however, when the thought occurred to him that it never could be perfect, he would become extremely anxious and agitated. Ironically, his work took him around the city quite a lot and he began to avoid such trips to avoid seeing all the imperfections.

Another form of these perfectionistic thoughts revolves around a sufferer worrying whether or not they can know everything about a particular topic. Obviously, they cannot and even if they could collect all the information on a specific topic, it cannot all be kept in a person's head at the same time because of normal forgetfulness. One research chemist had a more than ordinary interest in particle physics. While this subject had nothing directly to do with his work, he believed that it was important that he know everything about every type of atomic particle: the history of the research for each one, the names of the researchers, and all their latest published findings and theories. He would experience anxiety attacks as he worried about having forgotten the authors of a particular scientific paper or the subject, the paper's title, its exact conclusion, or even its publication date. He became anxious thinking about papers that might have been published without his knowledge, even though he subscribed to every journal. Rumors of new work could set off a new round of doubt and anxiety. His striving for closure and completion was not driven by any other consequences other than that they seemed necessary. By his own admission, he wished he could escape this endless cycle and realized no pleasure or enjoyment from it.

One other type of symptom in this category revolves around worries of whether or not a sufferer has said, done, or thought certain things in "perfect" ways. These worries should not be confused with obsessions where there is a fear of some negative consequence such as harm, danger, or embarrassment to oneself or others. There is simply doubt on the person's part about their past or present behaviors. The doubts suggest that they may have acted wrongly or inappropriately in some way that they often cannot identify. They may also be concerned that they have not expressed their thoughts exactly or said what they really meant.

Common accompaniments to perfectionistic obsessions involve difficulties in making decisions about even the smallest things and in being able to set priorities. The desire to do these tasks "perfectly" ends up paralyzing people and rendering them unable to accomplish almost anything at times.

NEUTRAL OBSESSIONS

There is a group of obsessional thoughts that seem somewhat different in character from those in the groups previously discussed. These are types of meaningless or nonsensical thoughts which, while distracting and annoying, are not connected with the idea of the occurrence of harm seen in most other obsessions. They usually involve the person noticing or paying attention to normally unimportant happenings or objects related to themselves, others, or their environment. They may also include repetitive internal questions about things which are unimportant and for which there may be no answer.

The real distress arising from thoughts in this category comes more from the individual's inability to simply stop thinking about them. It is obviously upsetting to feel that you cannot control what is going on in your own mind. Also, the thoughts tend to ruin a person's concentration and distract their attention to the point where they are unable to function efficiently. Among the most frequent subjects of these thoughts are electrical or mechanical devices. Sufferers get stuck obsessing about the way things such as motors, computers, appliances, and locks are able to work. They feel driven to understand the principles behind these things and can feel a lot of anxiety if they cannot. They believe that if they fail to perfectly understand these concepts, they will eventually get into some type of difficulty. One individual found himself obsessively thinking about how the hinges on doors worked, and could not stop staring at them or even going so far as to go right up to them and examine them. Sometimes, these preoccupations can focus on other people or even on the sufferer themselves. A female patient of mine could not, at times, stop thinking about the way people's mouths moved when they spoke or smiled, the lengths of pauses between their words, and the way they gestured. She therefore avoided conversations with others and had to even limit watching TV or listening to the radio. She also became preoccupied with people's birthmarks and found herself in some uncomfortable social situations due to her staring at them. Other sufferers I have known have obsessed about such things as their own breathing, blinking, or the way their minds worked. Similar to these thoughts are those that involve being excessively aware of sounds in the environment, such as ordinary noises or background music of the type played in offices or stores. Other people have reported being unable to stop thinking about the sizes of objects, such as the heights of buildings, the layout of streets and railroad tracks in their towns, the location of furniture or other objects in their homes, or how the landscape in a particular place was laid out. Endless and meaningless thoughts of numbers, words, and tunes also fall into this category.

There is one other type of obsession that I believe belongs in this group, which seems to be almost pure doubt. It is seen in people who think up numerous questions about things that either cannot be answered, are rhetorical questions, or are unimportant. Some examples are "Does grass grow at night?" or "How do I know what I think I know?" or even, "How do I know I'm not really standing when I think I'm sitting down?"

∾ Different Forms Compulsions Can Take

∾ *Nothing is more powerful than habit.*
—*Ovid*

Habits are at first cobwebs, then cables.
—*Spanish proverb*

Habit is stronger than reason.
—*Santayana*

A s mentioned earlier, compulsions can be generally defined as any mental or physical activities that relieve the anxiety caused by obsessions. (There are exceptions, where meaningless activities can be performed for no special reason, or have been done for so many years that the original cause of the anxiety has actually been forgotten and the compulsion is done merely out of habit.) Compulsions fall into two large categories—mental compulsions and compulsive actions. I have divided these into the following twelve categories which may overlap, because the OCSDs are by no means "neat" disorders. Despite this, I believe that this list can both take in and differentiate between most compulsions. The categories are as follows:

1. Decontamination Compulsions
2. Hoarding Compulsions
3. Checking Compulsions

4. Magical/Undoing Compulsions

5. Perfectionistic Compulsions

6. Counting Compulsions

7. Touching or Movement Compulsions

8. Self-Mutilative Compulsions

9. Body-Focused Compulsions

10. Grooming Impulsions/Compulsions

11. Mental Compulsions

12. Protective Compulsions

DECONTAMINATION COMPULSIONS

This group makes up one of the better-known categories of compulsive behavior. These compulsions involve the protective or preventive acts that an individual does to avoid harm they fear will come to them or others due to obsessions about contact with toxic substances, dirt or grime, bacteria, viruses, etc. Contamination actually takes in a much wider range of things, some of them even magical and superstitious, such as a fear of contamination via thoughts or words. The anxiety-relieving compulsions can include different forms of cleaning and avoidance behaviors, such as hand washing, showering, disinfecting or sterilizing, house cleaning, throwing things away, creating off-limits areas, and clothes changing.

The best known subgroup in the contamination category has to do with a fear of disease-causing agents, such as bacteria or viruses, which may cause a disease such as AIDS, cancer, hepatitis, or TB. Some experience only a feeling of "dirtiness" that cannot really be explained. Cancer used to be one of the more common fears until AIDS came along. The new treatment resistant strain of TB is just lately starting to gain in popularity. Individuals themselves often speak of the word "contamination." This is not the same thing as having a phobia, because phobias are much more limited in terms of what a phobic fears and avoids. Another difference is that "magic" and superstition are frequently involved in OCD but not in phobias.

Another large subgroup experiences anxiety over anything to do with the bathroom or elimination. Extreme hand washing and even a change of clothes follow urination and/or defecation. Many sufferers try to regulate themselves to defecate just before they are due to shower to avoid having to shower again. In more extreme cases, they may hold their urine or feces to the point of serious discomfort or else avoid eating or drinking at times to cut down on bathroom visits. After defecating, many will wipe and wash themselves excessively to the point of becoming sore and irritated. Many cannot sit directly on toilet seats and may hold themselves just above the seat, cover it with numerous layers of paper, or spray it with a disinfectant. Using public toilets or even toilets in other people's homes is often out of the question. This frequently limits how far individuals can travel from home since they cannot be too far away from their own bathrooms. Touching doorknobs, faucets, stalls, or any part of the toilets is usually out of the question. Just walking on the floor in a public toilet is something to be feared, as the "dirtiness" would then be tracked wherever the person went, particularly into their car or home.

An illustration of the complicated type of ritual one hand washer went through will shed some light on these types of behavior. Martha had many complicated rules for her excessive hand washing, which she performed several dozen times per day. The soap had to be either a brand new bar in an undamaged wrapper that had not been allowed to touch anything else or had been stored in such a way that no one else could have used it. She had to hold the soap by only one corner, and wash the bar thoroughly, while making sure it didn't accidentally touch anything. If it fell on the floor or brushed the edge of the sink, it had to be washed all over again (many washers prefer liquid soap dispensers to avoid this).

The faucets were usually washed and rinsed several times before they could be touched, and were sometimes washed in between every hand wash, depending on how "dirty" she felt things were at a particular time. It should be added that by "touching," I mean that they could only be turned on or off if she used a paper towel or a Kleenex between her hand and the tap. She would then begin to wash each hand in a special pattern a certain number of times, each part being done in a particular order. She would count as she did this, to be certain she had spent the time necessary to make the wash thorough enough. Some individuals may also count, think up special mental pictures, pray, or repeat certain words while doing these other things. Two patients I have treated bought special types of faucets that would not get their sinks or counter tops "dirty" by causing water to splash back out of the basin.

In Martha's case, paper towels had to be used for drying purposes, since they could obviously be thrown out after one use. The roll itself had to be kept in a "clean" zip-top plastic bag between uses and kept in a special "clean" corner she had created. If an ordinary cloth towel was used, it had to go right into the laundry after only one use. Even these precautions are not enough for certain individuals who must let their hands air-dry and cannot use towels of any kind. Some people fear recontaminating their hands after washing and must get someone else to turn off the faucets for them. The complications vary from one person to another.

Many washers need to be taught, while in treatment, how to wash and shower either because they have never done these things in an average way or because they have forgotten how to do so. It should be said here that I consider the average hand wash to be no more than fifteen seconds maximum in length. I also instruct patients to shower for no longer than ten minutes and to not specifically wash their hands while doing so. In extreme OC cases, handwashes can go on for an hour or more, and three- and four-hour showers are not uncommon. It is not unusual for some hand washers to wash fifty or sixty times a day, and there are certain people who have washed up to two hundred times a day, to the point of exhaustion. I know of one particular case where a patient washed his hands for thirty-six hours straight without pausing. As with hair pullers, washers can develop repetitive strain injuries in wrists and elbows from prolonged scrubbing and washing. Some even develop knee problems from standing at the sink for hours at a time.

Many washers can easily use several bars of soap daily and some even buy it by the case. The use of several rolls of paper towels per day is also common, as cloth towels may not seem clean enough and cannot be reused. Following showers, some avoid towels entirely and use hair dryers, stand in front of heaters, or just wait until their bodies air-dry. Such washing habits soon lead to skin damage and hand washers can often be spotted by their bright red, chapped hands, which can sometimes be at the point of bleeding and scabbing. Some have hands that look as if they are encased in red gloves reaching up to their wrists. Antiseptic soaps, alcohol, peroxide, and even disinfectants such as Lysol, are frequently used excessively on the hands and even the body, causing further damage. Several individuals I have seen in treatment have gone as far as to pour undiluted bleach over their hands, causing chemical burns. Many go to dermatologist's offices and get treatments for allergic dermatitis or eczema by the unsuspecting physicians.

Compulsive hand washing is obviously a futile exercise, since it provides short-term relief that only lasts until the sufferer touches something that increases their anxiety again. Once a washer is "clean," they will usually find themselves worrying about how to stay that way. This is, of course, impossible, but their doubt and anxiety make them so shortsighted that they cannot see this.

A lot of compulsive washing is not directly caused by touching things the person thinks are "dirty" or "contaminated." It often happens because the washing ritual itself is not performed in exactly the right way and must be started over again many times. Or because of the person's strong obsessive doubts, they will wash several times because they cannot be absolutely sure that their hands are 100 percent clean. One patient inspected his hands very carefully after each wash for even the slightest speck of dirt, worrying doubtfully as to whether that spot he saw on his skin was a discoloration, a vein, or a bit of dirt. Disposable surgical gloves or even plastic bags are used by some in an attempt to cut down on these tedious washing rituals. These can be used while doing chores or touching contaminated things, and then discarded after one use. Sometimes, other family members are "forced" into helping the sufferer, by checking areas of the body they cannot see by themselves and to tell the sufferer what they want to know, using only particular words or phrases. Why this is bad for the sufferer is dealt with in chapter 6.

Sometimes particular areas of the body or personal possessions are singled out for the cleanliness treatments as well or are overprotected in some way and kept in pristine states. I have noticed that such people seem to be very concerned about their hair becoming contaminated. Eyeglasses and contact lenses are another area of sensitivity. Some of our patients have given up wearing their glasses entirely, even though they have a vision problem, simply because the glasses have fallen on the floor. Contact lenses, which must be disinfected, are especially difficult for those with contamination problems. The procedure may be repeated many times, usually preceded by extensive hand washing. Even the carrying case must be disinfected over and over. Quite a few sufferers either wear their lenses too long to the point of irritation or don't wear them when they should, because taking them out or putting them in would just be too difficult. Many female sufferers are particularly protective of their purses and are unable to set them down or put them on the floor. One of my patients used to boil her jewelry after each wearing, as well as her keys and pocket change at the end of the day. Perhaps by picking out only a few things to protect, sufferers feel that they can better establish control in a world full of contamination.

Compulsive washers also avoid objects that are most likely to collect contaminants. Such objects usually include public items that other persons often touch, such as public toilets, handrails, light switches, pay phones, doorbells, vending machines, mailboxes, doorknobs and handles of all kinds, water fountains, water taps, and money. As mentioned before, floors frequently present a lot of problems. Anything that comes near or touches the floor becomes automatically "dirty" as well. This includes pants cuffs, shoes, and shoelaces. Many washers cannot touch their own shoes, much less tie them, and prefer to wear slip-ons, or ones with Velcro closures. Many cannot touch the cuffs or bottoms of their pants legs. In the homes of some washers who live alone, you may sometimes see their floors littered with dropped objects and belongings that fell and could not be picked up again because of contact with the "dirty" floor. Things which become "dirty" and which are not possible to wash or clean are usually thrown out—sometimes even valuable things such as jewelry. For some, as a further step in this contamination process, things that have touched items that have touched the floor can also then become contaminated.

A fairly common aspect of contamination fears involves a sort of misconception about the way contaminants spread. Even a few drops of a fear-producing substance can seem like enough to contaminate an entire house. Even touching an object that touched a contaminated object can be enough. As a challenge to such thinking, I usually ask patients if they could paint their whole house with a few drops of paint, because this is what they are suggesting can happen. They imagine that even the smallest amount of contamination will somehow coat every surface in their home.

It almost goes without saying that social contact is extremely difficult, if not impossible, for many in this category. Simple things we take for granted such as handshakes, hugs, kisses, or touches are sources of great anxiety. A sneeze or cough in the vicinity of someone with such fears can take on the proportion of a major calamity. The result is, of course, increasing isolation for those in this group. Some become virtual recluses, shunning all human contact, hiding in their apartments or homes, and having everything delivered to them. Others who live with families can hole up in their rooms, seldom coming out for anything, even using the toilet. I have had a number of such sufferers who, on their first visit to my office, would stand in a corner of the room rather than sit in one of the chairs. They hold their hands at their sides, being careful not to touch anything. Others have brought plastic bags to sit on or place over their hands. These individuals represent a very extreme subgroup and generally require rather intensive and strong interventions. This could include inpatient therapy with a gradual reintroduction to their homes later on.

One other set of behaviors I have observed among those with contamination fears has to do with shopping in stores. Many with this type of OCD will not buy the first item at the front of a shelf or on top of a stack of merchandise because it may have been handled or touched by others. Also, cans or packages of food that are not perfect are also shunned, because the damage, however slight, may have allowed bacteria to get in and spoil the contents.

Fears of Contamination: Source Unknown

Sometimes the sufferer cannot exactly say just what makes certain objects contaminating. Their only explanation is vague and may be limited to "I just feel that it is." When asked whether their fear involves bacteria, viruses, or poisonous chemicals, they usually shrug and answer, "I don't know. It's just dirty." Many of these people are more bothered by the idea of certain things as being "disgusting." Others simply dislike the textures of various substances, such as things that are sticky or greasy to the touch. In a few instances, the problem is the notion of getting something on oneself that smells bad, such as something fishy, or that has a perfumed or chemical smell. In some cases, there was once a reason for the avoidance, which over the years has become obscured or forgotten entirely, and which is still practiced only out of habit.

Fear of Contaminating Others

Problems with contamination usually go in one of three directions. The person fears that harm will come to them and only worry about that, with no regard for others, or they experience fears that harm will come to others (with no regard for their own safety), or finally, that harm might come both to them and others. When feeling contaminated, such persons as those in the last category, may not only believe that they are personally in danger, but also that they are a danger to loved ones, strangers, or even to public figures. One individual believed he himself was contaminated in some vague way, and that his contamination might kill, by eventual indirect contact, the pope or the president, whom he believed were elderly or frail. He avoided touching mailboxes, pay phones, and other public objects to keep the contamination from accidentally being spread to them in a chainlike fashion. Other people often seen as vulnerable can be elderly or ill individuals or people smaller or weaker than the sufferer, such as children or adults of small stature. This can make it rather difficult for some sufferers to be effective parents, because they cannot touch or hold their children, something that seriously deprives both the parent and the child.

Another type of problem relating to contamination is one in which individuals fear to leave their fingerprints, perspiration, or some type of undefined "essence" on objects in public. The fear, in this case, is that these substances will be harmful to others, although some of these particular sufferers may also become anxious about "losing" a part of themselves and leaving a part of themselves behind that cannot be recovered. I have also seen a few individuals who worried that if a crime were somehow committed in a particular location where they had left fingerprints, they would be traced and wrongly blamed for it.

Other Persons as Contaminators

Sometimes, the compulsive may single out one other person, such as a relative or an acquaintance, as the contamination source. One man believed his mother was contaminated and avoided everything she touched. If she came to visit, he would spend hours scrubbing and cleaning everything his mother had touched that was washable or would avoid or throw away things that weren't. He would, of course, avoid touching his mother at such visits and go as far as directing her where to sit and what not to touch. Going to her home was out of the question. This gradually became so bad, in his mind, that he could not go anywhere near his mother's town, for fear of coming into contact with someone or something she may have touched. Cars, trucks, manufactured goods, and even mail and newspapers that might have come from his mother's town would cause him serious anxiety, and he finally became housebound because of this. He spent days locked in his bedroom with the windows closed and with paper stuffed into the cracks around the door to keep out airborne contaminants.

Contrary to common psychoanalytic theory, there does not necessarily need to be any connection between such thoughts and the type of relationship the person has with the parent. I have seen several similar cases where the contaminating person was only slightly known or a total stranger to the patient, but was someone who simply "looked dirty" or "bad." With the increase in the number of homeless people seen in public, many individuals in this group have found it difficult to walk city streets or use train stations for fear of coming near or touching such people. I have treated patients who commute from the suburbs to the city who have found their jobs in jeopardy due to lateness or absence as a result of fear of running into a "dirty" person. Many compulsive patients fear that each one of these people is an AIDS carrier or has such things as body lice or TB. One teenage girl saw a boy in school she felt was unclean. It should be added here that she was not acquainted with the boy and did not even know his name. She did not want to go into classrooms where he may have sat, through school corridors he may have walked, into the cafeteria, and so on. Next, she avoided the neighborhood around the school. This compulsion escalated to the point where eventually she could not venture out of her home into the town where she lived, since there was no way of knowing where he may have gone or what he may have touched.

Family Members and "The Rules"

Special strict cleaning or decontamination rules may also be applied to other family members. Upon coming home, such family members may be forced to remove their clothes in some distant part of the home, such as the garage or basement, and then have to shower (sometimes for as long as an hour) and immediately change into clean ones. Shoes must be taken off before entering the house. Clothes must go right into the laundry, and in some cases, different family member's clothes must be segregated and washed separately. Hands must be washed after certain activities, no matter what. Family members may sometimes be forced to wash almost as often as the washer. Sometimes the sufferer will not allow other family members to do laundry themselves or any other type of cleaning chore around the house. They fear the risk of someone else doing a less perfect job than they would do. In other cases, family members must do all cleaning chores under the direction of the sufferer who wishes to avoid any of the actual touching of dirty things. Contaminated articles must be discarded and replaced, even if this involves great expense. Sufferer's rooms are usually off limits to other family members, not only for reasons of privacy, but also because others might accidentally contaminate things. Failure of the other family members to do as the sufferer commands can lead to fighting, arguments, tantrums, and even pleading and tears on the part of the compulsive in an effort to manipulate and control. Frequently, these tactics work as the sufferer trains the rest of the family to accept this level of control.

At the other end of the scale from those who take control of everything and who must do everything themselves, are those who have become so helpless and immobilized due to their symptoms that they can hardly do anything for themselves. I have witnessed extreme cases where the sufferer is confined to a room in the family home, venturing out only to wash or use the bathroom (sometimes even limiting themselves to only defecating and urinating in containers in their rooms) and forcing family members to bring them their meals, do their laundry, and perform any other errands.

Control of the family can even extend beyond the immediate home setting. Sometimes, in cases where the sufferer believes the source of contamination to be environmental and tied to the locality, families may be forced to sell their homes and move to new ones distant from the feared source.

Although the family may actually cooperate for a time, there is a great deal of anger and resentment, and in some cases, this boils over into conflict eventually leading to a family or marital breakup. This is particularly true where the sufferer is so involved in trying to manage their fears themselves that they are unwilling to seek help. Additionally, these arguments only serve to worsen the sufferer's symptoms due to the stress involved.

HOARDING COMPULSIONS

Some of those with OCD save or collect things to great excess. Compulsive savers, packrats, or hoarders, as they are commonly referred to in the OC world, may collect only certain types of things, or they may save everything. Please understand that I am not talking here about collectibles, which are valuable or important such as art, coins, or stamps. Hoarders generally tend to save things that are of little or no value, or if they do have value, they tend to save in ridiculously larger quantities than would ever be necessary. The main obsessive thought that causes sufferers to do this is their worry that if they throw a particular item away, it will be lost forever, and they may one day be in need of it in order to be able to use it, or to be able to remember it, or something connected with it. There is an inability here to discriminate between what is or will be useful or necessary, and what is not. Some hoarders can freely admit that the things they are saving are broken or damaged and unusable. They go on, however, to insist that they will someday repair the items and either make use of them or give them away.

A related reason for hoarding resembles the type of over-responsible thinking seen in protective compulsions. It is the idea that each thing they save and/or repair might be useful to others (rather than themselves), and that the hoarder would be responsible (and therefore blameful and guilty) for another person not having this vital item should the need arise. They rationalize that what they are doing is actually "recycling," and they are performing a community service by conserving resources. In actuality, there is no need for what they have saved, there is no one to give the items to, and the hoarder is burdened with a house full of junk.

A famous example of compulsive hoarding gone completely out of control is the story of the Collyer brothers, Langley and Homer. Earlier in this century, Langley managed to fill a mansion on Fifth Avenue in Manhattan with tons of trash, literally to the ceilings. The two brothers purchased the property in 1932, with the idea of turning it into an apartment house. When Homer became blind in 1933, the two of them moved into the building. The other brother, Langley, had two main occupations. These were caring for his blind brother and compulsive hoarding. He would go out on nightly expeditions to scavenge from the trash around the neighborhood. Their home soon became filled with discarded furniture, old ice boxes, baby carriages, animal bones, old clothing, and other assorted refuse. Among the debris were also eleven pianos and a Model T Ford that Langley had carted into the house in pieces.

The building was soon filled to overflowing. Langley rigged numerous booby traps, using tons of trash, to protect them from break-ins. Both were ultimately found dead in their home in 1947. Langley was killed when a huge heap of heavy items (perhaps one of his own booby traps) collapsed on top of him, and Homer, now an invalid, died of malnutrition and dehydration with no one to care for his needs. Homer was found first, but it took police three weeks to locate Langley's body underneath all the trash. An estimated 120 tons of refuse, junk, and human waste was removed from the building, an amount which had taken Langley fifteen years to accumulate.

There is an element of doubt in hoarding which you do not see in the type of saving seen in Obsessive-Compulsive Personality Disorder (see chapter 10). In both groups though, much of what is saved would be considered useless. Some of the things commonly saved include newspapers, magazines, lists, pens, pencils, empty boxes, pamphlets, old greeting cards, junk mail, outdated books, and even assorted labels, string, rubber bands, plastic containers, bottles, and bottle caps. In the most extreme cases, I have seen people save such things as empty matchbooks, used tissues, old cigarette butts, bird feathers, paper cups, paper towels, lint, and hairs. Many of these people will even rummage through the trash the way Langley Collyer did, and bring home obvious junk that seems useful or repairable. As the story of the Collyer brothers teaches us, savers can accumulate large amounts of things, creating storage problems and fire or health hazards. Their houses can take on the appearance of having been ransacked, with floors knee-deep in trash and debris, rooms filled wall-to-wall with overflowing paper bags and cardboard boxes. Ironically, the majority of people who save things compulsively rarely use or look at these things. Their security comes from merely having the things around "just in case" and in not having to make decisions about what to discard.

There are some who hoard for what looks like perfectionistic reasons, for a feeling of closure or completeness. They must save "everything" of a particular type or at least everything they can find. When prevented from doing so, they become anxious and obsessive about what they are missing.

An offshoot of hoarding is seen in people who are compulsive about remembering or not missing names, faces, facts, or events. In a way similar to the savers, they work for hours and even days to study, read, and memorize all facts in certain categories and get very anxious if they cannot remember everything. One sufferer I met had actually memorized all the names and complete specifications of all the world's fighter aircraft, which he then had to keep studying daily in order not to forget the information. The thought of forgetting any of these facts caused him great anxiety. In addition, he had to save a very large library of books on the subject and constantly keep it updated as new types of aircraft were manufactured. He would read them repeatedly and drill himself on the facts.

A behavior typically seen within this group is compulsive listmaking. Although some merely record everyday things such as errands to do or names and addresses, some listmakers perfectionistically record things they are likely to worry and obsess about. This could include incidents where harm might have occurred to themselves or someone else. One patient kept a list of every time he thought he might have run someone over, so he could verify it if he was ever accused of doing so. Another kept lists of things to double-check. Such lists can be quite long and detailed, and the information can include names, addresses, dates, facts, etc. Hoarders may have drawers full of lists, some going back years and in no particular order. When many of my compulsive listmakers have had to confront their habit in therapy, they are often forced to admit that they are unable to remember much of what the old lists contain. The names they saved no longer mean anything and the events are long forgotten.

Beyond the hoarding of facts, there are also those who have compulsions to hoard memories and experiences. We all like to hold on to certain moments in our lives and savor certain experiences, wishing they would last forever. However, this group of hoarders goes far beyond that. Generally, the experiences they wish to hoard tend to be small and insignificant. They appear to be indiscriminate about which ones to save, because they wish to save either all of them or everything in particular categories. I recall one person who constantly agonized about his inability to watch all the channels on TV at the same time, because he feared he was missing things that were all going to happen "for the last time," and he would not then be able to "save" all the memories. When watching the TV, he would anxiously switch from channel to channel the entire time, never really watching anything for more than a few seconds and getting more and more anxious because he wasn't seeing or remembering it all. The occurrence of a historic event on the TV would send him into extremely high anxiety states, as he was not able to watch the coverage on all the different channels simultaneously. Another example was a woman who wished to hoard her eating experiences. She could not even eat a piece of fruit without thinking that it was the "last time" she would see or eat this particular item. She would therefore agonize over how she could save the experience, often not eating the food at all and saving it until it had rotted. Some sufferers also become concerned with doing things for the "first time," for basically the same reason as "last timers."

One man was constantly picking up papers in the street, memorizing the writing on them, and saving them so he would not forget. After several months of this, he had collected quite a pile of trash and scrap paper in his home. If he saw signs, posters, or labels in public he would have the urge to memorize these as well, becoming very anxious at the thought that he might forget any of them. This thinking occupied many hours of his day, finally incapacitating him. In the later stages of his problem, he avoided going to stores, particularly grocery stores, for fear of all the labels he would then see and then have to memorize. Some memorizing compulsions may also be the result of obsessive fears of having Alzheimer's Disease. Forgetfulness is feared as a sign that the person has the disease, and the ability to memorize well is a way of double checking that this isn't so.

There are two types of compulsive behavior which resemble hoarding but aren't. The first takes in a group of individuals who cannot throw things away due to a severe and doubtful fear that together with legitimate trash, they may accidentally throw away something important, such as money, jewelry, important papers, photographs, etc. Rather than make such a mistake, they either just store their trash away or painstakingly and repetitiously comb through every item they discard before finally taking it out of the house. Typically, even though they know it is illogical, they will look into the seams of paper bags and envelopes before throwing them out, to check for important items that might be lodged there. Unlike hoarders, they do not have doubts which suggest that the things they save might actually be useful someday.

The second group encompasses those who accumulate large amounts of useless trash and disposable items simply because of chronic procrastination. These people seem to lack the ability to manage their time or to set priorities. They would like to organize their living spaces but can never seem to get around to it. The time they could be using to clear things up gets used for other unimportant or low priority activities. The more things pile up, the more they want to avoid dealing with them. They are happy enough to work on things when a therapist, a friend, or helpful family member steps in, but would never attempt to do so on their own.

CHECKING COMPULSIONS

In OCD, checking can be defined as compulsive, repeated, and often extreme attempts to make certain that a particular event has or has not taken place, or that some special state of affairs does or does not exist. Often, the event or state of affairs can have some kind of a disastrous consequence, and sufferers become extremely anxious if the checking is not performed or is done improperly. This must be differentiated from normal checking, which is a part of everyday life. The average person probably checks many things but not usually more than once. If they forget to check or are prevented from doing so, they will not experience extreme anxiety or interrupt their normal activities to go back and do it.

Checking is actually a circular kind of a process, involving four steps. These steps are

1. having strong doubts: feeling anxious about not being certain of something seen as important. You sense a lack of information.

2. the urge to check or question: the compulsion to obtain more information in order to get rid of the anxiety and doubt and to therefore feel certain, safe, or protected.

3. the physical or mental act of checking.

4. elimination of the doubt, and temporary relief from the anxiety, both of which do not usually last very long (sometimes only a few seconds or minutes), leading to further doubts, and thus, further checking.

Unfortunately, the pathological doubt of OCD is not the type that simply goes away. As can be seen, the checker may relieve his or her anxiety for a short time, but the doubt soon returns, and the whole cycle starts over again. The sufferer may agonize over persistent doubts about what was checked, or whether what was checked was checked properly. It is a nagging type of doubt that gnaws at a person, sometimes escalating to the point of great emotional and even physical pain. The relief gained by checking may only last a minute or an hour or may not be reached at all, until the person has checked dozens of times or over one long stretch of time. "Yes, but . . ." and "what if . . ." are always waiting around the corner. Very often when the doubt is set aside, it is only because a newer, seemingly worse threat turns up, and the previous doubt seems less important.

Checking may be done as a single act or as a special complex ritual of which there are many varieties. (Yes, there is an overlap with the Magical/Undoing category.) It can be a simple physical inspection by eye, or by touching, tasting, smelling, or listening. It can sometimes merely be the asking of a question of another person about the doubtful subject, where the OCD sufferer questions his or her own ability to know something. It can also take place mentally, with a person reviewing or rehashing the facts over and over. Counting often accompanies checking as a way of determining if the check was done for long enough, done the right number of times, or in the right sequence of steps. (See Counting Compulsions later in this chapter for more details.)

The doubt that the checker feels is of a very special type, and often does not seem to be logical or to make any sense to others. As you will see from some of the examples that follow, many of the things checked are very unlikely to ever happen. This may be because the checker seems to be basically confused about the difference between the possibility of something happening, and the probability, or the odds of its actually coming to pass. We can mostly all agree that while just about anything is possible under the right conditions, the chances of most of these things happening can be very rare and certainly are not worth taking precautions against. To many with OCD, if something even has the remotest chance of happening, it must be guarded against. At times it looks like checkers are trying to create overcontrolled, risk-free worlds for themselves, where doubt and danger do not exist. This would appear to be in response to their obsessive doubts, which are so strong and seem so real that only perfect certainty will suffice. However, we all know how little certainty there actually is in the world.

Allen relates some of his checking compulsions, many of which are typical (parts of his account also appear in the sections on Morbid and Religious Obsessions in chapter 8):

Allen's Story

⌒ *It would take about one-and-a-half hours of senseless checking to get to bed and about two-and-a-half hours just to shower. I typically got four-and-a-half to five hours of sleep a night. I checked things on my desk (things had to be perfectly straight and I kept counting to see that everything was there). I checked to see if lights were off (I could never accept they were). I checked that doors and windows were locked, oven knobs had to be perfectly lined up to the "off" position (the line on the oven knob had to line up perfectly with the line on the stove). I'd also check many things in the car to see if everything was off (usually twenty minutes), put letters in and out of envelopes because I wasn't sure if I really did put the right contents in. I'd even push very hard on light switches to make sure they were off. With everything I checked, I always had to force myself to get away, and I never felt satisfied that I had checked correctly.*

Checkers Checking Themselves

For some checkers, the object of their checking is limited to themselves. One patient, for example, whose checking grew out of contamination fears, checked her hands hundreds of times per day, examining them for the slightest foreign particle that she feared might be something contaminating to her and lead to her death or the death of others. Since her fears revolved around bodily excretions, the times following urination or defecation were most difficult for her. Not only did she check herself for specks even more closely at these times, but she also attempted to get other family members, as well as a close friend, to assist her by having them examine her lips, tongue, and teeth. She would stick out her tongue in front of a mirror many times every day to check for the presence of feces, even though she could not explain how it might have come to be there.

Another type of self-checking has often been observed in individuals who have actually been treated for cancer, or who simply have fears and doubts about getting cancer. People in this group examine one or more areas of their body in great detail, searching for any bumps or discolorations or to make sure the areas are identical to those on the other side of their body. Freckles and other blemishes are often great causes of doubt and fear for such people. They sometimes push, probe, and poke themselves so hard that they can cause bruises, irritation, and even draw blood at times. This, of course, always backfires on them, since the marks of their checking then become possible "signs" of the cancers they are looking for. When the area to be checked is one that is out of sight, they often use mirrors or enlist the help of family members to do the checking for them. As expected, this behavior leads to much tension and often to family fights. Mirrors actually seem to be dangerous as sufferers grow to fear looking in them, because they always see something on their bodies.

As time goes on, members of this group of checkers actually go in the opposite direction and become afraid to touch themselves, because their fear and doubt lead them to constantly imagine that they feel something every time they place their hands on themselves. Just scratching an itch, scrubbing in the shower, drying with a towel, or adjusting clothing can be enough to set off a whole new bout of checking.

Those with fears of cancer and other diseases also obtain the help of medical specialists, and can often persuade doctors to check them regularly and to put them through unnecessary complicated and even painful tests. The doubting is so strong here that even the reassurance of a physician may only last as long as the person is in the doctor's office. Within a short time, they even begin to doubt whether the doctor checked them correctly or whether they remembered to tell the doctor perfectly about this or that sensation. Public health messages about checking oneself for such things as breast or testicular cancer tend to have a very negative effect on this group of people. They just don't know when to stop. This type of advice about how to perform monthly self-examinations somehow gets twisted and transformed into the sufferer making several frantic examinations daily.

Self-checking is usually an important feature of BDD. Doubts about whether various features or body parts are ugly or misshapen drive this behavior, not the fear of disease. Those with BDD will frequently check themselves directly, with mirrors, or by asking others to check them or answer checking questions about their bodies. They pinch or poke offending folds of skin to test for looseness, compare the size and shape of body parts on one side of the body to those on the other side for symmetry, check the way clothes fit, study whether their teeth are crooked, stare at their scalp to see if their hair is thinning, etc.

Besides their bodies, sufferers may also check their own behavior in response to obsessions in the Harm, Danger, Loss, or Embarrassment category (see chapter 8). They may frequently check what they write for obscenities written accidentally, or continually review the things they say for anything which might embarrass another person or themselves. As a group, they carefully watch their own behavior for any possible inappropriateness. As one of my patients who spotted the paradox here put it, "You end up doing abnormal things to be sure you aren't abnormal."

Other Types of Checking

Checkers will commonly check certain household objects where there is any possibility of something dangerous happening. Among the most common of these are stoves, toasters, irons, hair dryers, coffee pots, electrical plugs in general, light switches, thermostats, water taps, doors, and windows. The checking here involves looking over and/or touching these things anywhere from two or three times, to several dozen times per session, to make sure they have been closed, turned off, unplugged, or locked.

Light switches and appliances are seen as the potential cause of fires or explosions, although the person has never had such a thing happen to them and can't explain how it would. Gas stoves seem to cause the most anxiety. Household items may be repeatedly gazed at or turned on and off dozens of times to verify that they cannot cause harm. If electrical, they will probably be unplugged when not actually in use. I have seen a few cases where sufferers took coffee pots or hair dryers to work with them or left them outside their houses when they were away to ensure that the house would not burn down. One particularly inventive patient would actually have her husband take Polaroid pictures of the kitchen stove before they left for a vacation so she could reassure herself while they were away.

One example is Anna, who checked her stove when going to bed or leaving the house. She feared that leaving it on could cause her house to burn down, although she could not explain how this could happen or why it didn't happen when she baked things for several hours. Her fears at bedtime were serious, but her fears on leaving the house unattended were even worse. She would check the stove for about an hour at a time before going out, staring at the knobs to make sure they were off and touching them to be certain they hadn't moved (at bedtime, fifteen minutes was sufficient). Things gradually worsened to the point of jeopardizing her job due to morning lateness and also due to daytime sleepiness from staying up all night to check.

Doors and windows are seen as possible ways for harmful intruders to enter the house and steal valuables or harm family members. They can be opened and closed or locked and unlocked repeatedly. Many individuals constantly check the faucets in their homes to make sure they are tightly closed, because they fear a flood will result from their carelessness. In another case, a woman, who feared an intruder might be hiding in her home, would check the entire house for hours before bedtime, even looking in such unlikely places as her drawers and behind furniture. Tied up with these fears is the issue that the checker will be blamed as the irresponsible and negligent one if an accident occurs, and along with suffering a loss, will be forced to live with the terrible guilt. Guilt and an overly strong sense of responsibility is a driving force for many with OCD.

It is not unusual for checkers to accidentally break things in their quest for certainty. Knobs or handles are frequent objects of breakage, due to compulsive overtightening. A number of my patients have routinely broken jar lids or the necks of bottles in the same manner, trying to be certain that they are completely closed.

As mentioned earlier under hoarding compulsions, some sufferers feel that they must keep checking to relieve their fear of having accidentally thrown important things away. They will typically examine everything to be discarded with extreme carefulness, if they are ever actually able to throw anything away. Envelopes, boxes, or bags must be examined in detail and even taken apart, to be certain that nothing is accidentally caught in a seam. Even after all these precautions have been taken, sufferers may still agonize about having thrown something away and feel guilty and overly responsible.

Many checkers become overly concerned about their personal possessions. When away from home, they will continually feel and pat their pockets to see if they have forgotten or lost something important. They will frequently open their wallets and purses to examine the contents. When getting up from chairs or leaving vehicles, they will first pause and look all around to be certain of whether or not they have left something behind.

Another very common area of checking revolves around writing out checks, paying bills, and putting them in the mail. Sufferers will reread the checks they write and study the math in their check registers dozens of times. When they finally do get past this step, they may check to see that they placed the check and bill in the envelope correctly. They may then take them out of the envelope and put them back in repeatedly before finally sealing it. Even then they may tear the envelope open, check the contents, and reseal it. When finally mailing it, they will open and close the mailbox door repeatedly, to make sure the envelope went in correctly. This may not put an end to things though, as they can go on to worry about whether or not they put the stamps on the envelope or if they put on the correct address.

Cigarettes can also cause checkers a great deal of anxiety. Checkers who smoke or who live with smokers can be seen to keep ashtrays filled with water. Burned matches must also be soaked with water. Cigarettes are frequently flushed down the toilet that then has to be checked again and again.

Checking Can Get Serious

While the average person might check something once and be satisfied, a checker can never be totally sure that he or she has made a proper inspection, even after dozens of tries. The need for perfection is very strong here due both to the presence of a pathological doubt that won't quit and also the fear of the consequences.

The checker's fear and doubt are so strong, and their ability to process information so weak, that only perfect proof could ever be satisfying. Paradoxically, through their own efforts, they make such perfect proof impossible to obtain. Since fear drives checkers, they frantically rush their efforts and then feel careless and distracted. This, in turn, makes them feel as if they checked poorly, leaving them dissatisfied, which is most likely why stress appears to worsen checking. The doubts are so stubborn that checking for some becomes a never-ending cycle that can grow to take over a person's entire life. At times, it seems as if the more information a checker gets by checking, the more doubtful they become.

Checking can frequently bring even more things to a checker's attention that they otherwise would not have noticed and can expand to fill hours of a person's day. Many find their worst times revolve around going to bed, or having to leave home to go to work, appointments, or vacations. Many checkers must get up as many as three hours early in order to be able to get all their checking done and not be late for work. Many usually are, anyway. Loss of jobs due to lateness is one major way in which checking can ruin an individual's life. Capable and intelligent people are thus sidelined and kept unemployed.

An example of checking can be seen in the case of a teenager, Ted, who, before he could use the bathroom in his house, had to check the closet in that room thoroughly to make sure that no harmful person was hiding there. The checking became so involved and tedious after several months that his whole day's activities would revolve around his visits to that room, which he naturally tried to limit. No amount of pleading, explaining, or lecturing by his parents could convince him to stop. He began to arrive progressively later at school, to the point where the principal contacted his parents. Eventually, he was unable to attend school at all. It went as far as his needing home tutoring for an entire school year, prior to receiving treatment for the disorder.

"Seeing" or "Hearing" Things

In some cases, checking can result from dysperceptions. These are described as actual sensations by sufferers and seem to go beyond just having doubtful thoughts. It often occurs among OCD sufferers when they are driving, a problem area also mentioned previously. Many persons have reported that after getting sensations of movements, blurs, or shadows on the edges of their field of vision, they have stopped their cars and walked around or made U-turns and have gone up and down the street many times to check for a person or animal they may have run over. In some cases, they would also thoroughly inspect their cars for dents, marks, or stains which might prove that they had actually hit something. Driving after dark can contribute to the doubt so strongly, and create so many more opportunities for dysperceptions, that many sufferers eventually give it up. Trash or objects in the street are also the cause of fear, as doubt seemingly transforms them into people or animals that were possibly run over.

An example which illustrates this point is the case of one patient who had difficulty driving his car, because he worried that the chances were very high that one of his tires might throw up a piece of broken glass or a stone that would kill a pedestrian. Along with this, he also feared accidentally running over pedestrians and interpreted the sensation of each bump in the road as possible evidence of his having done so. He would also have a type of dysperception, where he sensed shadows or movement on the edges of his vision, and immediately jumped to the conclusion that these were pedestrians whose movements he hadn't been entirely sure of. Since he couldn't be sure where these supposed pedestrians had been, he became doubtful as to whether or not he might have run them over. As a result, he would stop his car every few blocks and get out and search all around to get rid of his doubts about whether or not this had really happened.

Dissatisfied with the fact that he couldn't check perfectly enough, he would frequently phone the police to ask whether such an accident had been reported in the area where he had been driving. (See the section on Dysperception in chapter 11.) At one point, his calling became so excessive that the police traced his calls and actually visited his home to warn him to stop or face arrest, as he was obstructing police operations. This warning stopped the phone calls. He would also comb the newspapers daily and listen to the radio to see if any accidents were reported. If he heard of one, he would become very frightened, thinking that he had been responsible for it.

Whenever he saw police cars, fire trucks, or ambulances along his route, he would also become scared and assume that they were coming from the scene of some accident he had caused. He always had to drive the same routes coming and going, to make sure that he had even more chances to check. As his problem became worse, he would even become frightened at the nearby sound of other cars' horns, ambulance sirens, flashing lights, or the noise of brakes, thinking that someone had died in an accident he had caused. He would get the urge to visit the scene and ask if anyone had seen him commit the act.

All this constant checking did nothing to calm his fears, and he gradually became more anxious about anything to do with driving, until he was finally no longer able to do so. Ironically, on one earlier occasion he actually had an accident and he rear-ended another car. He handled it with no problems and went on his way. The difference here is that he knew he had actually hit someone— there was no doubt and therefore no anxiety. When asked why he could not tell the difference in less definite situations, he said, "Well, I really don't know, I just can't be sure."

A variation of the doubt about running others over is where the individual frequently hears cries for help or assistance coming from such unlikely spots as mailboxes, sewer openings, dumpsters, store display cases, train tracks, holes in the ground, etc. In such cases, the person often misattributes normal sounds to the calls of someone in trouble, and the doubt prevents them from shrugging it off. They will hang around these spots, looking and listening for the victim, afraid that if they leave the harm that may result will be their responsibility.

Those with fears of AIDS, who try to avoid anything resembling blood, frequently think they see red dots or glints of red on many surfaces or even themselves. Even really tiny specks that seem slightly "reddish" or are of no identifiable color at all can be cause for alarm. Often, they will stare at them doubtfully, in an attempt to know absolutely what the specks or spots are really composed of.

Another common dysperception is the "feeling" of having accidentally dropped something, such as keys or coins out of a pocket or purse. One individual would constantly stop and look behind himself while walking, to check for items he was afraid he had dropped. He would often exactly retrace the routes he had just taken in hopes of being able to verify if there were any "lost" objects. He also looked back around corners for the same reason and constantly patted and touched his pockets. Additionally, he also had a lot of trouble when throwing things out, because he felt doubtful as to whether he was accidentally throwing out other important things as well. He would spend long periods of time combing through his trash, tearing envelopes, boxes, and paper bags apart so he could check inside the seams for important items which might have become stuck there. It should be noted that these things were also checked before they were thrown out in the first place. Some of those with this problem often resemble compulsive hoarders, because they deal with their doubt by compulsively not throwing things out.

The doubts that go with dysperceptions can be so strong at times that some persons are seen to switch lamps on and off hundreds of times. This is because only by seeing the room totally lit or dark and comparing the two many times, can they be sure that the lamp is actually off.

Checking Things Out of Curiosity

Checking may also be the result of a compulsive desire to satisfy a special curiosity or out of a desire to memorize something perfectly and never forget it. One man had a strong interest in the workings of many different kinds of locks and doorknobs, and he felt the urge to study and look at as many as he happened to notice or that caught his eye. He even had the urge to take them apart, to examine their inner workings. Naturally, when these were not in his own home, it led to a few embarrassing moments. Another individual constantly looked up historical facts and dates in reference books, to check whether or not her memory of them was accurate. She would become so fearful about forgetting facts that she stopped watching TV, reading the papers, or even reading signs or package labels in stores. She had the urge to save everything that had some information written on it and also to keep reading it over and over to check her memory. Items saved included newspapers (huge stacks of them), can and jar labels, packages, junk mail, old greeting cards, and even litter in the street that had any printing on it. This checking is a variation on compulsive hoarding.

When a Checker Is Unable to Check Something

There is a myth that if a checker is prevented from checking, he or she will "flip out" or go crazy. It is true that checkers who cannot check, or are prevented in some way from doing so, can develop strong feelings of anxiety or anger. They do not, however, become dangerous to themselves or others. Some try to get around this by doing mental checking rituals in their minds, as a sort of second best substitute, and imagine themselves checking instead. Certain types of checking are purely mental anyway and cannot be prevented in any case. An example would be those who replay past situations in their heads.

Checkers may also make others behave in a repetitive way, such as always having to answer their questions with exactly the same words each time. Another alternative sufferers have is to get someone to do the checking for them, either by asking directly or by subtly maneuvering the other person into doing so. A very subtle type of checking involves the checker arranging to be accompanied in a particular situation by another person functioning as an observer who would "know" and warn the sufferer simply by their own reaction if anything dangerous or unusual were occurring. Most often, this observer is unaware that they are being used in this way.

In a variation of this, the checker, in front of a listener, "innocently" mentions or recounts a situation they are doubtful about and then watches for a reaction. Even if the listener gives no particular response, the checker will feel satisfied, thinking that if something really were wrong, they would be able to tell by the listener's reaction. Therapists, family members, or friends trying not to give reassurance must be aware of this, since even by only passively listening to questions or particular statements, they are still contributing to the illness. Unfortunately, family members do sometimes try to be helpful by preventing their loved one from checking, and great anxiety, resentment, and family fights can result. Why this is a very poor strategy is discussed in chapter 6.

MAGICAL/UNDOING COMPULSIONS

Magic

Obviously, those with OCD can have fears and doubts about almost anything. Many of these things cannot be commonly prevented, or they are so unrealistic and bizarre that no average person would ordinarily try to protect themselves or others against them, much less think of them. Those with OCD are constantly being barraged with thoughts that serious harm will come to them and/or others, in many cases from sources that even they must acknowledge are "crazy" and strange. The sufferer's need for control in the face of these fears is great, but they believe that ordinary protective measures cannot help them. The normal means of control don't apply in their magical world. The result is that with these types of fears, people feel that they must therefore resort to something beyond any ordinary precaution to have a sense of security and control, that is, magic. It appears to be their only possible alternative.

Superstition and magic create connections between things which according to logic don't connect within the real world. Numbers, words, and actions appear to control events in the present and future. Bad luck or good luck can be spread by thought, by touch, or simply by association. Those with this type of OCD realize that their behaviors are unrealistic and sound crazy to others, but they do them anyway to relieve their anxiety. Because magic figures into a fair proportion of OCD, it is most likely the reason that so many have been misdiagnosed as schizophrenic.

Magical thinking and the practice of magic have been a part of human behavior and society since prehistoric times. In an unforgiving world, where people felt small and powerless in the face of natural forces, it gave them a sense of comfort to believe they could explain the unexplainable and influence or control the apparently uncontrollable. Life would have seemed too insecure and frightening for them without this comfort. To not have magic would have been unbearable for them. When it appeared to work, it was, of course, only due to coincidence, but the belief in it was reinforced. When the magic didn't work, blame was probably placed on the fact that the ritual wasn't performed correctly or perfectly enough, or the magician was not pure enough. It was something not to be questioned. Our ancestors superstitiously believed that by carrying out special behaviors in particular ways, known as rituals, they could control such things as the weather, the occurrence of sickness or death, success in hunting or harvesting, and good fortune in general. It was also a way to directly petition or appeal to the gods or spirits which they believed were the power behind nature.

While belief in magic has declined quite a bit since the birth of science, a good deal of it still persists in many cultures and even among educated people. It might be safe to say that there is a predisposition and even a need for magic and superstitious thinking among human beings. Within limits, it can still be a part of a normal life. The popularity of horoscopes, good luck charms, and psychics in our own society bears witness to this. However, even in primitive societies where magic controls people's actions and decisions on an everyday basis, it is regarded as a tool and does not paralyze its users. In OCD, unfortunately, its use expands far beyond the normal limits. Beginning as a way to control anxiety brought on by obsessions, it gradually escapes the user's control, taking over their life, and generating greater anxiety than it was originally supposed to relieve.

Like the magic of old, compulsions in this category can involve all sorts of superstitious and ritualistic behavior, giving the sufferer a sense of control and security in their doubtful world of obsessions—one which to them seems filled with danger. What these compulsions all have in common with each other and with ancient magic is that they are performed for the purpose of preventing bad events in advance, or for undoing events or thoughts that have already occurred. We refer to these as "undoing rituals." One other similarity to other types of magic is that ritual steps must be kept rigidly "pure" and perfect, and cannot vary, or else they will not work. Additionally, rituals must be performed while in the correct state of mind, with no interfering or wayward thoughts. Because anxiety typically hampers the performance of almost anything, sufferers find it very difficult to get their rituals to be perfect. They get the steps in the wrong order, forget to do something, or an unpleasant obsession or image intrudes during the ritual, thus "contaminating" or destroying the magic. Unless the obsession allows them to have another chance at the ritual, a lot of careful planning or activity can be ruined in an instant. If it is a ritual that can only be done at a special moment or on a specific day, there might not be another chance for days or even weeks to try it again. An entire day, a month, or even a coming year can be "ruined." This is how rituals, themselves, become sources of anxiety in a circular sort of way.

Praying

Compulsive praying is a common type of magical procedure. One individual, for example, could only carry out an activity such as putting on a piece of clothing or turning a light on or off, if a special prayer she had invented had been recited first. Those who pray compulsively may do so to protect their own health and safety or the health and safety of friends or family members, or to protect themselves from being sinful or from falling into a state of sinfulness. As with other rituals, the prayers must be recited in a special order, or they must be done all over again.

Sometimes the appearance of a bad word or unlucky number, a morbid obsession, or an unpleasant image in the person's thoughts while praying will also cause the individual to have to begin all over again, as this is thought to ruin the prayer and make it imperfect and invalid. As mentioned earlier, when performing rituals, the person's anxiety often leads to making mistakes (as it does for checkers), and since the rituals must be "perfect" to do any good, the result can be several hours of more ritualizing. Sometimes, as a last resort, people with religious rituals and morbid fears will seek out priests, ministers, or rabbis to be forgiven or reassured that they are not "sinful" or "evil" for having morbid thoughts or for ritualizing. Typically, even when this reassurance is given, the obsessions and compulsions continue, since no amount of assurance can ever be enough in such cases, nor can such strong doubts be so easily erased. The person with such a problem just cannot seem to process the information or hold onto it mentally for very long.

Sometimes, what begins as a genuine religious practice can become incorporated into compulsions. Real prayers, such as The Lord's Prayer, the Hail Mary, or various Psalms, can be recited repetitively and compulsively to prevent bad luck or unpleasant events. Often, unless they are done perfectly, or with no other "bad" thoughts in mind, they will have to be redone. This process can sometimes last for hours.

Other types of magical compulsions also bear a strong resemblance to the magical practices of old. These would include washing off bad thoughts or ideas, performing actions or thinking thoughts in reverse, touching things in special ways, wearing special clothes or charms, or stepping in special ways or on special spots when walking.

Many sufferers find themselves having to redo common everyday activities if a "bad" or "harmful" thought coincides with them. When they are redone, it must be with a good or "perfect" thought in mind. They will walk in and out of rooms numerous times, pick things up and put them down again, reopen and close doors, windows, and packages, take off clothes and put them back on again, etc., as many times as it takes to get it right. Maria's account provides a picture of what this can be like.

Maria's Story

〜 *Dealing with my OCD is very complicated and difficult for others to understand. It involves the actual thoughts I am thinking at a specific time when I am performing an action. The thoughts mean everything. They mean life or death to me. They determine my fate. My own thought will decide if that action or the object involved will be a threat to me. By this, I mean that if I have a bad thought while doing an action, then the thing I just did or touched is contaminated. It can be as simple an activity as putting on an article of clothing, turning a light off or on, eating a raisin, drinking that last cup of soda, etc. The only way for me to be protected is by first making sure that I am conscious of what I am thinking about at the split second I am performing an act. After that, the only way to break the spell is by then redoing the act. As a rule, I must always know what I am thinking about at all times. Unfortunately, I always seem to have a bad thought when I consciously try to have a good thought. I can easily contaminate anything that is around me, an article of clothing, a step that I am walking on, a pen, paper, food, a house, etc. If I have a bad thought while putting on a shirt and continue to wear that shirt, I have to take it off and put it back on with a good thought. If I don't, the shirt and the whole day are both contaminated. This means that whatever I eat and drink, where I go, and whoever I meet are also contaminated. If I have a candy bar and have a bad thought while eating the last piece, I must buy another candy bar and eat a fresh piece with a good thought in mind. I must undo that terrible curse I have placed on myself. The only thing that will make me safe is by redoing the act and having a better thought. By not doing the act and staying with the bad thought, I feel that the thought will take over my body, and that my body will now be contaminated. It is now poisoned and this terrible thought will happen to me. If I have a bad thought while I am sneezing, I even have to go and inhale some pepper so that I will be able to sneeze again while having a good thought. The thoughts can also harm someone close to me. The result I fear usually involves getting cancer, especially leukemia. The rules and belief patterns that I have set for myself are the only way I can ensure the protection of myself and the ones I love. To not undo the thought means that the worst will happen. I feel cursed by these thoughts.*

Numbers

Numbers also play a special role in magical compulsions. Lucky and unlucky numbers figure into many symptoms. They can be the common ones, such as 7, 11, 13, 666, etc., or they can be special ones particular to the sufferer. Multiples of these numbers may be either good or bad, and odd or even numbers may also be significant. Most often, odd numbers are thought of as bad because they lack symmetry and are uneven. Bad numbers may have to be canceled out by good numbers or simply by counting to or looking at higher numbers. Other magical behaviors often have to be performed a special number of times or on special dates. Midnight, noon, or the first or last days of the month or year are the most common times that figure into these rituals. Certain times of day, when they appear on a clock, can also be lucky or unlucky, depending on which numbers a person's obsessions fasten on to. Actually, the digital clock has contributed a lot to these types of obsessions and compulsions. Those with magical touching rituals frequently incorporate numbers into their behavior and have to touch certain objects a special number of times in order for them to be effective.

The special mental arrangements of things such as numbers, information, words, names, and special images make up another subtype of magical ritual. As a mental compulsion, this type of behavior is generally not visible to others, yet it can be as serious and agonizing as any other OC symptom. At times it can be much more complicated than rituals involving only numbers. Alice vividly describes this type of symptom.

Alice's Story

ᥟ *It all started when I was about seven years old. I was in either first or second grade. My first recollection is of counting three separate incidents, one on each finger of my right hand. This continued for approxi-*

mately one year until it became unbearable. During this year, I would con-
stantly go over these three incidents in my mind. Feelings of guilt flooded
me. I would label each finger (in my mind) with a key word so as not to
forget or let go of the things that had happened in the past. The things I
kept track of were not major. One Saturday I broke down crying, ran to
my mother's bedroom, and told her about the three incidents that I could
not get off my mind (or my fingers). From then on, I felt compelled to tell
my mother about everything that occurred, every thought I had. This pat-
tern continued into my adult years. Counting occupied my every waking
thought. I had gone from three fingers to all ten, counting every incident,
each spoken word, anything I felt compelled to tell my mother. I HAD to
tell her, or something awful might happen to her. She had to know every-
thing that happened in my day. By her being aware of all my actions and
thoughts, she would be okay, and no harm would come to her. But I was
not allowed to forget ANYTHING. Anything that slipped away might one
day come back and hurt her. I could not dare FORGET anything. Through-
out the day I would go over and over the things I had to keep track of. As
the day went on, so did my counting. I could count as high as I had to by
memorizing the ten things and reusing my fingers. I often thought if I "cut
off" my fingers, maybe this nightmare would end.

I always thought I was so aware of what was going on around me, but
now realize that I was so busy concentrating on my counting that I missed
out on what was really happening out there in the real world.

After years of keeping track on my fingers (until I was twenty-one), I
finally stopped using them. Instead, I pictured boxes on the floor. I guess I
wanted to keep track of EVERYTHING that was going on, instead of just
picking out the incidents that seemed threatening. I usually had about
twelve boxes, anything that would happen in my day I would mentally
put into one of these boxes. It was almost like having a chart in my mind
and adding to it all day. Any little thing that happened, or everything I, or
someone else, said, had to be put in order and put in a box. At times
twelve boxes were not enough—I would sometimes go up to as high as
sixty or one hundred. Then, as if I took the chart home with me, I would
go over everything I kept track of to make sure it was all in order. This
took such time and energy. But it had to be done and as soon as possible
before anything else added to the new chart I was already setting up at
home. This would take two to three hours if I was not interrupted. Other-
wise, I would have to work the interruptions into the order of the new
chart I was just starting up at home. I would have to have my boxes every-
where I went. I set up new sets of them throughout the day. The boxes held
me up — without them I had a fear of falling. So many boxes, I tried to

put them behind me, literally, so I could concentrate on one set of boxes at a time. Finally, I kept track of all the boxes in my head. For hours, I would stare off into space, but my mind was very busy organizing, rearranging, going over and over every thought, action, movement that I and everyone else had made. I was in my box world, trapped in my box world. My body would tremble as I went through these daily rituals. My heart would pound, my hands sweat. The more I tried to control things, the more my rituals were controlling me.

Thinking back, I wonder if I at times put myself in a box. I believe I ignored a lot of things, almost as if I were inside one of my boxes, safe from any outside harm. Nothing could get to me in here. Any criticism from anyone would reflect off the sides. I was shielded. I had my barrier from any harm from the outside world.

An example of someone with magical number rituals can be seen in the case of Arlene, a part of whose story also appears under "Body-Focused Obsessions" in chapter 8.

Arlene's Story

ᴄ᷍   *My OCD started twenty years ago when I was thirteen years old. My dad was in a horrible motorcycle accident. It was an awful experience for the whole family. For months I obsessed about the randomness of the whole thing. If he had been in the exact same spot a few seconds sooner or later, the accident would not have occurred. I became afraid to make any minute decision because the tiniest action or choice on my part could result in destruction. I started to develop a system on which to base my decisions and that system involved numbers. I have realized all along that my numbers will not necessarily "keep me safe," but it has come to the point where I can't imagine functioning without them.*

Every month, I create a different number pattern that I use for that month. I have a time-consuming ritual to develop and memorize these numbers. They represent all sorts of things: specific times and dates, letters of the alphabet, directions, colors, etc., and I use this information to make decisions. I know people often think I'm not paying attention to them or that I'm distracted, and that is because I may be counting something, timing something, or doing calculations in my head. I am very obsessed with clocks, especially digital ones. Doing things at the "right" time is very important. The first thing I do when I go somewhere new is try to locate a clock. I check my watch or a nearby clock at least once every five minutes or so no matter where I am.

I followed my number scheme rigidly, regardless of the consequences, logic, or how it made me feel. Looking back, I am sad at how much time I have spent doing things I didn't really want to do because of my numbers, but nevertheless, I am still unwilling to let them go. The thought of that is too frightening!

PERFECTIONISTIC COMPULSIONS

Because compulsives are popularly known as perfectionists, most people think of behavior in this category when the word "compulsion" is mentioned. In the case of OCD, though, perfection has gone way beyond the point of being a virtue as we commonly conceive of it. Also, it is not pursued simply for the satisfaction of seeing something done well. This type of perfectionism paradoxically cripples sufferer's lives and actually keeps them from producing or accomplishing much of anything or making any kind of decision.

It would appear that this desire for perfection is an attempt by sufferers to control the doubt which accompanies OCD, as well as an attempt to impose some kind of a structure on one's mental life which seems to be constantly shifting. There are so many ways imaginable for harm to come to oneself or others, and the doubts are so strong and pervasive, that only by doing things perfectly can they be eliminated. In the face of such perceived danger, "almost" will never be good enough to make a sufferer feel secure. Naturally, the sufferer believes that the anxiety and the need to double-check will be eliminated once the doubt is gone. This coping strategy sounds good in theory, but since we are not perfect and do not live in a perfect world where everything can be controlled, it does not work in practice. Repeated failure does not seem to keep these sufferers from trying, however. As in the case of those who perform magical rituals, the doubt leads to endless double checking, numerous repetitions, and even greater levels of doubt and anxiety. Simple tasks can take hours to accomplish when they are redone two or three hundred times.

Another of the more difficult tasks for those in this subgroup is having to make a decision. Even the most inconsequential decisions can cause tremendous agony since they must be made perfectly. Naturally, such individuals can generate long lists of alternatives and exceptions among which they feel unable to discriminate. Even the choice of what to wear or eat can cause serious dilemmas.

Another path leading to perfectionism might be the presence of intrusive magical thoughts telling the person that they must do everything perfectly in order to prevent some type of bad event from superstitiously happening or to avoid the possibility of being a "bad" or "evil" person. Sufferers usually cannot explain how being perfect will protect them or others; they just "feel" that it will.

A third subcategory within this group would be those who have a "need" for order and symmetry. Sloppiness and asymmetry seem to bother and offend them. If they see things that do not look properly ordered or arranged, they will find themselves thinking about them continuously and often cannot get on with other business until something has been done about it. Those with more extreme forms of this problem will experience strong anxiety. Their perfectionism can apply to their appearance, their possessions and their room, or the house they live in. It can even go further, as can be seen among those who rearrange, clean, and order the possessions, rooms, or homes of others.

Often, other people may not be allowed into a sufferer's room or home for fear that things will be touched, moved, used, or dirtied. The rooms can be seen to be spotlessly clean, with items on shelves in size or alphabetical order, drawers all closed and with their contents perfectly arranged and aligned, and all the hangers in their closet alike and the same distance apart. Certain possessions or areas in their homes may be singled out to be kept absolutely pristine—areas where no one, not even they, can touch or enter once they have been made perfect. Sufferers may spend many hours each day cleaning and straightening things. They will often stay up through the night, unable to go to sleep unless everything is made perfect.

Acquiring new possessions can also be extremely difficult. One man would shop endlessly to find articles of clothing which were sewn perfectly, with the patterns matching up exactly at the seams. When he found them, he would take them home, store them in his drawers in their plastic bags, and never wear them in order to keep them in their "perfect," unused state. The idea of their being used and showing wear caused him to feel anxious. He dressed in old, worn clothing instead. When we finally got around to unwrapping and examining this pristine clothing collection in a therapy session at his home, we made the ironic discovery that, over the years, in some cases the pins keeping them folded had rusted, ruining them. This example illustrates the way in which compulsions relieve a sufferer's anxiety in the short run but bring about opposite results in the long run. Buying things in general for such people means never selecting items that are dented, bruised, scratched, folded, or repackaged. A common practice they have is to never buy items on the top of a stack or at the front of the shelf.

When some people in this group write or type, they end up redoing their work many times in order to get the letters or the content "perfect." Crossing things out or erasing would not be acceptable to them since it would leave marks or smudges. When forced to erase, they will often wear a hole through the page. While reading, the person may reread the same line or paragraph over and over to make sure it has been perfectly understood and that nothing has been overlooked by mistake. A behavior that sometimes accompanies rereading is compulsive underlining or highlighting. The sufferer wants to perfectly remember everything that might be important in a book, but due to their inability to discriminate the important from the unimportant, they often end up marking most or even the entire book.

The need to be "perfectly" understood can go far beyond merely writing. Some worry that they may not have communicated with others in an exactly correct way. Their fear of being misunderstood could lead others to think badly of them. In her account, Jessica describes this set of symptoms.

Jessica's Story

~ *I am a wife, mother of four, and a licensed child care provider. I always kept our home neat. If an item was missing, it had to be found. I was always so meticulous—no clutter and everything in order. I also had to put my life in order. Looking into the past, I wanted to correct or at least explain everything so that it was understood perfectly and clearly. I feared I would be misunderstood. I was so afraid an image would exist of me that wasn't so. Growing up, I was always told, "What will people think?" Therefore, I did not want them to think any other way than the way it actually was.*

I had never done anything in my past of which I should be ashamed, but it was not "perfect." I was always cautious, had a lot of friends, didn't date much, or get into many different relationships. I always just liked having that special someone in my life. I started to contact people from my past as well as the present to explain my feelings and make amends. I wanted to be understood perfectly. I would go over issues so that I would be reassured that what I said couldn't be misleading to their understanding, especially if we got on a subject that could reflect on me personally or my beliefs or disbeliefs. I was overly concerned about my image. I had to be sure the person didn't misconstrue anything I told them.

My compulsion to protect "my good image" became so great in the third month of my fourth pregnancy (which was also right after my father passed away) that I could not turn it off. I had to be sure everything was understood, that nobody took me or something that I said the wrong way. The "What if?" kept tormenting me. I contacted some people to explain why I was so withdrawn when I had bulimia—contacts to make amends, contacts to explain perfectly and clearly anything I felt needed to be clarified about me or my beliefs. I would contact the person by phone and then continue to call to explain over and over again. Sometimes a new thought would replace an old one and then I would be left thinking the person with whom I was talking didn't understand clearly or took it another way and then I would explain it over and over again, so that I could be reassured

everything was understood perfectly and in order. I would check by asking,
"You do know," or "you do understand," or "you didn't take it wrong, did
you?"

    I always had notes and read what I had to say to the person so I would-
n't forget what I had to say or leave anything out. I even started to tape
conversations so that I could play them back and hear all the details to
reassure myself of what I said and that I did go over all the necessary
details. I would write letters that would take days to complete and would
keep them in case I needed to add to them. I would do them over and over
in fear the person I was writing to wouldn't be able to make out a certain
letter or word. I started to print and make each letter carefully and would
still have to do them over again. I didn't trust the post office, so on a few
occasions I actually took the letter to the person and read it to them. I
would always question them to ascertain if they understood what I was
saying. I always made copies of all letters and cards that were sent.

    I lost a few friends over this. They could no longer put up with my
explaining to them over and over and doubting their understanding. Some
felt I questioned their intelligence. I couldn't trust that they did understand
and not misconstrue everything. I didn't doubt myself and what I knew. I
never experienced so much emotional pain as I endured. It is hard to
understand how a part of you (in your thinking) can take over and try to
make you believe its false alarms—where you have to battle with it and
convince it and actually prove to it that it is wrong. It is as though another
person lives within your mind and torments you until you carry out the
compulsion, using the "greatest" fear one has as a motivating force.

Attempting to memorize everything about a particular subject in order to
learn it perfectly has also kept quite a few sufferers up late at night. This compulsion has also been mentioned previously under hoarding compulsions, with
which it overlaps. Many an intelligent person with OCD has failed or dropped
out of school because of such symptoms. Those who do manage to stick with it
and graduate usually end up totally exhausted, as they must expend several
times more effort than the average student to even do average work.

    There are some who direct their perfectionism at their appearance. This is
different from those with BDD, who are convinced that their appearance is
defective in some way. Clothing, makeup, nails, and hair must be perfect, not
just presentable. One female patient of mine would not even walk outside her
home to get the mail unless she was made up, her hair was done, had on a "perfect" outfit with all seams aligned, and had her nails flawlessly polished. The
mere thought of being seen by others in a less than perfect state is enough to
cause strong feelings of anxiety. There is one form of this that is sometimes mis-

taken for BDD, in which sufferers repeatedly cut their own hair in an attempt to make it perfectly symmetrical. Even when their hair is nicely cut by a professional, they will go home and try to recut it, often cutting it to excess and ruining their appearance.

In his account, Charles describes what this compulsion was like.

Charles's Story

〰 *In my senior year of high school I slipped into an increasingly downward spiral of self-destructive behavior that I would later come to attribute to OCD. With my graduation steadily approaching, I felt that it was incumbent on me to look my best for the ensuing ceremonies. The hairstyle obtained was met with the usual self-conscious dissatisfaction. However, instead of simply grinning and bearing it as I had always done in the past, I felt compelled to rectify the matter by improving on the barber's handiwork myself. My actual appearance or even the unanimous approval of others would not alter my twisted perception that something looked "wrong." What does matter is the fact that once I began cutting my hair, it became virtually an impossibility to stop. Over a period of months I would trim my hair incrementally, never feeling quite satisfied with the results. Since the process was so gradual and done in secret, it wasn't until I was bordering on baldness that anyone began to notice. Even when my family and friends implored me to stop my "habit," I saw nothing wrong with my actions. I was convinced that as soon as I got my hair "right," I would then be able to stop. In the meantime, I would conceal my appearance from the general public by wearing several hats. Being quite thin as I was, my baldness would lead one to assume that I was going through cancer treatment. At this point, I had entered college, although my attendance in classes was minimal. I was so consumed with my appearance that I would seldom leave my house. On those days that I actually reached the campus, I would often wind up spending my class time in front of a bathroom mirror, incessantly wetting down and brushing my hair. This particular action was repeated so often and with such force that the flesh of my scalp would often become raw and occasionally bleed. Even then, I would still continue. It was not long after that, I finally arrived at a near-hysterical realization that something was very wrong with me.*

The ensuing months were spent in a desperate attempt not to give in to my tendency toward injuring myself in this way. This ultimately proved futile, for as soon as any tangible hair growth had been achieved, I would resume cutting. By this time I was overwhelmed with depression and guilt. I had little appetite and achieved little sleep. I dropped out of college and lived as a hermit. The allegorical hitting of rock bottom occurred when I was hospitalized for internal bleeding from an ulcerative condition which I had been living with for some years. No doubt it had been exacerbated by the OCD related stress.

What is sometimes referred to as "obsessive slowness" is probably in many cases a mislabeling of someone who is extremely perfectionistic. It should be made clear that this is not simply slowness for its own sake. People will often perform the most ordinary activities at an excruciatingly slow pace, broken down into many tiny steps to make sure that nothing has been done incorrectly or that no steps have been left out. Some may take more than a half hour to wash their face or to shave or even put on a single shoe. Counting rituals will sometimes be incorporated into their activities, to make sure that they have spent enough time at them to ensure perfect performance.

Also under this heading are those we refer to as having the problem known as "scrupulosity." These are the individuals who must always be 100 percent correct and morally perfect. This applies not only to religious issues for them, but also extends to all their dealings with others. They must always tell the truth and be 100 percent painfully honest, even if it causes them difficulties. Some will confess to doing things they are not even sure they did, just in case they might have done them. They are also seen to frequently correct others. Some will enforce punishments on themselves and levy strict penalties in an effort to control their sometimes-imperfect performance.

I have seen cases among Orthodox Jews where the ritual preparation of food under kosher conditions became a great cause for doubt and anxiety for those with symptoms in this category. They feared negligently mixing ingredients that they are forbidden to combine and would thereby contaminate their food. This would then make it unacceptable to eat and cause their family and themselves to violate religious law. Needless to say, those with such symptoms usually end up not being able to prepare food at all, due to the extreme stress it causes.

Another variation seen among members of the perfectionism subgroup is the need for a certain "just right" feeling when performing certain activities, in order that they may achieve a kind of closure or feeling of completeness. It is not uncommon for them to repeat ordinary activities until they feel "just right." Even certain thoughts must be rethought for the same reason. Sometimes there is a magical sort of requirement as to how many times something must be repeated for "rightness" to be achieved, or there are only certain times when things must be done if they are to feel "just right." This need for a "just right" feeling is also seen in the pulling of particular hairs in TTM and in the performance of tics in TS. One less common variation takes the form of having to look at things in the environment in special ways—lining them up visually or tracing them with one's eyes until it feels as if it has been done properly.

While it was mentioned earlier that perfectionistic compulsions are not done just for satisfaction, it is a factor that does sometimes affect treatment. Just as those who play slot machines will keep playing despite continued losses, so will compulsive perfectionists keep working at their compulsions, even though they cannot make or keep things perfect. The satisfaction or "high" that some sufferers obtain from only occasionally getting things "just right" is enough to keep them going. This may actually keep them from pursuing treatment, as the occasional momentary satisfaction may be just rewarding enough to make them not want to give up the behavior.

COUNTING COMPULSIONS

OCD sufferers count for a variety of reasons. One reason may be that it helps them keep track during compulsive double checking, which may have to be done a certain number of times in each case, to ensure that it was done either for long enough or with the proper number of steps. Second, counting may also relate to magical beliefs in lucky or unlucky numbers. These can be connected with all sorts of occurrences they can supposedly control. As mentioned earlier in the section on magical compulsions, bad luck numbers are frequently canceled out by counting to or gazing at higher or "good luck" numbers.

A third reason for compulsive counting may also be that some individuals simply get an inexplicable urge to count, without its relating to anything or to accomplishing a particular task. They may not simply count consecutive numbers. They may count by twos, threes, fours, or they may count in multiples of other numbers. Others may count almost anything that goes on around them or inside them. Among the internal event counters are those who count the number of breaths or steps they take or the number of times they chew their food.

TOUCHING OR MOVEMENT COMPULSIONS

Compulsive touching of things or moving in special ways can be carried out for a variety of reasons. One of the most common reasons they are performed is for "magical" or superstitious purposes. Those who use these behaviors magically must move their bodies or touch things in particular or repetitive ways in order to control a "bad" thought or event, to undo the possibility of one, or to prevent one from happening—to help ward off bad luck for themselves and/or others.

The possibility of these happenings seems very real to them at times, and they are frequently assaulted by doubtful obsessions telling them that these things may occur. Logically, they can state that the thoughts don't make sense or have little possibility of occurring, but the anxiety is strong and a movement or a touch have become their habitual means of dealing with it. Sufferers try, using magic, to create a connection between two things that don't ordinarily connect—some type of movement or a special way of touching things, and a negative event in the real world. The reason they have resorted to magic is because they can see that there are no logical or realistic options for preventing such unlikely events.

In other cases, we see sufferers moving or touching things more out of habit. They cannot explain why they do it. They may simply say, "If I don't do it, I feel uneasy or nervous." There may even have been a superstitious reason at one time in the past, but it has faded over time. Some feel a sense of being incomplete, rather than of uneasiness or anxiety. These people have a need for closure in such cases. If they don't carry out the compulsion, something will be "missing" for them, leaving them with an unsettled feeling.

A third reason for moving or touching compulsively may be to simply satisfy an urge. There is no bad consequence for not doing these things other than that if they are not performed, the sufferer will feel a need to do them persistently nagging at them, sort of like an itch that needs to be scratched. There is a strong resemblance between OC sufferers in this category and some of those who suffer from TTM or Tourette's Syndrome (TS) (see section in chapter 12 on OCD and Learning Disabilities for a further discussion of the relationship between OCD and TS). In each of these last two categories, there are subgroups of sufferers who also report that their respective tic or hair-pulling behaviors are preceded by a distinct urge which must be satisfied. Because the urge is accompanied by a rising internal feeling of tension, the activity can be delayed, but it cannot ultimately be resisted. Furthermore, some types of repetitive touching or movement compulsions show strong similarities to some of the ticlike movements of TS, as well as the type of frequent head and face touching and hair tugging or twirling that those with TTM do, even when they are not actually pulling hair. While TTM would not be mistaken for TS, there can be somewhat of a gray area between this disorder and TS. This can sometimes lead to some rather puzzling diagnostic situations. Discovering which is which can require a keen knowledge of both disorders. It is interesting to note that some of the drugs that have been helpful in the treatment of TS can sometimes be useful to augment the medications of OC sufferers in this category. (See chapter 4 for a detailed discussion of medications.)

Regardless of the reasons why they are done, these compulsions must be done frequently and in very specific and often ritualistic ways that can overlap with magical compulsions. If they are done incorrectly, when the person is in the wrong frame of mind or just doesn't "feel right," the sufferer must start all over again and keep doing them until they are done right. This can grow to the point of having to do several hundred repetitions of a touching or movement compulsion at a time. I have seen people with such serious and frequent touching rituals that they have developed thick calluses on their fingertips. Some objects must also be touched in certain places. Touching the edges or corners of things is commonly observed. One type of movement compulsion that is particularly unusual in appearance is where sufferers must reverse certain actions they have just carried out. An example would be having to walk out of a room backward. These behaviors can resemble a film being run in reverse.

Sufferers in the three categories mentioned above seem to carry out these behaviors in the same ways and in similar types of situations. Some of the most common occasions where these types of compulsions can occur are when walking through doorways, going up and down stairways, opening or closing doors or drawers, opening or closing boxes or bottles, sitting down or getting up from a piece of furniture, going from one room to another, washing or getting dressed, or getting in or out of a car.

Sufferers whose behaviors put them in this category of compulsions can be seen to do a variety of activities. They may include tapping door posts with certain fingers of one hand; always starting out on the same foot when going through a doorway or climbing the stairs; having to step on special spots on the floor when walking through their homes; holding a door or drawer in a special way when opening or closing it; transferring objects from hand to hand when picking them up or before using them; and putting clothing on and taking it off repetitively when dressing.

A common occurrence for those who have these compulsions is "getting stuck." This usually happens when they are making a transition from one position, place, or floor surface to another. Some examples would include their trying to get up from a chair, walk through a doorway, or move from a carpeted surface to a bare floor and then not being able to get their ritual "just right." They may stand outside their front door or on the threshold of a room for half an hour touching the door post or doorknob repeatedly, unable to enter because they cannot perform the ritual perfectly, or because, as mentioned above, it just doesn't "feel right" as they are doing it. This "just right" feeling is often indefinable, something a sufferer cannot put into words but can recognize when it is present.

There is one other type of compulsion that I am including here, although it does not specifically involve touching or often even an observable movement. This is where a sufferer has to gaze or look at certain objects or spots in their environment when coming near to or walking past them. It is not unusual to see this type of behavior in those who carry out other compulsions in this category.

274 ～ *Obsessive-Compulsive Disorders*

One patient had to stop and look at a particular spot on his driveway when walking to or from his house. He also had to look at a particular mark on his kitchen wall each time he walked through that room.

SELF-MUTILATIVE COMPULSIONS

This is not as well known a category as many of the others in terms of its association with OCD. There are some who might challenge whether or not it even should be categorized as part of the OCD spectrum, but I believe that self-mutilation should be classified as a type of body-focused compulsion because of certain resemblances between it and TTM.

Compulsive self-mutilation can take many forms and has been known to include the cutting or scratching of one's body, burning oneself with matches, cigarettes, or caustic substances, or poking oneself in the eyes, to name a few. In rare cases, extreme behaviors have been observed such as the destruction or amputation of parts of the body.

Such compulsions should not be confused with several other manifestations that look superficially similar and can also be performed in ritualistic ways. One of these would be actual suicide attempts, where the slashing of wrists, for example, is done strictly for the purpose of causing death. Another category, not to be included here, would be those less serious suicidal gestures designed to get attention and help from others. This is where depressed and disturbed individuals will scratch or cut their bodies (in such spots as their wrists) shallowly enough to cause some bleeding but which are not life threatening. These types of gestures may be done frequently, whenever such individuals are feeling distressed, need help, and cannot communicate this to others in any other way. A variation on this would be where certain individuals believe they are bad or evil and do these things to punish themselves.

Another somewhat rarer type of behavior that can look like self-mutilation is where an individual actively attempts to distract themselves when they are feeling anxious. I have witnessed patients who, when feeling extremely anxious and panicky, will actually scratch or cut themselves with their fingernails or implements to draw their attention away from the fear. This is sometimes seen in certain people who suffer from panic disorder. They do it to prevent a panic attack from occurring or to stop one in progress. I have even seen them go as far as pouring irritating substances on the cuts and scratches to make the experience even stronger.

In compulsive self-mutilation, we also see sufferers cutting or hurting themselves to relieve a sort of drive or urge, not unlike the type seen in some of those with TTM. There seems to be no particular thought process behind it. If they attempt to resist, it nags at them persistently. Also, as seen in TTM, performing the act of mutilation itself seems to cause individuals little or no pain, and they often report going into a state that resembles self-hypnosis or a kind of dissociation. Furthermore, following the mutilation, there is a feeling of satisfaction or relief. It might be that this activity is tied into some sort of release of endorphin (body-produced, opiatelike substances) in the brain, which can cause pleasurable sensations. I have heard some case reports of these behaviors as well as TTM being successfully treated with opiate-blocking drugs. Much more needs to be discovered about self-mutilation, as little is known at the present time.

BODY-FOCUSED COMPULSIONS

A person can be compulsive about wanting to double-check or control their appearance or the workings of their body. These compulsions make up a group of behaviors whose purpose is to relieve the doubt and anxiety of obsessions about the body (see Body-Focused Obsessions in chapter 8). The source of many of these compulsions is BDD, also known as "imagined ugliness," which is dealt with in several other sections of this book. The BDD-related compulsions include the checking of one's own appearance in the mirror for imperfections, questioning others about these feared defects, trying to hide or correct the defects oneself, and finally going for medical help to ask about and then possibly correct the defects surgically.

This personal account of BDD is a good illustration of someone with a body-focused compulsion.

Amanda's Story

ᔐ *I think my problems began following the death of my mother from cancer when I was thirty-one. I kept having visions of the way her face had come to look older, "smaller," and sunken in over a short period of time. I started seeing changes in my own face and lines around my eyes. I would study my face in the mirror for hours looking for changes. I would touch my face, feeling for lines. I even wanted not to have the normal creases that other people have. At times I hated those mirrors. I'm not a violent person, but I felt like breaking them. I ended up putting sheets over them. Even then I used to peek underneath just to get a glance. I had to question people all the time, asking, "Does my face look sunken to you? Do I have creases around my nose?" If I saw someone looking at me, I thought they were thinking that I looked like an old lady.*

I searched for solutions to the problems I saw in the mirror and kept thinking of plastic surgery as the only answer. It was like listening to a bro-

*ken record. I was even dreaming about it. I started to listen very carefully
to every little thing people said to me to see if they were really saying things
about the way I looked. It became so intense that I had no sense of reality. I
was totally absorbed with obsessing about my face. I thought I was losing
my mind and losing touch with reality. I opened up to a few close friends
about my problem, but nobody could really understand the nightmare I
was going through.*

*On the day of my uncle's funeral, I ended up being hospitalized because
I couldn't stop crying all day. It wasn't just because of his death. I just
wanted to die from the anxious feelings from within. My brother and his
girlfriend had me admitted to a psychiatric ward and there the doctors
immediately started me on medications to sedate me. I was later released
and returned home. I felt less anxious, but I felt like I was walking in my
sleep. After six months of sitting at home like a vegetable, I got deep into
my own OCD world. I had terrible side effects from the medication,
including even more crying, depression, and paranoia. All the fears and
traumas returned. My doctor wanted to increase the medication, but I
went off it completely. I don't think he really knew how to help me.*

*As I got more desperate, my thoughts returned to plastic surgery as a
cure. I went to one doctor and he turned me down, saying I was too young
and didn't need it. Another said he would do my eyes, cheeks, and lips. It
sounded like the answer to my prayers. I had it done. I was very relieved
after surgery and thought my problems were finally over. Eight months
later, the swelling from the operation finally went down and I then started
thinking about other facial areas, especially my neck. I returned to the sur-
geon's office and had liposuction done around my neck and chin. After
that, I started complaining that my cheek implants (which were implanted
during an earlier operation) had slipped, so I had them corrected too. I was
also having collagen injections in between all these surgical procedures.
Naturally, I went broke spending every penny I had or could lay my hands
on having all this done. When I realized that surgery wasn't helping, I
finally hit rock bottom as the reality of my actions really hit me. I was at a
dead end. I knew something was not right with my thinking and I took
myself for help, something I probably should have done in the first place.*

One type of compulsive hair cutting can be classified here as a body-focused
compulsion; however, it belongs under perfectionistic compulsions if its main
aim is to achieve symmetry and perfection of style. The focus then is on perfection, not ugliness. When people feel that their hair is "ugly" regardless of what
others say, this falls under BDD. It can be seen as different from perfectionism
because these sufferers always feel ugly no matter how they cut or shape their

hair. They are not necessarily aiming for perfection; they are simply trying to escape obsessive thoughts of ugliness.

A certain type of skin picking should be included under body-focused compulsions. As with hair cutting, it can fall under perfectionistic compulsions when the sufferer is trying to have a perfectly clear complexion. When a person mistakenly interprets the normal small blemishes we all get as severe acne, and takes drastic measure to open, cut, and squeeze, we would classify this as a body-focused compulsion. Others looking at the blemishes (before picking) would say they are negligible and unworthy of attention, or that they are merely minor skin imperfections and not blemishes or pimples at all. Again, the thoughts revolve around how the acne makes a person look "ugly" and not that their skin is imperfect.

What is likely a common but not well-known form of body-focused compulsion is the urge to check if one's own body is working or functioning properly. For some, it may focus on the workings of various organs such as the heart, gastrointestinal tract, or any of the five senses. In others, it can involve the workings of external body parts such as the head, arms, legs, etc.

Where the focus is internal, sufferers may study their inner workings compulsively, taking their own pulse, temperature, blood pressure, studying their excretions, etc. These self-exams can be very extensive, happen frequently, and last for very long periods of time. All this activity revolves around the idea that these organs may not be working the way they should. Many of those who suffer from these doubts will put themselves through uncomfortable and expensive medical tests and procedures, all of which turn out to be unnecessary. They may be so well acquainted with different types of symptoms that they can convince most physicians to refer them for these tests. The physicians, not wanting to accidentally overlook real medical problems are, of course, only too willing to go along with this.

Where the focus is on external parts such as the head, arms, legs, feet, hands, fingers, or toes, you may see a lot of self-conscious double-checking. Several patients have worried that others noticed that they did not walk normally and would try to concentrate on how they did this while they were out in public. This, of course, would lead to their actually walking strangely and then attracting the type of attention they feared in the first place. Others will sit and watch their arms, head, or hands move to see if they are working normally or to try and figure out how these parts work.

GROOMING IMPULSIONS/COMPULSIONS

Hair pulling, skin picking, and nail biting are universal. Human beings as a species are just as prone to scratching, picking, pulling, peeling, squeezing, and biting as any other. It is quite normal for average people to be peeling sunburns, picking at scabs, tweezing hairs, squeezing pimples, biting their nails and cuticles, picking their noses, etc. They may do these things absentmindedly in public or deliberately in the privacy of their own homes, cars, or offices. Everyone does these things to some extent, and while they may deny it, these activities can be pleasurable in small ways. Activities of this type are so universal that some have theorized that they are most likely instinctive self-grooming behaviors, probably hardwired into the circuitry of the brain as permanent resident programs. This programming is probably an evolutionary leftover, somewhat like the appendix, even though it appears that it may serve some useful functions at times. These functions could possibly include providing self-soothing or distraction when under stress, temporary relief from boredom, satisfaction at having improved one's appearance in some small way, etc. There are many models for this to be seen in the animal kingdom. These are known as "displacement behaviors" and are frequently seen when animals find themselves in stressful situations where they are trapped or uncertain about how to act.

The difference between these little instinctive personal activities and having a disorder is really a matter of degree. When a person performs them to the point where it interferes with their daily ability to function or begins to damage their appearance in some way, we can rightly say that they have crossed over the line that separates the normal from the abnormal. For instance, those who pull large amounts of hair differ from those who merely pull or tweeze a few cosmetically. In the former case, eyebrows, eyelashes, or scalp hair may be completely removed. I use the term grooming impulsions/compulsions to describe this group of symptoms. While they do resemble normal self-grooming behaviors, and may still serve some of the same purposes, they have escalated out of control to a level where they have become self-destructive and have taken on a life of their own.

Symptoms in this group are well known among specialists as being difficult to treat, possibly because they can have an almost automatic quality at times, and partly because of the feeling of satisfaction a sufferer often gets while doing it. It is paradoxical that even as someone may be saying how much he or she hates what their habit is doing to their appearance, they will also tell you about the momentary pleasure it gives them. Those looking in from the outside often wonder whether hair pullers feel pain when practicing their habits. Interestingly, those who do these things almost never report any painful sensations as they carry out the behaviors. It may be that they have become so used to the pain that they no longer take notice of it, or perhaps they are somehow causing the release of natural pain-killing substances (endorphins) within the brain which block the sensations and may even produce sensations of pleasure. I have heard sufferers use the phrase "but it feels so good" when trying to explain the reason for their habits. A description of this sensation is evident in Erica's account:

Erica's Story

∽ *It is very difficult for someone who does not suffer from this disorder to understand how hard it is to just stop or get control. I deal with it twenty-four hours a day. I find it difficult to concentrate at anything I do. It is hard to keep the responsibilities of my job in my mind, and I always feel in some way that I have to concentrate on fighting my disorder. I think my trichotillomania started in sixth grade. I pulled all of my eyelashes and eyebrows out. It was very humiliating and a terrible sense of shame overcomes a person. It is so hard to know what to say when someone very puzzled asks you, "Why on earth would you do something like that? Why can't you just stop?" I eventually grew them back in around seventh grade. About five years ago, I again pulled all of my eyelashes and eyebrows out. I was a senior in high school and this was even more humiliating. It is hard to describe the feeling that one gets when pulling from an OCD person's point of view. It's almost like a "high" sensation. I remember days in high school when I knew my eyebrows were starting to grow back in and I would look forward to going home and pulling on them. It's almost like an addiction, I feel, in some way.*

As mentioned in chapter 1, hair pulling falls into two categories: those who pull automatically (an impulsion), and those who pull deliberately (a compulsion), although many hair pullers do both at various times. Those who pull on purpose tend to know in advance that they are going to do so. Their type of pulling may in some ways resemble OCD more than that of the automatic (or impulsive) pullers. There are some who have suggested that automatic pulling is closer to some of the complex ticcing behaviors seen in Tourette's Syndrome, which seem to be more like direct physical urges. I have heard some automatic pullers endorse this idea themselves, on learning about Tourette's. This is also no doubt true of those who bite their nails and pick their skin. Perhaps these two approaches to picking, biting, or pulling may be two different problems altogether.

Many of these deliberate grooming behaviors seem to include elements of compulsive perfectionism. Those who pull hairs frequently pull ones which feel "just right" (or "wrong," as the case may be) or look different from their other surrounding hairs, ruining either the tactile or visual symmetry. Some TTM sufferers pluck out hairs in an effort to make their eyebrows or hairline even or symmetrical. Their anxiety about this usually causes them to keep pulling out more and more hair, and rather than a perfect or even look, they succeed in creating bald patches in their hairline or removing large portions of their eyebrows. Some who bite at their nails or cuticles may also be trying to perfectly trim off excess pieces in order to achieve symmetry, smoothness, or a neater

280 ～ *Obsessive-Compulsive Disorders*

look. A percentage of those who pick their skin or squeeze blemishes to excess are often trying to perfectly clean and clear up their complexions. Naturally, the behavior always turns out to be paradoxical, as the excessive pulling, picking, squeezing, and biting only make things worse rather than perfect. It also ends up producing a kind of circular reaction where the more they work on themselves, the worse they make themselves look. The more self-conscious they become, the less they feel like being seen by other people. This results in more time spent at home alone where they again have more opportunities to study and work on themselves.

There is a very tactile aspect to this group of behaviors. The "feel" of whatever body area the sufferer habitually touches is extremely important to the whole process. Which hairs get pulled, what particular bit of skin or nail is bitten, or which bump or blemish on the skin is squeezed or picked is frequently determined by touch. Sufferers will frequently touch, feel, or stroke the spots for a while before acting on them, searching for something that feels "different" in terms of texture or length. Hairs that are frequent targets for pulling are often those that are curly, stiff, or wiry. A vicious cycle may result for some who pull out hairs and are then further tempted to pull by the short, new bristly ones which feel different from surrounding ones. Bits of skin, cuticles, or nails that get bitten or pulled are usually the ones that are rough, sharp, or protruding. Once the hair, skin, or piece of nail, etc. is removed, the tactile aspects continue to be important. Often, the person will bite or chew whatever they have removed, or else they may touch it to their lips, roll it between their fingers, or play with it in some way before finally discarding it. Some hair pullers seem to enjoy biting the root bulb off from the pulled hair or crushing it between their teeth for the feel of it. For some, the tactile aspects do not even end here, as instead of throwing the item away, they may swallow it. Another tactile feature experienced by quite a few TTM sufferers is that the urge to pull is often touched off by an itching, burning, or tingling sensation in the area they usually pull from. In some cases, the itching just referred to may be the sensation that can accompany the regrowth of new hairs. This unfortunately can also lead to a circular chain of behaviors starting with pulling, feeling an itch when the hair grows back, and then pulling some more.

Another important aspect is the visual one. Sufferers can frequently be seen engaging in lengthy visual inspections of their chosen spots either directly or using a mirror. Hairs can be selected for pulling because they are a different color, have a split end, or look curlier or stiffer than neighboring ones. With bits of skin, nail, or cuticle, those that are seen to stick out or appear to be different in shape or color are the ones that get pulled or bitten. Those who pick at blemishes look for such things as redness, enlarged pores, blackheads or whiteheads, or raised spots or bumps on their skin. As with the tactile aspect, visual involvement may continue for some even after the act, as they closely inspect what they have removed and what they have done to themselves.

Some sufferers in this group may also employ implements. Tweezers, scissors, cuticle trimmers, nail clippers, pins or needles, toothpicks, small knives, razor blades, hand or pocket mirrors, etc. are often employed to aid in removal. I have a collection of such implements in my office, which have been turned over to me at the start of therapy.

Here is a firsthand account of TTM that I think gives a good picture of how agonizing this can be. It combines several different aspects of the types of sensations and thoughts that drive hair pulling:

Jean's Story

∾ *My name is Jean and I have Trichotillomania. I feel like an alcoholic desperately trying to stay sober and not succumb to the urge of drinking, or in my case, pulling out the hair that has a different texture—the one that catches my eye. Pulling out hair is like an addiction to me, and the fact that I pull out my eyelashes, eyebrows, and hair from my head makes me feel ashamed and embarrassed. I began this strange habit at the age of thirteen, when my father told me to pull out the small, black facial hairs growing from my mother's chin. I felt a sense of relief when I pulled out her hair, almost as if I was removing her imperfections. I liked the release of tension so much that I soon began to pull out my eyelashes. It hurt at first, but I liked the pain. In retrospect, I wonder if I was attempting to remove my imperfections.*

Always an overachiever, I made all A's almost every year up to my senior year in high school. I cannot stand to make mistakes and everything in my life needs to be balanced and in symmetry. I remember standing in front of the mirror, impulsively pulling out eyelashes. If I pulled out some from my left eye, I had to pull out some from my right eye. My madness continued and I found myself unable to stop pulling out hair. By the time I was seventeen, I had several bald spots that could not be camouflaged. I used eye pencils to darken my eyelids and draw in eyebrows, but nothing could adequately cover up the marks of my self-mutilation.

I graduated second in my class, but I was embarrassed and reluctant to speak in front of an audience. My mother insisted that I get a videotape of the ceremony, but I have yet to watch the tape. I saved no photographs of the time when I looked the worst, and I still hope to forget those painful times of humiliation, strange looks, and embarrassment.

My parents could not understand or relate to my problem, simply because it seemed so rare and odd. My father punished me for pulling out my hair in a desperate attempt to make me stop. He checked my eyes and hair weekly with a lamp shining over my eyes. I continually lied to him, saying, "No Dad, I swear I haven't pulled out any hairs" for fear of losing privileges. Once I had to sit on the steps blindfolded, because I was warned that I would be blind if I did not stop pulling out my eyelashes. I have learned to deal with my anger and resentment toward my parents. They simply tried to treat an abnormal behavior with typical parental discipline. Once they realized that they did not have the capabilities to help me, I was taken to a psychologist.

I would like to note here that I have come across a type of hair pulling that can only be termed "pseudo-trichotillomania." I had a patient who tugged on her hair in response to doubtful obsessive thoughts about whether or not it might be falling out. This frequent tugging resulted in much hair being pulled out, and while it resembled TTM in this way, it had no other similarities.

Nail biting (onychophagia) and cuticle biting are probably rather widespread and are commonly thought of as unimportant nervous habits. This is, no doubt, why many who do this to serious excess go unnoticed or fail to recognize it as a disorder themselves. This behavior can become rather serious, as sufferers tear away large pieces of skin or nail, creating bleeding wounds and unsightly sores. I have also come across a number of people who bite or chew the skin further down on their fingers or on the edges of their hands. One further behavior that ought to be included in this group is that of biting the inside of the cheeks which has lately come to my attention in a few cases, and I now routinely ask OC patients if they do it.

Skin picking may also be another seriously under-recognized problem. Those who compulsively engage in it may be doing it for different reasons. As mentioned at the beginning of this section, many do it in order to make their skin perfect looking, without a single blemish or irregularity. Those who actually have true acne problems or bad complexions, and react to them by picking and squeezing, belong in this category. Those who claim to have ugly skin problems, but who have no real visible blemishes and pick at every tiny speck, spot, or bump probably belong in the BDD category. They may also believe that other areas of their bodies are unsightly as well (see the section on Body Dysmorphic Disorder in chapter 1).

Skin pickers will often spend long periods of time standing before mirrors studying their faces. I have met many who revealed that these sessions could last for several hours unless interrupted, and that afterward, they typically had very little sense of how much time had elapsed. Along with using their nails to pick or dig at the blemishes on their skin, they may also resort to the use of a variety of implements to help them in their work. Their reddened and scarred skin is often a giveaway. Generally, they end up making themselves look worse, vowing not to do it the next time, but giving in anyway at the next sign of a pimple or blemish. Sometimes they rationalize their behavior, saying that they won't mark themselves up or cause infections because "I'll be careful, and this time will be different." The feelings of anger and disappointment directed at themselves and the humiliation of having to be seen by others after such an episode can frequently lead to feelings of depression and hopelessness in many sufferers. Attempts are often made to hide these behaviors from spouses or family members. Women who pick their skin have the advantage of using makeup; however, men with this behavior frequently resort to cosmetics as well. Adhesive bandages are also used at times, although these are not as invisible. Many will not leave the house or even answer the door without their cover-up.

Ken has provided a compelling and probably typical picture of what impulsive skin picking can be like, and how it affects an individual's life.

Ken's Story

⤳ *I know where every mirror is between my office and the train station and, as a matter of fact, I would often take a certain direction so that I would pass more mirrors, because what I would do, of course, is stare into them at myself. I think that is what the skin picking is all about, my obsession with my appearance, and if I see a blemish it's about getting rid of that blemish or increasing the healing of it, and this way I'll look better. So it's all about how I look, improving how I look, and checking on how I look.*

I guess this all started when I was in college, a pivotal time for me. It was my first time living away from home, the college scene, dating, and how so much of our society bases their opinions on appearance. Companies hire people often on their appearance, and not so much on their resume, just the first impression. For whatever reason, I picked up on the fact that appearance is very important in our society. I guess I'm an average looking fellow, and I guess my OCD and the picking is about not being satisfied with anything that isn't perfect.

I know in college I started breaking out and I guess it disturbed me more than most people. I had all these pimples and whiteheads and blackheads. I quickly found that by squeezing them and paying them extra attention I could accelerate what I thought was the healing process. I remember standing in front of the mirror, and this was every possible moment I wasn't busy with school or my friends. I'd be in front of that mirror sometimes for whole evenings. It would start about eleven P.M. and go on until about four or five in the morning, usually in the bathroom. I hoped that no one would come in and see me. I would look for the tiniest flaw, the tiniest blemish and Lord knows I would see them and start picking at them. My main goal was to get out any pus or whitehead or ingrown hair or clogged pore.

If you notice, all those things are not perfect and my job was to get rid of that. I really thought, at the time, that if I was to get rid of these things my skin would be clear naturally, but like most other OCD problems, your plan often backfires. I think that OCD is like trying to do something and actually doing something quite the opposite of what you're trying to do. It actually produced the opposite result. The excessive picking made my skin much worse. The red marks, the scabbing over, and the bleeding was just a major problem that probably would not have occurred had I left my skin alone.

That's where all the guilt and shame come from—having that problem. It's tough enough as an adolescent or young adult to have bad skin, but compounding it and making it even worse was the thing I was feeling most badly about, the fact that I was actually creating a bigger problem than there was. People in my life noticed this and I guess my folks were most upset about it. I remember when my younger brother was a teenager and had an episode where his skin was very bad. My mother didn't seem to take it very well. I remember her making excuses for my brother's skin. She would say that the problem was that he had poison ivy and it's not going away. There was something wrong with her saying that he had acne or that he had pimples so she had to describe it as poison ivy. That may have set a little seed in the back of my brain, that having bad skin is unacceptable.

No one causes OCD. It's not like I caused it or my mother caused it. We are not responsible for having OCD. No one is responsible for causing it, but maybe there are certain circumstances that could be a trigger or perhaps serve as a catalyst for the onset of the problem.

With this mirror picking that started in school, it got worse and I started to use implements. Lord knows I really felt that digging deeper was the way to get rid of these things. I became more and more dissatisfied with my appearance and of course I had to fix it. I went for the implements, such as toothpicks, tweezers, and I especially liked needles too because they would serve to puncture any imperfection on my face and then I could squeeze that spot. My family saw that it was a problem and did everything they could to stop it. I, on the other hand, defended it. I really felt that it wasn't so terrible, that it was only one of my habits and actually that I needed to continue doing it.

I really knew, deep down, that it was not healthy and that it was bothering me quite a bit more than it was bothering others. The strange thing about OCD is that we defend the behavior, even if it hurts us, especially in the beginning. I did have a lot of fights with my family because of it and the behavior escalated. The fighting made it worse. It was more than just verbal. My folks would pull the mirrors off the walls, and they would think that by taking the mirrors down I wouldn't pick. Obviously, that didn't work because there are mirrors in other places, like the back of a spoon, top of a toaster oven, reflection in a window pane. There are so many places and I found them all. Removing light bulbs didn't work either. There are windows during the day and there are always ways to see yourself.

There was a lot going on which only escalated the problem. It wasn't helping me that I was being berated, belittled, and demeaned. It was a sickness, although I didn't know it at the time. For years I got up in the morning and without even thinking, my brain would be on automatic pilot. I would jump out of bed and run straight to the mirror. It didn't make a difference what was going on, I had to get to that mirror. Even before my vision cleared, I was in front of that mirror. I remember so many nights when I came home from school or work that I'd have my heavy coat on and I would run straight to the bathroom without taking it off. I'd be standing there in front of the mirror with my coat on doing my thing. It didn't make a difference if I was boiling hot in that coat.

In addition to the skin picking, I became concerned about the impression that others had of my skin. I think this is another part of the illness, where I'm preoccupied by other people's thoughts about my skin. Were they looking at it? Do they think it's bad and what kind of impact would that impression have? If I saw a person impeccably dressed and groomed, I would think that's a smart cookie and here I am with bad skin. It's such an amazing sort of distorted logic. I became obsessed with other people's appearance and I would look to see if their skin was bad and wonder if perhaps they were pickers too.

Stress does seem to be a factor in grooming impulsions, much as it is in the other OCSDs. Seen in the context of grooming behaviors as performed by other animal species, this makes sense. Many animals will frequently begin to groom themselves when faced with stressful situations that they cannot resolve, or when faced by a more dominant and threatening member of their own species. A number of people I have met typically disappear into the bathroom and pick at blemishes whenever they have had an argument with a friend or spouse or a bad day on the job or at school.

(I have not included a separate self-help section on skin picking and nail biting, but I would refer sufferers to the TTM self-help section in chapter 3. The methods outlined there are just as applicable to these problems and can be used with only a little adaptation.)

MENTAL COMPULSIONS

Doing compulsions in one's mind is far more common than most people imagine. Their existence has led to great confusion about treating classic OCD on the part of both practitioners and researchers. Some of them believe in the existence of "pure obsessives"—people who have no compulsions. I disagree with this for the following reason. I find it very difficult to believe that a person could experience something as foreign and disturbing as an obsession and then not feel compelled to do anything about it. It seems to me that it is not human nature for people to just "sit there and take it," or to simply notice such an unusual mental happening and then just ignore it. Most sufferers I have questioned who deny having compulsions had to admit that there were at least a few double checking or undoing, mental activities that they performed in response to the anxiety the thoughts produced. Resistance to one's own symptoms is, in fact, one of the main features of OCD. As mentioned earlier, obsessions are thoughts that cause anxiety, and compulsions can be anything that relieves the anxiety caused by obsessions. By "anything," we mean either mental or physical acts. Compulsions can be strictly mental or physical, but it is highly unlikely, in my experience, to have none at all.

Those who treat OCD and believe in the existence of people with pure obsessions are negligently taking the risk of missing the important presence of mental compulsions. They may not ask key questions or will fail to notice when patients are describing important parts of their disorder. As a result, with symptoms going untreated, these sufferers will not fully recover.

The variety observed among mental compulsions is only limited by the imagination. As described, mental compulsions will usually serve one of two purposes—to double-check if harm has occurred or will occur to the sufferer or others, or to undo harm that could occur to the sufferer or others. A common example of a type of double checking that is purely mental is where the sufferer reviews past situations to try to remember or determine if something bad or harmful has really happened. This is often seen among people who suffer from obsessions of having run people over with their cars. One individual would continually go over particular driving incidents, trying to decide if he had struck a nearby pedestrian, jogger, or bicyclist. He would visualize his mental list of these events and then think through each one in sequence, almost as if he were watching them on tape. He would even run them backward and forward if he felt especially doubtful. If he forgot any of the details, he would get especially anxious.

The bulk of mental compulsions seem to be for the purpose of magically undoing or preventing harm. One of the simplest forms of this type is where the sufferer has to think a morbid or unpleasant thought in reverse to cancel it out. Those who do this describe it as "running a movie in reverse." A variation on this can be the rethinking of "bad" thoughts to "redo" them in a positive way. An example of this would be someone who must think of "nice" or "good" words or numbers to counteract thoughts of the names of illnesses or the names or images of people who died or were disabled by a particular illness, or unlucky numbers or words like "death" or "possession." Instead of words, some think of positive mental images or pictures.

Some mental compulsions involve the use or manipulation of information. There are those who feel they must memorize or make mental lists of facts, dates, names, etc. In some cases, they worry that they may need this information to protect themselves or others, will need it for some important project, or simply must have this information present in their minds in a way that resembles both perfectionistic and hoarding compulsions.

A type of mental compulsion related to this group is seen in those who create mental maps of places to prevent feelings of anxiety or uneasiness. They may not like the way those places look, but unlike those who try to make their homes or possessions perfect or symmetrical, these people get compulsions about things they are only able to manipulate in their imaginations. A place may be the town they live in or some other place or even a particular building.

One further type of mental compulsions relates to the checking of one's own thoughts. These may often be a response to morbid sexual or violent obsessions. Upon having these obsessions, sufferers attempt to check their own reactions to them, to see if they actually feel comfortable with them, or else feel disgusted and upset. The reasoning here is, "If I like thinking about such things, then they must be my own real thoughts and desires." OCD sufferers who are troubled by thoughts suggesting that they may be gay often attempt to prove to themselves that they aren't. They may look at members of their own sex and check their own internal reactions to see if they feel sexually aroused in any way that would prove they are homosexual. Some will even go so far as trying to monitor their own reactions while actually having sex. These sufferers have also been known to obsess about their appearance, their choice of clothing, the way they gesture, or the way they carry themselves. As they continually examine themselves in detail they ask, "Would a gay person look or act like this?"

Those who suffer from morbid violent obsessions do similar things. They will mentally conjure up images of killing or maiming others, and then carefully study their own reactions to see if they would really be capable of doing such things. They may view violent movies, videos, or news reports to see if they actually enjoy them, as another way of checking their own possible murderous tendencies. They do this in the belief that only a real murderer or sociopath would enjoy these things.

PROTECTIVE COMPULSIONS

The constant desire to warn or protect others seems to be a response to obsessive thoughts of harm that go far beyond what would be considered average and also represents a kind of thinking where the sufferer feels overly responsible for things most of us would never assume blame for. Along with difficulty in figuring out just how risky certain things are, many with classic OCD have difficulty in determining just how responsible they are for the safety and well-being of others. Like most other types of compulsion, this group focuses on possibilities of harm coming to others, within an almost endless variety of sources. It differs from some of the other groups in that sufferers with these symptoms are less concerned with harm in the present, but try to either prevent harm in the future or discover whether harm may have happened in the past (and to repair it if possible). The compulsions generally involve checking one's own memory for the possibility of harm having taken place, or warning others, or protecting others or oneself from possible future harm.

Some of the items in this category might well be placed within the double-checking compulsion category, however, sufferers in this group are somewhat different in character from other types of double checkers. The harm to be protected against or to be discovered is always perceived by sufferers as directly or indirectly resulting from their own neglect or incompetence, no matter what the actual source. Since others are involved, the sufferer may either act to stop themselves from being the actual cause of the harm or may believe that it is their responsibility to warn or save others from sources of harm caused by others or present in the environment. The ultimate fear here is that one could be responsible for harm happening to someone else and would then have to live (or not be able to live) with overwhelming feelings of personal guilt if it actually happened.

This group of symptoms should not be confused with what is referred to in OCD treatment as "hypermorality," which is really more concerned with following particular ethical, religious, or societal rules and guidelines perfectly, and which should really be categorized under perfectionistic compulsions. Questions of morality rarely enter into these compulsions. These behaviors would seem to be at the opposite end of the spectrum from sociopathy, a disorder in which individuals can behave criminally and harmfully toward others without the slightest shred of remorse or regret. They would also appear to be the opposite of morbid impulsions (see chapter 8), which are thoughts prompting a sufferer to harm others.

There is a great deal of variation within this group of symptoms. To begin with, the group of people to which they fear harm is coming may include family, friends, casual acquaintances, or even total strangers. Harm may come to the very young or the very old or both. Those who are ill, handicapped, smaller or weaker, or who are in some way defenseless, may also be targets for the sufferer's protective efforts. Also, the harm which others are to be protected from may, for some sufferers, always fall into a single category of happening, such as a particular disease or type of accident, while for others, it may take in practically any type of bad occurrence they are capable of imagining. The seriousness of the harm is another aspect of this group of symptoms which shows wide variation. It can range from protecting others from being inadvertently insulted, to having to protect them from sexual abuse, or even fatal accidents.

Those with protective compulsions will constantly do things to protect others, often at great material or personal cost to themselves. They feel as if they can never be too careful and seem to always be on the lookout for a potentially harmful event. Even the merest suggestion of the possibility of harm in the past or the future can send them into a whirlwind of frantic activity to protect others.

Most sufferers in this group will begin their compulsive activities with themselves. They will repeatedly recheck their memories, looking for facts or thought pictures which will tell them if someone else was harmed, an activity that can consume hours at a time. To help the checking process, people may keep long and extensive lists of every doubtful or potentially harmful situation they can recall. The lists will usually contain every relevant fact that can be remembered. Ironically, the lists are seldom looked at. The fact of simply having them and knowing that they are there can be enough to relieve anxiety. I have known sufferers who had accumulated hundreds of such lists that they carefully saved and guarded. The loss of a list can result in tremendous anxiety, even if the individual has never really looked at it. Often lists can be kept for so long that the sufferer can't actually recall the events recorded. A paradox of these lists can be that when a sufferer finally does anxiously look one over, they can experience even more anxiety due to wondering if they really did get all the facts or if they truly recorded things correctly. One individual had a fear of having possibly caused serious traffic accidents in the past and kept detailed records of the dates, locations, and relevant facts relating to the supposed events. He would read over his lists several times daily, reviewing them in his mind, never being able to determine whether or not anything had actually happened. As mentioned above, he was one of those who had several lists that were years old and about which he could not remember anything except what he had written. He held onto them anyway, "just in case."

Another compulsive activity often seen among members of this group and related to doubt is repetitive questioning. Sufferers will endlessly review doubtful situations for others in the hope that the listeners will tell them if it sounds like something harmful may have happened or is going to happen. Although no answer can eliminate the doubt, sometimes there may be relief at simply having told someone. The relief comes from the idea that if they had said something that sounded serious to the listener, they would have seen some kind of a reaction.

Some types of this questioning can become very subtle, particularly where the sufferer's fears involve the possibility of having harmed someone well known to them. One young woman had ongoing doubtful fears of having accidentally poisoned various guests who ate in her home. She worried about having mistakenly added household chemicals to the food, or that broken glass from previous kitchen accidents might somehow be in what she was preparing. She would sometimes call her guests back, either late at night or early the next morning, using some made-up excuse. Although she didn't come right out and ask them if they were all right, she got relief from her anxiety simply by hearing their voices and knowing that they were well enough to answer the phone. She also believed that if anyone else in their home was unwell, they would tell her about it.

A variation on questioning is compulsive confessing. Usually, the sufferer feels they must recite a long list of every little thing they may have done to harm others. In this way, they may accomplish one of two anxiety-relieving things. First, if they really did do something harmful, they will have given a warning either to protect the other person or to prevent themselves from causing further harm. Second, if they did not do anything wrong, the other person listening to the confession would tell them so and thus reassure them.

Those who fear that they may have run people over (see section on Checking Compulsions in this chapter) would be included in this group, demonstrating all the typical symptoms. A frequent response to these doubts is simply to stop driving. At the height of her problems, one sufferer told her husband to sell her car because she would never drive again. Where fears involve thoughts of having run people over in past situations, even not driving again cannot help. Sufferers will spend hours reviewing the past and asking others about what might have happened. For those who have no choice but to continue driving, it is common to see them driving back and forth many times past areas where the doubtful incident occurred, as they constantly check their rearview mirrors. Situations where visibility is limited, such as backing up or parallel parking, are particularly difficult, and night driving is usually avoided as much as possible.

More extreme examples of behaviors in this category involve those who worry about others being hurt by potentially dangerous objects lying around outdoors. You will typically see these people picking up broken glass, rusty nails, tacks, razor blades, which they see lying in the street. Their fear is that children or other unsuspecting individuals will be hurt by these objects, and that if they don't pick them up, the harm that results will be entirely their fault. One man felt it was his duty to warn civic authorities of any potential public hazards he might have spotted while traveling around his town. He would constantly call in reports of potholes, cracked sidewalks, broken tree limbs, and other such things. In one instance, he reported his fear to the local railroad that some of the steps at one of their platforms might be loose. As a side note, this same individual would become involved in following people on the street who were elderly and appeared frail. He would feel immediately responsible for them and would shadow them at a distance until they reached their destination. He believed that if any harm should come to them once he had noticed them, it would be his responsibility.

For some sufferers, their fears may concentrate on only one or several people who are close to them. One woman would suffer continual doubts about her husband's safety. She would begin every day by cautioning and warning him before he left for work and would continually call him at work to make sure he had arrived safely and was feeling well during his workday. Upon his arrival home, she would question him in detail to make sure nothing had happened to him while he was away. If he showed the slightest sign of illness, she would strongly overreact, always insisting that he see a doctor, taking his temperature and pulse frequently, and administering numerous remedies. She would try to dissuade him from taking business trips, and when this wasn't possible, would suffer severe anxiety the entire time he was gone. If his trip involved flying, the anxiety was even worse. Within this group, it is also not unusual to see sufferers act in these same overprotective ways toward their children. Constant monitoring of their children's health, plus frequent unnecessary calls and visits to the pediatrician are common.

It is not unusual for children with OCD to question their parents repeatedly, asking if mother or father will be "all right" or if anything is going to happen to them. As in the previous case above, they will also try to prevent their parents from leaving home on trips or normal local errands or failing that, question them closely about the exact time of their return. Of course, if a parent returns even a few minutes late, serious anxiety usually results. One young boy would spend long periods of time every night lecturing and warning his mother about the potential hazards she was supposed to watch out for the next day. One may also hear such children reporting obsessive thoughts about the possibility of someone breaking into their home and harming their family. These thoughts are frequently accompanied by extensive checking of the house before bedtime to look for unlocked doors and windows.

TEN

OCSD—Or Not

The question often arises as to whether what are commonly known as compulsive shopping, drinking, and gambling are considered to be types of OCSDs. This is a complex question for which there is currently no firm answer. While they appear to have some elements similar to classic OCD or BDD, they may actually have a closer relationship to the grooming impulsions (TTM, skin picking, and nail biting). One similarity is that in both groups you have individuals who find it extremely difficult to control an impulse. Also, grooming, shopping, drinking, and gambling are basically normal activities that are satisfying and pleasurable to begin with. They can all provide an escape, a needed stimulation, or lift, even though they may eventually be harmful when done excessively. Individuals with these types of problems start doing these things to feel a kind of relief, but in a circular way, end up becoming dependent on them. This is because the activities are taken to such an extreme that they actually cause unhappiness that the sufferer must relieve by practicing them further. Obviously, activities such as these can also be carried out in a moderate way over a lifetime by many people who do not become addicted to them. Some, however, may be more at risk than others due to some type of biological predisposition. It may be though that despite these superficial similarities, shopping, gambling, and drinking may only appear similar to the grooming impulsions. Only further research will reveal whether such a relationship exists.

As mentioned earlier, compulsive shopping, drinking, and gambling would appear to be less like classic OCD and BDD. Activities associated with classic OCD and BDD are those which are unpleasant, repulsive, senseless, or even disgusting to the person doing them, even from the beginning. They do not seem natural or appealing in any way, and they are done in order to relieve anxiety and doubt—not to give the person some kind of "high," lift, or pleasure, as would buying things, drinking, or betting. Recent studies have shown that the brains of those with compulsive gambling problems may have lower levels of brain chemicals that control excitement and arousal. One theory suggests that persons with this type of problem may experience lower than normal levels of alertness, leaving them feeling dull or bored, and that they require stimulating activities to raise levels of this chemical to the point where they may feel more normal. The brain messenger chemical in this case is norepinephrine, not serotonin, the one implicated in OCD (see chapter 12). This may further indicate that OCSDs and this other group of disorders may represent different biological families.

Within classic OCD, there are behaviors that look like compulsive shopping but which are actually compulsive hoarding problems. These individuals buy large amounts or quantities of merchandise that they then store away for some future use that never occurs. They try to keep these items pristine and unused, but paradoxically, many of the things they save end up deteriorating in storage. There is an actual belief on their part that they need or will need these things. This behavior differs from compulsive shoppers who buy things they know they don't need or who simply give away the things they purchase.

There are those with OCSDs who have developed what appear to be drinking problems. However, this can be regarded not as a compulsion, but as an attempt at self-medication. I suspect that there are many people attending AA meetings who suffer from OCSDs and who are not getting proper treatment. Alcohol can, for short periods, relieve anxiety and reduce OC symptoms, although it is not without its side effects. These would include addiction, sleep disturbance, and depressed moods.

OBSESSIVE-COMPULSIVE PERSONALITY DISORDER (OCPD)

There is a great deal of confusion in people's thinking concerning the difference between classic OCD and OCPD. To help you understand the difference between them, I have included here the official DSM-IV diagnostic criteria for Obsessive-Compulsive Personality Disorder, which you may compare with those for classic OCD listed in Appendix C.

> A pervasive pattern of preoccupation with orderliness, perfectionism, and mental and interpersonal control, at the expense of flexibility, openness, and efficiency, beginning by early adulthood and present in a variety of contexts, as indicated by four (or more) of the following:

1. is preoccupied with details, rules, lists, order, organization, or schedules to the extent that the major point of the activity is lost,

2. shows perfectionism that interferes with task completion (e.g., is unable to complete a project because his or her own overly strict standards are not met),

3. is excessively devoted to work and productivity to the exclusion of leisure activities and friendships (not accounted for by obvious economic necessity),

4. is over-conscientious, scrupulous, and inflexible about matters of morality, ethics, or values (not accounted for by cultural or religious identification),

5. is unable to discard worn-out or worthless objects even when they have no sentimental value,

6. is reluctant to delegate tasks or to work with others unless they submit to exactly his or her way of doing things,

7. adopts a miserly spending style toward both self and others; money is viewed as something to be hoarded for future catastrophes,

8. shows rigidity and stubbornness.

Having read this far, you are probably thinking of certain people who are frequently referred to as "compulsive" by others. These are the individuals who are famous among friends and relatives for having the cleanest, most dust-free homes about which they are fanatical, or who are always spotlessly clean, quickly changing their clothes or washing themselves if they get slightly dirty. They make you take off your shoes when you walk on their carpeting, or they are right there with a coaster for your glass. Or perhaps their records or books are all in alphabetical order, or the books are arranged in size order, or their clothes by color. A good example of this type of person is the character Felix Unger, made famous by Tony Randall, on the TV show *The Odd Couple*. These people are known as obsessive-compulsive personalities.

Unfortunately, many practitioners and laypersons alike are unable to tell the difference between the two problems. Some believe that they are basically the same, or that the OCPD paves the way for classic OCD. In reality, surveys have shown that only about 6 percent of those with classic OCD also have OCPD. Although many do not agree with the theories of Sigmund Freud which relate to OCD, it is interesting to note that he was one of the first to point out this difference between the obsessional (anal) character, and what was then called Obsessive-Compulsive neurosis.

While there appears to be a strong resemblance between OCPD and perfectionistic compulsions, there are definite differences. The easiest way to tell the difference between the two is by remembering that in classic OCD, the obsessions are repulsive, intrusive, and create doubt and fear. They are strange and repulsive to the person's true self. There is also an attempt to resist them. In the case of someone with OCPD, the ideas held and the things done are not disturbing and are seen by the person as normal and an integral part of life. These people don't believe that what they are doing is unusual or odd, and don't see their behavior as harming their lives or keeping them from enjoying themselves. They do not feel embarrassed by their own behavior and do not in any way try to hide it. Most of those with OCPD think that any problems they may have are the fault of others. Their behavior, may in fact, be a source of pride to them. Many compulsive ways are thought of by society as being positive and are rewarded and encouraged. Neatness and cleanliness, for instance, are often praised as good things. Just look at television commercials for laundry detergents, deodorants, cleansers, and soaps to see how having the shiniest floor or the whitest wash on the block are considered to be very desirable and deserving of praise. Workaholics in this category are also praised as conscientious and hard working. They earn a lot of overtime, receive promotions, and enjoy the praise and compensation. Unfortunately, they may alienate their families and have no lives outside their jobs. Those with OCPD enjoy what they do, feel it is a part of them, and could not imagine not doing it.

As mentioned before, a major difference between the OC personality and the OC disorder is that the person with the disorder cannot simply choose *not* to arrange, check, clean, or do what they must do. They feel they have to do or undo many things because of the strong fear or guilt they know will follow if they don't. On the other hand, someone with OCPD may only feel discomfort, annoyance, or frustration if kept from carrying out the cleaning, saving, or arranging activities. These activities are a natural part of their everyday life and are even seen as necessary or pleasant, unlike the disorder, where they are seen as stupid, "crazy," or pointless by the person carrying them out. A person with OCPD would never consider stopping or giving them up. Interestingly, most of those with OCPD who see me are brought in by someone else, usually a family member or spouse. The person with OCPD will say things like, "I don't have any problems. They're the ones with the problems." The greatest harm that occurs to those with OCPD is to their relationships. These people can be very critical, extremely controlling, and generally difficult to live with. They frequently find themselves divorced or abandoned by angry and resentful spouses, family, or friends who cannot put up with always having to be controlled.

Usually, those with OCPD don't wish to change for reasons of their own, and thus I have not found them to be terribly motivated in therapy. When they do change, it is mostly for practical reasons, such as to prevent their spouse from divorcing them or losing friends.

SCHIZOPHRENIA

Unfortunately, for those with classic OCD, laypersons and health professionals have been confused about the difference between the hallucinations and delusions of schizophrenia and the sometimes illogical and/or superstitious nature of obsessions. According to Freudian theory, classic OCD was supposed to be an individual's last ditch defense against becoming psychotic, and if you took away a sufferer's symptoms, they would slip into this other disorder. This is no longer believed to be true.

The only similarity between classic OCD and schizophrenia that we know of is that they are both brain biochemical disorders. The similarity ends there. According to current biological theory, schizophrenia is the result of a disturbance involving the brain transmitter chemical dopamine and its receptors. Classic OCD, on the other hand, is believed to largely involve the transmitter chemical serotonin (see section on the biological effects of OCD on the brain in chapter 12). Drugs used to treat schizophrenia increase levels of dopamine in the brain, while those commonly used to treat OCD help serotonin to remain longer around receptor sites where it is needed. This is not to say that other brain chemicals may not be involved in either disorder—neither disorder has yet been fully understood.

Classic OCD and schizophrenia are also different in terms of where sufferers believe their odd thoughts come from. Those with classic OCD recognize that these thoughts are being generated from within their own minds. Schizophrenics tend to believe that thoughts are being broadcast to them from external sources, such as other people or entities such as God or the devil.

Another difference between classic OCD and schizophrenia is in terms of the degree of belief. Those with schizophrenia truly believe in the existence of what their delusions and hallucinations tell them. There is little or no doubt in these persons' minds. Their insight, contact with reality, and ability to reason are poor. OCD, on the other hand, revolves largely around doubtful thoughts: OCD was once known as "the doubting sickness." One of the reasons that classic OCD is such a hidden problem is that sufferers know they're not crazy, that their thoughts don't make sense, and that others would think they were crazy if they revealed what was going on in their minds. They have not lost touch with reality. They know who they are and where they are. Many sufferers preface talking about their thoughts by saying, "I know it sounds crazy, but. . ."

BDD represents a somewhat different case. With BDD, there are times when a person's sense of reality appears questionable, since there is often a very high degree of belief that seems practically unshakable. BDD sufferers often deny that there is even a problem with their reasoning. While there may still be only a little room for doubt on a BDD sufferer's part, it often tends to be a lot less than that seen in classic OCD. It has been suggested by some that BDD may actually be two separate disorders. One type may be closer to classic OCD, in that there is room for doubt on the sufferer's part, as well as some insight that their thinking may not be entirely logical. The other variant may, in fact, bear a closer resemblance to schizophrenia, where there is practically no insight and the sufferer's firmly held ideas are closer to delusions. One difference between both types of BDD and schizophrenia, however, is that in BDD, sufferers do not believe their thoughts are coming from outside sources, but are seeing them as their own.

In the public view, however, there is very little difference between OCSDs and schizophrenia. Ignorance on this subject is widespread. As one sufferer explains:

Stanley's Story

∼ *You tell somebody you have a mental illness and the first thing that comes to their mind is this vision of you being hauled away in a straitjacket by some kooky psychiatric doctors in white coats. When I first talked with my cousin on the phone about my OCD, he treated it like it made me a "psycho." I was not offended, but I had to explain to him what it was like having OCD. I had to explain to him that my illness did not make me "crazy."*

While I don't want to confuse the issue, it should be mentioned that it is possible to have both an OCD and schizophrenia. Different estimates we have of how common schizophrenia may be in those with OCD appear to differ widely. What is probably the best estimate, and which is based on the Epidemiological Catchment Area Survey data, suggests that around 12 percent of those with OCD also suffer from schizophrenia. Where both problems exist in a person, it may take the diagnostic skills of an expert to identify which symptoms belong to which disorder and to decide what must be done in either case.

ELEVEN

~ *Accompaniments to OCSDs*

People with OCSDs can also suffer from other types of psychological problems. In addition to the primary symptoms we have already reviewed, there may also be secondary symptoms. They may not be seen in every Obsessive-Compulsive person, but they are present often enough to consider them as important factors in these disorders.

DEPRESSION

Depression is often seen to accompany OCSDs. By depression, we mean feelings of sadness, hopelessness, helplessness, a loss of the enjoyment of life, or a lack of energy and drive. Physical symptoms may include general feelings of unwellness, insomnia or excessive sleep, decreased or increased appetite, and fatigue. In the case of classic OCD, there are those psychiatrists and psychologists who suggest that the disorder is the result of anxiety and depression rather than the opposite. There is simply no evidence for this belief. The fact that we can sometimes, within particular patients, successfully treat the depression alone with some of the more common antidepressant medications, without bringing relief from the OC symptoms, strengthens the case against this point of view.

There may be very great feelings of frustration, isolation, and helplessness that come from not being able to gain any real control over the constant unpleasant symptoms that seem to take over a sufferer's entire life and prevent normal functioning. There is also the separation from others, a loneliness resulting from not being able to share thoughts or feelings for fear of being mislabeled or misunderstood. Not being able to hold a job or maintain a relationship would make anyone feel helpless and hopeless. Depression may also result from the rejection and anger of friends or family members who are unable to cope with that person's symptoms.

It should also be mentioned that there are biological-type depressions (known also as endogenous depression) which are chronic and persistent in some people who also happen to have an OCSD. This type of depression is not caused by a reaction to the OCSD, however. Generally speaking, these biological depressions are frequently seen to be a lot more serious than those that are simply a reaction to having an OCSD. One way we can tell that we are dealing with a biological depression is by observing whether or not the depression subsides as the OCSD subsides. Medication can sometimes help us to tell the difference. This happens when the OCSD is relieved by medication, but the person still reports feeling depressed, rather than liberated. Frequently, the depression will have to be brought under control before any headway can be made with the OCSD. This is because the fatigue and hopelessness that accompany it will prevent the sufferer from fully participating in behavioral therapy. Both OCSDs and many biological depressions are believed to be caused by disturbances of serotonin, a neurotransmitter chemical in the brain, which suggests a possible link between them (see chapter 12).

In some cases, there are those who have suffered chronic low to moderate level depressions throughout much of their lives without having much of an awareness of it. That is, they have always felt that way and have no experience of other mood states with which to make a comparison. Often it is not until the depression is relieved that people finally recognize the cloud that has been hanging over their lives and can then understand the effect it has had on them.

ANXIETY

Feelings of general anxiety and fear are another frequent secondary symptom of classic OCD and BDD. Those with classic OCD and BDD frequently report distress, fear, and a kind of restlessness that is hard to describe. Physically, symptoms of anxiety may include rapid heartbeat, dizziness, shortness of breath, excessive perspiration, tightness in the chest, nausea, feelings of unreality, headaches, or cold hands. Naturally, along with these symptoms comes great difficulty in coping with the anxiety itself.

These types of anxious symptoms need to be differentiated from Panic Disorder (PD), where a person experiences acute attacks of fear that seem to appear out of the blue and believes, for a few minutes, that they are "going crazy," losing control of themselves, are suffering a heart attack, or are unable to breathe. PD may occur coincidentally in those with OCD. One statistic suggests that about 13 percent of OCD sufferers also suffer from PD. We currently understand that PD is more of a "fear of fear" or an anxiety sensitivity. It is actually the result of the person misinterpreting harmless internal sensations and mistaking them for signs of something catastrophic happening to them, thereby making the sensations worse in a sort of circular way. I have listened to many individuals with classic OCD or BDD mistakenly describing the anxiety they feel as "panic attacks," when in reality it is a fearful reaction to their obsessions. These two disorders are not somehow the result of anxiety. It is really the other way around.

PERFECTIONISM

I believe that the perfectionism seen among many of those with OCSDs is actually a very understandable reaction to having persistent and severe doubts. When a person is "perfectly" doubtful, the only thing that will bring relief is "perfect" certainty. Certainty, of course, can only be achieved through total control of things, and this in turn requires perfectionism. A person faced with doubts about serious embarrassment, harm, death, or destruction to themselves or others is probably not going to settle for "pretty good" or "almost certain" when trying to prevent such things or attempting to decide if any of it may really be possible. This is very different from the perfectionism that is observed in Obsessive-Compulsive Personality Disorder, where perfectionism brings a kind of pleasure or satisfaction and is practiced for its own sake. OC perfectionism cuts across many groups of symptoms and is seen in many varieties of OCSDs.

Those with classic OCD and BDD are frequently characterized as being rigid and controlling in their approach toward their environment and with others around them. While not all sufferers have this characteristic, it is typically seen among those who are also perfectionistic (see the sections on perfectionistic obsessions and compulsions in chapters 8 and 9). How else can you pursue perfection, if not rigidly? There can be no flexibility or compromise. Obviously, this rigidity is not a very endearing quality and is what makes perfectionistic sufferers difficult to get along with.

Perfectionism is also the cause of a great deal of the anxiety associated with OCD and BDD. This is obviously because human beings are imperfect and cannot really be perfect in the pursuit of anything. The relationship is like a vicious circle. The sufferer feels anxious about some obsessive thought, tries to compulsively and perfectly reassure him/herself that the worst will not happen, makes mistakes in doing the compulsions due to anxiety and jitteriness, then feels even more vulnerable and less reassured, and finally ends up feeling even more anxious than before.

Perfectionism can also figure into TTM, skin picking, and nail biting. Sometimes these activities must be done until they give a "just right" or perfect feeling. In some cases of TTM, particular hairs may be singled out for pulling because they are the "perfect" ones, or because pulling them will make the sufferer's hair more perfect.

GUILT

Exaggerated or unwarranted feelings of guilt are both among the hallmarks of classic OCD. As mentioned earlier, two of the main divisions of classic OCD involve thoughts of harm coming to yourself or harm coming to others. It is among members of this latter group that we see the strong guilt that is so frequently associated with the disorder. Generally, the sufferer has frequent powerful doubts on the theme that something that they have done or will do will lead to harm for others because they were or will be careless or negligent in some way. This harm can include such things as accidentally insulting others, causing accidents, hitting others accidentally, starting fires, inadvertently stealing things or acting illegally, poisoning others, running people over, etc. The list could include almost any harmful thing that one person can do to another. They then tell themselves that since they are to blame, they must then feel very guilty about it, and that this guilt will be so great that they will not be able to stand it and will therefore suffer tremendously. Thoughts of possible punishment or jail are not even as troublesome as the fear of this guilt. The fact that what they may have done was accidental is never thought of as an excuse. The thinking here is rigidly black and white. A term sometimes used to characterize this thinking is "hyper-responsibility." In cases where the harm to others could involve death, some may even go so far as to say that if they knew for certain that they really were to blame for such a thing, they would kill themselves.

For the above reasons, many sufferers constantly walk around in fear of this guilt. As is usual with obsessive thoughts, compulsions designed to bring relief soon follow. These compulsions usually involve extensive double checking, avoidance, and an all-around scrupulous control of any particular behaviors.

Along with the exaggerated guilt comes the misguided idea that the sufferer is obviously a "bad person" and that the OCD is a punishment for it. These sufferers may even further punish or deprive themselves of things they enjoy because they believe they are undeserving of them.

ANGER AND AGGRESSIVE BEHAVIOR

Aggressive behavior can be observed, at times, in some classic OCD and BDD sufferers. Most of it is probably due to several reasons, one of which is the fact that having these disorders can be a maddening and frustrating experience. This frustration can build up over time to high levels in some sufferers, particularly where their every goal in life is being ruined by the illness. Their lives revolve entirely around keeping up with the demands of their symptoms, and they may be unable to hold jobs, have relationships, or live independently. Typically, they have a great deal of self-hatred, jealousy of others who are able to live normally, and a dislike of life in general. It doesn't take much to set them off, as they seem to walk around with a perpetual chip on their shoulder.

Another reason we see anger and aggression is due to the frustration and upset that occur when rituals and other types of compulsions do not go perfectly. This may be either because the sufferer is unable to get them right, or because others in their lives have interfered with their performance. There is no adequate description of what a superstitious sufferer feels when a carefully planned ritual goes wrong at a crucial time, or when a ritual that has taken hours to construct falls apart because of a single stray obsessive thought or some other interruption. It can ruin a day, a month, or even a year.

Family and friends can find anger directed toward them when they interrupt a compulsion. Inadvertently walking into the room of a perfectionist or someone with contamination fears can cause no end of upset. The room may have taken hours or days to arrange or decontaminate perfectly. Moving or touching the belongings of these sufferers is seen as being just as bad. Refusing to help perform a ritual can also be the cause of a bad scene. Often, sufferers depend on family or friends to do such things as answer fearful questions, say or do certain things to help complete a compulsion, touch things, or do chores they fear to do themselves. Obsessively doubtful individuals may also display aggressive behavior toward others close to them when those people become disgusted with being asked the same questions over and over and finally refuse to answer any more. One young man would typically shove and slap his mother when she would not reassure him and answer questions he believed were vital to relieving his anxiety. A young woman would nag and scream at her husband until he agreed to wash areas of the house she felt were unclean, and that she could not approach herself.

Worse yet is when well-meaning people take it upon themselves to break up or prevent compulsive activities in an attempt to "cure" a sufferer, messing up things that have been carefully arranged, dirtying "clean" places or objects, or saying things the sufferer fears to hear. Finally, anger may be caused by others constantly nagging sufferers to get help or even insulting, threatening, and berating them for having the illness.

Verbal aggression might be directed toward oneself, others, or objects. It could include yelling, cursing, and being insulting. Physically aggressive behavior by a person with OCD is usually directed at family members, and although it can reach serious levels, very rarely ends in anything more than pushing, shoving, or slapping. There may be a biological basis at least to some of this anger seen among certain sufferers. Neurobiological studies seem to indicate that the brain messenger chemical, serotonin, which plays a role in the OCSDs, also has a part to play in moderating anger and aggression (see chapter 12). Studies of the composition of spinal fluid appear to indicate that impulsivity and aggression increase as serotonin levels decrease. It has also been suggested that there is a correlation between lower serotonin levels and suicide attempts. In addition, one of the brain structures implicated in OCSDs, known as the caudate nucleus, is known to regulate impulses involving sex, anxiety, and aggression. It may be that difficulty in controlling anger may, in some cases, be the result of a dysfunction affecting this structure (see chapter 12).

Although the aggression may start as a way of letting out strong frustration, it can also become a "tool" which some classic OCD and BDD sufferers use to control family and friends to get them to help with rituals or avoidance. Such individuals can only feel comfortable when they control all those around them, even if it means using intimidation.

DYSPERCEPTIONS

Many classic OCD sufferers report experiencing things through their senses that they cannot feel certain about that cause them anxiety and doubt. These are known as dysperceptions. They are different from the hallucinations seen among psychotics, who feel sure about what their senses mistakenly tell them. The dysperceptions can occur in seeing, hearing, touching, tasting, or in the sense of smell.

A type of visual dysperception often seen (and which was mentioned in the section on double checking in chapter 9) is the sensation of seeing people, objects, or movement out of the corner of one's eye. If this were happening to you, you might think, for example, that you could see something out of the corner of your eye while driving a car. You would then become doubtful and wonder if it could have been a pedestrian, an animal, or some familiar object. This in turn could lead to repeated efforts to verify what you think you may have seen and possibly even hit. Typically, you might stop short, pull over, and get out of the car and search everywhere for the person or animal you may have run over, or check the car all over for dents, marks, or bloodstains. Sometimes, you might continue to drive back and forth past the spot or around and around the block, trying to be certain of whether or not you saw what you thought you saw.

These sensations might then spread to many other situations, such as developing fears of backing out of driveways or pulling out of parking spaces. Frequently, the individual with this type of dysperception may give up driving altogether. A different type of sensory dysperception also related to driving is seen in the person who, when riding over bumps, potholes, or debris in the road, may constantly become confused about the sensation and become doubtful as to whether they may have run over a person or animal.

One other type of visual dysperception worth mentioning concerns the sensation that minor or barely noticeable physical changes have recently occurred in one's environment and for which there is no explanation. Those who notice such things are constantly seeing marks, scratches, or dents on objects or surfaces in their homes, cars, or workplaces. These may be imperfections of damage already there, or the marks may be barely noticeable. They will study or think about them repetitively or in great detail, wondering how the marks got there or who made them. They may even believe that furniture, decorations, or equipment has possibly been hidden or moved slightly or to new locations. This can almost resemble paranoia at times, as sufferers may try to explain these supposed changes by suggesting that someone else did it to make them "crazy." When they are questioned more closely, however, they can admit to having some doubts about this.

Auditory dysperceptions are also frequently seen in those with classic OCD. Common ones include the hissing of escaping gas, cries for help coming from unlikely places, operating noises of appliances supposedly turned off, water running or dripping, prowlers in the house or yard, etc.

Dysperceptions involving the sense of touch may accompany contamination obsessions and also morbid aggressive or sexual obsessions. It is common for those who fear being contaminated or contaminating others to experience sensations of things touching or brushing against them, or to feel as if they have reached out and touched something or someone they shouldn't have. It is also common for them to feel things "jumping out" and landing on their skin, giving them an itching or "crawling" sensation at times. They may also experience localized sensations of tingling or burning where something contaminated could have touched them. Those with morbid obsessions are sometimes troubled by sensations of having touched or struck others in hostile or sexually improper ways.

It is not uncommon for some sufferers who fear becoming infected with AIDS to experience the sensation that strangers may be deliberately sticking them with contaminated hypodermics, when they are in crowded settings. One individual who worked in a rundown and drug-infested neighborhood would become quite fearful when walking past hypodermics lying in the street, because he would get sensations that he was perhaps stepping on them and that they were sticking him through the soles of his shoes. People will often check their bodies for needle marks following these supposed encounters. An example of a different form of these sensations was seen in a delivery driver with classic OCD who had constant doubtful thoughts that he had struck or hit people with packages he was delivering. He would either apologize to them compulsively or later would get the urge to go back and question them about whether or not he had caused them an injury. At one point in his disorder, things worsened to the point where he would get sensations of having bumped into or having struck people he passed in the street.

Over the years, I have encountered several sufferers who were often doubtful about whether they were eating something that was harmful. They would experience doubts about the taste or texture of the foods that they had eaten. These sensations frequently led to fears of drugs or poisons being put in their food. Unlike those who suffer from paranoia, they usually could not explain who might be doing it or why this would be happening. Some doubtfully wondered if someone might just be doing it as a random criminal act and would cite well-known examples of how poisoned items were planted in drugstores and supermarkets. They frequently ended up throwing away perfectly good meals.

Dysperceptions of the sense of smell may typically involve the sensation that one is smelling cooking gas, leading to continual checking of the stove and its knobs to see that they have been shut off, or smelling smoke from a fire possibly caused by a cigarette extinguished hours before in another room. One sufferer constantly thought she smelled exhaust fumes every time she drove her car. This led her to sniff and smell her car's interior compulsively and to drive with the windows open, even in the coldest and most unpleasant weather. She would constantly badger her mechanic to find the "leak" in her exhaust system (which he was only too glad to try to do, at her expense).

Anorexia nervosa, which is included here as part of the Obsessive-Compulsive spectrum, may often involve dysperceptions of the body. It has many similarities to BDD and may actually be a form of BDD. Due to a visual dysperception, anorexics often believe that they are grossly overweight, in spite of looking like near-skeletons. Looking at themselves in mirrors or photographs does not seem to convince them that they have a distorted self-image. One of the main sources of dysperception for anorexics can be the way the abdominal muscles normally relax and stick out immediately after eating. They interpret this temporary change as proof that they are "getting fat," which they believe actually happens as they eat. When asked in therapy to bring in pictures of overweight people, anorexics will typically cut out and bring in pictures of those of normal weight. A physical sensation of fatness or fullness may also go along with the visual dysperception and lead to even stronger efforts at self-starvation.

BDD, too, is most certainly the result of dysperceptions. Sufferers see all sorts of defects in their appearance which are either not visible to others or are so minor that they would undoubtedly escape notice if attention were not called to them. Their perceptions of themselves as ugly or deformed are not unlike anorexics looking at their emaciated bodies and seeing fat.

Note: Primary anorexia nervosa, not resulting from another psychiatric illness or physical disorder, is viewed by myself and many others as being an OCSD, probably a type of BDD as mentioned above. The symptoms often include obsessive thoughts of being overweight followed by compulsive self-starvation, ritualistic food preparation, double-checking one's body or weight, and/or sexual disturbances.)

PHOBIAS

A phobia is a simple fear of a person, situation, place, or thing. Typical phobias include fear of dogs, insects, drowning, flying in a plane, getting an injection, seeing blood or injuries, etc. Phobias are very common among classic OCD sufferers. One source estimates the lifetime occurrence of phobias in OCD sufferers as being 27 percent.

Phobias can range from very specific to very general types. Some 13 percent of those with OCD also suffer from Panic Disorder with Agoraphobia. Those with agoraphobia, one of the more common phobias seen, fear to travel far from home or go places alone because they might have a panic attack. Panic attacks are defined as sudden brief episodes of extremely intense fear. Sufferers misinterpret normal physical symptoms of anxiety as signs that they will lose control or become incapacitated in some way either in a public place or a place away from home with no one around to help. They fearfully believe that they are having heart attacks, strokes, going crazy, fainting, becoming nauseous or incontinent, etc.

Phobias and compulsions are related in a number of ways. Both use escape and avoidance as solutions to dealing with that which is feared. The main difference, however, is that the phobic individual can usually choose to avoid the feared situation more easily than the compulsive individual, because the phobia is not attached to as many things or situations and is not being generated by repeated intrusive thoughts.

One note here on the treatment of phobias. Simple phobias are best treated with behavioral therapy, but do not, by themselves, generally require medication. A different form of behavioral therapy known as "systematic desensitization" is the best-known method, and one which has been shown to be very effective. Newer and more rapid methods of treating phobias are also starting to make their appearance. Some phobias are now being eradicated in as little as one three-hour session through intensive and concentrated gradual exposure to the actual situations. This may ultimately be the most efficient approach.

PROCRASTINATION AND SLOWNESS

Procrastination is a very frequent and serious problem among those with classic OCD and often costs sufferers numerous jobs and relationships. As discussed earlier, most of those with the disorder suffer from strong doubt and perfectionism. This doubt causes some individuals to hesitate when making decisions for fear of not making the "perfect" decision, since the wrong choice could lead to harm or hardship for themselves or others, and finally, to guilt about their mistake. Making a decision is thus seen as taking an unacceptable risk. This causes many sufferers to agonize endlessly about even the most simple of questions. Roberta, a homemaker, would take as long as a half hour to decide what brand of breakfast cereal to buy. She would stand frozen in the supermarket aisle going back and forth mentally as the time went buy. Grocery shopping could easily become an all-day affair. Otherwise intelligent and capable people become paralyzed and accomplish little in life due to being so inefficient. Those whose rituals are extremely difficult and complicated may tend to go a step further and put off doing anything that could bring on the urge to do them. Procrastination is thus used as a way of coping with symptoms. Others fear not making the "perfect" decision in certain situations because they will possibly miss out on something important if they don't and will never get the particular opportunity again. Paradoxically, sufferers will often avoid or delay about such things for so long that they end up missing out on opportunities anyway. They do not seem to grasp that often not making a decision is the same as making a decision.

Another path that leads to procrastination is seen in those who perform frequent or complicated rituals and as a result are forced to put off doing other important things in their lives. These people are also frequently late for work or appointments. Mike, a building superintendent, had such complicated prayer rituals that when he first came to see me, he had to begin preparing three days in advance so that he could arrive on time for a therapy session. Amazingly, he made it, but at great emotional and physical cost to himself. It actually took him an hour just to put one shoe on. Another problem is that those who are extremely obsessive often cannot concentrate well and have difficulty focusing on making decisions or taking action. This is again true among those who have a serious depression accompanying their OCD, and who, along with concentration problems, lack the energy or interest to make or carry out decisions. If you feel depressed, it is often easier to put things off than to do something.

Because of the doubt that accompanies classic OCD and BDD, sufferers generally seem to have difficulty setting and deciding on priorities in their lives. They may be seen to neglect such things as filing their income tax returns, getting haircuts, visiting dentists or gynecologists regularly, or taking care of medical problems in a timely way. Such important self-care and life-maintenance often fall by the wayside when preoccupied sufferers fill up their lives with trivial activities.

None of the above should be confused with the slowness frequently associated with the performance of compulsions. This problem is sometimes referred to as "obsessive slowness" for reasons that don't make any sense, since it is the doing of compulsions rather than the obsessions that causes sufferers to take excessive time to perform everyday tasks. It makes it sound as if sufferers are somehow obsessing slowly. Aside from this poor choice of words, the term "obsessive slowness" doesn't really describe anything. Slowness can actually be the result of a number of different compulsive behaviors. Those who are compulsively slow may look a lot like the procrastinators but are not really trying to avoid things. They are actually trying to do things, but these things take up a lot more time than for the average person. In such cases, it is not unusual to see people who need an hour to wash their face or even longer to comb their hair. The simplest tasks can sometimes take hours and can be quite excruciating. One motive here is to do things "perfectly." This may involve doing each step ultracarefully and slowly or many times. As in procrastination, doubt and the resulting perfectionism are what are behind many forms of slowness. Only when something is perfect can doubtfulness be eliminated. One example of this was Larry, a garage mechanic. He had many doubts about whether he was accidentally damaging the cars he was supposed to be repairing and would install and remove parts either very slowly or several times over. Even individual screws or bolts had to be tightened or loosened up to a dozen times each, to ensure that the job was done perfectly. Reading is another area where compulsive slowness is frequently seen. Here the doubts are about whether the reader has accidentally skipped sentences or paragraphs, leading to painfully slow reading or lengthy rereading.

Slowness can also be the result of either magical thinking or the need for closure. As in all magic, a ritual must be performed perfectly, or bad luck or harm will result. Sufferers can become highly anxious about getting things right, since so much is riding on their doing so. It is therefore almost inevitable that one of two things will happen. One, is that they will make mistakes and have to keep repeating their ritual. The other is that the stress will cause an intrusive negative thought or image to interrupt things. This will then contaminate the magic of the ritual and cause the sufferer to have to start all over again. This kind of repetition can obviously take up a lot of time. In the case of the need for closure, sufferers must stick with certain activities until they are completed, no matter how long it takes, in order to avoid feeling anxious and uncomfortably incomplete. Another type of closure seen among OC sufferers is the need for what is known as the "just right" feeling. Certain activities must be repeated until they feel "just right." Only the sufferer can say what this is, in their particular case, if it can be put into words at all. Since this feeling may not be easy to achieve, the result can involve many repetitions. It is similar to a type of need frequently seen in those with TS.

One further note on procrastination: it can be especially insidious when it keeps sufferers from actually getting down to the business of working on their symptoms. They just cannot seem to manage their time well enough to be able to attend therapy sessions regularly, to get to each session on time, or to find time to do behavioral homework, whether prescribed by a therapist or as part of a self-help program.

TWELVE

~ Causes and Contributing Factors of OCSDs

~ OCD was once thought to be strictly psychological in origin. Those who practiced psychoanalysis believed that obsessions were a type of neurotic defense against unconscious impulses. Compulsions were thought to be an unconscious way of defending oneself against unacceptable aggressive impulses toward one's parents. This aggression, that had to be controlled, was supposedly the result of early experiences related to one's toilet training. While this theory makes for interesting literature, it does not represent the most recent knowledge gained through scientific methods. Its suggestions defy common sense and logic and merely represent pure speculation by Sigmund Freud. It has never led to any true understanding of the problem, nor has it produced a viable treatment. It has led to many sufferers and their families feeling as if they were somehow to blame.

True scientific developments over the last thirty years have gradually begun to reveal that the disorder has origins that appear to be both genetic and neurobiological. Genetic studies, although still rather preliminary, appear to statistically point to a pattern of genetic inheritance within families of classic OCD sufferers. Some theorists now believe that there may be an underlying genetic tendency for OCSDs to be able to occur in certain individuals. This would be referred to as a "predisposition." The actual onset of an OCSD would then, according to the theory, be triggered by some "precipitating" event. The types of events that may act as a trigger are still being studied and debated.

There is a new theory about a possible precipitator or trigger of classic OCD, which also suggests that it may be biological. It is still preliminary but may ultimately represent a breakthrough for some. It comes by way of studies of a related disorder known as Sydenham's Chorea (see the section entitled Brain Illness or Injury in this chapter, under the heading

Sydenham's Chorea). This disorder is sometimes seen among those who have had bouts of rheumatic fever. Its symptoms resemble OCD in a number of ways and may include compulsions to count, touch, repeat the words of others, or to curse repetitively.

SEROTONERGIC THEORY OF OCD

While there have been many speculations and hypotheses as to the actual mechanism behind OCSDs, probably the most widely accepted and most durable is the serotonergic theory. This theory largely owes its origins to the results stemming from the early use of the drug clomipramine (Anafranil) to treat classic OCD, beginning in Europe in the late 1960s. Clomipramine is an antidepressant drug that is known to have effects on two different neurotransmitter chemicals: norepinephrine and serotonin.

Neurotransmitters are chemicals that help transmit electrical impulses between nerve cells (neurons). Normally, serotonin is stored in chambers known as vesicles near the endings of certain neurons (see Fig. 12.1). When the neuron is stimulated by an electrical nerve impulse, the vesicles release their serotonin into the gap that typically exists between neuronal fibers (see Fig. 12.2). This gap is known as the synaptic cleft. The serotonin then travels across the synaptic cleft and fits into receptors on the other side, on the ends of the fibers of the neighboring neuron, much like keys being inserted into their locks. This next allows the electrical nerve impulse to cross the synaptic cleft and continue on its travels through the brain to its final destination. When the impulse has jumped the gap, the serotonin is then taken back into the vesicles to await the next impulse and for the cycle to begin again. This last activity is known as "reuptake." Theory holds that in OCD, the serotonin is released into the synaptic cleft, but before the nerve impulse can properly jump this gap, reuptake happens prematurely and a proper electrical transmission between nerve cells does not take place. When this takes place simultaneously at multiple nerve cell junctions, we have a brain dysfunction.

There are those cognitive theorists who argue that classic OCD is not a biologically based problem, but is instead a matter of people's mistaken evaluations of their obsessive thoughts being abnormal and dangerous to themselves or others. The claim is that everyone experiences morbid or unpleasant thoughts from time to time, but people with classic OCD, not unlike those with panic disorder, misinterpret such thoughts.

There is certainly a strong element of this in OCD, but there are also several strong sources of evidence, which run counter to this as a total explanation. These seem to back the theory that classic OCD is a neurobiological problem

Fig. 12.1 ～ Serotonin Release

Nerve Cell Transmission

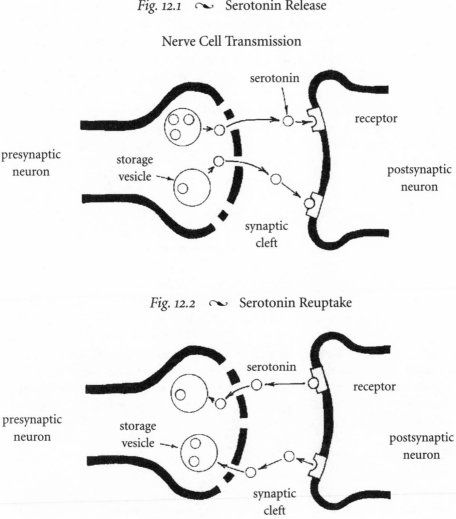

Fig. 12.2 ～ Serotonin Reuptake

involving the serotonergic system (and possibly other neurochemical systems) of the brain and include the following.

Studies Using Drugs which Relieve OCD Symptoms

The leading theory of the biological mechanism behind OCD holds that a dysfunction involving the neurotransmitter serotonin is responsible. This theory first arose in the late 1960s when patients, treated with the drug clomipramine (Anafranil) for the depression accompanying their OCD, were seen to experience a lessening of their OC symptoms. Anafranil is known to affect serotonin functioning in the brain by blocking premature reuptake. When serotonin is released by the vesicles into the synaptic cleft, the medication prevents it from being taken back up too quickly, making it more likely that it will lock on to a receptor on the other side of the cleft. Furthermore, it was found that improvement of symptoms could be correlated with increased blood levels of the drug. Since that time, other, newer, serotonin-active drugs besides Anafranil (see chapter 4) have been found to relieve OC symptoms, while drugs that affect other specific brain chemicals do not. This finding would seem to bolster the serotonergic theory. These results have been confirmed quite a number of times through double-blind studies designed to rule out placebo effects.

Disorders Found in Animals that Are Similar in Appearance to OCSDs

There are several disorders in animals which have recently been thought to resemble classic OCD and TTM in humans, and which may provide further models for the study of the disorder. One of the best known is Canine Acral Lick, seen in several breeds of dogs, particularly Labradors. Dogs who have this problem are typically seen to repetitively lick their paws, removing fur and even skin in some cases. Experimental studies in which these animals have been treated with Prozac have shown positive results. It has also been shown that cats with brain lesions in the area known as the caudate nucleus demonstrate perseverative and stereotypical behaviors. (See the next section in this chapter, What Actually Happens Within the Brain to Cause the Symptoms of OCD?, for a description of the caudate nucleus.)

Studies of Illness or Brain Damage

Studies of humans who have suffered illness in, or damage to, specific areas of the brain, and who then show OCD-like symptoms as a result are discussed in the section entitled, "Brain Illness or Injury," in this chapter.

Drug Studies

Studies have been conducted using drugs that can actually worsen or increase OCD symptoms. For example, studies have been carried out in which classic OCD patients successfully taking Anafranil have been administered the drug metergoline, which hinders serotonin activity. Results showed a worsening of anxiety and OC symptoms, probably the result of Anafranil's effects being undone. Another compound known as mCPP (m-chlorophenylpiperazine) has been used experimentally to help shed light on the serotonin theory, yielding interesting results. This chemical is known to oppose serotonin activity. Studies have shown that when those with classic OCD are administered mCPP orally, their symptoms worsen. When the drug is administered to normal control subjects, no changes are seen. Furthermore, when the compound was given to sufferers who had been taking the drug Anafranil for long periods of time, OCD symptoms and anxiety were not seen to increase. This study has led some to speculate that some type of abnormality in the action of brain serotonin may be connected in some way to OCD.

PET Scan Studies

PET (Positron Emission Tomography) scan studies yield moving color pictures, showing the rates at which various areas of the brain consume glucose (the fuel of brain and body cells) which has been radioactively tagged. Findings from these studies, whose work is still rather preliminary, have indicated that those with classic OCD show higher than normal metabolism rates in particular brain areas (the frontal cortex and the basal ganglia), as compared to those without it. The scans also show decreased metabolic rates in the same areas following the improvement of symptoms via the use of medication or behavioral therapy.

Studies of the role of serotonin, itself, raise some rather intriguing issues. Lower levels of serotonin breakdown products in spinal fluid have been shown to be connected with behavior that is more aggressive and impulsive, as well as with suicide attempts. The opposite has also been demonstrated. Excessive levels of serotonin activity have been linked to greater behavioral restraint, anxiety, and inhibition—all hallmarks of OCD.

Although TTM may be considered a disorder within the OCD spectrum, there is some evidence that it may involve other neurotransmitter systems beyond the serotonergic. One of the main pieces of evidence is the effectiveness of such drugs as Lithium and the newer antipsychotics in treating certain TTM sufferers.

WHAT ACTUALLY HAPPENS WITHIN THE BRAIN TO CAUSE THE SYMPTOMS OF OCD?

In actuality, aside from classic OCD, there are no firm theories about the circuitry of the OCSDs. It is an area of research in which much work needs to be done. In the case of classic OCD, there are several interconnected areas of the brain which are suspected to be the sites where symptoms originate, and together they make up what is believed to be a kind of circuit. They are (1) the

Fig. 12.3   ⌒   Location of Brain Areas Thought to Be Involved in OCSDs

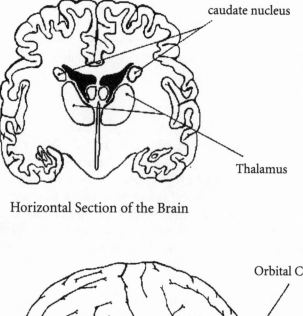

Horizontal Section of the Brain

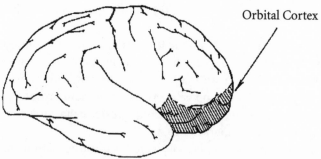

Right Side of the Brain

orbital cortex, which is part of the frontal area of the brain found just above the eyes, (2) the basal ganglia, a collection of structures deep within the brain, and (3) the thalamus.

The orbital cortex is a part of the "older" brain (in the evolutionary sense) and is involved in the regulation of anxiety, impulse control, meticulousness, personal hygiene, perseveration, and the starting and stopping of behaviors. The basal ganglia, as mentioned above, are actually two groups of structures, one on either side of the brain. One of these structures, the striatum, is of particular interest to OC research. The striatum is involved in the regulation of sensations, the ability to perseverate on or to shift to other tasks, the regulation of thought,

Fig. 12.4 ᗡᐧ Diagram of Brain Circuit Thought to Be Involved
in OCSDs

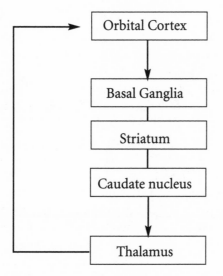

and the ability to smoothly carry out tasks that are automatic. It has been suggested that the striatum also controls older behavioral programs such as grooming, checking, etc.

To be even more particular, within the striatum there is a further substruc-
ture that may figure into OCD—the caudate nucleus. In a normally functioning
brain, the caudate nucleus works as a sort of filter or "gate" that allows only
important impulses and thoughts to get through to the conscious level to be
acted upon. Only impulses that are generally the strongest and most important
are supposed to be able to get through the gate, so that things that really are
deserving of our attention, such as serious threats, will be given priority and
dealt with.

Our third area of interest is the thalamus. It receives the impulses that the
caudate nucleus has allowed to get through and then sends them on to the
frontal area of the brain, of which the orbital cortex is a part. It acts to help drive
activity by sending the signal to the frontal area, telling it that there is something
which needs to be acted upon. One current theory holds that there is a dysfunction in the circuits of the caudate nucleus within the striatum. In OCD, the
"hinges" on the gate within the caudate nucleus are believed to be somewhat

loose, which allows too many sensations and thoughts to leak through to consciousness. Normally, these sensations and ideas would be suppressed without any (or at least very little) deliberate conscious effort. Because these thoughts and sensations are not ones that we normally experience, they are perceived as disturbing. Their escape is also believed to control the next stage in the circuit. They then move to the thalamus, which routes these improper and disturbing signals to the orbital cortex as priorities that need to be acted upon. The OC sufferer is forced to make a conscious (but unsuccessful) effort to suppress these odd disturbances, which results in feelings of anxiety.

PET scans of the brains of OCD sufferers show greater than normal metabolic activity in a part of the caudate nucleus, the basal ganglia, and the frontal area. Other disorders, which have features that resemble OCD (Tourette's Syndrome, Sydenham's Chorea, and Huntington's Chorea), are all associated with the basal ganglia. Those who have developed lesions in this area of the brain show symptoms similar to OCD. PET scans of the frontal area have shown the existence of a much higher than normal metabolic activity in that region as well. This activity in sufferers at rest was seen in some cases to be greater than in normal subjects who were engaged in deliberate problem-solving tasks. When symptoms are lowered, either by drug treatment or behavioral therapy, there also appears to be a decrease in metabolic rates in a direction toward more normal levels in the orbital cortex, the caudate nucleus, and the thalamus.

The question we come to now is just what exactly is happening within the actual brain structures themselves to cause them to function improperly? The current and most widely accepted theory holds that OCSDs are the result of a disturbance relating to the activity in the brain of the neurotransmitter chemical serotonin. This disturbance is believed to take place at the microscopic cell level.

BRAIN ILLNESS OR INJURY

In looking over scientific studies and observations dating even from the last century, there appears to be some evidence that injuries to or illnesses of the central nervous system can be connected to at least a percentage of OCD cases. Since OCD is believed to be a brain chemical dysfunction occurring in certain structures of the brain, it is logical to assume that damage to those specific areas could potentially result in OCD. However, there are no more than a handful of reports for many of the types of injuries and illnesses of the nervous system associated with OCD.

The causes listed below have been included either because people ask about them frequently or because they have been most commonly reported in the literature.

Head Injury

Many individuals question whether that childhood fall that knocked them unconscious could have caused their OCSD. Documented reports of head injuries resulting in OCD-type symptoms are rare. While such an occurrence might be possible, it would be a very rare occurrence, since a brain injury powerful enough to damage structures deep within the brain would most likely have caused other more serious disabilities and losses as well. Although they do exist, not enough is known about these cases to say anything conclusive. From the available data, all that can be concluded is that head injuries do not seem to be commonly associated with the onset of OCSD symptoms as a precipitating factor.

Brain Tumors

As with head injuries, there are very few reports of OCD symptoms resulting from brain tumors of any type.

Von Economo's Encephalitis

While most people have never heard of this disorder, it may actually have been responsible for many cases of OCD. Between 1915 and 1926, there were a series of flu epidemics that affected millions worldwide. This type of encephalitis was associated with that flu epidemic and is also believed to have been the result of a virus, although no organism was ever found. There were numerous case reports of individuals developing classic OCD and other neurological disturbances following their recovery from this disease.

Sydenham's Chorea

This disorder has recently received a great deal of attention by researchers, as it is believed that it may lead to an understanding of the causes of at least some cases of classic OCD, as well as tic disorders. Sydenham's appears to be the result of having had rheumatic fever and affects about 20 percent of those who have had the illness. It is believed to be an autoimmune disorder in which the body's own defenses attack certain minute areas of brain tissue. Sydenham's patients display many repetitive, OCD-like symptoms. Studies of Sydenham's have, in the last several years, led to the discovery that sudden onset cases of classic OCD in children may also be the result of an autoimmune disorder following streptococcus infections. It is theorized that the antibodies produced by the child's body cause the damage which then results in the symptoms of classic OCD and tics (see chapter 5, section on Childhood OCSDs and Strep Infections).

Epilepsy

There seems to be some connection between OCD and the types of epilepsy that are centered in the temporal lobe of the brain. Research studies using EEGs (electrical brain wave recordings) have shown a greater than expected incidence of temporal lobe abnormalities in those with OCD. However, these have all been studies using small groups of people and such results may not apply to the larger OCD population. More research is necessary. There do appear to be some similarities between temporal lobe epilepsy and classic OCD. One example would be the experience of being forced to think certain things. It is also interesting to note that some studies of those whose EEG's indicate temporal lobe epilepsy have been shown to have high scores on tests rating obsessionality.

What we can tell from all the above causes is that, based upon a limited number of studies, there does appear to be some relationship between infections of the central nervous system and OCD. Connections between OCD and such insults to the brain as physical injury or tumors would seem to be much weaker and therefore less likely.

As is often the case, we frequently see other types of brain damage accompanying some of these illnesses. One young man I know of suffered brain damage following a severe case of measles at age three and engaged in compulsive double checking and hoarding. Along with these symptoms, he had also suffered mild retardation.

TAKING ILLEGAL DRUGS

Those with OCSDs who have had past histories of illegal drug use often ask if that could have caused their disorder. The answer to this question is that not enough is yet known about the effects of various drugs on the biological mechanisms of the brain thought to be associated with OCSDs. While it is known, for instance, that cocaine does affect the serotonergic and dopaminergic neurotransmitter systems, it is not known how this might be linked to an OCSD, if at all. It is interesting to note, however, that cocaine and other drugs that stimulate the central nervous system have been known to cause repetitious or stereotypical behaviors that resemble classic OCD.

There have been a number of individual case studies that speculate about the association between the use of certain illegal drugs and the onset of classic OCD. One larger-scale study, published in 1993 by Rosa M. Crum and James C. Anthony of Johns Hopkins University, found a greater-than-expected risk of OCD among adult users of both cocaine and marijuana, as compared with adults who were not illegal drug users. The authors themselves noted, though, that there were some limitations to this study, and that further research was called for.

DEVELOPING OCD DURING OR AFTER PREGNANCY

The triggering or worsening of OCSDs in some women during pregnancy or immediately after delivery is a phenomenon that has been observed by many clinicians. There are studies that would also appear to support this connection. Why this occurs is a difficult question to answer, mostly because so little is known about it. It is quite likely that there are several possible paths to the development of OCSDs in relation to a pregnancy. While at least one study has shown that there is no particular relationship between classic OCD and post-partum depression, it may be that both problems are different expressions of some hormonal or biological shift affecting serotonin systems in the brain. In the case of a depressed mood, remission is usually seen as time passes or is relieved through the use of antidepressant medication. With OCSDs, this does not seem to be the case. Once they emerge, they become chronic problems.

It is commonly accepted that stress appears to worsen OCSD symptoms and tendencies. If a certain percentage of women are predisposed to having an OCSD, then the stresses surrounding pregnancy could possibly be precipitators. Some women experience stress in regard to pregnancy even before becoming pregnant. Problems can arise from such things as having difficulty conceiving or having to undergo numerous tests or fertility-enhancing procedures. Difficult pregnancies or miscarriages may be another stress-producing factor. (Actually, any of these things can produce stress not only for the woman, but also within a marital relationship.) Another source of stress could be the sudden responsibility of having a child (or an additional child) and this might act as a precipitator, touching off the OCSD.

What is unknown is the number of women whose OCSD seemed related to pregnancy and who may have already had a predisposition toward the disorder. Many women may already have had mild preexisting cases without recognizing it. Upon questioning a number of my female patients, I have often uncovered past histories of minor obsessions or some compulsive behaviors.

It is not unusual for pregnant women with classic OCD to have morbid obsessions or impulsions about either accidentally or purposefully harming their unborn child or new baby. These can be disturbing thoughts about dropping the infant, drowning it in the bath, smothering it, stabbing it. This should not be confused with the normal worries that many pregnant women may have, such as the potentially harmful things they might accidentally do to endanger the fetus, or the nervousness and uncertainty a new mother feels when handling the infant on her own in the first few weeks after giving birth.

These symptoms are quite treatable, and pregnant women and new mothers experiencing morbid thoughts and impulsions should seek treatment for them. Even if they are nursing and cannot take medication, they can still benefit from behavioral and cognitive therapies.

HEREDITY AND OCSDs

Whether OCSDs are hereditary is still not entirely clear. Until only a few years ago, when OCSDs were considered to be rare disorders, they were not believed to be hereditary in nature. The preliminary scientific data we have does seem to begin to point to a genetic link, but we must be careful not to draw hasty conclusions without more information.

One line of evidence for a genetic cause can be seen in twin studies. In these, it has been observed that there is a greater occurrence of classic OCD in pairs of twins who are identical, as compared with twins who are fraternal. Studies have shown that the rate of occurrence of classic OCD in identical twins is nearly double that for fraternal twins.

A second line of evidence is that we see a higher incidence of classic OCD within certain family trees than would be expected simply at random. Third, a higher rate among children of those with classic OCD versus children of those without the disorder has been observed. Two small studies done in 1989 (Swedo et al., 1989; Pauls et al., 1989) showed risk levels of 25 percent and 21 percent, respectively, for close relatives (parents and siblings). This works out to about a one-in-four chance of having classic OCD if a parent has the disorder.

I almost hesitate to include this information here, as some of those with OCD can be very suggestible and may focus too closely on the numbers and become fearful of having a child. The data we have is not yet strong enough to use for making decisions of this type. Please do not interpret this as being engraved in stone. It may also be, as mentioned in other sections of this book, that what is really inherited is a biological risk factor which is then triggered by other environmental factors. This would mean that even though you have inherited the potential for the disorder, you may not necessarily develop it. All this is very theoretical, and the final word is certainly not yet in.

Obviously, these cautions will still not prevent some people from acting on such preliminary information. The decision to have or not have a child is a very personal one. I would not base such an important decision on it. When patients ask me for my advice on this subject, I remind them that there are many good, intelligent, and productive people with OCD. Even if they have a child with OCD, early detection and treatment (if necessary) would surely make for a better experience in dealing with it than they probably had. Plus, the child will have something their parent may never have had—a good role model for facing the disorder. It may also reflect OCD-like thinking to believe that one must have a "perfect" child. No child should be expected to live up to a standard like that.

Many more studies are in progress and should help to clear the picture eventually. The problem with studies of this type is the difficulty in finding and properly interviewing relatives of those with OCD, as well as being able to correctly diagnose them for OCD, based solely on those interviews.

At the present time, no gene has yet been identified with OCD and there is no genetic test. Based on the current directions in research, my hunch is that a genetic basis will be found. While it is unscientific, my observations from my own patient intakes and interviews reveal, in most cases, the presence of relatives who certainly sound as if they suffer from OCSDs, depression, or other disorders of mood or anxiety. Genetic counselors I have spoken to seem to be aware of the possibility of inheritance of OCSDs, but they can only shrug their shoulders when it comes to making predictions for their clients.

OCSDs, STRESS, AND STRESSFUL EVENTS

There are questions whether an OCSD may be caused by some stressful event or be affected by stress. As mentioned previously in several sections, it would appear that those with OCSDs start out with a predisposition for them. For some, the disorder begins as early in their lives as they can remember. For others, it may come on gradually or suddenly at a later point in their lives. Stress, as we know, plays a role in many physical and psychological disorders. I have seen quite a number of people with a sudden onset OCSD, who can connect the event with some stressful condition or happening in their lives. It is difficult to say in these cases whether stress acted as a precipitator in someone who was already genetically destined to have it, or whether its appearance was just coincidental.

It is easy to see why many sufferers make the mistake of thinking that stressful events are the overall cause of their problem, due to the coincidence of the two events. To those who hold such beliefs, I would ask the following: since we obviously all go through stressful times in our lives, why don't we all therefore have an OCSD? Also, how can we explain the fact that there are many with OCSDs who are unable to link the onset with something stressful? It would seem to me that some type of special predisposition, whether genetic or otherwise, would be the explanation.

It can be observed that already existing OCSDs do seem to be worsened by stress, and most would agree that it represents some type of factor. Even where a sufferer's symptoms are under good control biologically and behaviorally, this can sometimes be temporarily overridden when the stress is great enough. The actual type of stress seems to be less important. I have seen people's symptoms worsened by fatigue, hunger, illness, job stress, relationship problems, or financial pressures. In quite a few of my female patients, the regular occurrence of premenstrual hormone changes also brings on a predictable, temporary worsening of their symptoms. Sufferers under stress may experience an upsurge of their compulsions because these behaviors are well-practiced ways of relieving anxiety. As such, they can automatically be called on at stressful times. For those still in the grip of their OCSD, a vicious circle can be created where the stress of symptoms only serves to create more symptoms, which in turn create more stress.

HABITS, LEARNING, AND DEVELOPING OCSDs

OCSDs are made up of both behavioral and biological components. It is most likely that genetics can predispose an individual to develop an OCSD, some biological event triggers it, and behavioral and environmental factors help to determine the way in which the fear and avoidance develop and are maintained.

There have been numerous theories about just what the behavioral and environmental factors are that affect OCSDs. In the case of classic OCD, the actual types of fears and rituals themselves are probably not inherited. The evidence of numerous children with OCD who show completely different symptoms from parents who also have the disorder can confirm this.

The question of how specific individuals come up with their own particular type of obsessive fear is not one that has a single answer. Simple phobias, which are an entirely different disorder, must be learned and become established directly via unpleasant experiences, or by seeing them modeled or demonstrated by others. For instance, one can develop a phobia of insects following a severe sting leading to an allergic reaction. You can also see individuals develop a similar fear if they have a parent who is strongly phobic of insects, who visibly panics whenever an insect comes close, who is constantly on the lookout for insects in the house, and who is always warning family members about the danger of insects. Classic OCD is contrary to a simple phobia. Sufferers can develop fears of things that are ordinarily regarded by society at large as dangerous, such as AIDS, or as common superstitions, such as the numbers 666 or 13. However, they can also come up with fearful thoughts of things which neither they nor anyone else would ever normally think of, much less worry about, or which would be considered outlandish or totally illogical. OCD differs from phobias in that sufferers can sometimes fear things that they have never heard of before, and which have never happened to them or anyone else they know.

It is probable that several different paths can lead to the fears of OCD. Remember the basic definitions of obsessions and compulsions: obsessions are thoughts which cause fear and anxiety; and compulsions are any physical or mental actions which relieve the fears and anxiety caused by obsessions.

The fearful content of a person's obsessions may well have input from any one or more of the following sources:

Culture and Social Peers. Fears that are common within a culture or a person's social group can become incorporated into obsessions. These could include superstitions practiced by others around the person or information available to everyone via word of mouth, TV, or newspapers, to name a few. Within our society, some examples of these would include fears of AIDS, cancer, asbestos, or electromagnetic fields.

Family and Friends. Fears that are shared within a person's family or circle of friends can be a strong influence. Fears of sickness or injury can often be present in families where there have been unpleasant experiences or losses due to such things. In some families that have lived through economic hardship such as the Great Depression, it is not unusual to see hoarding behaviors, which could then be incorporated into the next generation's obsessions.

Biochemical Disturbances. Strange or bizarre fearful thoughts that no one else shares are also common. A sufferer's biochemical disturbance allows material which would normally be filtered out to leak through into their consciousness. (See earlier section in this chapter entitled, "What Actually happens Within the Brain to Cause the Symptoms of OCD?")

Trauma. Traumatic or very upsetting events can sometimes provide the basis for an obsession. It is important to note though, that while some of those with OCD can trace the start of their fearful thoughts to some stressful event, the symptoms that follow may or may not be about the event itself.

The question of how sufferers come up with their particular compulsions, and what keeps these behaviors going or even increasing, is another matter. Behaviorally speaking, because compulsions are behaviors that relieve anxiety, it is rewarding, in the short run, to perform them. The rewarding nature of an escape from something unpleasant is known technically as "negative reinforcement." According to behavioral theory, behaviors that are rewarded tend to be repeated and may even increase as time goes on. The punishing experience of what these compulsions tend to do to a sufferer's life in the long run does not immediately serve as a deterrent, because negative consequences either take time to accumulate or are further off in the future, something clearly not on the mind of someone anxiously trying to relieve a strong fear.

Those with classic OCD or BDD never remain in fearful situations long enough to see that their fear would subside if they did absolutely nothing about it. This is because the compulsions cut off their contact with the fear, thus creating a vicious circle. Each time a fearful obsession occurs, anxiety goes up, a compulsion is performed, the anxiety is relieved, and the compulsion is strengthened, because it worked temporarily to relieve the fear. It becomes more of a habit because it was rehearsed, and the fear is strengthened because the sufferer avoided it before they could find out that it wasn't dangerous or realistic in the first place. As a result, the next time the fearful thought occurs to the sufferer, this whole cycle will be even more likely to occur again. To sum all this up, avoidance relieves anxiety in the short run, but keeps it going and even increases it, in the long run.

Some people may point out that performing compulsions can sometimes lead to more anxiety rather than less for some. This is especially true for those who have such serious anxiety to begin with that they cannot concentrate well enough to do their compulsions, or those who are so perfectionistic that they often cannot get their compulsion to be flawless enough to suit their standards. One other example of this can be seen when sufferers try to perform compulsions under pressure, or when they are in a rush.

As with other disorders of the OC Spectrum, TTM is also driven by behavioral factors. Hair pulling may fill a biological need for those who may have difficulty regulating the way they handle sensory input. It seems to help the sufferer when they are either understimulated (bored or lacking in physical stimulation) or overstimulated (emotionally stressed or feeling some type of localized physical sensations). A study published in 1990 by Dr. Charles Mansueto found that in a sample of TTM sufferers, 45 percent reported that hair pulling reduced tension, while 34 percent reported that they found it stimulating and energizing, and that it relieved boredom and inactivity. Similar findings were also observed in a study published in 1993 by Dr. Gary Christensen and colleagues. In this study, negative mood states or sedentary activities were each found to be components important to pulling. Hair pulling may also help those sufferers who experience obsessive perfectionistic thoughts about their hair having to be perfect in some way. Pulling may either provide needed stimulation through the various senses (sight and touch, for instance) or reduce stimulation by allowing the sufferer to fall into a relaxed state as they pull. It can also satisfy perfectionistic obsessions by eliminating hairs which, to the puller, don't seem to belong with their other hairs. Because pulling provides these different types of satisfying outcomes, a positive connection is created with it, ensuring that it will take place again when the same circumstances reoccur. This is known, in behavioral terms, as "conditioning."

While current theory suggests that those with OCSDs are born, and not made, we should not totally discount the influence of early learning and environmental factors. In the case of classic OCD, BDD, and perfectionistic hair pulling, being brought up in a household where certain OC-like traits are promoted is probably not the best atmosphere for someone with a predisposition toward the problem. Families who show a great deal of strictness, rigidity, and perfectionism probably do encourage sufferers to be more so. Children with classic OCD who are over-protected, or taught to be cautious and not take risks, might also have their symptoms worsened by adopting such attitudes toward life, as well as their own obsessive fears. Where habit and learning do play a direct role in classic OCD, it is in the development and maintenance of compulsions.

UPBRINGING AND OCSDs

There is no evidence that an OCSD is caused by environmental factors alone. If this were true, then everyone with an unhappy childhood would have one. Con-versely, I have met many people with OCSDs who had a happy and uneventful upbringing. This is not to say that an unhappy childhood may have no effect on someone already predisposed to an OCSD, since stress can be a precipitating factor. Living in a household where there is constant yelling, fighting, or upset might be likely to make for a more tense, avoidant, and uncertain individual. Stressful events may trigger the onset of an OCSD or possibly worsen what was only a rather low-level problem, even if they were not the actual cause.

Quite a number of patients I have seen would probably have needed therapy anyway due to the influence of their early home environments, even if they had not been afflicted with an OCSD. This does not mean that people should be encouraged to sit around blaming their parents or others for their troubles, while not making efforts to help themselves. I try to teach my patients that despite whatever happened in their lives previously, they are still fully responsi-ble for themselves in the present. The clock cannot be turned back. It is too late for their parents to raise them all over again, and the past, sadly, must be accepted, however dislikable it may have been. Blaming and accusing your par-ents will never change the past for you.

Not only may upbringing cause other problems in addition to an OCSD, but it can also make it difficult for a person to work at therapy. Often, those raised with certain unhelpful or illogical beliefs or attitudes find it difficult to participate in therapy or form a working relationship with a therapist. An example would be a sufferer raised by parents who were emotionally or physically abusive. As patients, they may find it especially difficult to trust a therapist and put themselves in that person's hands. They may find it difficult to get close to anyone. Another example would be those who have not been raised to be independent. Those who are instead dependent on others to help them get through life, have the most difficulty in taking responsibility for their own recoveries. They become negative and helpless. Their friends and families make the therapy contacts. They let others make follow-up calls to the psychologist or psychiatrist that they should be making for themselves, and they have these same others call the helping professional when they are having a difficult time or not following through on therapy.

One other influence I have witnessed is among those who have lived in homes where things were chaotic and unpredictable on an everyday basis. Parents with anger control or substance abuse problems frequently create homes like these. The reaction I have seen among those with classic OCD can be an increased need for a sameness and control in their everyday lives, which is also reflected through their symptoms. I have witnessed problems with symmetry and perfectionism associated with such upbringings.

ALLERGIES AND OCSDs

There is currently no evidence in the scientific literature on OCSDs that would indicate any connection between these disorders and allergies. I have run across several unscrupulous practitioners over the years who had attempted to convince sufferers that the OCSD was the result of allergic reactions to substances in their work or home environments. These people were encouraged to make changes to their homes, which were often expensive and inconvenient. These changes did not help and left the sufferer feeling victimized and angry.

This is not to say that individuals cannot become obsessed with their own real allergies. It is possible to incorporate anything within classic OCD, whether real or superstitious. It also does not mean that the stress of real health problems resulting from allergies cannot worsen a person's OCSD. It does mean, though, that at the present time, one should not believe anyone telling them that treating their allergies will surely "cure" their OCSD.

ATTENTION-DEFICIT/HYPERACTIVITY DISORDER (ADHD) AND CLASSIC OCD

Classic OCD is not currently classified as a learning disability or as a type of ADHD. Sometimes it appears to be similar, due to difficulties with concentration, attention, and information processing. Many of those with OCSDs, in general, have had histories of poor school performance and classroom behavior difficulties due to their symptoms. Sometimes, the poor concentration caused by obsessive thoughts or doubts that leads to rereading has been mistaken for ADHD.

ADHD sufferers have also been known to double-check their work or act in compulsively perfectionistic ways when performing tasks. This is not because they have true OCD, but because their lack of concentration and attention frequently causes them to make more than the average share of mistakes or omissions, or at least make them fearful that this is happening, because their attention may have wandered. In those with ADHD, these behaviors are more a way of compensating for their problem, rather than a sign of classic OCD.

This is not to say that there is no relationship between classic OCD and ADHD. While I cannot vouch for their accuracy, I have seen studies in which rates of ADHD have been shown to be as high as between 30 percent and 40 percent in male children and adolescents with serious classic OCD. Rates are generally said to be lower for females. While I have not seen rates of ADHD this high among my own patient group, I have seen both problems coexisting in several cases, and the two problems had to be treated separately, with different approaches. As mentioned earlier, these figures may be inflated by misdiagnoses confusing classic OCD with ADHD.

ADHD is also known to have an association with Tourette's Syndrome (TS) (a close, but rarer relative of classic OCD), occurring in about 50 percent of those with TS. In turn, TS is also known to have a strong association with classic OCD, with OC symptoms occurring in roughly 50 percent of TS cases.

It is interesting to note that classic OCD, ADHD, and TS all share problems involving the same two brain neurotransmitter systems, serotonin and dopamine. The disorders appear to differ somewhat though in the way they respond to pharmacological treatments. Antidepressants are used to treat classic OCD and sometimes ADHD. However, ADHD seems to respond best to low doses, while classic OCD seems to require higher doses. ADHD is seen to respond to the use of stimulant medications such as Ritalin, Cylert, Adderall, and Dexedrine, which cause the release of dopamine in the brain. However, these same drugs tend to cause a worsening of tics in TS, since TS responds to such antipsychotic drugs as Haldol, Orap, Risperdal, and Zyprexa, which block dopamine receptors.

It is also known that in certain cases of OCD, augmenting medications with antipsychotic drugs can cause further improvement. Antidepressant medications used to treat OCD by blocking the reuptake of serotonin (see the first section in this chapter on the "Serotonergic Theory of OCD") do nothing for the other two disorders, however. Whether these three disorders share some sort of common genetic or biological factor, or have some other relationship, has yet to be determined. Research in this area is still quite limited.

~ THIRTEEN

~ Finding Resources and Getting Help

W hile there are still insufficient resources for those with OCSDs, the overall picture is gradually improving year by year. The efforts of the OC Foundation and the Trichotillomania Learning Center have contributed greatly toward the goals of making certain that all OC sufferers understand their disorders, help them to know that they are not alone, and enable them to find proper help. The last ten years, in particular, have seen the rise of better informed consumerism in seeking mental health care and of a growing self-help movement.

SUPPORT GROUPS

Support and self-help groups can be extremely helpful. They help you see that you are not alone with the pain and difficulty you experience. In addition, they help remove the stigma, shame, and embarrassment by encouraging you to meet with others who, despite their disorder, are also decent, ordinary human beings. Support groups provide a setting where you and other people can speak publicly about what was once a most closely guarded secret. By accepting these others as ordinary people, you learn to accept yourself. You also learn to accept the fact that this disorder really is a presence in your life, albeit an unwelcome one.

Groups are also a good place to pick up helpful lessons and techniques. It is said that the best way to learn something is to teach it to someone else. As you pass along the knowledge you have gained in therapy or self-help, you are learning it anew and reinforcing your own lessons. While attending a group, one person can often find an inspiring role model in another person who has fought their way to a recovery, can copy them, and perhaps work their way up to eventually being a model for someone else in turn.

One other advantage to groups is that they are a good source of word-of-mouth information as to who in your area offers the best treatment for OCSDs. This is obviously more reliable than picking someone out of the phone book.

There are quite a variety of groups to choose from these days. They may meet weekly, biweekly, or monthly. There are patient support groups sponsored by many of the large hospitals and clinics that treat OCSDs, groups affiliated with the Obsessive-Compulsive Foundation, and the 12-Step groups which go by the name of Obsessive-Compulsives Anonymous and which are based upon the original format developed by Alcoholics Anonymous. We are also starting to see the formation of numerous groups for TTM affiliated with the Trichotillomania Learning Center. There are psychoeducational groups run by professionals, designed to teach sufferers and their families about the disorder, and there are groups run by those with OCSDs for fellow sufferers.

I have been running a monthly psychoeducational group since 1986, where I try to pass along the latest information in the field of OC treatment, answer specific questions about treatment, and get sufferers talking to each other. My clinic also sponsors groups for the families of those with OCD, women with trichotillomania, and groups for adolescents with OCD. Our clinic may be a bit more active in this respect than some others, but hopefully, if you look around, you will be able to find a group in your area. The OC Foundation maintains a list and will be happy to help you locate one.

If nothing is available close by, start your own group. Find a meeting place, such as a church, hospital, library, or synagogue. Sometimes, friendly mental health practitioners will donate meeting space in their offices. Put an ad in the community service column of your local newspaper (such ads are generally printed free). There are enough fellow sufferers out there, and you'll soon have members. Call the OC Foundation or the Trichotillomania Learning Center for the materials and support they can provide. The OC Foundation even prints a newsletter for self-help groups called *Check It Out*. For a small fee, you can also get an excellent book on how to start a self-help group from the Anxiety Disorder Association of America. Many groups have started this way.

For those of you who own computers, there is now yet another way to network with fellow sufferers. OCD bulletin boards currently exist on the Internet (Prodigy and America Online are both sources for these) and provide a way of attending group meetings electronically (see the section on Resources Online in this chapter).

One other important note on this subject. There are those who shy away from groups because they anxiously believe that if they hear others discussing their own symptoms, they will somehow take on the symptoms they have heard.

This is simply untrue. Those with OCD generally do not take on entirely new symptoms simply by hearing about them. The only grain of truth here is that sometimes, hearing someone with similar symptoms worrying obsessively about a favorite obsessive topic of yours may give you a new slant on it. I do not think this is a good enough reason to avoid a support group. You could just as easily have thought up this new variation on your own anyway or else run into it coincidentally out there in the everyday world. You might as well stay home and avoid everyone in that case. Let's face it, you cannot seal yourself off from the world in some kind of a shell and expect to recover. Getting well always involves risks, and this is one worth taking.

ORGANIZATIONS THAT CAN HELP

You may know someone locally who has had a successful treatment for OCD who can give you a referral to his or her practitioner. Self-help groups are frequently a valuable source of inside information as to which practitioners are effective. If such a local grapevine isn't available, you will have to look elsewhere. As mentioned above, probably the least helpful method is to blindly pick someone out of the phone book. Instead, write or call one of the following organizations or their local affiliate.

1. Obsessive-Compulsive Foundation
    337 Notch Hill Rd.
    North Branford, Connecticut 06971
    Phone: (203) 315-2190
    Fax: (203) 315-2196
    E-mail: *info@ocfoundation.org*
    Website: www.ocfoundation.org/

Not enough good things can be said about this organization, its helpfulness and good attitude, and the things they do for OCSD sufferers. They will even mail their newsletters in plain envelopes and extend free membership to the disabled, so there is no excuse not to join. The OC Foundation maintains an extensive nationwide referral list and may have several names for you. They publish a valuable newsletter and also offer an extensive list of books, pamphlets, audiotapes, and videotapes. Their annual membership meetings, held at different locations around the country, are informative and important experiences. The OC Foundation is represented around the country by local affiliates that can give you the best tips on where to seek treatment within their area. These currently include:

(NOTE: The names, addresses, and phone numbers of these organizations and their contact persons may be subject to change. In case of any problems, contact the OC Foundation for newer information.)

The OCF Metro Chicago
2300 Lincoln Park West
Chicago, IL 60614
Phone: (773) 880-2035
E-mail: *ocfmetchgo@aol.com*
Contact persons:
    Ms.Susan Richman, President
    Ms. Judith Parente, Executive Director

OC Foundation of Philadelphia
c/o AATC, 112 Bala Avenue
Marion Station, PA 19066
Phone: (610) 660-0549
Contact persons:
    Ms. Gayle Frankel, President
    Ms. Anna Mae Yurkanin, Co-President

OC Foundation of Rhode Island
110 Wilcox Avenue
Pawtucket, RI 02860
Phone: (401) 431-8633
Contact person:
    Ms.Patricia Parent, President

Minnesota Affiliate Obsessive-Compulsive Foundation
2395 University Avenue West, Suite 304
St. Paul, MN 55114
Phone: (612) 646-5615
Contact person:
    Ms. Sharon Lohmann

OC Foundation of Texas, Inc.
P.O. Box 110
Friendswood, TX 77546
Phone: (281) 482-2147
E-mail: *wing1pray@aol.com*
Contact person:
    Ms. Donna Friedrich, President

OC Foundation of Michigan, Inc.
P.O. Box 510412
Livonia, MI 48151-6412
Phone: (313) 438-3293
E-mail: *ocdmich@aol.com*
Contact person:
     Ms. Roberta P. Slade, President

OCF Greater Boston Affiliate
115 Mill Street
Belmont, MA 02478
Phone: (617) 855-2252
E-mail: *egan@OCD.McClean.org*
Contact person:
     Ms. Denise Egan, President

Central New York OCF Affiliate
P. O. Box 74
Whitesboro, NY 13492
Phone: (315) 768-7031
E-mail: *CNYocf@dreamscape.com*
Contact person:
     Mr. Scott Carlsen, President

OCF of Jacksonville, Inc.
P.O. Box 16892
Jacksonville, FL 32216
Phone: (904) 726-0918
E-mail: *janericjul@aol.com*
Contact person:
     Ms. Janis McClure, President

Central New Jersey OCF Affiliate
60 McAfee Road
Somerset, NJ 08873
Phone: (732) 828-0099
E-mail: *AllenWeg@aol.com*
Contact person:
     Ms. Ina Spero, President

OCF of San Francisco Bay Area
P.O. Box 31444
San Francisco, CA 94131-0444
Phone: (415) 337-4160
Contact person:
    Mr. Scott Granet

2.   The Trichotillomania Learning Center, Inc. (TLC)
1215 Mission Street, Suite 2
Santa Cruz, CA 95060
Phone: (831) 457-1004
E-mail: *trichster@aol.com*
Website: www.trich.org

The understanding and compassion with which this organization is run is truly remarkable. It publishes a unique and helpful newsletter and has an extremely comprehensive information packet available to new members. TLC sponsors an excellent yearly retreat for sufferers, which provides a safe environment where those with TTM can explore the issues of having their disorder, and which is an extremely moving experience. For those who suffer from TTM, it is an experience not to be missed. TLC has begun to establish local affiliates and may be able to provide local referrals.

3.   Association for the Advancement of Behavior Therapy (AABT)
305 Seventh Avenue, 16th Floor
New York, NY 10001-6008
Phone: (212) 647-1890
Website: *http://www.aabt.org*

This is an organization for cognitive/behavioral therapy professionals and consumers can contact them for referrals. Members are listed in their directory by states, towns, and specialties, of which OCD is one. Those who treat OCD probably treat BDD, and possibly TTM.

The following organizations do not directly provide referrals, but are of particular value to OCSD sufferers. They are as follows:

4.   Obsessive-Compulsive Anonymous World Services (OCA)
P. O. Box 215
New Hyde Park, NY 11040
Phone: (516) 741-4901
Website: *http://members.aol.com/west24th.index.html*

This organization sponsors numerous OC self-help groups that employ a 12-Step approach to coping with OCSDs. The approach here is more spiritually based along the lines of AA. They have been extremely helpful to many sufferers and provide one-on-one sponsorship by more experienced members. In addition to self-help, their meetings can be a good place to network and find local treatment information. They also have several valuable publications, and there are no membership fees. Send a stamped self-addressed envelope for information.

5. OC Information Center
    Madison Institute of Medicine
    7617 Mineral Point Rd., Suite 300
    Madison, WI 53717
    Phone: (608) 827-2470
    Website: *www.healthtecsys.com/mimocic.html*

This center is the absolute best source for articles about OCSDs. They have what may be the world's most extensive collection of both popular and scientific articles, any of which can be ordered by mail or phone. They can also perform computer searches on specific OC topics, the printouts of which can be ordered at very reasonable cost. Their staff is very knowledgeable and helpful, and never too busy to take the time to work with you.

6. National Institute of Mental Health (NIMH)
    c/o Research on OCD
    Building 10, Room 3D41
    10 Center Drive
    Bethesda, MD 20892
    Phone: (301) 496-4812
    Website: *http://www.nimh.gov/publicat/ocd.html*

A valuable source of reliable information about the latest OC research findings. Also a good source of information on PANDAS. You can also inquire about participating in one of their research protocols if you are interested.

7. Tourette Syndrome Association, Inc. (TSA)
    42–40 Bell Boulevard
    New York, NY 11361-2874
    Phone: (718) 224-2999
    E-mail: *tourette@ix.netcom.com*
    Website: *http://www.tsa.mgh.harvard.edu/*

TSA is the only place to go for information and support should TS or a tic disorder accompany your OCSD. This large association has great resources that include a very informative newsletter, many publications, and videotapes, which can be extremely helpful. They are also the best source for information concerning education laws and children with OC Spectrum problems. Local affiliates often provide help with school advocacy.

8. OC & Spectrum Disorders Association (OCSDA)
   18653 Ventura Boulevard – Suite 414
   Tarzana, CA 91356
   Phone: (818) 990-4830
   Fax: (818) 760-3748
   Website: *www.ocsda.org*

OC&SDA is a California-based organization which provides information about treatment resources to residents of that state. They also provide support for members, sponsor regular conferences, pursue mental health legislation, and maintain a good informational website.

9. Anxiety Disorder Association of America (ADAA)
   6000 Executive Boulevard, Suite 513
   Rockville, MD 20852
   Phone: (301) 231-9350
   Website: *http://www.aada.org*

The ADAA offers a referral booklet which includes professionals and support groups. It offers many publications and tapes dealing with the various anxiety disorders. They hold an excellent annual convention with offerings for patients and professionals alike.

10. Recovery, Inc.
    802 North Dearborn St.
    Chicago, IL 60610
    Phone: (312) 337-5661
    Website: *www.recovery-inc.com*

Founded in 1937, this organization sponsors a nationwide chain of nonprofit, nonsectarian support groups. Their structured meetings are run by nonprofessionals, and they teach their members a very useful form of what closely resembles cognitive therapy. Meetings are devoted to teaching and practicing practical problem solving for emotional disturbances. The membership includes those with mood and anxiety disorders among others.

11. Child Psychopharmacology Information Service
6001 Research Park Boulevard - #1568
Madison, WI 53719-1179
(608) 263-6171
Website: *www.psychiatry.wisc.edu/cpis.htm*

This organization maintains a collection of useful and reliable information concerning the use of psychiatric medications in children.

12. Scrupulous Anonymous (SA)
One Liguori Drive
Liguori, MO 63057-9999
Website: *www.liguori.org*

SA is devoted to assisting Catholics suffering from obsessive moral scrupulosity. They publish a helpful newsletter, as well as other works on this subject.

RESOURCES ONLINE

There are also many valuable OC, TTM, and TS Internet sites for those of you who are online. Please take note that given the changing nature of the Internet and its sites, it is difficult to keep a list like this up to date. Web addresses and site contents are subject to change over time. Also, please note that inaccuracies and misinformation are likely to appear within news and chat groups. Be cautious before you act on what you are told there. In the interest of your being a good consumer, it is advisable that you use information from reputable major sites, as well as your own mental health professionals, to check on what you are told at these locations. These sites have been listed for *informational* purposes only. Being listed here does not constitute an endorsement for any particular site or its contents.

Some of the better sites currently available would include:

· The home page of the OC Foundation can be found at :
www.ocfoundation.org
· The home page of the Trichotillomania Learning Center is at:
www.trich.org

- The website for Tourette Syndrome Association is at:
  www.tsa.mgh.harvard.edu/
- The home page of the OC & Spectrum Disorders Association is located at:
  www.ocsda.org
- The website for Western Suffolk Psychological Services, my own clinic, can be accessed at:
  www.wspsdocs.com
- The website for the Obsessive-Compulsive Information Center can be found at:
  www.healthtecsys.com/mimocic.html
- The web address of the Child Psychopharmacology Information Service is:
  www.psychiatry.wisc.edu/cpis.htm
- The OCD NEWSGROUP site is located at:
  alt.support.ocd
- The TRICHOTILLOMANIA NEWSGROUP is located at:
  alt.support.trichotillomania
- The TS NEWSGROUP site is at:
  alt.support.tourette
- Prodigy's On-line Bulletin Board Service for OCD can be accessed at: (jump)medical support bb; choose topic "anx/dep/ocd"; then look in the subject area for subjects beginning with "OCD."
- America Online's OCD Chat on Wednesdays at 9 P.M. to 12 midnight EST, which can be reached by using the keyword:
  PEN>chat rooms health-conference room
- The best general site for OCD with extensive links to other sites is at:
  www.fairlite.com/ocd/ocd text.shtml
- A very large and rambling collection of links, as well as anything and everything related to OCD, is titled "Again and Again: Obsessive Compulsive Disorder Websites" and is located at:
  www.interlog.com/~calex/ocd/index.html
- Another good central site with information and links relating to ocd can be found at:
  www.mentalhealth.com
- The best central site for TTM with links to other sites is at:
  http://www.fairlite.com/trich/
- A mailing list is sponsored by the OC & Spectrum Disorders Association for teenagers from ages 13 to 19 who suffer from OCD, TTM, TS where they

can be free to express themselves to those in their own age group, make friends, and get support. It can be subscribed to at:

> *www.angelfire.com/il/TeenOCD/*

- An excellent website for psychopharmacology is at:

  > *http://uhs.bsd.uchicago.edu/~bhsiung/tips.html*

- The OCD-L mailing list on the Internet. To become a subscriber, e-mail them at:

  > LISTSERV@VM.MARIST.EDU.

  Leave the subject line blank and in the body of the e-mail type: SUB OCD-L and follow it by typing in your real name.

- The National Institute of Mental Health OCD site gives basic information about OCD, treatment, and the latest research at:

  > *www.nimh.gov/anxiety/anxiety/ocd/index.htm*

- Mental Health Net—Obsessive-Compulsive Resources (including trichotillomania) lists many on-line resources for OCD and TTM and rates them for usefulness.

- The Association for the Advancement of Behavior Therapy site contains a lot of information about this organization's activities. It is a good source for referrals, and the site has links to other mental health sites:

  > *www.aabt.org*

- The Anxiety Disorder Association of America website is at:

  > *www.aada.org*

- Obsessive-Compulsive Anonymous (OCA) website is located at:

  > *http://members.aol.com/west24th/index.html*

- The Recovery, Inc. website is located at:

  > *www.recovery-inc.com*

- Scrupulous Anonymous maintains a website at: *www.liguori.org* At this site you can get on the mailing list for their newsletter. To get it, e-mail them your mailing address and the name of the newsletter you want (Scrupulous Anonymous) at:

  > *newsletter@liguori.org*

- A site for partners of those suffering from mental illnesses which contains tips, stories, information, and resources is located at:

  > *www.lightship.com*

- The Yale University home page for OCD and TS is located at:

  > *www.info.med.yale.edu/chldsty/tsocd.htm*

- The OCD Resource Center is a website sponsored by two drug companies (Solvay Pharmaceuticals, Inc. and Pharmacia & UpJohn Co.). It contains general information on OCD, a Club OCD for children, and a Physician's Forum (accessible only to physicians). Information kits on OCD can also be ordered here. It can be found at:

www.ocdresource.com

- An excellent site for books, audiotapes, and other materials and information about cognitive therapy is run by the Albert Ellis Institute and is located at:

  www.rebt.org

- The site Medication A-M contains a list of links to discussions of commonly prescribed medications and the effects they are likely to have. Listings include medications frequently prescribed for OCD at:

  http://www.algy.com/anxiety/drugsam.html

- The Medicine Program website offers a program run by volunteers, whose purpose is to connect patients who lack the means to purchase medications with free medical assistance programs. The site provides an application that can be downloaded and mailed in. There is a processing fee of $5.00 for each medication requested. The address is:

  http://www.themedicineprogram.com/

- A site which contains information on newly approved drugs and lets you register for participation in OC drug testing programs is located at:

  www.clinicaltrials.com

- A really excellent site containing extensive information about special education laws that will assist you in obtaining educational help for a child with a handicapping condition is located at:

  www.wrightslaw.com

GETTING THE RIGHT TREATMENT

When you finally do get a name, whatever the source, be sure to check out the practitioner's credentials. Don't be afraid to conduct a mini-interview with them when you call. You have the right to assertively question their ability to help you. Be sure to ask the following types of questions when you call the practitioner:

1. "What degrees do you hold and are you state licensed?" (Avoid the unlicensed, as they are unregulated, uninsured, and you will have no protection if you feel you have not been treated properly.)

2. "Do you specialize in OCD (or BDD or TTM as the case may be)? What are your qualifications, and have you had any special training in the treatment of my disorder?"

3. "How long have you been in practice? How many cases of my disorder have you treated? How many cases of this are you currently treating?"

4. "What is your orientation?" (Ask this question only if you are calling about getting therapy, not medication. The correct answer should be—behavioral or cognitive/behavioral.)

5. "Do you endorse the use of behavioral therapy together with medication?" (Ask this if you are calling a psychiatrist. The correct answer should be "Yes.")

6. "Do you endorse the use of medication (if necessary) together with behavioral therapy? (Ask this if you are calling a behavioral therapist. The correct answer should be "Yes.")

7. What techniques do you use to treat disorders such as mine? (Ask this if you are calling about therapy, and make sure the answer is—Exposure and Response Prevention for OCD and BDD, and Habit Reversal Training for TTM, skin picking, and nail biting. A therapist who uses these techniques is probably trained in cognitive therapy as well, but ask if they have training in this approach anyway.)

8. What is your fee? Are your services covered by insurance (if this is an important factor in affording therapy)? *Note:* Check your own insurance coverage before you call to make sure you are covered for outpatient mental health services. Also find out about how much coverage you have.

9. How often would you have to see me? (Once per week is about average, unless you are looking into intensive short-term therapy).

10. On the average, how long does the treatment take? (This may be a difficult question to answer if there are other problems to be solved in addition to an OCSD.)

If you're already in treatment, but feel it is the wrong one, first, and most important, talk it over with whomever is treating you. They at least deserve this courtesy and may be able to correct the situation. A sign of a good therapist is someone who listens with an open mind, helps you to see all your available options, and then discusses them with you objectively. Consider your own role, too. If your OCD has not been dealt with thus far in your therapy, it may be that you have not fully disclosed it and are waiting for your practitioner to ask the "magic questions" that will permit you to finally bring up the problem. If you have been in your current therapy only a short time, don't be overly impatient or hasty if you have told all, and know you are being treated with the latest methods. Some people hop from practitioner to practitioner, never letting any one work with them long enough to do any good. If, however, you have been in treatment say a year or more and have seen no real progress toward your OCSD goals, you should reconsider whether this is the right therapist for you.

Some practitioners, unfortunately, are still ignorant of the latest behavioral or medical advances. It is their ethical duty to stay abreast of these developments in their fields. If yours doesn't, it may be time to consider whether this person is really acting in your best interests or is simply trying to hang on to you as a patient. I have heard reports of patients being told, "I don't believe in behavior therapy and besides, it won't really get to the underlying root of your problem," or "I think medication is dangerous and it doesn't work for these types of problems." I once heard of a therapist, who told a patient, "I don't think your problem is serious enough for behavior therapy to be able to help you." Conversely, I have also heard of a therapist, who told another patient, "You're too seriously ill for behavior therapy to be able to help you."

Some therapists may acknowledge the OCD, but then tell you that you must work on other personal issues first, in order to make progress. You may end up seeing them for some time, working on other things and even resolving them, but never really getting around to the OCD. Some therapists procrastinate because they don't feel qualified to actually treat your problem and are too embarrassed to admit it. They may even use your other problems as an excuse. I have always believed that unless the OCD is dealt with first, you won't be able to properly concentrate on other issues in your life, no matter how important they may be.

You may encounter a therapist who has some knowledge of behavioral therapy and, despite your lack of progress, tells you, "Those other doctors won't be able to do anything for you that I haven't done." Such a therapist may have tried a few techniques with you, but nothing intensive or comprehensive. Don't be misled by this. Someone well versed in treating OCSDs will have more than one or two types of assignments to give you. They will have a real program for you.

It may be that your practitioner is of a theoretical background that will not be helpful in treating your OCD. They may not be trained in behavior therapy, for instance, but may still believe in it and be willing to make a proper referral for you. You can show them this book or publications from the Obsessive-Compulsive Foundation or the Trichotillomania Learning Center. It is a bad sign if they won't look at the information or discuss it with you. If you approach them assertively as a consumer and don't immediately put them on the defensive, they just may listen to you and perhaps even learn something.

Luckily, the majority of therapists are ethical and caring people. It is a bad sign if a therapist immediately attacks or, even worse, dismisses your idea without a good discussion. If they belong to that unfortunate minority, don't wish to be confused by the facts, and won't discuss it with you, you may just find yourself on your own when it comes to finding another practitioner. Don't let yourself be browbeaten into staying or made to feel guilty or ignorant for wanting to end the relationship if it is not therapeutic for you. It is not hard to make OCSD sufferers feel guilty, and they can, at times, be easily manipulated. You are allowed to set your own priorities, but at least listen to what the therapist has to say about unfinished work. Weigh the facts yourself. If you wish to set up a consultation with another practitioner, don't be afraid to do so. That is certainly your right. You can then have the two of them communicate with each other. Following therapy for your OCSD, you might even go back to your previous therapist to work on some of those other problems. As I have said, you are the consumer. If the therapy is not working for you, speak up and then take action if you must. Don't let anything stand between you and your recovery.

MAJOR TREATMENT CENTERS

In some cases, symptoms may have become so severe that self-help and local outpatient treatment just aren't enough to do the job. Sometimes, local intensive inpatient treatment for these more severe cases just isn't available. There are also times when a second opinion about diagnosis and treatment is desirable, such as when treatment is at an impasse, or there is uncertainty about the diagnosis. At such times, the question is—"Where to go?" The following is a list of major nationally recognized treatment centers. The professionals who head them are generally considered to be leaders in the field of OCSD treatment. It may take some doing to get to one of these centers; however, in complex or severe situations, a trip to one of them for a consultation may be just the thing to do. You might even decide to stay and get treatment. Call several to compare them—not every program is right for every person. These programs are listed for informational purposes only. Being listed here does not imply an endorsement for any particular program or its personnel.

Brown University School of Medicine
Butler Hospital
345 Blackstone Boulevard
Providence, RI 02906
Phone: (401) 455-6209
Website: *www.butler.org/opt.htm*
Evaluation and treatment for OCD and TS.

Duke University Program in Child and Adolescent Anxiety Disorders
Box 3527
Duke University Medical Center
Durham, NC 27710
Phone: (919) 684-4950
Website: *www2.mc.duke.edu/depts/psychiatry/pcaad*
Inpatient and outpatient evaluation and treatment of childhood OCD and
    PANDAS.

Eastern Pennsylvania Psychiatric Institute (EPPI)
Medical College of Pennsylvania
Dept. of Psychiatry
3200 Henry Avenue
Philadelphia, PA 19129
Phone: (215) 842-4010
Website: *www.mcphu.edu/*

McLean Hospital—Obsessive-Compulsive Disorders Institute
Hill House
115 Mill Street
Belmont, MA 02478
Phone: (617) 855-3279
Website: *www.mclean.harvard.edu/ocdinstitute.htm*
Intensive residential care for those 17 years or older.

New Hampshire OCD Inpatient Program
Hampstead Hospital
218 East Road
Hampstead, NH 03841
Phone: (603) 329-5311

Oregon Health Sciences University
OCD Specialty Clinic
3181 SW Sam Jackson Park Road
Portland, OR 97210
Phone: (503) 494-6176

Rogers Memorial Hospital
34700 Valley Road
Ocohomowoc, WI 53066

Phone: (800) 767-4411
          (414) 646-4411
Website: *www.rogersmemorial/org/ocinfo*
Residential and day treatment programs.

Sierra Vista Hospital
OCD Program
8001 Bruceville Road
Sacramento, CA 95823
Phone: (916) 423-2000
Partial hospitalization program.

St. Louis Behavioral Medicine Institute
Anxiety Disorder Center
1129 Macklind Avenue
St. Louis, MO 63110
Phone: (314) 534-0200
Website: www.*info@slbmi.com*
Inpatient, outpatient, and home-based care available.

Stanford Medical Center
OCD Research Unit Clinic
Department of Psychiatry
Stanford, CA 94305
Phone: (650) 723-5154
Medication and research protocols.

UCLA—Neuropsychiatric Institute
Child and Adolescent OCD and Anxiety Program
740 Westwood Plaza – Rm. 68-251A
Los Angeles, CA 90024
Phone: (310) 825-0122
Website: *www.npi.ucla.edu/caap/contact.htm*
Evaluation and short-term treatment for childhood OCD, TTM, TS, and tic
    disorders.

University of Illinois – School of Medicine
Institute for Juvenile Research
Pediatric OCD and Tic Disorder Program
907 South Walked MC 747

Chicago, Il 60612
Phone: (312) 413-9093

Western Psychiatric Institute and Clinic
University of Pittsburgh Medical Center
Center for the Treatment of OCD
3811 O'Hara Street
Pittsburgh, PA 15213
Phone: (412) 624-4466
Website: *www.wpic.pitt.edu/*

Yale Adult OCD Clinic
Connecticut Mental Health Center
Yale University School of Medicine – Department of Psychiatry
Phone: (888) 622-CNRU
              (203) 974-7543
Website: *http://info.med.yale.edu/psych/cnru/ocd.html*
Free inpatient and outpatient care for OCD is available to those 18 and over.

Yale Child Study TS/OCD Clinic
Yale-New Haven Hospital
Phone: (203) 785-5880
Website: *www.info.med.yale.edu/chldsty/tsocd.htm*
Inpatient and outpatient care

The following program specializes in the treatment of BDD:

Body Image Program
Butler Hospital
345 Blackstone Boulevard
Providence, RI 02906
Phone: (401) 455-6466
              (401) 455-6613
Website: *www.butler.org/bdd.htm*
Free evaluations are available, as well as treatment for adults and adolescents
    with BDD.

OBSESSIVE-COMPULSIVE DISORDER
SYMPTOM CHECKLIST

Please rate the following symptoms in terms of their severity. Rate them from 0 to 6 according to their current severity and their greatest severity in the past. 0 represents no problem whatsoever and 6 represents the most severe possible.

Only endorse items which apply to you due to: (1) their having been performed excessively, (2) their undesirability, (3) your attempts to resist, and (4) their having interfered with your functioning in some way.

Please note that an overlap exists between some categories, as certain types of obsessions and compulsions fit into more than one.

A. AGGRESSIVE OBSESSIONS/IMPULSIONS

Thoughts of:	*Current*	*Past*
Actively harming others intentionally	_____	_____
Harming yourself intentionally	_____	_____
Going crazy and harming others	_____	_____
Violent or repulsive images	_____	_____
Blurting out obscenities or insults	_____	_____
Writing obscenities	_____	_____
Acting out in antisocial ways in public	_____	_____
Having insulted or offended others	_____	_____
Acting on impulses to rob, steal from, take advantage of, or cheat others	_____	_____
Rejecting, divorcing, or being unfaithful to a loved one	_____	_____
Deliberately hoping that others will have accidents, become ill or die	_____	_____
Other _____	_____	_____

B. SEXUAL OBSESSIONS/IMPULSIONS

Thoughts of:	*Current*	*Past*
Forbidden or perverse images or impulses	_____	_____
Sex with children	_____	_____
Sex with animals	_____	_____
Incest	_____	_____
Being homosexual or acting homosexually	_____	_____
Doubt about your sexual identity	_____	_____
Sex with religious figures or celebrities	_____	_____
Acting sexually toward others	_____	_____
Doubt about possibly having acted sexually toward others	_____	_____
Doubt about possibly having been acted upon sexually by others	_____	_____
Other _____	_____	_____

C. CONTAMINATION OBSESSIONS

Centering around harm coming to self _____ others _____

Fearful thoughts of:	*Current*	*Past*
Bodily waste or secretions, e.g. feces, urine, saliva, perspiration, blood, semen	_____	_____
Dirt or grime	_____	_____
Germs, or viruses	_____	_____
Environmental contaminants (asbestos, lead, radiation, toxic wastes, etc.)	_____	_____

Household chemicals (cleansers, solvents, _____ _____
drain openers, insecticides)

Auto exhaust or other poisonous gases _____ _____

Garbage, refuse, or their containers _____ _____

Grease or greasy items _____ _____

Sticky substances _____ _____

Medication, or the effects of having _____ _____
ingested medication in the past

Your food or drink having been adulterated _____ _____
or tampered with by others

Broken glass _____ _____

Poisonous plants _____ _____

Contact with live animals _____ _____

Contact with dead animals _____ _____

Contact with insects _____ _____

Contact with unclean or shabby _____ _____
looking people

Contracting an unspecified illness _____ _____

Contracting a specific illness _____ _____

Hospitals, doctor's offices and health care _____ _____
workers

Spreading illness to, or contaminating others _____ _____

Leaving or spreading an essence or trace of _____ _____
yourself behind on objects or others

Being contaminated by thoughts of harm _____ _____
happening to yourself or others

A specific person, or place felt to be _____ _____
contaminated in some nonspecific way

Being contaminated by certain words _____ _____

Being contaminated by the names of _____ _____
certain illnesses

	Current	Past
Being contaminated by seeing an ill or disabled person	_____	_____
Being contaminated by the memory of a person who has died	_____	_____
Being contaminated by certain numbers or their multiples	_____	_____
Being contaminated by certain colors	_____	_____
Your belongings being contaminated by having been present or used when something unpleasant was occurring	_____	_____
Being contaminated by evil or the devil	_____	_____
Other _____	_____	_____

D. RELIGIOUS OBSESSIONS

Thoughts of:	*Current*	*Past*
Being deliberately sinful or blasphemous	_____	_____
Doubtful thoughts as to whether you acted sinfully or blasphemously in the past	_____	_____
Fears of having acted sinfully or unethically	_____	_____
Doubting your faith or beliefs	_____	_____
Unacceptable thoughts about religious figures, religion, or deities	_____	_____
Thoughts of being possessed	_____	_____
Thoughts of having to be perfectly religious	_____	_____
Other _____	_____	_____

E. OBSESSIONS OF HARM, DANGER, LOSS, OR EMBARRASSMENT

Centering around harm coming to self _____ others _____

Thoughts of:	*Current*	*Past*
Having an accident, illness or being injured	_____	_____
An accident, illness or injury happening to someone else	_____	_____
Accidentally losing control and harming others	_____	_____
Causing harm to others through your own negligence or carelessness	_____	_____
Never being able to be happy, or never being able to get what you want in life	_____	_____
Doubt about whether you somehow harmed or injured others in the past	_____	_____
Being deliberately harmed by others	_____	_____
Being rejected by a loved one	_____	_____
Being cheated or taken advantage of by others	_____	_____
Having somehow cheated or taken advantage of others	_____	_____
Having insulted or offended others	_____	_____
Objects in the environment having been moved or changed in unexplainable ways	_____	_____
Being trapped in an unsatisfactory life or relationship	_____	_____
Being looked at or noticed by others in a critical way	_____	_____
Acting inappropriately in public	_____	_____
Your own mortality	_____	_____
Your children not being your own	_____	_____
Other _____	_____	_____

F. SUPERSTITIOUS OR MAGICAL OBSESSIONS

Thoughts of:	Current	Past
Having bad luck	_____	_____
Bad luck happening to someone else	_____	_____
Lucky or unlucky numbers or their multiples	_____	_____
Lucky or unlucky colors	_____	_____
Lucky or unlucky objects or possessions	_____	_____
The possibility that thinking or hearing of bad events can make them occur to yourself or others	_____	_____
Certain words names, or images being able to cause bad luck	_____	_____
Certain actions or behaviors being able to cause bad luck	_____	_____
Being possessed	_____	_____
Places, objects or people associated with unlucky occasions causing bad luck by contact	_____	_____
The need to perform certain activities a special number of times	_____	_____
Lucky or unlucky mental arrangements of things	_____	_____
Other _____	_____	_____

G. BODY-FOCUSED OBSESSIONS

Thoughts that:	Current	Past
Parts of your body are ugly or disfigured in some way	_____	_____

Your body has scars or marks	_____	_____
Question how certain parts of your body work or function	_____	_____
A part of your body does not work properly or functions differently than it used to	_____	_____
Parts of your body are asymmetrical	_____	_____
Part(s) of your body is (are) too large or small	_____	_____
You are overweight or underweight	_____	_____
You will choke or vomit accidentally	_____	_____
You are going bald or have thinning hair	_____	_____
Part(s) of your body is (are) aging prematurely	_____	_____
Clothing does not fit certain parts of your body correctly (too loose or too tight)	_____	_____
Other _____	_____	_____

H. PERFECTIONISTIC OBSESSIONS

Thoughts of:	*Current*	*Past*
Questioning whether you have said, done, or thought certain things perfectly	_____	_____
Wanting to do, think, or say everything (or certain things) perfectly	_____	_____
Wanting to have a perfect appearance	_____	_____
Wanting your clothes to fit perfectly	_____	_____
Questioning whether you have told the truth perfectly	_____	_____
Making or keeping your home or possessions perfectly clean or pristine	_____	_____

Ordering things or making them
symmetrical

Wanting to know everything about a
specific subject or topic

Other _____

I. NEUTRAL OBSESSIONS

Thoughts of: *Current*   *Past*

Sounds, words, or music

Nonsense or trivial images

Counting for no special reason

Repetitive questions for which there are
no answers or which are unimportant

The excessive awareness of your own
thought processes

The excessive awareness of specific things
in your environment (sounds, colors,
objects, persons, etc.)

Other _____

J. DECONTAMINATION COMPULSIONS

For the purpose of protecting yourself _____ others _____

                                              Current   *Past*

Washing your hands ritually and/or
excessively

Bathing, or showering ritually and/or
excessively

	Current	Past
Disinfecting yourself	_____	_____
Disinfecting others or having them disinfect themselves	_____	_____
Disinfecting your environment or your possessions	_____	_____
Washing or cleaning items before they can be used or allowed in the house	_____	_____
Changing or having others change clothing frequently to avoid contamination	_____	_____
Discarding or destroying potentially contaminated items	_____	_____
Wiping, blowing on, or shaking out items before using them	_____	_____
Avoidance of certain foods which may be contaminated	_____	_____
Avoidance of specific persons, places, or objects which might be contaminated	_____	_____
Using gloves, paper, etc. to touch things	_____	_____
Having family or friends perform any of the above on your behalf	_____	_____
Performing, reciting, or thinking ritually to avoid or remove contamination	_____	_____
Excessive questioning of others about contamination	_____	_____
Other _____	_____	_____

K. HOARDING/COLLECTING COMPULSIONS

Saving things for yourself _____ others _____

	Current	Past
Saving broken, irreparable, or useless items	_____	_____

Buying excessive quantities of items beyond
an amount needed for reasonable usage   _____   _____

Retrieving from or searching through your
own or other people's trash   _____   _____

Inability to throw things out due to fear of
accidentally throwing important items away   _____   _____

Going to excessive lengths (including
extreme self-denial) to save money   _____   _____

Saving excessive quantities of informational
matter (newspapers, old lists, magazines,
junk mail, etc.)   _____   _____

Saving items simply because they belong to
yourself or loved ones   _____   _____

Having to own complete collections of
certain things, even if not important   _____   _____

Keeping extensive lists or records of certain
things   _____   _____

Other _____   _____   _____

L. CHECKING COMPULSIONS

To protect yourself _____ others _____

Done ritualistically _____ nonritualistically _____

Doublechecking:	Current	Past
Doors and windows	_____	_____
Water taps	_____	_____
Electrical appliances	_____	_____
Stoves	_____	_____
Light switches	_____	_____
Car doors, windows, headlights, etc.	_____	_____

Items to be mailed or mailboxes   _____   _____

Whereabouts of sharp objects   _____   _____

Extinguished cigarettes or matches   _____   _____

The arrangement of objects for symmetry   _____   _____
or perfection

Surfaces or objects for marks or damage   _____   _____

Objects, surfaces, or your own body parts   _____   _____
for contamination

Your own words or actions (to verify that   _____   _____
you did not act inappropriately)

Your own thoughts to determine if they   _____   _____
are (or were) appropriate

Your own thoughts to determine if they   _____   _____
are really obsessions or not

Your writing for obscenities or errors   _____   _____

Driving situations (to verify that you did not _____   _____
hit someone or something with a vehicle)

Your own or another's vital signs or body   _____   _____
(for signs of illness)

For possible hazards to children   _____   _____

The possibility that unspecified harm will   _____   _____
occur to yourself or others

The possibility that you may have harmed   _____   _____
yourself or others accidentally or through
negligence

Whether or not someone has acted   _____   _____
sexually toward you

Whether or not you have acted sexually   _____   _____
toward someone else

Whether your own thoughts or reactions   _____   _____
indicate that you are sexually attracted
to others in ways which are inappropriate
to you

For prowlers (in closets, under bed, etc.)   _____   _____

For objects dropped accidentally   _____   _____

That valuable items were not accidentally   _____   _____
thrown away

Container tops or lids for closure   _____   _____

That one did not injure another   _____   _____
through negligence

Your body for symmetry or perfection   _____   _____

Your appearance or grooming for   _____   _____
symmetry or perfection

Your own memory (by asking yourself   _____   _____
or others)

That you have made the perfect   _____   _____
decision

What you have read   _____   _____

Your paperwork or writing   _____   _____
for errors

That you have not touched something   _____   _____
hazardous or contaminated

Yourself or your environment for signs   _____   _____
of contamination

For sources of dangerous gases   _____   _____
or fumes

That you have not ingested foods which   _____   _____
are unhealthy or forbidden

Your food or drink for drugs or   _____   _____
chemicals put there by others or
by accident

Your phone for   _____   _____
eavesdroppers

Other _____   _____   _____

M. MAGICAL/UNDOING COMPULSIONS

To prevent harm to yourself _____ others _____

	Current	Past
Repetitive praying or crossing yourself	_____	_____
Counting up to or beyond certain numbers	_____	_____
Reciting or thinking of certain words, names, sounds, phrases, numbers, or images	_____	_____
Moving your body or gesturing in a special way	_____	_____
Having to mentally arrange certain images numbers, words, names, etc.	_____	_____
Having to physically arrange objects in your environment in special ways	_____	_____
Stepping in special ways or on special spots when walking	_____	_____
Repeating an activity with a good thought or image in mind	_____	_____
Performing actions or movements in reverse	_____	_____
Washing off ideas or thoughts	_____	_____
Rethinking thoughts	_____	_____
Thinking thoughts in reverse	_____	_____
Having to eat or not eat certain foods	_____	_____
Having to reread words, sentences, or pages	_____	_____
Repeating behaviors a special number of times	_____	_____
Performing behaviors an odd or even number of times	_____	_____

	Current	Past
Performing behaviors at special times or on particular dates	_____	_____
Repeating your own or other's words	_____	_____
Repetitively apologizing or asking for forgiveness	_____	_____
Gazing at or thinking of certain numbers or words to cancel others out	_____	_____
Gazing at objects in a special way	_____	_____
Touching certain things in a special way or a particular number of times	_____	_____
Other _____	_____	_____

N. PERFECTIONISTIC COMPULSIONS

To prevent harm to yourself _____ to others _____

To prevent feelings of dissatisfaction or unease _____

Having to:	*Current*	*Past*
Arrange objects or possessions in special or symmetrical ways	_____	_____
Keep new possessions unused and in perfect condition	_____	_____
Buy only items which are perfect	_____	_____
Keep your home or living space perfectly clean and orderly	_____	_____
Avoid using rooms, closets, drawers, etc., once they have been arranged perfectly	_____	_____
Keep your possessions perfectly neat and clean	_____	_____
Say things perfectly	_____	_____

Remember or memorize things perfectly
or in a special order   _____   _____

Read or reread every word in a document
to avoid missing anything   _____   _____

Know or learn everything about a particular
subject   _____   _____

Keep remaking decisions to ensure picking
the perfect one   _____   _____

Rewrite or write over numbers or letters
to make them perfect   _____   _____

Perform ordinary activities extra slowly
to get them done perfectly   _____   _____

Think of certain things perfectly
or exactly   _____   _____

Be perfectly religious   _____   _____

Punish or penalize yourself when you
do not behave perfectly   _____   _____

Be perfectly self-denying   _____   _____

Look at certain things in the environment
in a special or perfect way (visually tracing   _____   _____
or lining them up, etc.)

Be perfectly aware of everything going on
around you in your environment   _____   _____

Tell the truth or be perfectly honest   _____   _____

Perfectly confess about all your thoughts or
behaviors to others   _____   _____

Confess to having done wrongful
things whether you have done them   _____   _____
or not

Make one's appearance perfect (e.g. hair,
nails, clothes, makeup, etc.)   _____   _____

Cut your hair (to make it perfect or
symmetrical)   _____   _____

	Current	Past
Perform activities a certain number of times until they feel just right	_____	_____
Keep extensive lists or records of certain things	_____	_____
Only perform certain activities at perfect times	_____	_____
Other _____	_____	_____

O. COUNTING COMPULSIONS

To prevent harm to yourself _____ to others _____

Having to count:	Current	Past
While performing certain activities	_____	_____
To ensure an activity has been done a certain number of times or for a long enough duration	_____	_____
To ensure that an activity has been done an odd or even number of times	_____	_____
The numbers of objects or occurrences of certain things in the environment	_____	_____
Up to or beyond certain numbers	_____	_____
Simply to count (unconnected with any special idea or activity)	_____	_____
The occurrences of certain body functions (e.g., breathing, steps, etc.)	_____	_____
Other _____	_____	_____

P. TOUCHING OR MOVEMENT COMPULSIONS

To prevent harm to yourself _____ others _____

Done ritualistically _____ nonritualistically _____

Having to:	Current	Past
Gesture or pose in a special way	_____	_____
Look or glance at something in a special way	_____	_____
Move in symmetrical or special ways	_____	_____
Having to step in special ways or on special spots when walking	_____	_____
Tic, twitch, or grimace in a special way	_____	_____
Move in special ways while carrying out certain activities	_____	_____
Reverse movements you have just made	_____	_____
Repeat certain activities (e.g., sitting down, getting up, passing through doorways, or by certain locations) a special number of times, or until they feel right	_____	_____
Touch furniture before sitting down or standing up	_____	_____
Touch doors or drawers before opening or closing them	_____	_____
Touch the edges or certain parts of things	_____	_____
Touch doorways before walking through them	_____	_____
Touch things a certain number of times	_____	_____
Touch things in special patterns	_____	_____
Touch, move, or handle possessions a certain way before using them	_____	_____
Other _____	_____	_____

Q. SELF-MUTILATIVE COMPULSIONS

	Current	*Past*
Cutting or scratching yourself	_____	_____
Burning yourself	_____	_____
Poking yourself in the eyes	_____	_____
Biting yourself (e.g., insides of cheeks)	_____	_____
Other _____	_____	_____

R. BODY-FOCUSED COMPULSIONS

	Current	*Past*
Checking your appearance in the mirror for problems or imperfections	_____	_____
Checking your appearance or physical reaction to assure yourself about your sexual identity	_____	_____
Checking the way your body works	_____	_____
Questioning others directly or indirectly about your appearance	_____	_____
Seeking frequent medical consultations to check on your appearance or the workings of your body	_____	_____
Having to have your appearance improved surgically	_____	_____
Cutting your hair to excess or for long periods of time to make it perfect	_____	_____
Picking or squeezing pimples or blemishes to make your skin perfect	_____	_____
Other _____	_____	_____

S. GROOMING IMPULSIONS

	Current	*Past*
Hair pulling (from head, eyebrows, eyelashes, pubic area, body, etc.)	_____	_____
Skin picking or biting	_____	_____
Nail or cuticle biting, picking, or cutting	_____	_____
Picking or squeezing pimples or blemishes for the sensation of it	_____	_____
Other _____	_____	_____

T. MENTAL COMPULSIONS

Having to:	*Current*	*Past*
Make mental maps of places	_____	_____
Memorize facts or information	_____	_____
Make mental lists or arrangements	_____	_____
Know or learn everything about a particular subject	_____	_____
Keep reviewing past situations to try to remember or understand them	_____	_____
Think specific thoughts in special ways	_____	_____
Think about specific topics	_____	_____
Create specific mental images or pictures	_____	_____
Repeat your own or someone else's words in your mind	_____	_____
Think of sequences of special numbers or words	_____	_____
Rethink specific thoughts	_____	_____

Think certain thoughts in reverse   _____   _____

Other _____   _____   _____

U. PROTECTIVE COMPULSIONS

To protect yourself _____ others _____

Repeatedly:	*Current*	*Past*
Questioning others, or your own memory, to determine if you have harmed or insulted someone (recently or in the past)	_____	_____
Checking your own memory to determine if you came to harm in the past	_____	_____
Recording and collecting information about past events to help in determining if harm occurred to yourself or others in the past	_____	_____
Collecting and removing objects from the environment that could harm others (i.e., tacks, razor blades, nails, matches, lit cigarettes, glass, etc.)	_____	_____
Checking on the whereabouts of others to be certain that harm has not occurred to them	_____	_____
Trying to limit the activities of others to prevent harm from happening to them	_____	_____
Warning others repeatedly of potential harm or danger	_____	_____
Asking others if you will be safe or if things will turn out well for you	_____	_____
Asking others if they will be safe or if things will turn out well for them	_____	_____
Confessing to having done things you believe may have harmed others	_____	_____
Other _____	_____	_____

TRICHOTILLOMANIA, SKIN PICKING, NAIL BITING SYMPTOM CHECKLIST

Age: _____   Sex: M   F

Level of education: _____

Currently employed: Y   N

Occupation: _____

Do you   _____   pull out your hair
              _____   pick your skin
              _____   bite your skin
              _____   bite or pick your nails

Age when habit(s) first began: _____

Have you ever gone for help for your habit(s)?   Y   N

       Age when you first went for help: _____
       How many different times have you gone for help? _____
       Were any treatments helpful?   Y   N
       Which one(s) helped? _____
                                _____
                                _____
                                _____
                                _____

Have you ever tried any solutions on your own which were helpful?

Y   N   What were they? _____
                                _____
                                _____
                                _____
                                _____

Have you ever abused _____ drugs?
_____ alcohol?

Do you believe it was in response to your habit(s)?   Y   N

Do you have any blood relatives who have similar habits?

      Y   N   Unsure

      Does either parent pull/pick/bite?   Y   N   Mother or Father

      Indicate how many of the following relatives pull/pick/bite:
      _____ brothers
      _____ sisters

Maternal		*Paternal*
_____	grandfather	_____
_____	grandmother	_____
_____	uncles	_____
_____	aunts	_____

Has the picking/pulling/biting ever gone away on its own for a period of time?
Y   N

If "Yes" how long? _____

Have you ever been diagnosed with any other psychological problems?
Y   N

What were they? _____
_____
_____
_____

Do you have visible hair loss or other damage?   Y   N

Do you have bleeding or injured fingertips?   Y   N

Have you caused scarring on your face or body?   Y   N

For hair pullers:

From what areas of your body do you, or have you pulled hairs?

	Past	*Present*
head	___	___
eyebrows	___	___
eyelashes	___	___
beard	___	___
mustache	___	___
torso	___	___
arms	___	___
legs	___	___
pubic area	___	___

For skin pickers and nail biters:

From what areas of your body do you pick or bite skin or nails?

	Past	*Present*
cuticles	___	___
fingers	___	___
scalp	___	___
face	___	___
arms	___	___
legs	___	___
feet	___	___
toes	___	___

Do you ___ feel the urge to pull/pick/bite before you actually do?
___ pull/pick/bite without thinking about it or noticing?

Do you pull ___ occasionally
___ most days
___ every day

Circle the estimated number of pulling/picking/biting episodes per day:

1–5   6–10   11–15   16–20   21–25   26–30   over 30

For hair pullers:

Circle the estimated number of hairs pulled on a daily basis:

0–10   11–20   21–30   31–40   41–50   51–60

61–70   71–80   81–90   91–100   over 100

What is the average estimated time you spend per episode? _____

In which locations do the majority of the pulling/picking/biting episodes take place? (circle all that apply)

car   bedroom   kitchen   living room   bathroom

office   public places   family room   classroom

other _____

Are you most likely to pull when   ___   others are present
                                     ___   you are alone

During which activities do the majority of pulling/picking/biting episodes take place?

(number the ones that apply in order of where the most
pulling/picking/biting takes place)

Pull	Pick	Bite	
___	___	___	watching TV
___	___	___	listening to music
___	___	___	lying in bed
___	___	___	talking on the phone
___	___	___	working at a desk
___	___	___	reading
___	___	___	driving or riding in the car
___	___	___	doing homework
___	___	___	using the toilet

—	—	—	putting on makeup
—	—	—	fixing your hair
—	—	—	working at the computer
—	—	—	standing in front of a mirror
—	—	—	eating
—	—	—	riding in an elevator
—	—	—	sitting in class
—	—	—	riding on a bus or train
—	—	—	while on the job
—	—	—	any activity involving _____
—	—	—	other _____

For hair pullers:

Do you pull   1. ____   any hairs
               2. ____   ones that feel or look "just right" for pulling
                       (but cannot say exactly why)
               3. ____   only ones that feel as if they don't belong
               4. ____   (if you pull from the scalp) only ones from very
                       specific spots
               5. ____   A combination of the above (circle those that
                       apply below)

1   2   3   4

Are you more likely to pull hairs:

_____ when you are looking at them directly or in a mirror
_____ when you cannot see them or are in the dark, but can feel them
_____ both of the above

What specific qualities cause you to pull particular hairs?
(number the ones that apply in the order of importance to pulling)

    Visual qualities (qualities you can see)

         ____   color
         ____   split ends
         ____   curliness

___ location
___ length
___ other _____

Tactile qualities (qualities you can feel)

___ curliness
___ length
___ texture
___ location
___ other _____

What do you do with the hairs once they have been pulled?
(number the ones that apply in the order of frequency which you do them)

___ swallow them
___ chew them
___ brush them across my lips or cheek
___ throw them away
___ tie them in a knot
___ bite off the root bulb at the bottom
___ wind them around my finger
___ save them
___ play with them
___ break them
___ roll them in a ball
___ perform a ritual or ceremony with them
___ other _____

For nail biters:

What do you do with the nails once you have bitten them off?

___ swallow them
___ throw them away
___ chew them
___ play with them
___ save them
___ perform a ritual or ceremony with them
___ other _____

What moods or states generally lead to pulling/picking/biting?
(number the ones that apply in the order in which they affect you)

_____ anxious
_____ depressed
_____ angry
_____ tired
_____ relaxed
_____ rushed
_____ bored
_____ deep in thought or concentrating
_____ busy with some activity
_____ daydreaming
_____ close to falling asleep
_____ just waking up
_____ feeling distant or removed from things
_____ other _____

During what times of the day are you most likely to pull/pick?
(number the ones that apply in the order in which they apply to you)

_____ morning
_____ afternoon
_____ evening
_____ during the night

Do you use any implements to pull hairs or pick your skin?
Please list them in the order of frequency with which you use them.

_____
_____
_____
_____
_____
_____

What is your mood or state after you have pulled/picked/bitten?

_____ relieved
_____ angry
_____ anxious
_____ depressed

_____ relaxed
_____ satisfied
_____ distant or removed from what is going on
_____ other _____

For hair pullers:

What methods have you used to cover or hide areas from which you have pulled hairs?

_____ wig
_____ kerchief
_____ hat
_____ false eyelashes
_____ eyebrow pencil
_____ cut other hairs very short
_____ shaved whole head
_____ hair piece
_____ combed hair over it
_____ spray on hair
_____ not going out where anyone can see me

For hair pullers:

What reasons have you given others for your missing hair?

_____ I'm going bald
_____ I have alopecia
_____ I had an accident
_____ It was a side effect of medication
_____ It was a side effect of cancer treatment
_____ It was a reaction to a hair treatment
_____ It was an allergic reaction
_____ I tell them I don't know
_____ I won't discuss it with anyone
_____ other _____

For skin pickers:

What methods have you used to cover or hide areas which you
have damaged through skin picking?

_____ Band-Aids
_____ cover makeup
_____ covered with clothing
_____ not going out where anyone can see me
_____ other _____

For nail biters:

What methods have you used to cover or hide areas of your hands that
you have damaged through nail biting?

_____ Band-Aids
_____ gloves
_____ kept hands in pockets
_____ other _____

Have you caused any other physical problems for yourself as a result
of your habits?

_____ neck pain
_____ wrist strain
_____ elbow problems
_____ back problems
_____ calluses (hair pulling)
_____ scars
_____ other _____

How does (did) your family react to your hair pulling?

_____ punished me
_____ ridiculed me

_____ sympathized
_____ got angry
_____ ignored it
_____ took me for help
_____ told me I'd grow out of it
_____ got upset
_____ threatened me
_____ denied it was a real problem
_____ other _____

Has your problem ever caused you

_____ to be unemployed? How long? _____
_____ to lose a job?
_____ to lose a relationship?
_____ to not even try at certain job opportunities?
_____ to simply avoid relationships?

On a scale of 0 to 7, rate your expectation for recovery.
(0 = do not expect to recover, 7 = totally believe I will recover)
Please circle below:

0   1   2   3   4   5   6   7

OFFICIAL DSM-IV DIAGNOSES

The DSM-IV is considered to be the "bible" of psychiatry and gives the official definitions of all recognized mental disorders and dysfunctions.

OBSESSIVE-COMPULSIVE DISORDER (CODE 300.3)

A. "Obsessions" as defined by:

(1) Recurrent and persistent thoughts, impulses, or images that are experienced, at some time during the disturbance, as intrusive and inappropriate and that cause marked anxiety or distress

(2) the thoughts, impulses, or images are not simply excessive worries about real-life problems

(3) the person attempts to ignore or suppress such thoughts, impulses, or images, or to neutralize them with some other thought or action

(4) the person recognizes that the obsessional thoughts, impulses, or images are a product of his or her own mind (not imposed from without as in thought insertion)

"Compulsions" as defined by:

(1) Repetitive behaviors (e.g., hand washing, ordering, checking) or mental acts (e.g., praying, counting, repeating words silently) that the person feels driven to perform in response to an obsession, or according to rules that must be applied rigidly

(2) the behaviors or mental acts are aimed at preventing or reducing distress or preventing some dreaded event or situation; however, these behaviors or mental acts either are not connected in a realistic way with what they are designed to neutralize or prevent, or are clearly excessive

B. At some point during the course of the disorder, the person has recognized that the obsessions or compulsions are excessive or unreasonable. *Note:* This does not apply to children.

C. The obsessions or compulsions cause marked distress, are time consuming (take more than one hour a day), or significantly interfere with the person's normal routine, occupation (or academic) functioning, or usual social activities or relationships.

D. If another Axis disorder is present, the content of the obsessions or compulsions is not restricted to it (e.g., preoccupation with food in the presence of an Eating Disorder; hair pulling in the presence of Trichotillomania; concern with appearance in the presence of Body Dysmorphic Disorder; preoccupation with drugs in the presence of a Substance Use disorder; preoccupation with having a serious illness in the presence of Hypochondriasis; preoccupation with sexual urges or fantasies in the presence of a Paraphilia; or guilty ruminations in the presence of Major Depressive Disorder).

E. The disturbance is not due to the direct physiological effects of a substance (e.g., a drug of abuse, a medication) or a general medical condition.

Specify if:
   With Poor Insight: if, for most of the time during the current episode, the person does not recognize that the obsessions and compulsions are excessive or unreasonable.

BODY DYSMORPHIC DISORDER (CODE 300.7)

A. Preoccupation with some imagined defect in appearance in a normal-appearing person. If a slight physical anomaly is present, the person's concern is grossly excessive.

B. The belief in the defect is not of delusional intensity, as in Delusional Disorder, Somatic Type (i.e., the person can acknowledge the possibility that he or she may be exaggerating the extent of the defect or that there may be no defect at all).

C. Occurrence not exclusively during the course of Anorexia Nervosa or Transsexualism.

TRICHOTILLOMANIA (CODE 312.39)

A. Recurrent failure to resist impulses to pull out one's own hair, resulting in noticeable hair loss.

B. Increasing sense of tension immediately before pulling out the hair.

C. Gratification or a sense of relief when pulling out the hair.

D. No association with a preexisting inflammation of the skin, and not a response to a delusion or a hallucination.

OCSD READING AND VIEWING LIST

The following is a list of publications and videos you may find helpful in your own research on OCSDs.

RECOMMENDED BOOKS FOR SELF-HELP

- *Alone in the Crowd,* Joe H. Vaughan (order from the author at (913)-384-6966).

- *Blink, Blink, Clop, Clop, Why Do We Do Things We Can't Stop: An OCD Storybook,* E. Katia Moritz, Ph.D., and Jennifer Jablonsky, Child's Work/Child's Play, Secaucus, New Jersey, 1998. A book about OCD written for children. Can be ordered by phone at (800) 962-1141.

- *The Boy Who Couldn't Stop Washing,* Judith Rapoport, M.D., Penguin Books, New York, 1989. This is the first notable book written for people with OCD. Available in paperback.

- *The Broken Mirror,* Katharine A. Phillips, M.D., Oxford University Press, New York, 1996. A comprehensive guide to Body Dysmorphic Disorder.

- *The Doubting Disease,* Joseph W. Ciarrochi, Paulist Press, Mahwah, New Jersey, 1995. Focusing on obsessive moral scrupulosity. Available in paperback.

- *Drug Treatment of OCD in Children and Adolescents,* J. Jay Fruehling, Obsessive Compulsive Foundation, 1997.

- *Funny, You Don't Look Crazy,* Constance H. Foster, Dilligaf Publishing, (64 Court Street, Ellsworth, Maine 04605, 1993.

- *Getting Control,* Lee Baer, Ph.D., Little, Brown & Co., Boston., 1991. A self-help guide. Available in paperback.

- *Kids Like Me,* Connie Foster, Solvay Pharmaceuticals, 1997. A children's book about five children with OCD.

- *Learning to Live With Body Dysmorphic Disorder,* Katharine A. Phillips, M.D., Barbara Livingston Van Noppen, MSW, and Leslie Shapiro, MSW, Obsessive-Compulsive Foundation, 1997. An informative pamphlet.

- *Obsessive-Compulsive Anonymous (2nd ed.),* Obsessive-Compulsive Anonymous, New Hyde Park, New York, 1999. The original guide for those interested in the 12-Step approach. Available in paperback. Can be purchased through OCA (see chapter 13 for address).

- *Obsessive-Compulsive Disorder: A Survival Guide for Family and Friends*, Roy C., Obsessive Compulsive Anonymous, New Hyde Park, New York, 1993. Can be purchased through OCA (see chapter 13 for address).

- *Polly's Magic Games*, Constance H. Foster, Dilligaf Publishing (64 Court Street, Ellsworth, Maine 04605), 1994. A book for children.

- *The Secret Problem*, Chris Weaver, Shrink-Rap Press (P.O. Box 187, Concord West, New South Wales, 2138, Australia), 1994. A book for children.

- *Stop Obsessing*, Edna B. Foa, Ph.D., and Reid Wilson, Ph.D., Bantam Books, New York. 1991. A self-help guide. Available in paperback.

- *Teaching the Tiger*, Marilyn P. Dornbush, Ph.D., and Sheryl K. Pratt, M.Ed., Hope Press, 1995. An informative work for those who teach children with OCD, ADHD, and TS.

- *Tormenting Thoughts and Secret Rituals*, Ian Osborn, M.D., Pantheon Books, New York, 1998. A self-help guide. Available in paperback.

- *When Once Is Not Enough*, Gail Steketee, Ph.D., and Kerrin White, M.D., New Harbinger Publications, Oakland, California. 1990. A self-help guide. Available in paperback.

- *When Perfect Isn't Good Enough*, Martin M. Anthony, Ph.D., and Richard P. Swinson, M.D., New Harbinger Publications, Oakland, California, 1998. A self-help manual to aid in overcoming perfectionism. Available in paperback.

Note: Many of the above books may be purchased from the OC Foundation (see chapter 13 for address).

- *Feathers*, Renee Trachtenberg, 1998. A beautifully illustrated story for children with TTM. Can be ordered through the Trichotillomania Learning Center, Santa Cruz, California.

The following four booklets can be ordered from the Madison Institute of Medicine, Obsessive-Compulsive Information Center, 7617 Mineral Point Road, Suite 300, Madison, Wisconsin 53717 (608) 827-2470.

- *Obsessive-Compulsive Disorder: A Guide*, 1997.

- *Obsessive-Compulsive Disorder in Children and Adolescents: A Guide*, 1997.

- *Trichotillomania: A Guide*, 1998.

- *Depression and Antidepressants: A Guide*, 1999.

The following two publications can be ordered from Scrupulous Anonymous, One Liguori Drive, Liguori, Missouri 63057-9999 (800) 325-9521.

- *Helps for the Scrupulous*, Russell M. Abata, C.Ss.R., S.T.D., Liguori Publications, 1994. A guide for Catholics who suffer from moral scrupulosity and religious perfectionism.
- *Understanding Scrupulosity*, Thomas M. Santa, C.Ss.R, Liguori/Triumph, 1999. A guide for Catholics with OC symptoms relating to moral scrupulosity.

A free publication is available for those who suffer from moral scrupulosity. It can be obtained at:

Scrupulous Anonymous Newsletter
Dept. SA
One Liguori Drive
Liguori, MO 63057-9999

PERSONAL ACCOUNTS OF LIFE WITH OCD

- *Just Checking: Scenes from the Life of an Obsessive-Compulsive*, Emily Colas, Pocket Books, 1998. The author's account of her life with OCD. Available in hardcover.
- *Kissing Doorknobs*, T. Spencer Hesser, Bantam Doubleday Dell Publishing, 1998. A novel about a child's OCD and its effect on the family. Ages 12 and up.
- *Passing for Normal—A Memoir of Compulsion*, Amy Wilensky, Random House, New York, 1999. A first-person account of the author's experiences in living with OCD and TS.

COGNITIVE THERAPY SELF-HELP BOOKS

- *How to Stubbornly Refuse to Make Yourself Miserable About Anything—Yes, Anything!*, Albert Ellis, Ph.D., A Lyle Stuart Book, Carol Communications, New York, 1988.
- *A New Guide to Rational Living*, Albert Ellis, Ph.D., Wilshire Book Co., North Hollywood, California, 1975.

- *Overcoming the Rating Game*, Paul Hauck, Westminster/John Knox Press, Louisville, Kentucky, 1991.
- *Think Straight, Feel Great*, Bill Borcherdt, CSW, Professional Resource Exchange, Inc., Sarasota, Florida, 1989. To order, call: 1 (800) 443-3364.
- *You Can Control Your Feelings*, Bill Borcherdt, CSW, Professional Resource Exchange, Inc., Sarasota, Florida, 1993. To order, call: 1 (800) 443-3364.

RECOMMENDED BOOKS FOR PROFESSIONALS

- *Current Treatments of Obsessive-Compulsive Disorder*, Michele Tortora Pato, M.D., and Joseph Zohar, M.D., editors, American Psychiatric Press, Washington, D.C., 1991.
- *Grief Counseling and Grief Therapy (2nd ed.)*, J. William Worden, Ph.D., Springer Publishing Company, New York, 1991.
- *Impulsivity and Compulsivity*, John M. Oldham, M.D., Eric Hollander, M.D., and Andrew E. Skodol, M.D., editors, American Psychiatric Press, Washington, D.C., 1996.
- *Obsessive-Compulsive Disorder in Children and Adolescents*, Judith L. Rapoport, M.D., editor, American Psychiatric Press, Washington, D.C., 1989.
- *OCD in Children and Adolescents: A Cognitive-Behavioral Treatment Manual*, John March, M.D., M.P.H., and Karen Muller, B.S.N., M.T.S., M.S.W., Guilford Press, New York, 1998.
- *Obsessive-Compulsive Disorder: Contemporary Issues in Treatment*, Wayne K. Goodman, M.D., Matthew V. Rudorfer, Jack D. Maser, Lawrence Erlbaum Associates, Inc., Mahwah, New Jersey, 1999.
- *Obsessive-Compulsive Disorder: Theory, Research and Treatment*, Richard P. Swinson, M.D., Martin M. Anthony, Ph.D., S. Rachman, Ph.D., and Margaret A. Richter, M.D., editors, Guilford Press, New York, 1998.
- *Obsessive-Compulsive Disorders: Practical Management (3rd ed.)*, Michael Jenike, M.D., Lee Baer, Ph.D., and William Minichiello, Ph.D., editors, Mosby-Yearbook Publishers, Chicago, 1998.
- *Obsessive-Compulsive and Related Disorders in Adults: A Comprehensive Guide*, Lorrin Koran, M.D., Cambridge University Press, New York, 1999.
- *Obsessive-Compulsive Related Disorders*, Eric Hollander, M.D., American Psychiatric Press, Washington, D.C., 1993.

- *The Psychobiology of Obsessive-Compulsive Disorder*, Joseph Zohar, M.D., Thomas R. Insel, M.D., and Steven Rasmussen, M.D., editors, Springer Publishing Company, New York, 1991.

- *Treatment of Obsessive-Compulsive Disorder*, Gail S. Steketee, Guilford Press, New York, 1993.

- *Trichotillomania*, Dan Stein, M.B., Gary Christensen, M.D., and Eric Hollander, M.D., editors, American Psychiatric Press, Washington, D.C., 1999.

VIDEOTAPES

The following videotapes may be ordered from the OC Foundation (see chapter 13 for address).

- *The Touching Tree: A Story of a Child with OCD*
- *BDD: Body Dysmorphic Disorder*—by Katharine A. Philips, M.D.
- *Obsessive-Compulsive Disorder in School Age Children*—A two-tape set plus booklets, designed to educate school personnel about OCD.
- *Step on a Crack*—by A. Lorre. Highlights the stories of six OCD sufferers, their lives, their disorders, and their treatments.
- *G.O.A.L.* (Giving Obsessive-Compulsives Another Lifestyle)—An excellent program developed with the assistance of Jonathan Grayson, Ph.D. Includes a tape and a manual that instruct how to set up and run a professionally assisted behavioral treatment group for OCD.
- *Sharing the Hope*—Relates the experiences of three different families in coping with the diagnosis and treatment of OCD in a child.

The following videotapes may be ordered from the Trichotillomania Learning Center (see chapter 13 for address).

- *Our Personal Story*—A 90-minute documentary detailing sufferers experiences in living with TTM.
- *A Desperate Act*—An extremely moving personal revelation of one woman's life and struggles with TTM, delivered in front of an audience as a performance art piece.
- *Trichotillomania: Overview and Introduction to HRT*—A two-hour workshop on HRT by Fred Penzel, Ph.D.

The following videotape may be ordered from Michael McDonald Productions at (818) 881-3211.

• *Bending the Rules: A Guide For Parents of Troubled Children*—Professional advice for dealing with children with OCD and ADHD.

GLOSSARY

ADDICTION. The strong psychological or physical need for a habit-forming substance.

ADHD. Abbreviation for Attention-Deficit/Hyperactivity Disorder.

AGGRESSIVE OBSESSIONS/IMPULSIONS. Unwanted intrusive and repetitive thoughts about harming or murdering others or harming oneself. They may also revolve around doing other aggressive antisocial acts as well, such as destroying property or creating disturbances.

ANOREXIA NERVOSA. A type of eating disorder characterized by obsessions about being overweight, and the resulting anxiety, which is relieved by compulsive self-starvation.

ANTERIOR CAPSULOTOMY. A type of brain surgery which has been used to treat severe cases of classic OCD.

ANTERIOR CINGULOTOMY. A type of brain surgery which has been used to treat severe cases of classic OCD.

ANTIANXIETY MEDICATION. Medication that can relieve the feelings that accompany anxiety (*see Benzodiazepines* below). These are sometimes called "anxiolytics" or, less accurately, "tranquilizers."

ANTIDEPRESSANT MEDICATION. Medication that can relieve the symptoms of depression. Certain antidepressants also relieve the symptoms of OCSDs as well.

ANTIPSYCHOTIC MEDICATION. Medication that can relieve the symptoms of schizophrenia or other psychotic disorders. Some of these are also used to treat TS and can sometimes help in treating OCSDs when combined with antidepressants.

ANXIETY. A state of fear accompanied by one or more of a whole set of uncomfortable physical sensations, such as sweating, trembling, increased pulse rate, difficulty breathing, light-headedness, nausea, or dizziness.

ATTENTION-DEFICIT/HYPERACTIVITY DISORDER. (ADHD) A biologically based brain disorder in which sufferers cannot maintain their focus on a single task or inhibit their own behaviors very well, resulting in impulsivity, difficulty in concentrating on and staying with tasks, and seeking stimulation. Those with ADHD are often difficult to manage behaviorally at home and in school. It is first noticeable in childhood and can continue on into adulthood.

AUDITORY DYSPERCEPTION. In OCD, it refers to a person hearing ordinary sounds (usually indistinct) and doubtfully misinterpreting them, most often as something dangerous. An example would be a sufferer hearing a faint noise and assuming it is a deadly gas leak, or hearing a squealing sound while driving and assuming they have run over a child.

AUGMENTATION. When one drug is taken together with another in order to boost the first drug's action.

BASAL GANGLIA. The name given to a group of structures in a part of the brain known as the forebrain. One of the structures is the caudate nucleus, which is implicated as one of several problem areas in OCD. The caudate, together with a nearby structure called the putamen, makes up an area of the basal ganglia known as the striatum. One of the basal ganglia's functions has to do with enabling you to put together separate complex physical movements into a larger coordinated action. Problems in the basal ganglia can produce twitches, jerks, and tremors.

BDD. Abbreviation for Body Dysmorphic Disorder (*see below*).

BEHAVIORAL THERAPIST. A mental health professional with specialized training and experience in behavioral therapy, usually a psychologist.

BEHAVIORAL THERAPY. An approach to treating psychological disorders based on researched scientific principles of human learning and functioning. It is used to educate individuals in methods of self-control. It focuses on problems in the present rather than the past and determines success in terms of specific behavioral changes which can be observed and measured. One type of behavioral therapy, Exposure and Response Prevention, is effective in the treatment of classic OCD. Another type, Habit Reversal Training, has been used to treat Trichotillomania, skin picking, and nail biting.

BENZODIAZEPINES. A group of antianxiety medications. They can sometimes be helpful at the beginning of OCSD treatment where there is much anxiety present. They can be addictive.

BEZOAR. A mass blocking a person's digestive tract. It can sometimes occur in people with TTM who swallow the hairs they pull and that forms a blockage. Such hair masses are called "trichobezoars."

BIOCHEMICAL. Having to do with the chemistry of living things.

BODY DYSMORPHIC DISORDER. A disorder which belongs in the OC Spectrum, also referred to as "Imagined Ugliness." Sufferers have strongly held, disturbing beliefs that they are ugly, misshapen, or deformed in some way that is either not visible to others, or so minor that others would not believe that it could be so disturbing. The thoughts are persistent and obsessive, and sufferers try to relieve their anxiety about them in compulsive ways.

BODY-FOCUSED COMPULSIONS. Any behaviors that relieve doubt or anxiety resulting from obsessions about a person's own body.

BODY-FOCUSED OBSESSIONS. An intrusive, unwanted, or unpleasant thought having to do with the human body—either the person's own or the bodies of others.

BRAIN LESION. An abnormal anatomical change in the brain due to injury or disease.

BULIMIA. An eating disorder in which sufferers try to control their weight through compulsively vomiting food they have just eaten. Some bulimics also have problems involving binge eating that then leads to compulsive vomiting.

CANINE ACRAL LICK. A compulsive paw-licking disorder seen in dogs that is thought to resemble OCD in humans, and that has been successfully treated with select antidepressant medications.

CAUDATE NUCLEUS. Part of one of the basal ganglia known as the striatum. The caudate nucleus functions as a type of filter or "gate" and decides which impulses and thoughts are important enough to be let through, directed to, and acted on by the conscious mind.

CHECKER. A slang term for someone who compulsively double-checks things in order to relieve the doubt and anxiety caused by obsessions.

CHRONIC. When a disorder is always present to a greater or lesser degree but is not curable. A person can recover from certain chronic problems, such as OCSDs, but the potential for symptoms to return will always be there.

CLASSIC OCD. Once thought to be the only Obsessive-Compulsive type disorder, this illness is characterized by intrusive, repetitive, and often unpleasant thoughts known as obsessions. Obsessions result in anxiety that sufferers try to relieve using repetitive mental and physical actions known as compulsions. The disorder is chronic and probably hereditary.

COACHING TAPE. An audio tape recorded by a therapist or patient that encourages a patient to keep working on their therapy, and that may also instruct them in how to keep up their motivation.

CODEPENDENT. An unhealthy relationship between someone who is dysfunctional and another individual who becomes overly responsible for that person's functioning in life and their recovery.

COGNITIVE THERAPY. An approach to treating psychological disorders based on the theory that many emotional disturbances are caused not by other people's actions or by external situations, but rather by the illogical or extreme ways we view and interpret these things. This therapy attempts to treat disturbed emotions by teaching people how to spot the errors in their thinking and how to therefore have emotions that are more moderate and appropriate to whatever situations occur. When these skills are mastered, it leads to better coping.

COMPETING RESPONSE. A special type of muscle movement used as a part of Habit Reversal Training which is a treatment used for TTM, skin picking, nail biting, and tics. It is used to block and replace the physical movements that are part of the undesirable habit.

COMPULSION. Any physical or mental action that relieves the anxiety caused by an obsessive thought.

CONTAMINATION OBSESSIONS. Repetitive and intrusive thoughts occurring in OCD that tell a sufferer that they or others are or will become contaminated via germs, viruses, chemicals, people, thoughts, or in magical ways which will lead to bad luck, sickness, or death.

CONTINGENCY MANAGEMENT. A scientifically based approach to managing and shaping behavior by rewarding desirable ones and denying any type of reward or payoff for undesirable ones. This is a particularly important approach in getting young children (and sometimes older ones) to cooperate with behavior therapy goals.

CORRELATION. When two things have a mutual relationship, we say there is a correlation between them.

DECONTAMINATION COMPULSIONS. Compulsive washing, cleaning, avoidance, or disinfecting activities that are performed to help relieve fears of contact with dirt, germs, viruses, or chemical substances.

DEGREE OF BELIEF. In OCD treatment, this term is used to refer to the extent to which a sufferer believes that what their obsessions tell them is true.

DEPRESSION. A disorder of mood characterized by feelings of hopelessness and helplessness, accompanied by such physical signs as sleeping too much or too little, eating too much or too little, tearfulness, and fatigue. Sufferers tend to think negatively about themselves, as well as the past, present, and future. It may be caused by either unhappy life circumstances or a biochemical problem involving brain chemistry.

DERMATOLOGIST. A medical doctor who has specialized training in treating disorders of the skin.

DIAGNOSIS. The science of identifying a disorder based on its symptoms and signs.

DIAPHRAGMATIC BREATHING. A type of relaxed deep breathing commonly used by singers and those who practice yoga. It is also used as a part of Habit Reversal Training for the treatment of TTM, skin picking, and nail biting.

DOPAMINE. A brain neurotransmitter chemical involved in the control of voluntary movements. Problems with the regulation of this chemical have been implicated in OCSDs, ADHD, and schizophrenia. A shortage of dopamine in the brain causes Parkinson's Disease.

DOUBLE-BLIND DRUG STUDY. A type of experimental procedure where neither the participants nor the researchers know whether any of the participants are getting an actual drug or a placebo, until after the study is completed and the results are known (*see* Placebo *below*).

DOUBLE CHECKING. A type of compulsive behavior commonly used to relieve the anxiety caused by obsessive doubt. It can involve looking at things several times, questioning others repeatedly, reviewing past events mentally, or repeating tasks until the doubt is satisfied.

DSM-IV. The "bible" of psychiatry and psychology, published by the American Psychiatric Association. It sets down all of the guidelines for diagnosing psychological disorders and problems.

DYSMORPHOPHOBIA. An older term used to refer to Body Dysmorphic Disorder (*see above*).

DYSPERCEPTION. When someone misunderstands or misinterprets what one or more of their senses are telling them.

ECT. Abbreviation for electro-convulsive therapy (*see below*), also known as "shock treatment."

EEG. Abbreviation for electro-encephalogram, which is the recording of a person's electrical brain wave patterns to study for abnormalities that may indicate signs of brain problems such as epilepsy.

ELECTRO-CONVULSIVE THERAPY. Also known as "shock treatment," is a treatment that has been used to treat severe depressions that do not respond to medication. It is not considered appropriate for the treatment of OCSDs. It involves putting a person under anesthesia while delivering an electrical current to the brain, in order to cause a seizure. There is some controversy as to whether or not it may cause brain injury.

392 ᐈ *Appendix E*

ENDOGENOUS DEPRESSION. A form of depression that is the result of an individual's own disturbed brain chemistry and not due to unhappy life circumstances or illogical thinking.

ENVIRONMENTAL FACTORS. All those factors in an individual's external world which, in the case of OCSDs, have an influence on their symptoms. These may help or hinder symptoms, although they are not the original cause.

EOSINOPHILIA MYALGIA. A serious and potentially fatal reaction to the now banned amino acid L-Tryptophan that some individuals took in the belief that it would relieve symptoms of OCD. The amino acid, while not actually harmful in its natural state, was made so via a faulty manufacturing process.

EPILEPSY. A disturbance of the electrical activity of the brain, usually resulting in convulsive seizures.

EXPOSURE AND RESPONSE PREVENTION. The only behavioral therapy procedure shown to be effective in the treatment of classic OCD. It involves having sufferers gradually expose themselves to increasingly fearful obsessive thoughts and situations that will cause anxiety, while at the same time resisting the urge to do the compulsions they commonly use to relieve the anxiety.

EXPOSURE TAPE. An audio tape used in behavior therapy as part of the treatment of OCD and BDD. It is used to expose patients to the things they obsess about and helps them to gradually learn to tolerate the anxiety caused, without turning to compulsions to relieve that anxiety.

FLOODING. A slang term for Exposure and Response Prevention.

FRONTAL LOBES (OR AREAS). The front area of the brain, and in terms of evolution, one of the newest. It is an extremely complex grouping of different structures that contribute to the control of such things as language, recent memory, social behavior, sexual behavior, spontaneity, movement programming, spatial orientation, etc. It has connections to the basal ganglia (*see above*).

GAMMA KNIFE. A surgical device that uses tightly focused beams of gamma radiation to destroy tiny areas of body tissue. It is currently used in brain surgery for severe cases of OCD that have not responded to any other known treatment. Unlike other forms of psychosurgery, the skull does not have to be opened.

GLUCOSE. A sugar produced within the body by the breakdown of the foods we eat. It is the body's essential fuel that is burned to create the energy it needs to operate. It is the brain's only fuel source.

GROOMING IMPULSIONS. A term applied to a group of poorly controlled behaviors including hair pulling, skin picking, and nail biting, which seem to resemble grooming activities but actually result in localized injury.

HABIT. An automatic pattern of behavior established through repetition that is maintained because it is rewarding in some way. Compulsions gradually become habits as they are repeated and maintained, because they reward sufferers by allowing them to escape from feeling anxious.

HABIT REVERSAL TRAINING. A four-step program used for changing undesirable habits such as tics, hair pulling, nail biting, skin picking, etc. It was developed in the early 1970s by Dr. Nathan Azrin.

HABITUATION. In behavioral treatment for OCD, it represents the gradual decrease in a person's ability to react anxiously as a result of being repeatedly exposed to thoughts and situations they fear, and where no unpleasant consequences actually happen.

HALLUCINATION. A symptom seen in mental disorders such as schizophrenia, in which the sufferer sees, hears, smells, tastes, or feels things that do not really exist.

HEMATOLOGIC. Having to do with blood.

HIERARCHY. Used to design an individual program of behavior therapy treatment for classic OCD and BDD. It involves making a list of the thoughts and situations that cause a sufferer to feel anxious. Each is rated on a scale from 0 to 100, depending on how much anxiety they cause (0 = no anxiety, 100 = the highest anxiety possible). Therapy assignments are then drawn from this list in order of difficulty.

HOARDING COMPULSIONS. The urge to collect and save abnormally large amounts of things for which a person has little or no use, or even unrealistically large quantities of useful things.

HOT SPOT. Any situation that is likely to get your symptoms going, and that needs to be anticipated in order to be able to head off a lapse or a relapse.

HRT. Abbreviation for Habit Reversal Training (*see above*).

HYPERMORALITY. A compulsive need on a classic OCD sufferer's part to be certain that their behavior is absolutely and perfectly moral and ethical in every possible way, even to the point of causing themselves great difficulty or harm. Often, it is rigidly pursued to irrational lengths. It is practiced in response to a sufferer's doubtful obsessive thoughts that their behavior is not perfectly moral, and that something bad will then happen. It is sometimes referred to as "moral scrupulosity."

HYPER-RELIGIOSITY. A compulsive need on a classic OCD sufferer's part to be certain that their religious conduct is absolutely perfect according to whatever code that religion sets forth. Their perfectionism generally drives them far beyond anything their faith has intended, even to the point of not being able to successfully practice it at all. It is practiced in response to doubtful obsessive thoughts that they are not sufficiently religious, and that they will therefore suffer some bad consequence. It is sometimes lumped together with hypermorality and also referred to as "moral scrupulosity."

HYPER-RESPONSIBILITY. An overwhelming sense of responsibility for the health, well-being, and safety of others that is experienced by some sufferers of classic OCD. It is an extreme response to obsessive thoughts that if others come to harm, it will be the sufferer's fault, and that they will have to suffer extreme guilt if they do not take some sort of protective action.

HYPOTENSION. Low blood pressure.

IMAGINED UGLINESS. A term used to describe Body Dysmorphic Disorder.

IMPULSE CONTROL DISORDER. The official DSM-IV (*see above*) name for a group of assorted disorders that includes Trichotillomania, Kleptomania, Compulsive Gambling, Pyromania, etc. It is an illogical catchall sort of a group in which several probably unrelated disorders have been lumped together for convenience. It tells us nothing about the disorders and is probably best ignored.

IMPULSION. A type of obsessive thought that represents a call to action and can feel like an urge. Those with aggressive or sexual obsessions often get impulsive thoughts that tell them they want to do something socially unacceptable or criminal and that they are going to do them. Actually, in the case of classic OCD, they never do. In the case of grooming impulsions, sufferers can find themselves frequently thinking about performing their habits. The difference between this type of impulsion and those just mentioned is that grooming impulsions are immediately rewarding and are carried out, while aggressive and sexual impulsions are repulsive and punishing and are not carried out.

INPATIENT. A patient who stays in a hospital in order to be treated.

INTERACTION. In the use of medication, this term refers to the effects that drugs may have on each other when taken together.

INTRAVENOUS. When a drug or solution is delivered to the body through a vein.

INTRUSIVE THOUGHTS. Unwanted thoughts that force their way into a person's conscious mind. They may or may not be repetitive.

LAPSE. A slip on the part of someone who is in recovery or who is recovering. It usually involves going back to behaviors which were already brought under control.

LIMBIC LEUCOTOMY. A type of brain surgery which has been used to treat severe cases of OCD.

L-TRYPTOPHAN. An amino acid present in certain foods, that is the raw material of serotonin, a neurotransmitter chemical (*see below*). It is currently under an FDA ban due to manufacturing impurities.

MAGICAL THINKING. A variety of obsessive thoughts that superstitiously connect actions and behaviors on the part of the sufferer with unpleasant or negative consequences. The thoughts usually revolve around bad luck and the sufferer somehow having the power to make bad things happen to themselves or others by doing, thinking, or saying the wrong thing.

MAINTENANCE. The phase a person enters following their initial recovery from symptoms. A person who has reached this point must now work to maintain their recovery in order to stay well.

MENTAL COMPULSIONS. Any mental activity performed by a classic OCD sufferer that relieves the anxiety caused by obsessive thoughts. These should not be confused with obsessions.

METABOLIC. Refers to the chemical activity in the body's cells during which energy is generated for life processes, as food is used and broken down into simpler substances and waste products.

MONODRUG THERAPY. When a person's symptoms are treated with a single medication.

MORAL SCRUPULOSITY. A type of obsessive thinking and compulsive behavior that revolves around trying to be morally perfect.

MORBID OBSESSIONS. Any intrusive and repetitive thoughts that have to do with gruesome or repulsive subjects such as murder, mutilation, or sexual misbehavior. The thoughts may be concerned either with these types of things happening to the sufferer or being committed by the sufferer.

NEGATIVE REINFORCEMENT. When a behavior is rewarded by an escape from something unpleasant. Compulsions tend to increase because they can be rewarding in the sense that they allow those who do them to escape from the anxiety caused by obsessions.

NEURON. A nerve cell.

NEURONAL FIBERS. The "arms" that project out from nerve cells and connect them to other nerve cells.

NEUROTRANSMITTER. A chemical compound that is released into the spaces between nerve cells to enable them to send electrical signals across those spaces to each other.

NEUTRAL OBSESSIONS. Repetitive and intrusive thoughts that cause sufferers to focus on meaningless or unimportant things. These can be things in the environment, numbers, words, or even the person's own thoughts. They can cause anxiety because the sufferer cannot control them and because they make concentration very difficult.

NOREPINEPHRINE. A type of neurotransmitter chemical found within the brain that enables certain nerve cells to communicate with each other. Problems involving it can result in some forms of depression. Some of the medications used to treat OCSDs act on it and the transmitter chemical serotonin (*see below*).

OBSESSION. An intruding, unwanted thought that is usually unpleasant or negative in some way, and tends to cause anxiety. It is usually persistent and may keep repeating itself in different variations.

OBSESSIVE-COMPULSIVE NEUROSIS. An outmoded term which was once used to refer to classic Obsessive-Compulsive Disorder.

OBSESSIVE-COMPULSIVE PERSONALITY DISORDER. A type of disorder whose name unfortunately makes it easily confused with classic OCD. Unlike classic OCD, its symptoms are generally seen by sufferers to be desirable, an important part of themselves, and something they have no desire to stop doing. It can involve such things as perfectionism, a need to control others, hoarding, stinginess, etc. Only a small percentage of those with classic OCD also have this problem. Sufferers do not tend to do well in treatment as they do not believe they have a problem.

OBSESSIVE-COMPULSIVE SPECTRUM DISORDERS. A group of disorders once thought to be unrelated but currently believed to be linked biologically in a number of ways. The group includes classic OCD, Body Dysmorphic Disorder, Trichotillomania, compulsive skin picking and nail biting, Tourette's Syndrome, and most likely the eating disorders Anorexia Nervosa and Bulimia.

OCD. Abbreviation for classic Obsessive-Compulsive Disorder.

OCPD. Abbreviation for Obsessive-Compulsive Personality Disorder.

OCSD. Abbreviation for Obsessive-Compulsive Spectrum Disorder.

ONYCHOPHAGIA. A problem in which a person compulsively bites their nails to the point of causing serious pain and injury to themselves.

OPEN LABEL STUDY. An experimental drug study in which the participant knows that they are taking the actual drug and not a placebo.

ORBITAL CORTEX. The part of the frontal lobes of the brain that lies just above and behind the eyes. It is one of the "older" parts of the brain, in terms of evolution, and is involved in regulating such things as anxiety, impulse control, meticulousness, personal hygiene, perseveration, and the starting and stopping of behaviors.

OUTPATIENT. A patient who receives treatment at a clinic or a doctor's office, rather than staying in a hospital.

OVERVALUED IDEATION. Refers to the very strongly or deeply held magical or distorted beliefs sometimes seen in those with OCD or BDD. The stronger the beliefs, the more difficult it may be to get the sufferer to change them.

PANDAS. An abbreviation for Pediatric Autoimmune Neuropsychiatric Disorders Associated with Streptococcal infections. These are a subgroup of OC and tic disorders seen in children which are believed to be caused by antibodies the body produces in reaction to strep-throat infections. These antibodies are thought to cause these symptoms by attacking specific areas of the brain.

PERFECTIONISTIC OBSESSIONS. Repetitive and intrusive thoughts that cause doubt and anxiety about harm or danger resulting to the sufferer or others, due to not having done certain things perfectly enough.

PERSEVERATION. To keep working at something continually. In OCSDs, this refers to constant and repetitious thinking or behavior by a sufferer.

PET SCAN, OR POSITRON EMISSION TOMOGRAPHY. A medical device that takes moving color pictures of the brain as it burns glucose (the fuel of the body's cells) that has been treated to make it radioactive. It can show which areas of the brain are more active than others during different mental or physical activities, such as when symptoms are happening.

PHARMACOLOGICAL. Having to do with drugs.

PHOBIA. A learned fear which is the result of either having something unpleasant happen to you or witnessing a very unpleasant event.

PLACEBO. An inactive or harmless substance used as a control when testing whether an actual medication is effective or not. It helps to rule out whether it is simply the belief that one is taking an actual medication that produces any positive results in a drug study.

POLYPHARMACY. When two or more drugs are combined to treat a condition. This is usually done when no single drug is able to do the job.

PRECIPITATING FACTOR. In psychological disorders, this term refers to any stressful biological or environmental event which suddenly touches off an illness. For this to happen, individuals usually must first be predisposed to the illness (see *Predisposition*).

PREDISPOSITION. Being susceptible to a disorder due to such factors as genetics or those coming from the environment.

PREFRONTAL LOBOTOMY. A type of brain surgery used (and widely misused) in the past to treat a variety of psychological conditions.

PREOCCUPATION. To become completely engrossed in something to the point where it absorbs one's total attention.

PROCRASTINATION. Putting off or not getting around to doing or facing certain things, particularly those that would be difficult or that would produce anxiety. Often accompanies some types of classic OCD.

PROGRESSIVE MUSCLE RELAXATION. A method of relieving body tension and stress that teaches individuals how to gradually relax all the various groups of muscles in their bodies one at a time.

PROTECTIVE COMPULSIONS. Any mental or physical activities that must be performed to protect an individual and/or others from being harmed in some way. They are a response to intrusive obsessive thoughts that tell the individual something bad is happening or will happen.

PSYCHIATRIST. An individual who holds a medical degree, is licensed to practice medicine, and who has specialized training in the treatment of mental disorders through the use of medication. They are also usually trained in the use of psychotherapy, but do not always practice it.

PSYCHOLOGIST. An individual who is licensed to practice psychology and who usually has a Ph.D. or Psy.D. degree in psychology (some states allow people with MA degrees to be licensed). They have specialized training and experience in the treatment of psychological disorders using psychotherapy and may be trained in one of several different approaches. They do not prescribe medication. Those trained in cognitive/behavioral therapy are generally better able to treat OCSDs.

PSYCHOTHERAPY. Used in the treatment of mental disorders or life problems. It may take the form of any one of a number of approaches involving communication between the patient and a trained mental health professional. Its goal is to bring about a change in behavior or emotional responses.

PSYCHOTIC. Refers to schizophrenia or any disorder in which there is a loss of contact with reality (*see Schizophrenia*).

RECEPTOR. A special site on the surface of a nerve cell which, when it is locked onto by a transmitter chemical from a neighboring nerve cell, allows a nerve signal to jump from one cell to the other.

RECOVERY. The point at which a person's symptoms have been brought under control. They must then be kept under control through ongoing maintenance. It should not be confused with cure.

RELAPSE. When a recovering or recovered person has gone back to "square one," in terms of their symptoms, and has stopped practicing any of the self-control they have learned.

RELAPSE PREVENTION. A four-step process that a recovered person needs to follow to keep from falling back into their former state of illness.

RELIGIOUS OBSESSIONS. Any intrusive, repetitious, and unpleasant thoughts that have to do with religious matters. They can involve morbid or blasphemous subjects, and frequently, result in guilt.

REMISSION. When a sufferer's symptoms appear to have gone away.

REUPTAKE. A part of the cycle in which electrical nerve impulses are transmitted from one brain cell to another. In OCSDs, there has been a great deal of focus on the reuptake of the transmitter chemical serotonin. Serotonin is released by one nerve cell into the gap between itself and a neighboring nerve cell. It locks onto receptors on the other side of the gap which then triggers a nerve impulse in the receiving neuron. When its work is finished, the serotonin is drawn back up into the first nerve cell. This last step is known as reuptake.

REUPTAKE INHIBITOR. Any psychiatric medication which prevents a neuro-transmitter such as serotonin from being drawn back up too quickly into the nerve cell fiber from which it was released (*see Reuptake above*). It has been theorized that in the OCSDs, serotonin is not allowed to linger long enough in the gaps between nerve cells in certain areas of the brain. Reuptake inhibitors help keep the serotonin in these spaces longer in order to ensure proper nerve cell transmissions.

REWARD. In behavioral terms, it refers to anything an individual finds pleasurable or satisfying. Behaviors that are rewarded are likely to be repeated.

REWARD MENU. A list of possible prizes or other rewards that a person can choose from once they have performed certain behavioral therapy tasks. These prizes are used to help create motivation for doing the difficult things sometimes necessary for recovery. This approach is mostly used with young children.

RITUAL. Any type of compulsive behavior that must be performed in an exact series of steps that never varies. When done properly, it helps to relieve doubt and anxiety caused by obsessive thoughts, and often has a magical quality in the way it prevents harm or bad luck. If it is done incorrectly or imperfectly in any way, it must usually be repeated as many times as it takes to get it right. It can be performed mentally or physically. A ritual may take a few seconds or can last for hours.

RUMINATION. Thinking repetitively about something. This is not necessarily the same thing as an obsession. Those who are depressed will often ruminate about negative feelings and situations having to do with their depressions.

SCHIZOPHRENIA. A type of chronic brain chemical disturbance marked by delusions and hallucinations, some of which can cause great mental anguish and anxiety, as well as by disordered thinking and communication. Sufferers have very strongly held beliefs that what their senses and thoughts wrongly tell them is true. It is believed to involve the neurotransmitter chemical dopamine.

SEDATION. A drowsy or relaxed state which can be brought on by tranquilizing medications. Some antidepressant medications can also have sedating effects on certain people.

SEIZURE. A symptom complex of the brain disorder known as epilepsy. They are caused by an uncontrolled, chaotic discharge of electrical signals by certain areas of the brain. Seizures are marked by either a minor loss of consciousness (a petit mal seizure) or a severe loss of consciousness and muscle control (a grand mal seizure). Seizures also may be occasionally caused by psychiatric or other medications if prescribed or taken in excessively high doses, or where an individual has (unknown to them) a tendency toward epileptic problems.

SELF-EFFICACY. The belief in your own abilities to accomplish a task; in therapy, this would include such tasks as taking control of your own thoughts, feelings, and behaviors. A sense of personal power and effectiveness.

SELF-HELP. When an individual attempts to treat their own disorder by themselves along with the help of special books or tapes and/or the support of fellow sufferers acting as a group.

SELF-INJURIOUS BEHAVIOR. Behaviors such as hitting one's head against objects, slapping oneself, or burning, scratching, or cutting oneself. Some of these behaviors have also been referred to as compulsive self-mutilation when they occur as a part of an OCSD. They should not be confused with the disorders mentioned above. In OCSDs, they may bear a similarity to Trichotillomania, as they are often followed by a feeling of satisfaction or relief. These behaviors are also seen to accompany such disorders such as autism, mental retardation, and dissociative disorders (where sufferers lose their sense of being in reality).

SELF-MEDICATION. This refers to the use of alcohol, illegal drugs, or the abuse of prescription or over-the-counter medications to treat your own symptoms without the guidance of a trained physician. Addiction can frequently be a result.

SELF-MUTILATIVE COMPULSIONS. Repetitive behaviors that involve the person cutting, burning, or otherwise injuring themselves in some way. They may have the function of relieving feelings of tension or anxiety and may be related to Trichotillomania for this reason.

SELF-RELAXATION. Another term for Progressive Muscle Relaxation (*see above*).

SEROTONERGIC SYNDROME. A problem drug interaction that can result from taking a drug that works on serotonin (*see below*) together with a type of drug known as an MAO Inhibitor. Symptoms can range from mild to severe and include restlessness, muscle twitches, excessive perspiration, shivering, and tremors. This problem may also result from taking two different SSRI-type medications at the same time.

SEROTONERGIC THEORY. The theory that OCD is the result of a disturbance in the way serotonin is used by nerve cells in certain areas of the brain to communicate with each other.

SEROTONIN. One of a number of chemicals in the brain that enables brain cells to send messages to each other.

SEROTONIN-SPECIFIC REUPTAKE INHIBITOR. Any medication that selectively blocks the reuptake of serotonin by nerve cells in the brain (*see Reuptake above*).

SETBACK. A lapse (*see above*) or any temporary return to symptoms that have already been brought under control.

SEXUAL OBSESSIONS. Unwanted and unpleasant repetitive thoughts having to do with sexual subjects. They usually revolve around the person having unpleasant sexual things done to them, or else their doing unacceptable sexual things to others.

SIDE EFFECT. Any unwanted physical or mental effect caused by a medication. It may be harmful or merely annoying. It may also be only temporary or may last as long as the medication is taken.

SOMATOFORM DISORDER. A group of disorders listed together in the DSM-IV (*see above*) manual that are concerned with problems regarding a sufferer's body. It includes Somatization Disorder, Conversion Disorder, Pain Disorder, Hypochondriasis, and Body Dysmorphic Disorder (*see above*). It is unclear whether these disorders truly belong in the same category or are all possible members of the OC Spectrum.

SSRI. Abbreviation for Serotonin Specific Reuptake Inhibitor.

STEREOTYPICAL BEHAVIOR. Behavior which is repetitive and which is performed in exactly the same way each time it is repeated.

STIGMATIZED. When a person feels marked by society, or in their own eyes is seen as "bad," inferior, or undesirable. Many OCSD sufferers feel that their symptoms have caused them to be marked in this way.

STRIATUM. A pair of structures in a part of the brain known as the basal ganglia. These structures are, in turn, made up of the caudate nucleus and the putamen. These two areas within the striatum have been implicated as possible locations for the disturbance that results in classic OCD. The striatum is involved in the regulation of sensations, the regulation of thought, and the ability to smoothly carry out automatic tasks. It may also control such activities as grooming and checking.

SUBCAUDATE TRACTOTOMY. A type of brain surgery which has been used to treat severe cases of classic OCD.

SUDS, OR SUBJECTIVE UNITS OF DISTRESS. These are part of a scale that is used in behavioral therapy. Patients are asked to rate items on a list called a hierarchy (*see above*) from 0 to 100, indicating how anxious they would feel in situations where they would have to face their symptoms. It helps to determine which situations are more difficult than others, so they can be treated in order of difficulty.

SUPERSTITION. Thoughts or beliefs that are not based on the laws of science and rely instead on magic or supernatural thinking.

SUPERSTITIOUS OBSESSIONS. Magical thoughts that suggest supernatural-like connections between things that in reality have no connection.

SYDENHAM'S CHOREA. A disorder that afflicts some people following a bout of rheumatic fever. Some of its symptoms seem to resemble a combination of OCD and TS.

SYMPTOM. A sign or indication of a particular disease or disorder.

SYNAPSE. The region between two nerve cells across which nerve signals are transmitted from one cell to the other.

SYNAPTIC CLEFT. The tiny gap between two nerve cells at the point where the fibers of one come into near-contact with the other. It resembles the gap in a spark plug.

TARDIVE DYSKINESIA. A type of prolonged side effect seen in some individuals who have taken antipsychotic drugs for long periods of time. It involves the loss of control of certain muscles, often around the head, face, or mouth.

TCA, OR TRICYCLIC ANTIDEPRESSANT. A class of medications used to treat depression.

THALAMUS. Part of an area of the brain known as the diencephalon. It receives impulses that the caudate nucleus has selected as worthy of attention and action, along with sensory information from the spinal cord, and sends them on to the frontal area of the brain to be acted upon. It may be a part of the faulty circuitry implicated as a cause of the symptoms of classic OCD.

THERAPEUTIC. Something that heals or treats disorders.

THOUGHT-STOPPING. An older and outmoded method of treating obsessional thoughts. Patients were taught to vigorously think of the word "stop," whenever unwanted thoughts would occur, as a way of blocking them out. It has not proven to be particularly effective.

TIC. An intermittent, repetitious vocal utterance or motor movement seen respectively in Chronic Vocal Tic Disorder or Chronic Motor Tic Disorder. When both types occur together, you have Tourette's Syndrome. Tics can be very simple or such complex chains of activities that they do not even appear to be tics. There is usually an urge to perform them, and they can be repeated over and over the same way until it is felt that they have been done "just right." They can sometimes be temporarily suppressed but must be performed sooner or later. They are common among sufferers of classic OCD, can begin in childhood, and may be spotted long before the symptoms of the OCD itself make their appearance.

TTM. Abbreviation for Trichotillomania.

TOLERANCE. The gradually increasing resistance to the therapeutic effects of a particular drug, seen to develop over time with the continued use of that drug. This effect is seen in certain classes of medications, particularly those used for anxiety or sleep problems (but not antidepressants).

TOUCHING COMPULSIONS. The urge to touch things in special or ritualistic ways to get either a feeling of having done it "just right", or else to get some kind of magical control.

TOURETTE'S SYNDROME. A disorder of the Obsessive-Compulsive Spectrum which is marked by the presence of both vocal and motor tics (*see above*). Like many other OCSDs, the tics are preceded by an urge and may have to be performed until they feel "just right."

TREATMENT RESISTANT. When a disorder has not responded to any known standard treatment, it is said to be treatment resistant.

TRICHOTILLOMANIA. The compulsive pulling of head, facial, or body hairs, either deliberately or in a state of unawareness, or a combination of the two.

TRICYCLIC ANTIDEPRESSANT. A type of medication used in the treatment of depression. Two members of this group, imipramine (Tofranil) and clomipramine (Anafranil) have been used in particular in the treatment of OCSDs.

TS. Abbreviation for Tourette's Syndrome (*see above*).

UNDOING COMPULSIONS. Compulsive behaviors performed to neutralize or cancel out other behaviors, thoughts, or happenings which could cause bad luck or harm to the sufferer or others.

VESICLES. Storage chambers located at the ends of nerve fibers in which supplies of neurotransmitters are stored, waiting to be released when an impulse is transmitted between nerve cells.

VISUAL DYSPERCEPTION. In OCD, it refers to when a person doubtfully misinterprets or is unsure of what their eyes tell them, and assumes that it is something bad or harmful to them or others. An example would be a sufferer seeing a blur out of the corner of their eye while driving, and assuming that they must have hit a pedestrian.

VON ECONOMO'S ENCEPHALITIS. A type of brain disease associated with the worldwide flu epidemics that occurred between 1915 and 1926. It was believed to be caused by a virus, though none was ever found. Many sufferers developed OCD and other neurologic problems following their recovery from this disorder.

WASHER. A slang term for someone who has fears of contamination and who washes themselves compulsively.

WORD LOSS. A side effect seen in some people as the result of taking antidepressant medication. When it happens, the person sometimes feels that as they are speaking, a particular word is on the tip of their tongue, but they are unable to think of it.

YBOCS. An abbreviation for the Yale-Brown Obsessive-Compulsive Scale. This widely used scale measures the severity of the symptoms of classic OCD and was originally developed for use in OCD drug tests to measure improvement. There is also a children's version called the CYBOCS.

Frederick Penzel, Ph.D. is a licensed psychologist, and executive director of Western Suffolk Psychological Services, in Huntington, New York. He has actively specialized in the treatment of obsessive-compulsive spectrum disorders since 1982. Dr. Penzel is the only psychologist to sit on the Science Advisory Boards of both the Obsessive-Compulsive Foundation and the Trichotillomania Learning Center. He is a regular contributor to the newsletters of both organizations, and conducts numerous workshops and lectures in the United States and Canada for the benefit of professionals, mental health consumers, and their families.

If you have any feedback, questions or comments, Dr. Penzel can be reached at the following address:

Frederick Penzel, Ph.D.
Western Suffolk Psychological Services
755 New York Avenue
Suite 200
Huntington, NY 11743

Dr Penzel's clinic also maintains a website at www.wspsdocs. com

The site contains an extensive bibliography of books and videos relating to OCSDs, a large list of web addresses of interest to OCSD sufferers and their families, self-diagnostics, information on where to obtain free medication, and a substantial collection of articles on OCSD-related subjects written by Dr. Penzel and his associates.

AA. *See* Alcoholics Anonymous (AA)
acceptance(s)
  blocks to, 197–198
  definitions of, 196–197
  list of, 201–210
  of OCD by adults, 185, 193–210
  of OCD by children, 163
  OCSDs, treatment, and, 198–201
acne, from skin picking, 14, 282
acrylic nails
  as nail-biter habit blockers, 106
  as TTM habit blockers, 106
ADAA. *See* Anxiety Disorder Association of America
Adderall
  in ADHD therapy, 329
  drug augmentation with, 133
addiction
  definition of, 387
  to OCSD medications, 140
ADHD. *See* Attention-Deficit/Hyperactivity Disorder
adolescents
  ADHD in, 329
  facial skin picking in, 156–157
  OCD in, 332
  OCSDs in, 39, 152, 165–172, 332, 340
  online resources for, 340
  Tourette's Syndrome in, 340
  treatment centers for, 345–348
  treatment of, 174, 177
affective modality, in TTM, 10
"Aggravation List," as TTM reminder, 108
aggressive behavior, in OCD patients, 302–304, 315
aggressive obsessions/impulsions, 211, 212–215, 216, 224
  definition of, 387

Symptom Checklist for, 349
agitation
  in children, 154, 177, 178
  drug-induced, 122, 130, 132, 137, 138, 177
  medications for, 120, 122, 126
agoraphobia, in OCD, 307
AIDS, fears about, 219, 238, 244, 256, 305, 324, 325
Albert Ellis Institute, 342
alcohol abuse
  in OCSDs, 28, 140, 205, 294
  relapse prevention in, 77
  from Trichotillomania, 11
Alcoholics Anonymous (AA), 28, 81, 83, 206, 209, 294, 332, 337
Alice, personal story, 262–264
Allen, personal story, 214, 222–223, 250–251
allergic dermatitis, in washers, 240
allergic reactions, to drugs, 127, 130, 142
allergies, OCSDs and, 149, 328
Alzheimer's Disease, 248
Amanda, personal story, 219, 275–276
amantidine hydrochloride. *See* Symmetrel
Ambien (zolpidem), as sleep aid, 138
America Online, OCD bulletin board on, 332, 340
amino acids, 147
Anafranil (clomipramine)
  drug reversal of, 314
  effects on neurotransmitters, 312, 313–314
  in OCD treatment, 117, 118, 119, 120, 126, 127, 128, 129, 138, 403
  side effects of, 120, 132, 133, 134, 138, 177
anger
  in checkers, 257
  in OCD households, 328
  in OCSD patients, 28, 190, 302–304
animals, OCSD-like disorders in, 314

BDD. *See* Body Dysmorphic Disorder
    (BDD)
Beck, Aaron T., 81–82
behavioral therapist
    definition of, 388
    how to choose, 342–345
    role of, 24–25, 31, 182, 187, 190
behavioral therapy, xvi, 194, 388. *See also*
        Exposure and Response Prevention;
        Habit Reversal Training
    assignments in, 25, 29–30
    of BDD, 32–33, 37, 200, 201
    of biological problems, 46–47
    of children, 160, 167–169, 177, 178–182
    cognitive therapy use in, 19–21, 25, 31–32
    commitment to, 44–45
    for compulsions, 42–44
    costs of, 37, 38, 39, 40
    description of, 24–25, 388
    diagnosis in, 25
    hierarchy creation in, 25, 27
    homework for, 25, 29–30, 310
    inpatient vs. outpatient models of, 37–40
    intake and history in, 25–26
    intensive, 38
    lack of adverse effects from, 41
    medication use with, 45–46, 115, 141, 142,
        145–146, 194
    for nail biting, 33–36
    for obsessions, 42–44, 200
    for OCD, 17–47, 200
    for OCSDs, xvii, 17–47
    organization for, 336
    for pregnant women, 131, 322
    relapse prevention in, 25
    for skin picking, 33–36
    as sole treatment, 41–42
    steps in, 17–47
    symptom analysis in, 25
    systematic desensitization in, 307
    time frame for, 36–37
    for TTM, 33–36, 37
belief enhancements, for TTM, 109
Benadryl (diphenhydramine), as sleep aid,
    138
benzodiazepines
    addiction to, 140
    as antianxiety drugs, 137, 138, 387

definition of, 388
beta-blockers
    as antianxiety drugs, 140
    for headache therapy, 135
    in OCD treatment, 121, 137
Bethanacol (uricholine)
    for blurred vision, 138
    for dry mouth, 134
    for sexual dysfunction, 136
    for urinary retention, 135, 177
bezoar, definition of, 388
biochemical, definition of, 388
biochemical disturbances, in OCD patients,
    325
biological problems, behavioral therapy of,
    46–47
bipolar disorder
    drug therapy of, 126
    lithium therapy of, 120, 126
black-and-white thinking, about setbacks, 82
blocks, to acceptance, 197–198
blood
    pre-drug testing of, 125
    serotonin in, 116
Bobby, personal story, 158–159
Body Dysmorphic Disorder (BDD), xvi, 3, 4,
    5, 6–9, 199, 201, 233
    in adolescents, 156–157, 348
    anger and aggressiveness in, 302
    anorexia and, 306
    anxiety in, 300, 301
    audiotapes for, 71, 84
    behavioral therapy of, 25, 27, 29, 30, 32–33,
        37, 200, 336
    behaviors to resist in, 85–86
    in children, 164
    cognitive therapy of, 19–21
    compulsions in, 85, 275, 293
    description of, 7–8, 231–232, 388
    doubting in, 309
    DSM-IV definition of, 380
    dysperceptions in, 306–307
    environmental factors in, 327
    E&RP for, 21, 22, 32–33, 200
    fears in, 326
    hierarchy creation for, 27, 84
    incidence of, 6, 15
    medications for, 84, 117, 118, 122, 128, 133

of OCSDs in children, 152–159
diaphragmatic breathing
  definition of, 391
  in HRT, 34, 35, 99–100, 102
  for TTM, 87, 99–100
diarrhea
  drug-induced, 132
  treatment of, 134
diazepam. *See* Valium
diet
  drug-induced restrictions of, 121
  effects on OCD, 147–149
diphenhydramine. *See* Benadryl
disability benefits, for OCSD patients, 210
Diseases of the Nervous System (Breitner),
  xv
disinfecting, as decontamination ritual, 238,
  239, 240, 241
displacement behaviors, 278
distortions
  as acceptance blocks, 197
  setbacks and relapses based on, 81–82
dogs, canine acral lick in, 10, 314, 389
dopamine
  definition of, 391
  drug effects on, 320
  receptor blockage for, 329
  role in schizophrenia, 297, 400
Doreen, personal story, 226–228
double-blind studies, of drugs, 143, 314, 391
double checking
  in ADHD, 329
  definition of, 391
  by OCD sufferers, 31, 199, 248, 265, 271,
    275, 277, 286, 288, 302, 307, 320
doubting
  by checkers, 249, 252, 254
  by hoarders, 246–247
  by OCD children, 155, 171
  by OCD patients, 258, 265, 309
"doubting sickness," OCD as, 2, 297
Doyle, Arthur Conan, 211
dream activity, drug-induced increase in, 139
drinking
  compulsive, 293
  excessive, 1. *See also* alcohol abuse
drug abuse
  fears about, 158

medications for, 123
  in OCSDs, 28, 140
  from TTM, 11
drug augmentation, 119, 121, 133, 141, 329
  definition of, 388
dry mouth, drug-induced, 120, 132, 134, 177
Drysol, as antiperspirant, 139
DSM-IV, 13, 391
  criteria for OCD in, 54
  Impulse Control Disorders in, 9, 394
  OCPD criteria in, 294–295
  official diagnoses of, 379–380
  Somatoform Disorder in, 7, 401
Duke University Program in Child and Adolescent Anxiety Disorders, 346
dysmorphophobia. *See also* Body Dysmorphic Disorder (BDD)
  definition of, 391
dysperception
  by checkers, 255–257
  in classic OCD, 304–307
  definition of, 391

Eastern Pennsylvania Psychiatric Institute
  (EPPI), 346
eating, compulsive, 1
Ebola virus, fears about, 219
ECT, 391. *See* electroconvulsive therapy
  (ECT)
eczema, 240
EEG, epilepsy detection by, 320
Effexor (venlafaxine)
  assistance program for, 150
  neurotransmitter blockage by, 117
  in OCD treatment, 119
Eisen, ___, 6
EKG, recommended prior to drug therapy,
  125
electroconvulsive therapy (ECT)
  definition of, 391
  for OCD, 146–147
electromagnetic fields, fears about, 325
Elliott, Walter, 206
Emmelkamp, Paul, 40
emotional abuse, OCSDs and, 28, 328
endogenous depression, 28, 300
  definition of, 392
endorphins, hair pulling and, 278

urinary retention, drug-induced, 132, 135, 177
urination compulsions, 238, 251
  in children, 154

vacation, benefits to OCD patients, 67
Valium (diazepam)
  addiction to, 140
  in OCD treatment, 127, 137
Vanderbilt University, 144
Vasofem, use for sexual dysfunction, 136
Vasomax, use for sexual dysfunction, 136
venlafaxine. *See* Effexor
verbal aggression, by OCD patients, 303–304
vesicles
  definition of, 404
  serotonin storage in, 312
Viagra, use for sexual dysfunction, 136
videotapes
  on OCD, 180, 185, 385–386
  on Tourette's Syndrome, 337–338
violent thoughts, 212–213, 287
vision blurring, drug-induced, 132, 138
Visken (pindolol)
  as augmenting drug, 142
  in OCD treatment, 121, 128
visual dysperception
  in classic OCD, 304–305
  definition of, 404
vitamins, for classic OCD, 148
vocal tics, 403
vomiting fears, in children, 154
Von Economo's Encephalitis, 319
  definition of, 404
  OCD from, 319

washers
  decontamination compulsions of, 238–241
  definition of, 404
  self-identification of, 54

Websites. *See* under individual organizations
weight gain, drug-induced, 132, 137, 177
Wellbutrin (bupropion), as stimulant, 133–134, 136, 137
Western Psychiatric Institute and Clinic, 348
Western Suffolk Psychological Services, 340
When Things Fall Apart (Chödrön), 62–63
Worden, J. William, 208
word loss
  definition of, 404
  drug-induced, 139, 404
workaholics, OCPD in, 296

Xanax (alprazolam)
  addiction to, 140
  as antianxiety drug, 28, 138
  in OCD treatment, 127, 137

Yale Adult OCD Clinic, 348
Yale-Brown Obsessive-Compulsive Scale (YBOCS), 26
  definition of, 404
Yale Child Study TS/OCD Clinic, 348
Yale University, 6
  home page for OCD and Tourette's Syndrome, 341
YBOCS. *See* Yale-Brown Obsessive-Compulsive Scale
yeast infections, OCD and, 149
Yocon (yohimbine), for sexual dysfunction therapy, 136
yoga, as stimulation reducer, 106

Zoloft (sertraline)
  assistance program for, 150
  in OCD treatment, 118, 120, 126, 132
zolpidem. *See* Ambien
Zyprexa (olanzepine)
  in OCD treatment, 119, 121, 122, 126
  in Tourette's therapy, 329